Praise for *But Eno*

"A dizzying display of versatility. . . .
with tremendous respect—yes indeed, . . .
ity to switch (apparently seamlessly) from one form to . . .
prose enlivened by his distinctive wordplay and quirky opinions. He is good company whether you're looking for two quick pages and a smile, or want to linger."

—*The New York Times Book Review*

"A geyser of comedy for three decades."

—*USA Today*

"Witty and irreverent."

—*Washington Independent Review of Books*

"One of the funniest and most insightful writers in America. The word I wrote most often in my notes as I read the book was 'hilarious.'"

—*Book Reporter*

"This collection of Buckley's essays perfectly showcases and draws upon his many writerly voices. . . . His thoughts are pithy, trenchant, and perspicacious, and for all that, his essays are seasoned with a light dusting of self-deprecation, the secret to this book's exceptional charm. . . . Sublimely addicting."

—*Booklist*

"Prone to benign mischief, a literary twinkle in the eye, Buckley nails his targets."

—*Kirkus Reviews*

"[Buckley] excels in parodies of newspaper corrections, travel tips for small-aircraft passengers, and the comedic dystopia of an imagined inaugural speech from President Donald Trump."

—*Publishers Weekly*

ALSO BY CHRISTOPHER BUCKLEY

They Eat Puppies, Don't They?

Losing Mum and Pup: A Memoir

Supreme Courtship

Boomsday

Florence of Arabia

Washington Schlepped Here

No Way to Treat a First Lady

God Is My Broker

Little Green Men

Wry Martinis

Thank You for Smoking

Wet Work

Campion

The White House Mess

Steaming to Bamboola: The World of a Tramp Freighter

But Enough About You

(essays)

Christopher Buckley

Simon & Schuster Paperbacks

NEW YORK LONDON TORONTO SYDNEY NEW DELHI

Simon & Schuster Paperbacks
An Imprint of Simon & Schuster, Inc.
1230 Avenue of the Americas
New York, NY 10020

First Simon & Schuster trade paperback edition May 2015

SIMON & SCHUSTER PAPERBACKS and colophon are registered trademarks of Simon & Schuster, Inc.

Manufactured in the United States of America

1 3 5 7 9 10 8 6 4 2

The Library of Congress has cataloged the hardcover edition as follows:
Buckley, Christopher, 1952–
[Essays. Selections]
But enough about you : essays / Christopher Buckley.—
First Simon & Schuster hardcover edition.
pages cm
Includes index.
I. Title.
PS3552.U3394B88 2014
814'.54—dc23
2013019392

ISBN 978-1-4767-4951-8
ISBN 978-1-4767-4952-5 (pbk)
ISBN 978-1-4767-4953-2 (ebook)

For
Christopher Hitchens
1949–2011
Faithful Old Body

CONTENTS

OUT AND ABOUT

STATECRAFT

FAREWELLS

CRITICISM

LA BELLE FRANCE

But Enough About You

PREFACE

Make [the reader] laugh, and he will think you a trivial fellow. But bore him the right way and your reputation is assured.

—SOMERSET MAUGHAM

This irksome quote weighed on me as I cobbled together this collection. I'll willingly cop to being a trivial fellow, but I can say with a straight face that my goal has never been to bore the reader. Still, Mr. Maugham does have a point, blast him. Maybe I've been going about this all wrong. But I'm sixty-one now, so it's a bit late in the game to be worrying about that.

Some years ago I found myself on a panel with Bruce McCall, Steve Martin, and Wendy Wasserstein, three nontrivial artists well known to Thalia, Muse of Comedy. I forget what exactly our topic was, but it must have had something to do with the business of trying to make people laugh. I do seem to recall that before long we were all whingeing about humor's second-class status.

The nontrivial P. J. O'Rourke, one of the wittiest and smartest writers in the business, memorably remarked, "Humor sits at the Children's Table of Literature." Somewhere among P.J.'s abundant trove of *bon mots* is his observation that "Anyone can draw a crowd by standing up and shouting, 'I have cancer!' But try doing it with forty-five minutes of stand-up." When P.J. got cancer some years later, I couldn't resist calling him up to say, "Trying to draw a crowd, are we?" Happily, the cancer is now gone for good, and even without it P.J. continues to draw big crowds.

During the panel discussion, Wendy Wasserstein said that someone had once condescendingly told her that she really ought to try "serious" writing instead of comedy. "I said to him, 'Think writing funny is easy, do you? Really? *You* try it.'"

Well, only five paragraphs in and already wallowing in self-pity. We just can't get no respect. It's an old lament, and sometimes itself comic.

Toward the end of his life, Robert Benchley, one of the twentieth century's great practitioners of literary humor, became obsessed with the idea of writing something serious. Making people laugh—even to the point of reducing them to tears—was no longer enough for him. He had never wanted to be a mere "funnyman." (His coinage, I believe, and no compliment.)

Benchley was a keen student of British history. He resolved to write a book on the Queen Anne era of early eighteenth-century Britain, when the Enlightenment was popping up everywhere like spring bluebells. According to his biographer, this would be nothing less than "a new, analytical history."* Benchley amassed a library of one hundred books on the subject. Periodically, he would seal himself off in a hotel room with his secretary, a former hatcheck girl, to work on his elusive masterwork. (For the purpose of scholarship, not shenanigans, though to be sure Mr. Benchley was no stranger to those.)

His new analytical history did not eventuate. There's an amusing and telling quote in the biography courtesy of his son Nathaniel Benchley, author of a little novel called *The Off-Islanders* that became the basis for the movie *The Russians Are Coming! The Russians Are Coming!* Nathaniel's son Peter wrote a monster best seller about a vengeful shark, providing the Benchley dynasty with a trifecta.

Nathaniel notes that his dad was hampered in his quest to write history by a scholarly version of obsessive-compulsive behavior. If he came across some informational lead, he *had* to follow it, wherever it went. And then had to follow that, wherever *it* led. And so on. "At dawn he was still awake, the floor littered with books, determinedly reading some passage in a volume totally unrelated to the Queen Anne era." Lucky for him he lived before the Age of Google.

As for the bottom line: his biographer posits that Benchley's Scheherazade-style research kept him "from having to confront the fear

* *Laughter's Gentle Soul: The Life of Robert Benchley*, by Billy Altman. 1997.

that often gnaws at those who find themselves bearing the mantle of humorist—that, when the chips were down, he would find himself unable to write adequately on a serious topic."

More on that "mantle of humorist" in a moment. Meanwhile, my own theory is that most humorists—to use that awful word—find their way to Thalia's workshop after discovering themselves incompetent in other, more practical professions. (Cosmetic surgery, personal injury law, gun industry lobbying, etc.)

Benchley's career as a student at Harvard inclines me to this insight. He had to sit for a final exam in which he was asked to "discuss the arbitration of the international fisheries problem in respect to hatcheries, protocol, and dragnet and travel procedure as it affects (a) the point of view of the United States and (b) the point of view of Great Britain."

Benchley stared at the question, then took up his pencil and wrote, "I know nothing about the point of view of Great Britain in the arbitration of the international fisheries problem and nothing about the point of view of the United States. Therefore, I shall discuss the question from the point of view of the fish."* I like to think he got an A, but those Harvard profs can be sticklers.

As to "mantle of humorist." Mantle seems, gosh, an awfully grand term. In the pages of this book, I cite a *New Yorker* cartoon in which a Washington, D.C., politician scowls at his secretary as she approaches his desk, holding in outstretched arms a folded garment.

"No, no, Miss Clark! I asked you to bring in the Mantle of Greatness, not the Cloak of Secrecy."

That's more like it. I doubt Robert Benchley ever thought he was wearing a mantle over his shoulders. He'd have more likely called it a negligee.

As for "humorist" . . . I know a few folks who earn their daily bread by making people laugh, either with word processor or paint brush or on stage, and I can't remember a one of them ever referring to him or herself as a "humorist." Why would you? It's only asking for it. *You're a humorist? Yeah? Say something humorous.*

* *American Literary Anecdotes*, edited by Robert Hendrickson. 1990.

I've never called myself by the odious term, but I have heard these scrotum-tightening words, and shuddered. "Comic," on the other hand, or "Comedian" are another matter. They're straightforward job descriptions and in any case hardly apply to me, alas.

"Satirist"? Problematical. As the playwright George S. Kauffman permanently defined it: "Satire is what closes on Saturday night." *Satirist* is no insult, but it's a ten-dollar word. Would you put it on your passport application under "Occupation"? On your business card? Tombstone? Perhaps. *Here lies John Q. Jones. Husband. Father. Satirist.* Maybe that's it: a satirist is a dead humorist—who concentrated on pointing out everyone else's failings rather than his own. The old *saeva indignatio*: Latin for fierce indignation. It's on the gravestone of the greatest satirist of them all, Jonathan Swift. (It should be pointed out, I suppose, that he made *his* living as a preacher.)

One time before I gave a talk to a sizable audience in the Midwest, the gracious and well-meaning host introduced me as a "say-terist." He repeated the word several times, which surely had some folks wondering why—on earth—the lecture committee had invited a sex fiend to address them at eleven o'clock in the morning in the civic center. An elderly lady came up to me afterward and sweetly asked how old I was when I first decided that I wanted to be a "say-terist." I wasn't quite sure how to respond, so I said, "It's complicated."

I've done a bit of public speaking, too much of it in the service of trying to get people to buy my books. Trust me when I say: You're truly better off if they don't introduce you as a "humorist" or "satirist" or any sort of amusing person. Chances are the audience already knows about you. They're not a flash mob. They didn't just spontaneously gather in response to some tweet. (I can proudly avouch that my audiences generally do not consist of looters.) So they already know that you're not Stephen Hawking or Joyce Carol Oates or the author of the hot new analytical history on Queen Anne Style that everyone's talking about.

I've gotten some laughs over the years, but when I lie there wide-awake in bed at three a.m., it's not the laughs I remember, but the disasters. And there have been those, oh yes. Always—always—there's that guy or woman sitting in the front row, arms tightly crossed over the chest. The others might be laughing. Not him. No, no. He's staring, impassive as the Sphinx, unamused as Queen Victoria. He even looks a bit put out that everyone else seems to be finding it all so darned amusing. I can read this fellow's thoughts as clearly as I can the giant electronic news crawl in Times Square: THAT'S NOT FUNNY . . . THAT'S NOT FUNNY, EITHER . . . I'M NOT GOING TO BUY YOUR BOOK . . . ANDY BOROWITZ IS COMING NEXT MONTH . . . I'LL BUY HIS BOOK . . . *HE'S* FUNNY . . .

You know those "About the Author" paragraphs on the back flap or cover of a book? The paragraphs authors pretend they didn't write? *Considered one of the funniest, most brilliant, most original*— etc.—*writers of his generation* . . . Right—those. After a half-dozen books, I got bored saying the same thing (there wasn't much to say to begin with), so for this one, I just made it all up. Among other noteworthy fictional accomplishments, I wrote that I'd been "an advisor to every U.S. president since William Howard Taft." Why not?

By Day Ten of any book tour, you're a bit punchy. I was shambling like a sedated mental patient into a studio to do an AM radio drive-time interview. With all due respect to the fine professionals who do these for a living, AM radio drive-time interviews are typically not occasions of Socratic dialogue.

The host was sitting at his console speed-reading the "About the Author" paragraph on the back flap of my book. I knew that this was all he would know about me.

He looked up at me dubiously. "You were an advisor to William Howard Taft?"

"Yes," I said.

His brows beetled. "So . . . we could talk about that?"

"Sure," I said.

And we did. I haven't been asked back on his show, but I have no regrets. It was well worth it.

Book tours have a yin and yang to them. On the one hand, they're a narcissist's wet dream. You get to talk about yourself endlessly, again and again, until even you are heartily sick of yourself and your book. On the other hand, they tell you exactly where you fit on the food chain. On that same book tour, I happened to be following in the slipstream of another author—George Stephanopoulos. George was promoting his number one best seller memoir about his years working for President Clinton. I was promoting a comic novel about the UFO world, which was getting okay-but-mixed reviews.

At every airport along my Trail of Tears, my author escort would greet me, still flushed with excitement. "We just had George Stephanopoulos. You've never seen such crowds. We had to move his reading to the coliseum."

On my first book tour, I arrived one night for my reading at a venerable independent bookstore in Berkeley. It was all new to me and I was pumped and nervous. I needn't have been, for there was not one single person present. The embarrassed manager excused herself. A few minutes later, four of the fifty seats were suddenly occupied—I couldn't help but notice—by Hispanic persons. She'd gone into the stockroom and told the staff to go pretend to be my audience. It was very thoughtful of her. One of them even came up afterward and had me sign the book and then pretended to buy it at the cash register.

That was fifteen books ago. There are fewer empty seats now at the readings—but not to worry: there are still seats available for *you*. Book tours have their strange moments, but it's at the bookstores that you meet your readers, and I could hug every one of them. I don't know if George Stephanopoulos feels the same way about his readers, but then it would take him all day to hug everyone in that coliseum. Mine I can get hugged in no time.

But enough about you. Are writers more vain and sensitive—that is, insufferable—than people in other professions? Say, actors or musicians? Doctors, lawyers, architects, imams, hedge fund managers, elected officials, fashion designers, opera singers, models, university professors, submariners, dictators, fighter pilots, terrorists, funeral directors, comedians, spies, baseball players, football players, publicists, policemen, presidents, air traffic controllers, ship captains, plumbers? Buddhist monks?

Over the course of my life I suppose I've met or known most of the above types of people. (Actually, meeting a dictator is still on my bucket list.) So I can say with absolute authority: I have no idea. But it's probably safe to assert, if not asseverate (see "insufferable," above), that as a rule, writers tend to come labeled FRAGILE: HANDLE WITH CARE. This can variously be cause for amusement, nonamusement, or reaching for the nearest blunt instrument.

As W. H. Auden put it, "No poet or novelist wishes he was the only one who ever lived, but most of them wish they were the only one alive, and quite a number fondly believe their wish has been granted." Auden himself was perhaps a unique case—of justifiable narcissism, if we take his fellow poet Stephen Spender's word for it. Justifiable, that is, by virtue of utter self-confidence untainted by jealousy.

Spender said of his great friend, "He just thought he was cleverer than anyone else, but without arrogance really . . . He knew exactly what he was doing, and he was totally indifferent to what anyone said about it . . . For instance, when he was so attacked by Randall Jarrell in 1947 he said, 'He must be in love with me; I can't think of any other explanation.'"*

In the pages of this attractively packaged and *very* reasonably priced book, you'll come across some writers I've personally known or encountered or studied. Joseph Heller and I became pals somewhat improbably after I wrote a respectful but far from glowing review of one of his novels. Joe had a healthy ego, no question. A writer once lamented to him that he would never write a book as good as Heller's *Catch-22*. Joe replied, "Who has?" Not bad. If Joe had been a narcissist *qua* narcissist, he would never have written me the thank-you note for the unglowing review that inaugurated our friendship.

You'll also find Ray Bradbury in here. I didn't know Ray well, but I admired him greatly, not only for his genius as a storyteller, but also for the abundant joy that he brought to the business of writing. His electric zest seemed to act as an ego-jamming device. He so loved writing that it was infectious. And he was generous. He took pleasure in the success of fellow writers, especially younger ones.

Contrast Joe Heller and Ray Bradbury, then, with another writer

* *The Writer's Chapbook*, edited by George Plimpton. 1989.

who makes a brief appearance in here, Gore Vidal. If Joe Heller was a yellow jacket and Ray Bradbury a bumblebee, Vidal was a black widow spider, dripping venom. Yet you can still purr with guilty delight over his imperishable *mal mot*: "Whenever a friend succeeds, a little something in me dies." And was he not also author of the schadenfreude-perfect remark: "It is not enough to succeed. Others must fail"? Chuckle, as I do, but rest assured: these were sincere sentiments. He meant it.

I didn't know him personally, but P. G. Wodehouse appears in these pages. Wodehouse was an anomaly as authors go, on two counts: first, he cheerfully admitted to reading reviews of his books. (Joseph Conrad: "I don't read my reviews. I measure them." Noel Coward: "I love criticism just so long as it's unqualified praise.") Second, Wodehouse was incapable of holding a grudge. Extremely rare in writers.

After Wodehouse made his innocent but ill-advised wartime broadcasts from Berlin while he was an internee, he was mercilessly savaged back home in England. Among the voices howling for his head on a pike was A. A. Milne. And yet after the war Wodehouse made friends with almost all those critics, some of whom had publicly called for him to be tried and hanged for treason. Of Winnie-the-Pooh's creator, Wodehouse would later write privately, "We were supposed to be quite good friends, but, you know, in a sort of way I think he was a pretty jealous chap. I think he was probably jealous of all other writers. But I loved his stuff. That's one thing I'm very grateful for: I don't have to like an awful person to like his stuff."*

Sean O'Casey famously bestowed on Wodehouse the title of "Literature's performing flea." P.G. had the wit, to say nothing of grace, to remark, "I believe he meant to be complimentary, for all the performing fleas I have met have impressed me with their sterling artistry and their indefinable something which makes the good trouper."†

You'll come across Herman Melville in here. (I didn't know him

* *Fighting Words: Writers Lambast Other Writers*, edited by James Charleton. 1994.

† Ibid.

either, personally.) His ego, and lack thereof, presents us with a tricky dialectic, as evidenced by his alternately chest-thumping and demure correspondence with his friend Nathaniel Hawthorne.

There was nothing demure about Melville's near-contemporary author Theodore Roosevelt. (Roosevelt and I were great friends, but he never quite forgave me when I began advising William Howard Taft.) In the first volume of his magisterial—a word you don't get to use very often—biographical trilogy, Edmund Morris provides us with a Zen-perfect instance of egotism reduced to the irreducible "I." When TR was writing his book *The Rough Riders* in 1898, he splattered the text with so many first-person pronouns that the typesetters at Scribners had to send to the foundry for an extra supply of capital I's.*

Perhaps the best way to get to the bottom of why writers have such bottomless egos is to back up and pose the predicate question: Why do they write in the first place?

There's a lovely story—in this telling, courtesy of the poet Billy Collins. A friend of his was walking down Madison Avenue with the *New Yorker* icon Roger Angell. A passerby spotted Angell and stopped to tell him how much he admired him and what a terrific writer he was. After moving along, Angell said, "That's what it's all about."

"What do you mean?"

"That's what writing is all about," Angell said.

"What?"

"The love of strangers."†

Bingo? But I know a few cranky writers and I believe the *last* thing they crave is the love of strangers. If you stopped any of them on the street to gush, they'd tell you to f— off.

The notoriously irascible Evelyn Waugh is the standard-setter of this type. His insults of people who were just trying to pay him a compliment are eye-poppers. When a woman at a dinner party gushed to him about how she loved *Brideshead Revisited*, he re-

* *The Rise of Theodore Roosevelt*. 1979.

† http://daronlarson.blogspot.com/2011/01/love-of-strangers.html

turned her serve by telling her, "I thought it was good myself, but now that I know that a vulgar, common American woman like yourself admires it, I'm not so sure."* But then Waugh detested Americans, so we have to cut him some slack. Elsewhere, he put forth his view of the author-reader relationship less caustically: "I do not believe that the expenditure of $2.50 for a book entitles the purchaser to the personal friendship of the author."† Put Mr. Waugh down as non-craving of stranger-love.

Occasionally—rarely—we come across a writer who comes bracingly clean about motivation. Balzac once gleefully copped to what he hoped fame would bring: "I should like one of these days to be so well known, so popular, so celebrated, so famous, that it would permit me . . . to break wind in society, and society would think it a most natural thing."‡ How refreshing it would be to hear a writer of our own age put it just this way. Henry Kissinger, very much a writer as well as a statesman, was surely expressing a cognate sentiment when he said, "The nice thing about being a celebrity is that if you bore people they think it's their fault."

This book is dedicated to the memory of my late friend Christopher Hitchens, so it's apt to look for our answer to the pages of one of his great literary heroes, George Orwell. In Orwell's 1946 essay "Why I Write," he adduces "four great motives for writing":

> *(i) Sheer egoism. Desire to seem clever, to be talked about, to be remembered after death, to get your own back on grown-ups who snubbed you in childhood, etc., etc. It is humbug to pretend that this is not a motive, and a strong one. . . .*
>
> *(ii) Aesthetic enthusiasm. Perception of beauty in the external world, or, on the other hand, in words and their right arrangement. . . .*

* *Evelyn Waugh: A Biography*, by Christopher Sykes. 1975.

† *The Writer's Quotation Book, A Literary Companion*, edited by James Charleton. 1980.

‡ *Bartlett's Book of Anecdotes*, edited by Clifton Fadiman and André Bernard. 2000.

> *(iii) Historical impulse. Desire to see things as they are, to find out true facts and store them up for the use of posterity.*
>
> *(iv) Political purpose. Using the word "political" in the widest possible sense. Desire to push the world in a certain direction . . .**

Orwell goes on to tells us that he is by nature a "person in whom the first three motives would outweigh the fourth." He then adds that the twentieth century, in particular the Spanish Civil War, forced him into "becoming a sort of pamphleteer."

We use the word *Orwellian* to signify something futuristic, surreal, contradictory, and totalitarian. But *Orwellian* ought also to denote its eponym's unflinching and unsettling—even ruthless—insistence on the truth. This was a quality that Christopher himself evinced, despite occasionally shattering consequences. So in his memory, then, let Orwell have the last word; or as Christopher would say, *dernier mot*:

> *Looking back through the last page or two, I see that I have made it appear as though my motives in writing were wholly public-spirited. I don't want to leave that as the final impression. All writers are vain, selfish and lazy, and at the very bottom of their motives there lies a mystery. Writing a book is a horrible, exhausting struggle, like a long bout of some painful illness. One would never undertake such a thing if one were not driven on by some demon whom one can neither resist nor understand. For all one knows that demon is simply the same instinct that makes a baby squall for attention.*

Flattering, isn't it? But on the plus side, how many people in other professions get to break wind in society with impunity?

But enough about me. Over to you. This is a book of essays and other pieces, some of them memoirish, written over the last quarter century. That went by quickly, I must say. Kierkegaard is a philoso-

* *A Collection of Essays by George Orwell*. 1946.

pher whom I rarely quote and the spelling of whose name I always have to look up. He said that life is best understood backward but must be lived forward. I was originally going to title the book *What Was That About?* I'm still not sure. But with luck, the reader may find it boring in just the right way.

—April 29, 2013
Stamford, Connecticut

But Enough About You

There's no greater bliss in life than when the plumber eventually comes to unblock your drains. No writer can ever give that sort of pleasure.

—VICTORIA GLENDINNING

FREIGHTER DAYS

Call me Whatever. At eighteen I went to sea, not in Top-Siders, but in steel-toed boots, as a deck boy aboard a Norwegian tramp freighter. My pay was $20 a week, about $100 today. Overtime paid 40 cents an hour, 60 on Sundays. Not much, I know, yet I signed off after six months with $400 in my pocket. My biggest expense was cigarettes ($1 a carton from the tax-free ship's store; beer was $3 a case). I've never since worked harder physically or felt richer. The Hong Kong tattoo cost $7 and is with me still on my right shoulder, a large, fading blue smudge. Of some other shoreside expenses, the less said, the better.

Shipping out was a phrase I'd always thought romantic, probably due to reading Conrad and Melville. At boarding school I used to stand way out on the ice on Narragansett Bay, far from shore, and watch the big ships make their way through the channel toward open sea. I wanted to go, and finally bound a berth on an orange-painted tramp freighter named MV *Fernbrook*. She took me from New York to Charleston, Panama, Los Angeles, San Francisco, Manila, Hong Kong, Bangkok, Singapore, Sumatra, Phuket (then still an endless white beach with not one building on it), Penang, Port Swettenham, India, and, as it was still called then, Ceylon.

The final leg—Colombo to New York, around the Cape of Good Hope—was thirty-three days, longer than expected owing to a Force 12 gale in the South Atlantic. In such seas, the ship's autopilot cannot function; the steering has to be done manually. I took my turns at the helm in a state of barely controlled panic at the thought that thirty-one lives depended on my ability to steer a shuddering, heaving 520-foot ship through mountainous seas. When the next man relieved me, my hands shook so that I couldn't light a cigarette. Even some of the older men, who'd seen everything in their time, were impressed by this storm. Arvid winked at me. "Maybe ve sink, eh?"

They were Norwegian mostly, a few Germans and Danskers. The mess crews were Chinese. The one in charge of waking us for breakfast did so by going down the corridor, banging on our doors and shouting, "Eggah!" It took me a few days to decipher. Eggs. Breakfast.

We carried all kinds of cargo: a police car, penicillin, Dewar's whisky, toilets, handguns, lumber, Ping-Pong balls, IBM data cards. A giant crate of them slipped out of the crane strap and split open on the deck, just as we were making ready to depart San Francisco. A jillion IBM data cards, sufficient to figure out $E = mc^2$. As deckboy it fell to me to sweep them into the Pacific as the Golden Gate Bridge receded. In our modern era of recycling, this would constitute a crime worthy of being tried at the International Criminal Court at the Hague.

The crossing to Manila took three weeks. I didn't set foot onshore there until four days after we landed. As the youngest man, I drew consecutive cargo-hold watch duty. My job was to prevent the stevedores from stealing, a function I performed with spectacular lack of efficiency. They loved me, the stevedores.

At one point I'd been awake for seventy-two hours when a huge crate slipped its straps and plunged fifty feet to the deck. Out spilled an improbable thing: five thousand copies of *The Short Stories of Guy de Maupassant* intended for Manila's public schools.

The stevedores were confused as to whether the books were worth stealing and turned to me, their new best friend, for guidance. I was beyond caring. I told them, "Well, it *is* a good book."

At sea in those latitudes, the temperature on the ship's steel decks might hit 115 degrees. During my lunch break, I'd climb down the long ladder that led to the bottom-most reefer (refrigerated) hold, where it was pleasantly frigid and dark. Better still, there were hillocks of Oregon Red Delicious apples—I mean, mountains of them. I'd sit on top of a mound and munch away like a chipmunk in paradise. One day I consumed eight apples and emerged belching back into the heat and light to pick up my hydraulic jackhammer and resume chipping away at decades of rust and paint.

I remember standing in the crow's nest as we entered the misty

Panama Canal, and the queer sensation as the 4,000-ton ship rose higher and higher inside the lock. I remember dawn coming up over the Strait of Malacca; ragamuffin kids on the dock in Sumatra laughing as they pelted us with bananas; collecting dead flying fish off the deck and bringing them to our kindly, fat, toothless Danish cook to fry up for breakfast. I remember sailing into Hong Kong's harbor and seeing my first junk; steaming upriver toward Bangkok, watching the sun rise and set fire to the gold-leafed pagoda roofs rising above the jungle canopy; climbing off the stern down a wriggly rope ladder into a sampan, and paddling for life across the commerce-mad river into the jungle, where it was quiet and then suddenly loud with monkey chatter and bird shriek. I remember moonlight on palm fronds. I remember it all.

—*The Atlantic Monthly*, December 2010

ECRU, BRUTE?

One year and many dollars ago, I decided to move back to the house I grew up in. I don't have statistics for how many Americans are doing this, but it's quite possible, in this economy, that even some recent college grads are moving back in with the 'rents. It's also possible that for some parents, the words "Mom! Dad! I'm home!" no longer have quite the same heartwarming effect they once did.

I hadn't lived in the house since I was thirteen, before I went off to boarding school. That was in 1966, about the time I used to pedal my bike into town to buy the latest Beatles 45. So it's been awhile, but I can still summon a memory for every square foot of the house and grounds. The tree my friend Danny and I used to climb up to smoke cigarettes; the place on the beach where the seven-foot shark went after me; the living room where I burst into the grown-ups' cocktail hour one day, age ten, to announce, "President Kennedy has just blockaded Cuba." Never since have I caused conversation to come to such a screeching halt.

My original plan, after the last of my parents had checked out and moved, so to speak, to the Big Upstairs, was to hold my nose and spend whatever it took and put it on the market. (Did I say "market"? Sorry, just going for an easy laugh.) The brokers who bothered to return my calls came, looked around, and, as if reading off an identical script, said, "Nice bones, but it's very *dark*."

The house had almost burned to the ground fifteen years before. My mother, a lady of excellent taste, had used the occasion to redecorate along a color spectrum ranging from dark chocolate to milk chocolate. It looked great, but you needed a flashlight to find your way around even during daylight hours. There are probably still weekend guests from the 1990s wandering around lost, looking like Gollum, going, "*Preciousssss!*" It finally dawned on me that women of a certain age—Mum was then in her late sixties—aren't especially keen on bright ambient light.

So it was that I found myself on my hands and knees with Danny, crawling around the floor with paint chips. I make no claim to knowing anything about decor. My only aim was to brighten and lighten for the real estate agents.

"Well," I said to Danny, "let's start with white. How wrong can you go with white?"

It turns out that there are many, many versions of white. Danny and I fanned through Colonial White, Egg White, White Out, White Nights, Snow White, White Flight, Perry White, Teddy White, E. B. White, and Hast Seen the White Whale? Somewhere out there amid the amber waves of grain and purple mountain majesties and fruited plain, a dedicated group of Americans are working day and night to come up with four thousand different names for beige. If Isaac Newton had gotten his hands on a paint-chip wheel, the rainbow would consist of the following colors: Better Red Than Dead, William of

Orange, Lemon Tree Very Pretty, How Green Is My Valley, Danube Blue, Mood Indigo, and Violet Hush.

Danny and I finally settled on Ostrich Shell. Your basic off-white, but with a more exotic name.

I'd been told—rather, warned—that when you paint one room, it will look nice but will make the room next to it look as if raccoons have been living in it for the past decade. Indeed, this was the case. So we had to paint *that* room too, which made the room next to it look like the raccoons had been using it as well for their nefarious raccoony purposes. The Domino Effect. So we ended up doing all the rooms.

Which provided another teachable moment, because if you make the inside look new, then the outside will look like the House of Usher. So the outside got painted, too. Then the basement. Why the basement, you ask? Well, if the upstairs and outside look nice, you can't have a basement that looks like Abu Ghraib. The new basement is now bright off-white, or Crème de la Crème or Milk of Magnesia. Whatever. Now when guests go down into it, they no longer expect someone to leap out, put a hood over their head and waterboard them.

After it was all finished, I looked at it and thought, *Not bad. A person could live here.*

Danny ventured, "Your mom would be proud."

I considered. She was a woman of definite opinions, my mother.

"It's possible," I said. "It's also possible that she's going to appear at the top of the staircase in a nightgown, holding a candelabrum and pointing a finger at me, and moan, "*Ecru*, Brute?"

When I go downstairs for a glass of milk in the middle of the night, I turn all the hall lights on. But it feels like home again. And years from now, when my children are looking at these walls, scratching their heads and looking at paint chips, it'll be me on the landing, in my boxers—a truly frightening sight—moaning, "Magenta Dream? You *can't* be serious."

—*The Atlantic Monthly*, January 2011

THE NAZI OF THE QUIET CAR

I live on a train. A sad thing to admit, but there it is. It's a nice train, I'll say that much. It's called the Acela, a name meant to denote swiftness as well as "costs more than our other trains." It plies between Washington and Boston. My portion of the silver rails lies between Washington and New York.

I generally inhabit the car designated the "Quiet Car." Good old Amtrak, in its wisdom, finally decided, many, many years after the advent of the cellular age, to designate one car out of six for passengers who, oddly, prefer not to be unwilling bystanders at conversations in which they play no part. How my heart used to sink, in the early days, when the passenger next to me would lift from his briefcase a battery pack the size of a cinder block, attach it to his prototype cell phone, and bark, "CHARLEY, CAN YOU HEAR ME? *NOW CAN YOU HEAR ME? GREAT! OKAY—LET'S RUN THE NUMS!*"

The Quiet Car does not hide its light under a bushel. No. Prominent, explicit signs hang from the ceiling at five-foot intervals. They declare, unequivocally, that NO CELL PHONES ARE PERMITTED and that conversation must be kept to a minimum and in hushed tones. In addition to this copious and ostentatious signage, the conductor usually announces over the p.a. system in a stentorian voice, "LADIES AND GENTLEMEN, IF YOU CAN HEAR THIS ANNOUNCEMENT, YOU ARE SEATED IN THE *QUIET CAR*. NO CELL PHONES ARE PERMITTED IN THE *QUIET CAR* AND ALL CONVERSATIONS MUST BE CONDUCTED [pun intended, I wonder?] IN A *LIBRARY-LIKE ATMOSPHERE*."

Often the conductors add that there are *five other cars* where you can sit and play bongo drums or hip-hop music at full volume, whatever turns you on. You just can't do that in *this one car*. Not complicated, you'll agree?

I reflect that not once, in all these years, have I ever seen the famously garrulous Vice President–elect Biden in the Quiet Car. As senator from Delaware, he faithfully commuted on this train to and from Wilmington, Delaware, every day. I just googled "Biden" and "quiet car." The first match is from a newspaper report in September: "At 1:57, Biden took a seat on the first passenger car—not a quiet car . . ." I rest my case.

So, all perfectly straightforward, one might think. But no. Oh, no. Years of riding the Quiet Car, on which I have written maybe a half dozen novels, many articles, and now my blog, have turned me into something I never thought I would become: a Nazi. For it often falls to me, a generally gentle, timid soul, to be the enforcer of quietude. Sad, I agree. Really, my life used to be more exciting than this. Sex, drugs, rock and roll. Now I am become Shush, Destroyer of Conversation.

Invariably, just as one is settling into the cone of silence, there comes from two seats away an 80-decibel cell phone ring tone, sometimes "The Ride of the Valkyries." Sometimes cuter: the sound of a Paris police car; sometimes au courant: "Te Extrano" by Xtreme. Sometimes generically grating, like the air-sundering *oomp oomp oomp* that hits you as you walk by a disco in the meatpacking district.

So you brace, hoping the owner of the cell phone playing Wagner has simply neglected to put it on vibrate and will now press IGNORE. But no. No.

"Fred! Hey! Yeah, the meeting went great! But look, we gotta get Bill and Chuck in the loop or it's gonna be a total f— gang bang . . . What? *CAN YOU HEAR ME NOW?*"

As my dear late mother used to say, "Which words in the sentence 'No cell phones are permitted' did you not understand?"

And so the Nazi of the Quiet Car, his cone of silence shattered, must go to work.

"Sir?"

Look of annoyance. "Yeah?"

Pointing to the sign. (Semiapologetic tone.) "It's the Quiet Car?"

Aggrieved look. "Uh-huh?" (Translation: So?) "Fred, there's some *asshole* here telling me I can't use the phone. I'll have to call you back."

The Nazi of the Quiet Car returns to his seat, face flushing at having been publicly called an "asshole" in front of dozens of people.

Sometimes an intensifier is added before "asshole." On one occasion, the silenced party, one of Tom Wolfe's masters of the universe, declared to his conversational partner before furiously ringing off, "There's a *real asshole* on the train." He added in a knowing, wry tone, "There's *always* one."

Two weeks ago, when I suggested with a hint of asperity to a young gentleman sitting across the aisle, somewhere during his fourth conversation about truly nothing in particular, that he might go use his phone in another car, he replied, "You want to step outside? I'll beat the f— s— out of you." Whereupon he returned to his call with a "Where was I?"

Once, the director of the FBI himself got on in Washington. He sat down in the row in front of me. He was accompanied by three or four manly men, bulgy about the armpits. He proceeded to converse with them, in manly tones, in a fashion that could neither be described as hushed or library-like.

I exchanged "Oy, vey" glances with my my fellow suffering passengers, but none of them indicated readiness to take on the head of the Federal Bureau of Investigation. Normally, as a journalist, I would be interested, fascinated, even, to listen in on insider G-man chitchat. But their conversation was of the "So what's Jack up to these days?" with a bit of golf chat thrown in. Finally, the Nazi of the Quiet Car took a deep breath, screwed up his courage, leaned forward, and gently tapped the nation's top cop on the shoulder.

"Mr. Freeh," I whispered respectfully. "You are a great American, and I am your greatest fan. But this, sir, is"—I pointed—"the quiet car."

His retinue eyeballed me unpleasantly. I braced to hear "Freeze!" or "On the ground, NOW!" and the unholstering of Glock 9s. Director Freeh looked up at the sign. He seemed momentarily nonplussed. Possibly, it had been a while since someone had told him to shut up.

"Oh." He shrugged. And then, simply and without fuss, got up and moved, along with his meaty, scowling entourage, to one of the Unquiet Cars.

How I savored my little triumph. If I get an obituary, I hope the second paragraph will note, "He is said to have once shushed the director of the FBI." Yes, this is how I should like to be remembered.

—*The Daily Beast*, December 2008

FISH STORY

My wife, in her wisdom, decreed that we must have a fish tank in our bathroom. Like Rumpole of the Bailey, I refer to my darling as She Who Must Be Obeyed. So the only answer was "Darling, what an excellent idea. I am so excited to have fish in our bathroom."

I did not utter aloud the next sentence that formed in my mind: "How convenient for flushing them down the toilet after they have lived to the ripe old age of forty-eight hours."

She settled on a 38-gallon tank. It looked impressive. But even more impressive was the filtration system that theoretically keeps the water clear, so that you can actually see the fish. There is apparently some very deep thinking going on in the fish-tank-filter department. Ours looks like it could keep a human alive during open-heart surgery. And—as I found out when I had to disassemble it—you could almost certainly use it to cause a human being to die. Horribly. But I'll get to that part in a moment.

My darling was very excited. Together we picked out tchotchkes for the tank: plastic plants, a little fake coral head, more plastic plants, and of course the obligatory sunken ship and Diver Dan.

Then the colored gravel, the bling, if you will, of the aquarian world. We chose jewel tones: deep purple, crimson, with hints of turquoise. It looked gorgeous. But the best part of the gravel was yet to come. (More on that, too, shortly.)

What had we forgotten? we asked ourselves. Fish!

We selected a half-dozen goldfish of a type called ryukin, which sounds like an island that might start a war between China and Japan. Ryukins are hardy and comical-looking: fat little rascals, some with quadruple tails. Personality? To spare. Beguiling? Beyond—and then some. Whenever I come into the bathroom, which being sixty years old I do quite often in the course of a typical day, our ryukins wiggle those quadruple tails like Las Vegas dancers. Little minxes!

How could I resist constantly feeding them? It says on the food container—I quote—"Feed fish several times a day, enough for them to consume in three minutes." Within weeks, the ryukins were the size of blowfish. Not that you could actually see them, since the water was now opaque, as if someone had dumped a quart of buttermilk into it.

The lady at the fish store berated me for constantly feeding them. When I protested that the label said to feed them several times a day, she replied truculently, as if dealing with a mental defective, "Of *course* it says that. They want you to buy lots of food." Oh, I replied.

But the most fun part was cleaning the filter and the gravel. This was my "punishment" for being so stupid as to follow the feeding directions. And here my education continued, for now I learned the reason for all that gravel. The gravel acts as a sort of repository for what the fish didn't eat; and, of course, for what the fish *did* eat. But the gravel was merely the amuse-bouche. The main event was cleaning the filter.

Fortunately, my beloved has a medical degree in both infectious and tropical diseases. So when she observed the considerable quantity of . . . let's just call it "matter" all over me, she was able to declaim knowledgeably about the types of infections I was most likely to come down with: Bacterial seemed to be the winner, as opposed to viral, parasitic, or toxic. Of course, then you've got your "intoxications" to consider—microbial versus, say, biotoxic or chemical.

But there I go again, Debbie Downer. Is it worth it? Let me tell you: There's something about going to the bathroom and seeing those ryukins wiggling away, going, "Feed meee! No, feed *meeee*!" that brings a lump to my throat. But that could be the infection.

—*ForbesLife*, November 2012

COMMENCEMENT BUTTERFLIES

I have to give a speech at a commencement exercise next Sunday and I'm a bit nervous. Actually, quite nervous.

There will be about eight thousand people present. I once spoke to an audience of nine thousand people—in of all places, Bakersfield, California. It was inside a structure that resembled a zeppelin hangar, so it was at least a contained space in which such laughter as I might generate—during the coveted "humor" time slot of 8:45 a.m.—would ricochet about and linger and maybe encourage others to join in. In real estate it's location, location, location. In public speaking it's acoustics, acoustics, acoustics.

Next Sunday's event will be outdoors, and so my words will be going straight up into the trees, clouds, and roar of passing airplanes. And quite possibly, rain.

If you're a famous person like the president, or a movie star, it doesn't really matter. The audience will pay attention to you ex officio. And even if they aren't really listening, they'll pretend to be listening, because of who you are. I will not have this luxury. Many in the audience will, doubtless, be thinking, or whispering to each other, "Who *is* this guy?" And the audience will include parents, grandparents, and fidgety three-year-olds who need to go to the bathroom *right now*.

I'm also haunted by the fact that I spoke on this same ground at my own graduation day (a long time ago, during the reign of Emperor Augustus). Being young and oh-so-clever, I thought it would be witty to close my oration with a quote containing the f- word. I still wake up at three a.m. in a clammy sweat, remembering that golden moment. At the level of taste, it was on a par with Janet Jackson's Super Bowl wardrobe malfunction. No, lower. How proud my parents were. I wonder, did they nudge the parents sitting next to them and say, "That's *our* son!" My father's graduation present to me was a typewriter—remember those?—with the f, u, and two other relevant keys painted over with my mother's nail polish.

I've given one or two commencement speeches before, but not at universities. The first time was to my boarding school alma mater, a fine institution run by Benedictine monks. I was somewhat surprised to be invited, since I had recently written about my agnosticism in a newspaper of wide circulation.

"Are you *sure*?" I said warily to the lay headmaster.

"Absolutely," he insisted. "We definitely want you."

My extremely Catholic father, upon learning of the invitation, e-mailed me furiously to say that he was "appalled" that I had accepted such an "inappropriate" invitation. He added: "If I were a parent of one of the students graduating, I would walk out of the ceremony and urge the other parents to join me in boycotting you."

We'll put you down as undecided, leaning against.

I replied somewhat frostily that I had not sought this invitation, and indeed had tried to decline it. He dismissed that as irrelevant. We didn't speak for months.

Arriving at the headmaster's office on the big day, I was greeted by a low, ironic chuckle: "I must say, your selection as speaker has proven to be *most* controversial."

"Thanks," I said. "You certainly know how to make a speaker feel relaxed and full of confidence."

Had it all been a plot, to embarrass a lapsed alumnus? Catholics do know how to plot, as you know from history.

On the way to the stage, I was accosted by Father Damian, my old housemaster and English teacher. I retain abundant fondness for Father Damian, but he still has the power, forty years later, to instill in me paralyzing terror.

"Ah, Buckley," he said, giving me an appraising look. "You've put on *weight*, I regret to say."

The invitation to speak at the university arrived before Christmas, so I've had plenty of time to toss and turn at night, wondering what—on earth—to say to these very bright young people and their proud parents.

Last year's speaker was Tony Blair, former prime minister of Great Britain. I found his speech online and did a word count: 1,900 words. The year before Blair, the speaker was Hillary Clinton, then a newly minted U.S. senator. Her count came to 3,400 words. My goal is to be more Blairian than Clintonian.

I read some of my other predecessors' speeches. I was struck by their demure tone and their frank worry about boring the audience.

Fareed Zakaria (2007) ended his address: "Finally . . . you know, somebody once said to me, 'About halfway through your speech, say, "Finally." It wakes them up.'" I'm tempted to steal that.

Garry Trudeau (1991) said at the outset of his talk: ". . . the chief function of the graduation speaker has always been to ensure that graduating seniors are not released into the real world until they have been properly sedated." Might steal that, too.

Well, it's all rather nerve-wracking. My only consolation is the knowledge that the speaker is entirely secondary (or tertiary) to the proceedings. However dull, long-winded, or inappropriately profane the speaker might be, he or she is only a bit of parsley on the day's plate, not the main course. There's this consolation, too: every person in the audience will be about as happy as they've ever been. And ten minutes afterward, no one will even remember who spoke that big day.

That, at any rate, shall be my mantra next Sunday as I mount the scaffold and look out on the sea of faces. And on the umbrellas, thousands of them, popping open as the rain begins to fall.

—*The Daily Beast*, May 2009

REALLY-REALLY-REALLY TOP SECRET

What do you know: I see that my old friend Dennis Blair is up for the top U.S. intelligence job. The position used to be called "Director of Central Intelligence," but then it was decided that we need someone even more central, and if possible, more intelligent, so now our top spook is called "Director of National Intelligence."

Describing Admiral Blair as "my old friend" is putting it a bit strongly. I haven't seen or spoken to him since February 1983. Our friendship, if it was ever really that, consisted of spending nine days together, intense ones, on Air Force Two, flying between European capitals.

"Denny" Blair was then a bright and dashing young Navy commander, seconded (a British term, which, being affected, I use) to the National Security Council at the White House. I was chief speechwriter to Vice President Bush.

Remember the Cold War? Don't you miss the Cold War? It was *so* much more fun than this one. Anyway, the Cold War was running kind of hot in 1983. As we now know from declassified files, the Russians were absolutely convinced that sooner or later, Ronald Reagan would launch nuclear weapons at them. We also now know that Ronald Reagan would never have used "the nuclear option," even in retaliation. But in 1983, these facts were, as Don Rumsfeld would say, unknown unknowns.

Vice President Bush was dispatched to undertake a PR blitz and handholding mission to our allies in Europe. Some years earlier, NATO countries had petitioned the United States, asking us to deploy on their soil intermediate-range Pershing nuclear missiles and air-launched cruise missiles ("Al-Cums," in the grim parlance of Armageddon), in order to defend them against similar weapons already deployed by Russia.

Then, having asked us, the Europeans came under pressure from peace movements and the Soviet Union. They backed down and wanted to cancel the order, as it were. But the U.S. position was that these weapons were vital to maintain the balance of power. (Or if you prefer, balance of terror.) Mr. Bush's mission was to reassure Europe that the United States was not thirsting to initiate Armageddon, and to stiffen its spine so that the deployments could go forward.

We went to eight countries in nine days; or nine countries in eight days. I can't remember, my head is still spinning. It was grueling, but in the end, successful. NATO went through with the deployments and six years later the Berlin Wall came down.

But about my old friend Dennis Blair: This was a vice-presidential mission, but since it was unlike most vice-presidential missions, that is, actually important, the White House sent Commander Blair along with us to keep an eye on things. Being a typical White House staff, we of course naturally assumed that his real mission was to spy on us.

We were all very collegial. There is no "I" in T-E-A-M-A-M-E-R-I-C-A. (Oops—there is. Never mind.) But we did feel a bit . . . *supervised* by our NSC minder. I was informed that I would have to clear my speech drafts with him.

The vice president's chief of staff was himself a naval person: Admiral Daniel J. Murphy, former four-star admiral. "Murf," a nickname I never used to his face, was a genial type, Brooklyn Irish. He was also someone you didn't want to mess with, and when it came to bureaucratic in-fighting, he held a seventh-degree black belt.

Admiral Murphy was cordial with Commander Blair, but he, too, felt a little supervised. So there was a definite feeling of us-versus-them aboard Air Force Two as we winged from Brussels to Berlin to Rome to Paris to Geneva to London in order to make the world safe for . . . more nuclear weapons.

Commander Blair handed me back the draft of the big speech. He sort of tossed it at me in a brisk, naval way. He shrugged. "It's okay, but it needs to be peaced up a bit." We writers are—as you may have heard—a sensitive lot. This response was not the "By God, Buckley, this is absolutely dazzling" I'd hoped for. And what on earth was he talking about?

"Pieced up?" I said.

"Peace. Put in more about *peace*."

"Ah."

I shuffled off sullenly and groused to Admiral Murphy that Commander Blair was clearly an unlettered philistine who wouldn't know it if Shakespeare bit him on the rear end. Murf was a lion to his cubs, but there wasn't much he could do. He told me to suck it up.

Then, two days later, something very cool happened.

Commander Blair had given me back my draft of the next speech. Leafing through it, I noticed that it had somehow acquired two additional pages. What's this? I read the two additional pages. My eyes popped, my jaw dropped.

Commander Blair had accidentally paper-clipped to my draft a two-page TOP SECRET/CODEWORD (which is to say, truly secret) memo. How my little hands trembled as I held it. It's probably best not to reveal what exactly it said, even thirty years later. I have no great desire to join Private Manning of Wikileaks celebrity in his jail cell. Suffice to say that it concerned codes having to do with nuclear launch procedures, a topic about which our government is very protective, and very pissy when revealed.

I thought: *Hm*. I reviewed my options: a) sell it to the KGB, b) give it back to Commander Blair, or c)—leverage! Working at the White House turns any Pollyanna into Machiavelli.

I scurried off to share the gorgeous radioactive windfall with Admiral Murphy. "Thought you might be interested in this," I said, handing it to him.

Admiral Murphy had been a Navy aviator. He had commanded the Sixth Fleet during the Yom Kippur War. Been very high up at the CIA. He was not a man easily impressed. But his eyes widened. He exhaled in a naval sort of way. He said to me, "Where did you get this?" I explained. He folded it and tucked it away in his vest pocket.

Things were ever so collegial aboard Air Force Two after that. Commander Blair's editorial comments about my speech drafts were all variations on "My God, Buckley, this is brilliant, just brilliant."

For whatever it's worth, I think Admiral Blair (Ret.) is a splendid choice for director of whatever we're calling it now. After he left the White House, he went on to a brilliant Navy career. And who could resist a guy who once water-skied behind his own destroyer?

—*The Daily Beast*, November 2008

SUMMERS ON *SUZY*

College summers I worked as first mate and cook on a sailboat named *Suzy Wong*. She was a 42-foot-long Sparkman & Stephens yawl (two masts), all teak and mahogany and scrollwork dragons and Buddhas, topsides painted fire engine red, built in Hong Kong for four young American officers mustering out of the Navy and wanting to sail home. My father bought her in Miami, where the Navy vets landed after numerous adventures including being stuck in a monthlong sandstorm in the Red Sea.

To defray the costs, my dad chartered her to paying clients. Our home port was Stamford, Connecticut, on Long Island Sound. We would go anywhere the client wanted: Long Island, Newport, Block Island, Buzzard's Bay, Martha's Vineyard, Nantucket, Cape Cod, Maine. My best friend, Danny, was skipper.

Suzy was over a decade old now and, like any lady of a certain age, was starting to show the wear and tear. It took weeks of long days to get her ready for sea. By mid-June, neither Danny nor I had fingerprints left from all the sandpapering. She leaked from the top and from the bottom; the bottom leaks being more problematic. I was forever lifting the floorboards to see how much water had accumulated in the bilges. When you hit the bilge pump toggle switch, you never knew if you were going to hear the reassuring *rrrrrr* sound indicating that it was working.

On one memorable occasion, one of our charterers stuck his head through the companionway and asked, "Is the water *supposed* to be above the floorboards?" We were twenty miles offshore and, as usual, the marine radio—one's link to the U.S. Coast Guard—had decided to stop working.

Danny sprang into action. One of my enduring images is of Danny's legs protruding from the engine compartment, accompanied by a vigorous stream of profanity. The culprit was usually the stuffing box, where the propeller shaft penetrates the hull of the boat, providing ample opportunities for the admission of seawater.

There was always something. One time we had to dismantle a very unpleasantly clogged head (toilet) and carry it out onto the deck over the heads of the guests eating dinner, one of them a distinguished monsignor of the Catholic Church.

For refrigeration we had an icebox, which after five days would begin to smell, on occasion urgently. Another lasting image I have of Danny: his face a prune of revulsion as he extracts spoiled chicken parts. For cooking we had an alcohol stove and outdoor barbecue. The alcohol stove you approached as you would a live hand grenade. You had to prime the burner with a propane torch, then pump air into the stove's fuel reservoir in order to force the alcohol up onto the burner. Then you opened the valve and applied the match, at which point it could go either way. Often it went the bad way. For most of four summers, I had no eyebrows.

Steaks and burgers we cooked on the outdoor charcoal briquette barbecue. It hung over the stern (rear). One night, anchored in a swift current in the cold water of Maine, I was cooking some lovely juicy steaks for our guests. I cut into one of the steaks to see if it was ready, whereupon the entire barbecue swiveled 180 degrees and dumped four Omaha steaks and dozens of sizzling charcoal bricquettes into the swift-running current of dark water.

Danny and I leapt into the inflatable dinghy, fired up the outboard motor, which for some strange reason actually started, and buzzed off into the blackness in pursuit of the runaway steaks. We drove two over with the propeller, turning them from filet mignon into chopped steak. The other two were more or less intact. Fortunately our guests were too well gone into their martinis to notice that their steaks had been mutilated and finished off with outboard motor oil.

Most of our charterers were nice people, and we worked hard to make their time aboard *Suzy Wong* a good one. Sometimes this came about in a roundabout way. When we went aground, for instance, or got lost in a dense fog, or the floorboards started floating twenty miles offshore. Nothing, we found, made our guests happier than when these disasters ended well. Our incompetence in having gotten us into the difficulty in the first place was immediately forgotten, so grateful were they on learning that they were not going to die, after all. One time we got seriously lost off Block Island, with bad weather coming in. Our guests were a nice Belgian couple who spent the night hyperventilating and wondering if they would ever see Belgium again. When by some miracle we found the harbor entrance, they were so overjoyed that they broke out a bottle of brandy and toasted us on our navigational skills.

What we lacked in seamanship, we tried to make up for in other ways. We had no electric blender, but this did not deter us from making banana daiquiris for our guests. Many a cocktail hour found me squeezing bananas into mush with bare hands.

Other occasions called for different libations. One time we had aboard a middle-aged couple whose marriage didn't seem likely to make it to the Diamond Anniversary. Their dialogue could have been written by Edward Albee. Sometimes they got so angry at each other that they could converse only indirectly, through us.

Her: Chris, why don't you get Bob another drink. He's only had seven since lunch.

Him: Anything to numb the fact that I'm married to her.

It got so bad that Danny and I decided the only solution was tea. I mixed some pot—hey, it was the seventies—with actual tea in the coffee percolator and let it boil for an hour. I poured Mr. and Mrs.

Virginia Woolf each a steaming mug and before long they were curled up together in the cockpit, cooing at each other and going, "Isn't that an amazing sunset, sweetheart?" "Yes, sweetie, it is." Danny and I smiled. When they got off, I was a bit tempted to give them some of my tea. I wonder if their marriage made it.

Sometimes we'd say, "Would you like lobster for dinner tonight?"

They'd point out that we were at sea. "Where are we going to get lobsters?"

Whereupon we steered to the nearest lobster pot, which was usually never far. We'd pull up a pot, remove a few lobsters, and by way of payment, put a bottle or two of whisky or vodka in the pot. I always wanted to be there when the lobsterman pulled up his trap and found bottles of Johnny Walker Red and Smirnoff.

The summers passed quickly. We read Zen koans by candlelight. Drank wine from goatskins. Fished for squid in phosphorescent water. Shot off flares. Slept on deck under millions of stars. Made bonfires on beaches. Swam naked at night. Blew out sails. Took apart the engine. Scaled a sand cliff and rescued a kid who had gotten trapped. Drank rum to keep warm during a storm. Did foolish, dangerous things and howled because we were so scared, the only thing to do was laugh. Then came ashore and went about our lives and grew up and got old. I think of him whenever I come across the passage in Conrad:

> *A gone shipmate, like any other man, is gone forever; and I never met one of them again. But at times the spring-flood of memory sets with force up the dark River of the Nine Bends. Then on the water of the forlorn stream drifts a ship—a shadowy ship manned by a crew of Shades. They pass and make a sign, in a shadowy hail. Haven't we, together and upon the immortal sea, wrung out a meaning from our sinful lives? Good-bye, brothers! You were a good crowd. As good a crowd as ever fisted with wild cries the beating canvas of a heavy foresail; or tossing aloft, invisible in the night, gave back yell for yell to a westerly gale.*

—*Forbes FYI*, June 2005

THE DIRT ON DIRT

I seem to have taken up gardening.

I realize that this is not a declaration to cause goose bumps. I stipulate that, rhetorically speaking, it is not up there with "Once more unto the breach" or "Sic semper tyrannis." It's more on a par with "Checkout time is eleven a.m." or "Where did I put the car keys?"

How did this happen, I wonder? As a child, my summer chores included weeding my mother's marigold bed. She called it a "bed," but at the time it seemed as vast as the entire state of Connecticut. It did not instill in me a love of gardening. To this day, I cannot hear the word *marigold* without breaking out in hives.

If you yourself have not yet been ensorcelled by Horta, Goddess of the Garden, and turned into a haunter of the local nursery, let me report that as hobbies go, it's less expensive than collecting antique biplanes or Andy Warhol soup cans, but dirt, though dirt, does not necessarily come cheap.

When the landscape architect Le Nôtre presented the bill for the gardens of Versailles to Louis XIV, a shadow is said to have eclipsed the features of the Sun King. My own little patch of earth is as Dogpatch, comparatively speaking, but like *le Roi Soleil*, I went ashen when presented with a bill for sixty bags of cedar nuggets.

"Nuggets," I quipped to the fellow behind the counter. "I must say, *that's* apt." As you can see, I'm something of a wag.

He did not riposte, but then he was busy on the phone with the Fraud Alert Department of American Express, which was no doubt demanding zip codes, blood types, social numbers, and maternal birth dates. Once home, I placed each "nugget" individually about the garden with care befitting Murano glass mosaic tiles.

We of Hibernian persuasion have internalized the adage that to be Irish is to know that sooner or later the world will break your heart. But I have made a corollary discovery: The gardener, too, knows that Nature—and all the gods—is in conspiracy against him.

Squirrels, I am now aware, devote every waking hour between October and May to rooting out the bulbs that you laboriously interred in October. The bulbs, that is, that you ordered from exotic mail-order houses; that you soaked overnight in a homemade atomic elixir containing the most potent capsaicin-laden peppers known to science. While I prepare this fiendish brew, I wear latex gloves, face mask, and eye goggles. Saddam Hussein would have paid good money for my formula.

That sound you hear in my garden? That would be the squirrels, expressing gastronomic satisfaction as they dine, chittering, "Cayenne and habañeros! Sublime! *Magnifique!*"

I wonder: What countermeasures did the burghers of Amsterdam deploy against their squirrels during the seventeenth-century Dutch Tulip Bulb Mania? Did grown men weep on discovering that a squirrel had noshed on a tulip bulb worth more than the value of their house? It is not impossible that the arquebus- and sword-wielding soldiers in Rembrandt's celebrated painting *The Night Watch* were protecting tulip bulbs from seventeenth-century tree rodents. How gardening widens one's intellectual horizons.

Gardening is said to be a calming pursuit, yet there you find yourself, reaching for a pencil with which to scribble down the 800 number in the infomercial with the guy injecting compressed gas into gopher holes and then igniting it, causing thousands of divots to shoot violently into the sky, along with the remains of the very unpleasantly surprised gophers. How does the poem go? "One is closer to God in a garden than anywhere else on earth." Right.

In my next dispatch from my backyard Eden, I will discuss strategies and options after Hurricane Sandy has deposited fourteen cubic tons of sea salt on your perennials and fifty-year-old ornamental cedars. Hint: You're going to need a lot of gypsum.

—*ForbesLife*, April 2013

AUTUMN, INTIMATIONS

Season of mists and mellow fruitfulness, as Keats put it, before heading off to Rome to cough his life out in a *pensione* overlooking the Spanish Steps. According to my anthology, "To Autumn" is the most popular poem in the English language. And here I thought "Casey at the Bat" had that distinction. Well, I'm not a bit surprised: Everyone's a sucker for fall. If you grew up in New England, as I did, this was when you knew you were in the Right Place.

That apple smell, those burning leaves. Those younger than me—an ever-growing cohort—have no memory of setting a match to the piles of leaves our parents made us rake up. The Environment Police put an end to that, on the grounds that that rich, musky smoke would bring about another millennial winter. Such a distinctive smell, those smoldering leaves made. I'm reminded of it on bright sunny days when my ten-year-old sets fire to a leaf with his magnifying glass. It takes me back forty years. Rakes have been supplanted by blowers. The delicate *scritch-scratch* sound of tines combing the grass has been replaced with eardrum-straining turbines. Lawns now sound like the flight deck of aircraft carriers.

Ripeness is all, as Lear would say, and fall is when ripeness happens. While I was growing up, Dr. Bell lived next door. He had a magnificent vegetable garden, and by September his tomatoes were red and heavy on the vines. We would sneak in after dark, armed with a purloined salt shaker, and sit and gorge. We ate his corn raw, each kernel exploding with sugar juice. My mother used to serve us acorn squash with puddles of butter and brown sugar. As a child, I found this a credible delivery system for a foodstuff named "squash." Pumpkins made a hollow *thunk* when you tapped them. Gutting them was never my favorite part; the stringy innards clung tenaciously to the sides, so you had to shave them off. Back then most Halloween jack-o'-lanterns had quaintly similar eyes, noses, and mouths. Now I buy carving templates that transform your pumpkin to look like it was designed by the special effects crew of *Halloween 5*. What hasn't changed is the toasty smell of the candle-scorched insides, the thrilling pagan feel of the night.

People from other parts of the country who came to New England in the fall said, "Aren't the trees beautiful this time of year!" I shrugged. The trees were exactly what they were supposed to be this time of year. Nothing unusual in that. (Yankee *snobisme*.)

We would drive up to New Haven for the Yale-Harvard game. This was my introduction to tribalism. Those blazing autumn sunny days and the blue and crimson banners snapping in the wind seem vivid now. During the final down of one close game, I remember my father telling me that it was sad, because this was the last time these players would be on a football field. Looking back, it seems to me apt that my first intimation of mortality was imparted to me by my father at the time of year when things start to die.

Thanksgivings we drove up to Sharon, in northwestern Connecticut, my grandparents' house. When we arrived, I would tumble out of the rattly diesel Mercedes and race into the house to make mischief with cousins. As there were fifty first cousins, the opportunities abounded. In later years when I was older, the ritual was to hunt pheasant on Thanksgiving morning. Not much fun for the pheasant, but walking through those fields, listening to the tinkle of the dogs' collar bells, is one of my happiest memories. Of those Thanksgiving meals, I remember the pearled onions in cream, mince pies, and bottles from my grandfather's celebrated wine cellar being brought up and decanted. Some of these had been maturing since the First World War. Sometimes after it was poured into glasses a half-inch of purple mud would settle at the bottom. My aunts and uncles would ooh and aah over these pourings, but we of the younger gen caught them wincing and puckering when they drank.

Then, always too soon for me, it was time to go. These partings wrenched, for a full year might pass before I saw my cousins again. The good-byes in the crepuscular gloom of late November afternoons were, I now understand, rehearsals for later, more final, partings.

—*Boston*, October 2002

HOW TO BREAK INTO THE MOVIES IN ONLY TWELVE YEARS

The Wall Street Journal reported a while back that Tom Clancy went as ballistic as a *Red October* submarine because—brace yourself—the director filming one of Mr. Clancy's novels placed a reef in the middle of the Chesapeake Bay, for reasons of plot.

My first reaction was that this was surely so much *Sturm und Drang* in a teacup. But then I realized I was only being churlish. And worse, jealous. I had just recently gotten word that one of my novels had run aground—yet again—on a reef somewhere in Hollywood. It had been languishing nearly a decade in what is euphemistically called "development hell."

The novel was called *Thank You for Smoking*. Mel Gibson had optioned the rights to it in 1993, before it was published. It would be more accurate to say—as we Hollywood types do—that "Mel's people" had optioned it.

Mel's people couldn't have been nicer. In our first phone call, they could barely contain their enthusiasm. "This will be Mel's next movie. Absolutely." This was an assertion I would hear many times over the coming decade. Eventually the thrill somewhat wore off.

The problem, see, was that Mel and his people got themselves hopelessly sidetracked with two absurd and inconsequential projects. One was called *Braveheart*—I'm told that it sank without a trace at the box office. What was the name of the other? . . . *The Passion of the Christ*. Another commercial stinkeroo. Crater City.

I felt sorry for Mel, but at the same time couldn't help thinking, *You have only yourself to blame, my friend.* We never actually met, but as an honorary Mel person, I feel justified calling him "friend." The real tragedy, of course, is that if we actually had become friends, I might have been able to stop him getting into the car that night and getting arrested for driving while anti-Semitic.

So on reconsideration, I now feel Mr. Clancy's pain over that reef-mad director. Really, the gall of these so-called auteurs. Philistines. Let's hope he never gets to direct Proust's *Remembrance of Time Past*. He'd probably put a reef in the Seine next to the Ile de la Cité.

The *Wall Street Journal* article used the occasion of this artistic outrage to examine other books that were turned into movies. Remember Louis L'Amour, the great western novelist? L'Amour was the real deal, one of the most successful writers of his day. The *Journal* noted that he wrote more than one hundred books, of which nearly fifty—fifty!—were sold to the movies. One of the first was a western titled *The Broken Gun*. When it arrived on the big screen it was called *Cancel My Reservation* and starred Bob Hope.

Unlike Mr. Clancy, Mr. L'Amour was philosophical about it all. He just shrugged. He likened the process to selling a house to a new owner. The new owner, he said, had every right to redecorate. Take the money and let it go.

Ernest Hemingway, a writer of no small ego, was so embittered by his experiences with Hollywood that he formulated what could be called Hemingway's Rule for Dealing with those Celluloid SOBs. It goes like this: You drive your car up to the California state line. Take your manuscript out of the car. Make them throw the money across first. Toss them the manuscript, get back in the car, and drive back east as fast as you can.

I had pretty much given up all hope of *Smoking* ever being made. Mel and his people seemed hell-bent on their economically suicidal obsession to make a movie about some minor fracas in Palestine two thousand years ago.

And then one day I got a call from a twenty-four-year-old named Jason Reitman. He said, "I'm the guy they hired to f— up your book." He had me at hello.

Jason had not only read the book, but had also written a screenplay on spec (i.e., without commission). He sent it to Mel over the transom.

A few weeks later, Jason's phone rang. It was—Mel! Calling from his private jet. (Presumably while flying from the *Braveheart* bankruptcy hearing to the *Passion of the Christ* bankruptcy hearing.) Mel told Jason that his script was "brilliant." That it was *exactly* the script he'd been hoping for all these years. They would make the movie together. Absolutely. And that was the last Jason ever heard from Mel.

Some years passed after my call from Jason. Then one day a friend of mine from my White House days rang.

"There's this guy I know from Stanford Business School," he said. "He became chief operating officer of something called PayPal, which was sold to eBay for one-point-four billion. Now he wants to get into moviemaking and really wants to make *Thank You for Smoking*. Would it be okay if he called you?"

I told my friend that my rule has always been to accept phone calls from people worth some portion of $1.4 billion and who want to turn one of my novels into a movie.

David Sacks called the next day. I said I was tickled and please, be my guest. But I said he must first call Mel's people. And so David spent the year and a half on the phone with Mel's people trying to wrestle back the rights.

Mel's people explained that they had spent vast sums developing it, paying endless screenwriters to write unusable adaptations. Then there were all the Fed Exes and the photocopying and coffee and electricity and feeding the parking meter and the mocha frappuccinos and wheatgrass smoothies and cosmetic surgeries and all the rest. (In Hollywood this is called "overhead.") David told me that they seemed to be under the impression that he had pocketed the entire $1.4 billion himself.

They weren't being greedy. No, no. That doesn't happen in Hollywood. As David saw it, deep down they didn't want to sell it because—what if they did and David and Jason made it into a good movie? Mel would look like a schmuck. And if there's one thing Mel hates, it's looking like a schmuck. (Too Jewish.)

To make a long story slightly less long, David deployed all the skills he'd learned at Stanford Biz. And what do you know, he did it. He got the rights back.

Time went by, as time does. Nothing. I went back to assuming nothing would ever happen. Then one day I got an e-mail from a Washington friend who'd moved to Park City, Utah, to become a masseuse. The e-mail said, "Hey, great news about Aaron Eckhart!"

I wrote back, "*What* news about Aaron Eckhart?"

She e-mailed back: "He's been cast in the lead in your movie."

Shortly later arrived an e-mail from David: "Pigs are flying, snowballs are forming in hell! *Thank You for Smoking* is finally in production!"

Each day brought more cool news. They'd signed Rob Lowe. Robert Duvall. Sam Elliott. Katie Holmes (much in the news then, what with her fiancé Tom Cruise leaping up and down on Oprah's couch). Maria Bello. William Macy. Actors of the first caliber. I *was* impressed.

I serially relayed these names to my teenage children. They were . . . politely enthusiastic. *That's nice, Dad. (Yawn.)* Until another e-mail arrived, announcing that someone named Adam Brody had been cast. Upon hearing this, my sixteen-year-old daughter, Caitlin, began to hyperventilate. In the medical sense.

"Adam Brody?! Oh my God. *Oh. My. God.* Adam Brody!"

I had to look him up. He was in a TV show called *The O.C.*

A year later, I found myself at a dinner at the Toronto Film Festival sitting next to Adam Brody. One of the nicest young men I have ever met. Gracious, poised, natural, unassuming.

I told him how my Caitlin had ho-hummed at the names of the other cast members but that his had caused a call to 911. He smiled self-effacingly. He'd heard it before, surely.

I am by nature reticent. I would sooner chew off my right arm at the elbow than accost a celebrity or ask for an autograph. It took three martinis to screw up the courage. I reached into my pocket for my cell phone.

"I . . . don't suppose . . . ?" He nodded, sure.

I dialed and got Cat's voice mail. My heart sank like a Tom Clancy submarine. But it turned out even better, for now Cat could play the message for her friends: "Hi, Cat, this is Adam Brody. I'm just calling to say hi." God bless him, he did not add, "Your dad is drunk and totally annoying."

So it was all worth it in the end, even if it took twelve years. Sometime later, at one of the movie events, I was prattling on to an industry person about how Hollywood had certainly taken its time making the movie, blah blah blah. (Looking back, I wonder: Was this an unconscious attempt to bore him in just the right way?)

He listened patiently, then said with perfect deadpan, "It took over a hundred years to turn *Moby-Dick* into a movie."

To which all I could think to say was "Good point."

—*Time*, March 2006

INTO THIN HAIR

You need to do something when you turn fifty. What made me think this was losing three friends in the space of one month: one to AIDS, one to cancer, another to Lou Gehrig's disease. The eldest of these sweet souls was fifty years old. And now, weirdly, sadly, as I type these words, comes the phone call that my cousin Lee has died. She was fifty-one.

My father celebrated his demicentennial by sailing a schooner across the broad Atlantic. One friend of mine celebrated his by climbing the Grand Teton. Lacking a schooner and uneager to dangle from rocks, I sought a kinder, gentler way of marking the occasion.

Mulling this, I came across a piece in *The New York Times* about hiking the Tour Monte Rosa: a roughly eighty-kilometer oval trek around the Matterhorn. The article described how, with a bit of advance planning and a detour here and there, you could do the trek in comfort and style and not have to sleep in the spartan mountain huts alongside a lot of smelly Swedish backpackers. (As you approach fifty, other people's sweat becomes less appealing.) It takes seven or eight days, with just one longish thirty-kilometer day. I wouldn't return home with a tale to rival Jon Krakauer's *Into Thin Air*. But I would come back.

I proposed to my friend and fellow soccer dad Elan that he come along. Elan is superb company and can say "My friend has fallen into a crevasse, please dispatch a rescue helicopter" in five languages. "Why not?" he said.

We made multiple trips to the outfitters. I showed him the seven-dollar emergency space blanket that the prudent hiker brings along. He looked at me as if I had just presented him with a nuclear-biological-chemical-warfare suit.

"You never know," I said.

I urged on him a headlamp.

"Are we going *mining*?" he asked.

"You never know." I shrugged.

When I showed him the collapsible walking sticks, he became convinced he was the victim in a bait-and-switch exercise. What next? Ropes and crampons? In fact, we would need those for the short schlepp across the glacier on the first day. I decided to let the guide explain about that when we got there.

"Now," I said, "you'll want a knife."

"Why?"

"You've seen *Deliverance*, haven't you? It's even worse in the Alps."

Finally we arrived in Zermatt. There we arranged for the guide, bought more maps, entered emergency rescue numbers (Swiss and Italian) into Elan's cell phone, immersed ourselves in local knowledge, packed and repacked our backpacks, bought energy bars and extra batteries for the GPS. I'd been practicing my GPS navigation all summer. A year after we had first discussed the idea, we were ready.

The night before we were to set off, Elan announced, "I can't feel anything in my big toe." He said this was the familiar prelude to a spinal disc that periodically herniates. Manfully, he offered to press on with Plan A. I imagined the scene, somewhere at 10,000 feet along the Tour Monte Rosa, kneeling beside him as he was wrapped in his shiny space blanket like a ball park hot dog, telling him, "The radio says there's a storm moving in, so the helicopters aren't flying. Is the Advil working yet?" I imagined explaining to his wife and three children why I had crippled him for life with my insistence that we stick with Plan A.

There are few crises that cannot be improved with multiple bottles of wine. So it was that we hatched Plan B: Stay in Zermatt, sleep late, hike by day, swim afterward at the health club, then sauna and steam, followed by leisurely dinners, followed by Armagnac and Cohibas and billiards. Wake up the next morning and do it all over again, for ten whole days. Plan B actually sounded pretty good.

I hadn't been to Zermatt in forty years. This is one disadvantage of being fifty: being able to say, "I haven't been here in forty years." To the pretty young women behind the desk at the Hotel Monte Rosa, I wittily said, "Why, you weren't even *born* when I last stayed here!" Being professional, they reacted as if I had let loose an Oscar Wilde–level *bon mot*. This is one advantage of being fifty: young people humor you.

The Hotel Monte Rosa has been around since 1855, when it belonged to a man named Alexander Seiler. It was from this hotel that the twenty-five-year-old Englishman Edward Whymper and his six companions set off, at 5:30 on the morning of July 13, 1865. (Not July 14, as the bronze plaque on the front of the hotel proclaims. But then, bronze typographical errors are expensive to correct.) Seven of them made it to the summit. It was the first successful ascent. Three of them made it back to Zermatt alive.

In Whymper's book, *Scrambles Amongst the Alps*, he describes the scene: "Seiler met me at his door, and followed in silence to my room. 'What is the matter?' 'The Taugwalders and I have returned.' He did not need more, and burst into tears; but lost no time in useless lamentations, and set to work to arouse the village."

Our rooms on the second floor had balconies with flowers and looked out onto the main square and the little splashing frog fountain across from the Grand Hotel Zermatterhof. If it hadn't been for the casino they were building, I'd have been able to see the alpinists' cemetery next to the church, where Michel Croz is buried. Croz was one of the men killed on the way down on July 14. I remember as a child standing in front of his gravestone and reading the inscription on it, marking

the loss of a brave man, beloved by his comrades
and esteemed by travelers. He perished not far from here,
a man of stout heart, faithful guide

It's only a matter of time before they put slot machines and a craps table near the grave of a man like that. This is a disadvantage of turning fifty: coming back to a fairyland of your youth and finding that they've added a casino.

But the Matterhorn has not changed. It still takes your breath away when on the train ride up into Zermatt you look out the window and bang, there it is, the world's most recognizable mountain. Horace Bénédict de Saussure, a scientist and Alp-scrambler from Geneva, gave it its modern French name in 1789 when he crossed the St. Théodule pass into Zermatt and described in his book "the great and superb pyramid of Mont-Cervin which rises to an immense height in the form of a triangular obelisk of living rock, and which has the appearance of being carved by a chisel."

This living rock has killed almost three times more climbers than Everest, about five hundred, by one estimate. This sounds like a tragic accumulation, and of course it is, though the figure is equal to about five days of U.S. auto deaths.

I remember as a child being fascinated by the mountain, by Whymper, by Gustave Doré's engraving of the tragedy. I remember reading James Ramsey Ullman's *The White Tower* under my blanket with a flashlight and seeing the movie *Third Man on the Mountain*. My dashing uncle Reid—a four-pack-a-day smoker at the time—actually climbed the mountain. One of the people in his group refused to leave the summit, and remained, a suicide.

One day Elan and I were lying on our backs in the shale at the base of the mountain and looking up at the north face, thinking the identical thought ("No f— way"). Through binoculars, we made out two human flyspecks four-fifths of the way up, making their way to the top v-e-r-y slowly.

Wandering amid the tombstones in the alpinists' cemetery where the noble Croz was buried after they reassembled his remains, I came across the grave of a seventeen-year-old from New York City. He was killed on the nearby Breithorn in 1975. His ice ax is mounted on his gravestone, along with the words *I CHOSE TO CLIMB.*

Later that same day, as Elan and I strolled Zermatt's main street, we heard the buzz of a helicopter. People craned their necks upward at the cliffs looming above the town. We watched a man being lowered by a cable from the helicopter 500 meters up and leap—*leap*—onto the cliff face, where, through binoculars, we made out three more bright dots clinging to the rock face. For the record, my tombstone will display not an ice ax but the TV remote control changer and the inscription *I CHOSE NOT TO CLIMB.*

We did, on the other hand, choose to hike. Over ten days our aggregate came to 55 kilometers and 6,700 vertical meters. It doesn't sound like much, but we returned sweaty every day. We calculated our vertical as amounting to about eighteen Empire State Buildings, which sounds a bit more impressive.

The trails around Zermatt take you through some of the most beautiful scenery in the world. To the little village of Zmutt, to the Schwarzee (Black Sea, an immodest name for the pond near the base of the Matterhorn), the Mettelhorn, the Gornergrat. Soon the click-clack of our collapsible walking sticks on the rock seemed as natural as breathing.

One day we hiked up to Edelweiss (population: 2), perched on a cliff almost 360 meters above Zermatt. It's a bit of a hump. Before you reach Edelweiss, you come to a sheer vertical rock face. At the foot of it are little shrines, with battery-operated votive candles. One crucifix bears the words,

Zum andenken
OTTO GENTINETTA
Geboren den 25
August 1892
Hier verunglückt
Am 20 Juni 1900

Elan translated *verunglückt*: unlucky. He was only seven years old, poor little guy.

A few days later we hiked up to Edelweiss again. This time, Elan didn't stop. He's in much better shape than I, so I didn't catch up with him until I got to the restaurant with its porch overlooking the valley.

"You were moving fast," I said.

It was September 11, 2002. He'd done it without stopping, as a token anniversary tribute to the firefighters who went into the two towers. Looking down from the terrace, the thought was there between us. The people trapped in the upper floors who leapt to their deaths fell for ten seconds.

We finished our cups of *Hakenbutter* (hot, reviving red tea) and pushed on up another 300 meters to Trift (population: 3). It was foggy and windy and cold, which made us grateful for Hugo's hot potato-leek soup at the inn. Hugo and his wife and six-year-old son, Sebastian, run the place. Hugo used to guide on the Matterhorn. "Ninety times," he said, with that matter-of-factness that in the Swiss denotes pride. "Four hours up, four hours down."

Flaxen-haired Sebastian insisted that we play with him as we slurped soup and drank iced tea–lemonade. The fog cleared and Hugo produced an alpenhorn, Switzerland's second most conspicuous icon after the Matterhorn, and blew a haunting air called "Luzerner," which he aimed at a dozen hikers nearly invisible on a path 2,000 feet above. It was as soulful a sound as I've ever heard in Switzerland. The entire valley became a tympanum. In the distance, the hikers paused and waved.

After lunch we climbed another 300 vertical meters, until we came to a ridge under the Weisshorn, some 1,000 meters above Zermatt. Here we found enormous steel gates: avalanche barriers to protect the town below. Next to plunging 1,200 meters down the cheese grater of the Matterhorn, "Buried Under Avalanche" is right up there on my list of Ways I Would Prefer Not to Die.

Elan rushed on the long hike down. I could barely get him to pause for a photo beneath a spectacular rainbow. I wondered if this was another 9/11 homage, but at the bottom he confessed to inexplicable bad vibrations. It might have been the *foehn*, the warm wind that causes mood changes.

But now the late-afternoon sun was blazing as we click-clacked over paved streets to a garden restaurant where we sat and drank cold beer. That night we ate pasta and drank red wine at the Chalet da Giuseppe, which is where the locals eat when they want to have a good meal out. Giuseppe has been there for almost thirty years, smiling and shouting, "*Buona sera!*" at you when you walk in, and kissing and hugging the clientele, who, being Swiss, do not generally go in for a lot of public kissing and hugging. Giuseppe has deep smile lines, but his eyes looked exhausted from three decades of jollying local Lutherans.

Lord Byron fled London to Switzerland after an incest scandal. His verdict on Helvetia was that it was "a curst, selfish, swinish country of brutes." Having Swiss blood in my own veins, I do not subscribe to the Byronic position. I've known many Swiss, with great fondness. But there is a certain stolidity in the Swiss soul. We met an Italian woman who had lived in Zermatt for many years. She gave Elan her perspective, in Italian: "They survive, but they do not live."

On the way back to the Hotel Monte Rosa, we smoked cigars in the cold moonlight and found ourselves on the Hinterdorfstrasse, a narrow street lined with ancient chalets. We heard a preternatural screech from within and witnessed a ferocious engagement between bellicose cats. I dozed off to sleep with *War and Peace* on my chest and *A Clockwork Orange* dubbed in Spanish on the TV, and woke at 3:30 a.m.—a nightly event—to the sound of drunks spilling out of Grampi's Bar and Pizzeria. One night, Elan and I prepared water balloons to launch on the raucous hearties from our balconies, but we never did get a clear shot.

On the second floor of the Hotel Monte Rosa is a quiet wood-paneled room hung with etchings and photographs of men who either made the Matterhorn famous or died on it, or both. Here are Whymper, Charles Hudson, Lord Francis Douglas (he was related to

Lord Alfred Douglas, Oscar Wilde's lover), Douglas Hadow, Michel Croz, and Peter Taugwalder and his son.

There's also a photo of Sir Arnold Lunn. The face looking out is of an old but still spry man, carrying skis over his shoulder, grinning and squinting through small round spectacles. If you ski, you owe Sir Arnold thanks, because it was he, perhaps more than any other single person, who made it into a sport.

He was a remarkable Englishman. In his early twenties, climbing in Wales, he fell 30 meters and broke his leg so badly that for the rest of his life he walked with a limp on a leg three inches shorter than the other. Yet he climbed every mountain in the Alps, skied down some of them, and invented the slalom. He also wrote dozens of books—on mountaineering, the Swiss, and Catholicism.

He was a friend of my father's. Every year we would visit him in Mürren. (The town got its name from Hannibal, who was apparently impressed by the immense cliff on which it perches. You may have seen it in a James Bond movie.) Sir Arnold and Lady Phyllis lived in a grace-and-favor apartment provided by the Swiss government in recognition of his contribution to their national economy. When I was eight years old, I taught him how to use the elevator in his hotel. When Sir Arnold was eight himself, in 1908, he met the great Edward Whymper. So I shook the hand that shook the hand of Edward Whymper.

I brought Sir Arnold's book *Matterhorn Centenary* on our trip. It's a fascinating, unsparing account, and from it I learned the intriguing fact that Whymper, the Englishman who did more than anyone else to make the Matterhorn and Zermatt famous, was more or less detested in these parts. The reason had to do with the aftermath of the July 14 tragedy.

In Whymper's telling, here is what happened. Michel Croz was helping the Englishman Hadow place his feet securely when:

> *I heard one startled exclamation from Croz, then saw him and Mr. Hadow flying downwards; in another moment Hudson was dragged from his steps, and Lord F. Douglas*

> *immediately after him. All this was the work of a moment. Immediately we heard Croz's exclamation, old Peter and I planted ourselves as firmly as the rocks would permit: the rope was taut between us, and the jerk came on us both as on one man. We held; but the rope broke midway between Taugwalder and Lord Francis Douglas. For a few seconds we saw our companions sliding downwards on their backs and spreading out their hands, endeavouring to save themselves. They passed from our sight uninjured, disappeared one by one, and fell from precipice to precipice on to the Matterhorngletscher below, a distance of nearly 4,000 feet. From the moment the rope broke it was impossible to help them.*
>
> *So perished our comrades! For the space of half an hour we remained on the spot without moving a single step.*

The accident caused headlines and controversy. There were letters to the *Times*. Queen Victoria demanded of the lord chamberlain why mountaineering couldn't simply be prohibited by law. Taugwalder was accused of cutting the rope. Whymper defended him against that charge, but leveled others, implying that Taugwalder had deliberately tied himself to Douglas, an inexpert climber, with a weak rope. He also said that the Taugwalders had asked him to say publicly that they had not been paid for guiding, in order to arouse sympathy for them and to stimulate future business. But most damningly, Whymper told the inquest that as they huddled miserably through the long night, the Taugwalders acted so menacingly toward him that he kept his rock and ice ax at the ready. The implicit charge was that they were seeking to increase their notoriety—and guide business—by becoming the only survivors of the first successful ascent of the Matterhorn. Grim stuff.

The two Taugwalders were tainted by the odious charges until Sir Arnold Lunn published an article in the *Alpine Journal* exonerating them eighty years later. It wasn't until then, he wrote, that one Swiss confided to him, "*Whymper war nicht beliebt in Tal.*" (Whymper was not liked in the valley.)

So there you have the dirty little secret of Edward Whymper, Great Man of the Matterhorn: the locals hated his guts.

Sir Arnold wrote, "He was a friendless, and in many ways a pathetic man, and there was little, if anything, admirable about him excepting his mountaineering, but in spite of defects which I have not attempted to conceal, there was something great about the man. Many eminent mountaineers have contributed to the history of the Matterhorn by forcing new routes up its cliffs, but the Matterhorn remains Whymper's mountain, partly because he himself had something of the indomitable character of that great peak . . . To the end, he remained astonishingly tough. At the age of 62 he walked from Edinburgh to London, averaging 55 miles a day."

I spent some pleasant hours with Sir Arnold's book in the little room on the second floor of the Hotel Monte Rosa. There's a small library in the hall, donated by a New York lady. There I found a reissue of Whymper's own book, *Scrambles Among the Alps* (Dover Publications, New York).

After breakfast, Elan and I would take our tea there and plan our leisurely days. I couldn't remember when I had last had ten full days with no appointments or To Do list. No BlackBerry, no iPhone, just the clunky computer in the hotel foyer with intermittent Internet access. Bliss, truly. Elan called the trip our *piccola pausa*—little pause—the Italian term for the interval between courses.

Being unrushed, I began to notice things that might ordinarily have escaped my attention, such as the hotel's flower planters. They were old chamber pots. I wondered, *Might this one have been Whymper's?* Altitude does strange things to a man.

One afternoon we hiked to a glade by a small waterfall and made a picnic of crusty bread, Côtes du Rhône, luscious plump tomatoes, Gruyère and *Trockenfleisch* (slices of air-dried beef), and a bar of Toblerone. We hiked back into town and went to pay our respects at the Alpine Museum.

I was last there in 1962—before you were born—and remembered seeing the famous rope that had parted, sending Croz, Hadow, Douglas, and Hudson on their fatal plunge. It's still there. I was no less enthralled standing before it as I had been as an innocently morbid boy. I could find no reference to the Controversy. Whymper may have been *nicht beliebt in Tal*, but he still packs them in. One exhibit is a chair he sat in while having his hair cut.

There's a sad display of dried leather boots that belonged to climbers who never lived to unlace them. A photograph of a breathtakingly beautiful young Englishwoman who died on the Matterhorn in a terrible storm. Near the exit is a framed account by Teddy Roosevelt of his ascent of the Matterhorn in 1881, age twenty-two. (Winston Churchill also climbed it. *Everyone* seems to have climbed it.) Young TR wrote to his sister back home, "One of the chief reasons I undertook the ascent of the Matterhorn was to show some English climbers who were staying at the same hotel that a Yankee could climb as well as they could." Standing before this document, I realized that I, too, must make my ascent of the Matterhorn. National pride was at stake.

It was going on two in the afternoon when the next day we achieved the base of the mountain. Here would begin our path to the summit, 1,500 meters above.

I checked my water bottle, marked the spot on my GPS, and applied another coat of SPF. Whymper and the others had started from this very spot, as had so many others. Elan would remain behind. He had to call Barry Diller on his cell phone about some deal they were doing.

Thus I set off solo on my ascent of the north face. Ten minutes into it I had reached 60 meters up the trail. I thought of Michel Croz and *The White Tower* and *Third Man on the Mountain* and the seventeen-year-old who had chosen to climb. A helicopter buzzed by overhead on its way to the Hörnli hut to deposit climbers. It was a brilliant sunny-cool day. I felt superbly alive—not a day over forty-nine.

I began my descent. Elan was still on the phone with Barry Diller. It took Hugo eight hours to make it up and back. It took me fifteen minutes. Now, for the rest of my life I could say, "I climbed the Matterhorn." (Not with a bang, but with a Whymper.)

We hiked back down into town. I slept through until dawn, undisturbed by the Grampi's revelers. I didn't even have to get up in the middle of the night, which as you hit fifty, becomes another of life's accomplishments, along with conquering the Matterhorn.

—*Forbes FYI*, October 2003

SUBURBAN CRANK

For years, I lived in cities, where my conversation consisted of world events, politics, literature, art, science, and, to be sure, the latest gossip.

Now I live in the suburbs, and my conversation seems to consist of complaining. We had guests over the other night—solid, interesting people who could hold their own in any conversation about the latest developments in Europe or Mali, or John Irving's new novel, or the upcoming exhibit at the Metropolitan Museum of Pre-Columbian Erotic Ceramics.

Instead, I treated them to a diatribe on my property taxes. Then it was on to the heron—or, as I call it, the "f— ing heron"—that has turned my koi pond into its private sushi bar. I can go on at length on that topic, let me tell you. And would have, if the memsahib hadn't shot me a glance that said, Dear, why don't we move on from the heron?

So I moved on, to another subject worthy of Socratic discourse: the third-floor fire detector. See, it's right outside the bathroom door, and whenever someone takes a steamy shower and opens the door—*weeeoooo weeooo*—it goes off. And if someone happens to be using the phone and the alarm company can't call us, the next thing you know, there are six hook-and-ladder trucks and two ambulances wailing up the driveway, with sirens going and—

"Darling," memsahib interjects, "I think our guests need more wine. Why don't you go down into the basement and get some?"

"Yes, oh light of my life," I say huffily, feeling like Homer interrupted in mid-epic.

But as I reflect on my current conversational repertoire—the traffic on I-95 (don't get me started); the so-called weed remover that seems to promote weed growth (an outrage, really); the mole holes in the lawn (you could break an ankle); the dryer fan in the basement that no one ever remembers to turn off after the dryer is finished (it makes this *rrrrr-rrrrr* sound); the fireplace that every time you light turns the TV room into a smokehouse despite the new $700 chimney fan. . . . The evidence is, I stipulate, starting to mount: I have become a suburban crank.

I also talk about the weather. I never used to talk about the weather, unless it involved a hurricane or tornado. Then the other day, I was going on about the water bill and caught myself saying, "I'm seriously considering writing a strongly worded letter to the editor of the local paper." Memsahib said, "Good idea, darling. Why don't you?" I caught the look of pity on her face, oh yes. (Or was it . . . self-pity?) She has started to humor me. That wasn't supposed to happen for at least another twenty years.

How did this happen? Okay, so I moved to the suburbs. But there's some undistributed middle at work, surely. I keep up with things. I do. I read the papers every day—three, including the *Financial Times*. I admit I skim that one, since I don't understand most of it. To be honest, I don't hang on Angela Merkel's every word, try as I might. But that doesn't stop me from saying with a straight face, "The *FT*? Indispensable. Read it every day."

I read books—quality books, too, not trash. I can do the Sunday *Times* crossword, so long as memsahib is at my side. I went to college. I know stuff. Do *you* know the derivation of the word *mayonnaise*? Were you aware that it is one of the few words in the English language of Carthaginian origin? Didn't think so.

So, anyway, the other day, I drive over to Galt's to pick up some more three-quarter-inch river stone for the edging around the fish-pond. Because the lawn guys, when they do the leaf-blowing, always blow the smaller stones into the fish pond. Which totally freaks out the koi. I mean, one minute they're hanging out doing koi stuff, the next there's this underwater avalanche. And of course we wouldn't want the f— heron to think that his sushi bar has a badly edged border, would we? Nooo. So I tell the guy at Galt's—

"Darling."

"What?"

"I think your readers need more wine."

—*ForbesLife*, June 2013

BUT SERIOUSLY

Reality goes bounding past the satirist like a cheetah laughing as it lopes ahead of the greyhound.

—CLAUD COCKBURN

SUPREME COURT CALENDAR

The Court ruled, 5–4, that the police may open fire on vehicles speeding through the EZ Pass toll lanes provided they first fire "an attention-getting warning burst" into the air. In *Gonzales v. Texas Interstate Authority*, a San Antonio man sued when his car was riddled with bullets after he went through the EZ Pass lane at 38 miles per hour. Writing for the majority, Justice O'Connor noted, "While the presence of 187 bullet holes suggests zeal, even delight, on the part of the officers who disabled Mr. Gonzalez's vehicle, their actions were consistent with existing local statues providing for 'extraordinary measures' when dealing with EZ Pass lane violators."

The Court struck down, 7–2, a controversial Connecticut state constitutional amendment granting full civil rights to raccoons. In a sharp dissent, Justice John Paul Stevens, a moderate liberal, suggested that Justice Scalia "was off his meds" when he wrote the majority opinion. "The Founders," Stevens warned, "purposely left vague whether raccoons, *nihilo minus* of the fact that they carry rabies and upset garbage cans in the middle of the night, are second-class citizens." Furthermore, "this will—and should—inspire fear among Connecticut's porcupines, whose civil liberties have already suffered irreparable harm at the hands of juridical blackshirts." Supreme Court guards had to separate the two justices and a brief recess was called.

In *Krud Coal Co. v. Wrings Water from Rocks*, the Court ruled, 6–3, that a Colorado coal company that drained the entire water supply of a nearby Indian reservation in order to pump coal through its pipeline was not obliged to provide "compensatory hydration" to 2,300 Arapahoe left severely parched by the drainage of the aquifer that they have been using since A.D. 1000. In his majority opinion, Chief Justice Rehnquist pointed out, "there are three Coca-Cola machines on the reservation," and that the Arapahoe "are by reputation excellent rain dancers." In a withering dissent, Justice Ruth Bader Ginsburg pointed out that Justice Rehnquist owns 6 percent of the Krud Coal Company, "in his Cayman Islands account"; moreover, that it has not rained in that part of Colorado since 1974.

In *Bigelow v. M&Ms*, the Court ruled, 7–2, that a candy manufacturer could not be sued by someone seeking damages for adolescent acne. In a scathing majority opinion, Justice Scalia wrote, "Those who bring such suits deserve far worse than acne. They should, *per antiqua lege Romana*, be put in burlap sacks with wild cats—or, as Justice Stevens would no doubt prefer, raccoons—and thrown into the Potomac." In his dissent, Justice Souter said that the ruling violates the equal protection clause, "as not all Americans have access to cats and water, or pari passu, burlap."

The Court ruled, 5–4, in *Lamar Buford Podine v. State of Florida* that a state is entitled to seek compensation for the wattage expended in executions by electric chair. Writing for the majority, Justice Thomas cited the sixteenth-century precedent of "tipping the headsman." In a dissent, Justice Stevens wrote, "Earth to Clarence: this is the twentieth century. Or did you not get that memo?" Justice Rehnquist, who co-wrote the majority opinion with Justice Thomas, suggested that there should "definitely" be compensation if the electric chair in question was powered by coal.

The Court strengthened the hand of bank examiners by ruling 6–3 that they should be permitted to administer physical torture while conducting routine audits. In another banking-related case, the Court ruled along straight ideological lines as to whether Screen Actors Guild actors who use ATM machines should be paid residual royalties for appearing in the film taken by security cameras during transactions.

In a bitter dispute involving Chief Justice Rehnquist's basement parking space, the Court ruled, 8–1, that he should take "immediate steps" to repair the leaking crankcase of his 1997 Chevy Impala, which has been spilling oil onto Justices Kennedy's, Ginsburg's and Souter's parking spaces. Writing for the majority, Justice Souter noted, "The Founders clearly intended for high officials of the land to maintain undercarriages that were not 'inherently loathsome' (*Madison v. Conoco*) to their fellow man." Justice Rehnquist, writing for the minority, cited *Messy v. Ferguson*, "in which some court somewhere in like, Ohio or Iowa or one of those places," ruled that it was "legal, if not entirely considerate" for a person to empty a 45-gallon container of radioactive waste in the parking garage on the grounds that he had paid the full daily rate for the space.

—*Forbes FYI*, October 2002

THE ORIGIN AND DEVELOPMENT OF THE LOBSTER BIB

Volume II: Rome to the Present Era

A.D. 20—Pristinus, tunic-maker to the Roman emperor Tiberius Caesar, is tasked with protecting the imperial purple robe from stains caused by seafood particles during the emperor's prolonged feasts on the Isle of Capri. He devises a protective garment that he calls a "bibulus," because it also protects Tiberius's clothes from imperial drool caused by drunken gorging. The bibulus is embroidered with rubies in the form of a Mediterranean spiny lobster. Tiberius's mother, Livia, comments in front of the entire court that the garment makes her son look like a Zoroastrian hermaphrodite. Tiberius makes Pristinus eat the bibulus and has him thrown off the cliff from the imperial villa. The incident has a chilling effect on further lobster bib R&D.

564—Ergo of Fluny, a Benedictine abbot, oversees work on *Les Milles Malheures du Beurre*, a thousand-page illustrated manuscript depicting the evil effects of drawn butter spilled on priestly vestments. Ergo's interest in this theologically recondite area is due to a previous manuscript having been ruined by a monk-scribe prone to snacking, who dribbled food onto it, thereby ruining twelve years of communal labor. The book is denounced as heretical by Pope Indolent III on the grounds that melted butter on priestly garments is an outward manifestation of divine grease (*foi grasse*). Depictions of Ergo being lowered into the papal pot of boiling water become a popular motif among medieval artists.

622—Padraigggth Cro Ma Uch Na Gorbthflp, called Anapatrick, or more simply, Anapaddy, a Celtic slave from Ireland, saves his English owner when he falls into a pool of holy lobsters. Anapatrick loses a toe in the process, but is granted his freedom by his grateful master. As a sign of his manumission, Anapaddy is given a hempen apron crudely decorated with several lobsters of fierce aspect. The garment, remnants of which are on display at Trinity College, Dublin, is thought by scholars to have been both the first full-length bib as well as the first to depict multiple lobsters.

892—Grim the Odious, a highly unpopular Viking, begins using buxom women as human lobster bibs after his raids on English fishing villages. Grim decides that this is a superior method of shielding his breastplate from chunks of raw shellfish than using the flayed hides of defeated warriors. From this point on, contemporary accounts begin referring to him as Grim Mellowpuss.

1000—The Norseman Leif Ericsson lands in what is now Bar Harbor, Maine, thereby discovering the Western Hemisphere. He and his men are met by natives who, taking Ericsson's arrival as an ill omen, pelt them with rocks, driftwood, and the plentiful creatures that they call "stupid slow-moving things that turn pink when you drop them in hot water."

The creatures, whose names will eventually be shortened to "lobstahs," bounce harmlessly off the breastplates of the Vikings, but the gesture annoys the Norsemen, already grumpy after being blown thousands of miles off course by savage storms, so they slaughter the Indians. Afterward, the hungry Vikings eat the creatures, which have conveniently been shattered into edible pieces by the metal breastplates. For the next two centuries, Vikings will break lobsters by slamming them against their chests, but these "hard bibs" will soon give way to "soft bibs" as people become less violent in their dining habits.

1216—The English "red" barons and King John meet at Runnymede, where the barons assert their right to wear "bibbes" to protect their chain mail from being rusted by seawater dripping off "lobbesters and other such crustacean victualles that dribbleth from our mouthes whilst feastinge and whoringe." King John, weary from last year's meeting with barons at Runnymede, signs the document, which will become known as the Magna à la Carta, but he holds firm on his refusal to provide the barons with "moiste towelettes."

1240—A bib alleged to have been used by Jesus at the so-called Clambake of Cana is given to William of Dipp, a knight-crusader, by some Muslims he is about to behead, in exchange for not beheading them. The bib shows what appears to be a man's chest soaked in butter and the impression of two lobster claws. William gives the bib to an archbishop in return for a temporal indulgence and what is now Yorkshire. It disappears from history until 1389, when it reappears in the Convent of the Wretched Sisters of Penury in Umbria. They display the bib as a holy relic, drawing pilgrimages and donations. In 1395, the order changes its name to the Formerly Wretched Sisters of Penury and purchases what is now Umbria.

1994—Bowing to pressure from the Vatican, whose scholars can find no reference to a "Clambake of Cana" in the life of Jesus, the Extremely Well-Off Sisters of Penury allow a team from Cal-Tech's Jet Propulsion Lab and the Cornell Institute of Bibliological Studies to subject the bib to sophisticated spectrographic and carbon-14 analysis. The experts conclude that the bib is in fact a fake; moreover, that crustaceans were unknown in the Sea of Galilee. Nonetheless, the bib continues to be revered by many, in particular by a group of strict penitents who flagellate themselves with lobsters as part of their annual Lenten observance.

—*Forbes FYI*, May 2000

A SHORT HISTORY OF THE BUG ZAPPER

1506—Leonardo da Vinci invents the first bug zapper on May 3. Also on that day, he invents the first toaster oven, gyroscope, electric toothbrush, Q-tip, cheese knish, flush toilet, ball bearing, hypodermic needle, global positioning system, helium, heart-lung transplant machine, Botox, and the paper aeroplane. His "Device for the Immolation of Pests of the Air" is powered not by electricity, which he won't discover until May 7, but by nuclear energy, which Leonardo invented on May 2, along with fluoride, quarks, the submarine, the stop sign and pantyhose.

1552—Ivan the Terrible, the first Tsar of All the Russias, is distracted by mosquitoes while torturing boyars in the Kremlin. He offers a prize—not having your head chopped off—to anyone who proposes an efficient means of eliminating the *"proklyatj vozduh d'yavol"* ("f— devils of the air"). Oddly, no one comes forward with ideas. Ivan relents and changes the prize to life imprisonment at hard labor, but still no one voices a proposal. Furious, Ivan annexes the Tatar states of Kazan and Astrakhan. His subjects, too terrified to point out that this will accomplish little toward eradicating insects, praise him. Progress will not be made for another 350 years, when Stalin declares all mosquitoes counterrevolutionary and has them shot or sent to Siberia.

1752—Benjamin Franklin electrocutes a moth by tying it to a kite that he floats aloft into an electrical storm. He sends his friends in England a dissertation entitled "An Experiment on the Effects of Violent Lightning Bolts Upon a Specimen of Lepidoptera." His conclusion: A million volts of electricity will likely incinerate not only the moth but quite possibly the person holding the kite string. George III falls asleep while Franklin's treatise is being read to him, though this is attributed by court insiders to a surfeit of gin. A subsequent attempt to electrocute a rat by similar means fails when the rat bites Franklin and escapes.

1863—During the siege of Vicksburg, Lieutenant Homer Suds of the Union Army's Corps of Engineers is tasked by his commanding general with coming up with a way of "killing these swarms of goddamned bugs." Suds's method, still considered a masterpiece of battlefield improvisation, consists of honey, molasses, saltpeter, and unstable nitroglycerin. It dramatically reduces the local mosquito population, but is discontinued after it blows up a lieutenant colonel and two brevet majors who mistakenly dip their spoons into it, seeking to sweeten their coffee.

1934—The Düsseldorf electrician Heinrich Himmelring designs a prototype of the first truly modern bug zapper, called *Insektver-BrennnungsofenMaschine*. Powered by twin hydroelectric turbines, his IBM is capable of frying one million insects simultaneously, but fails to catch on commercially, since it causes massive brownouts (*lampedämmerung*) throughout North Rhine–Westphalia. Himmelring offers his services to Emperor Haile Selassie I of Ethiopia, but is frustrated when he cannot find a single electrical socket in the entire country. A treadmill powered by thousands of Somali "guest workers" not only fails to generate the required kilowattage but triggers war with Somalia. Distraught, Himmelring commits suicide by drinking tap water.

1942—Einstein writes FDR a letter in which he warns the president that "the German government is close to achieving a means of mosquito elimination utilizing blue lights and directed energy." Roosevelt orders the Office of Strategic Services to create facsimile zappers in order to deceive German agents into believing that the United States already possesses bug-incineration technology. The fake devices consist of boxes containing blue fluorescent lightbulbs and dwarves covered with shoe polish who make "Zzzt!" sounds.

1948—Jean-Pierre Blumière is charged by the French colonial authorities in Indochina with devising a means of keeping French generals from being bitten by mosquitoes during their daily four-hour lunches. Blumière's device, consisting of bulbs imported from Paris's red-light district, is effective, but the generals complain that the smell of the roasting insects is interfering with their enjoyment of the food.

1958—The documentary movie *The Fly* portrays a Montreal scientist's obsession with creating a means of killing houseflies by electric current. His experiment backfires tragically when the scientist's molecules are fused with those of a housefly that he is trying to teleport to the United States so it can torment Americans.

1966—As the Vietnam War escalates, the U.S. Navy secretly trains dolphins to eat mosquito larvae before they can hatch in the Mekong Delta and pester U.S. troops.

1967—Stoned hippies in San Francisco's Haight-Ashbury receive painful electric shocks and blistered tongues when they lick bug zappers, mistaking them for "psychedelic" black lights. Governor Ronald Reagan announces that it serves them right.

1991—The Sharper Image company introduces the "Mother of All Bug Zappers" in its spring catalogue. Sleekly designed to look like a cross between the bomb dropped on Hiroshima and a flat-screen TV, MABZ boasts patented nonclogging vertical killing grids and uses spent plutonium and argon gas, causing bugs to glow iridescently in up to twenty colors before succumbing painfully to radiation poisoning. Each time an insect drops to the ground, MABZ emits a tape-recorded squeal, "Help meeeeeee!"

—*Forbes FYI*, May 2003

SCRUTINY ON THE *BOUNTY*

Captain Bligh's Secret Logbook

No monster on the high seas has equaled the infamous ship captain William Bligh. And no movie fan can forget the scene in which Charles Laughton, the definitive Bligh in the 1935 film, instructs his crew to keep flogging a man. That he's dead makes no difference to Bligh, lips curled with unfettered malignancy.

"Everything you think you know about Bligh is utterly wrong," says best-selling writer Caroline Alexander . . .

—*USA TODAY*

February 2, 1789. Position 18°52′3″ S, 129°27′45″ W. Winds light, W by WSW. Seas 2–4 feet. Am much vexed on account of Mr. Christian. His mood-compass vacillates sharply between Hysterical Agitation and Sullen Lethargy. I had so wanted this Voyage to be special for him.

Last night upon seeing him brooding, I told him I would stand his Watch and to go below and curl up in his bunke with a saucy book and a tot of grog. Whereupon he expostulated at me with such Violence that all I could do was mutter, "I keenly regret that you should feel so, dear man," and retreat to my own cabin.

Calmed myself by redrawing the Admiralty charts of the North and South Atlantick, which I found to be rife with Errors.

Febr. 10. Upon examining the Log, I found that Fletcher, who of late hath taken to addressing me as "Captain Bilge," had put us on a course not for Otaheite but for the Greate Barrier Reefe—named by myself on my Voyage with the late Captain Cook, God rest his fine soul.

Not wanting to embarrass him in front of the other Officers, I quietly ordered the helm up 2 ½ points. Whereupon he appeared on the quarterdeck, wearing no Breeches but only a nightshirt and a most fierce look in his eyes, and proceeded to accost me in a manner alarming and disrespectful, calling me Names which Decency prevents me from here enumerating.

I could only reply abashedly, "But your course, good man, though indubitably well intentioned, would have set us upon Sharke Rocke!"

But he would hear none of it, and called *me* the sharke.

"Fletcher, Fletcher, Fletcher," I said to him with a soothing aspect, "pray lie down, and I shall send Surgeon to bleed you of this unbecoming Humour."

Thereat he threw his grog cup at my feet and stormed off, beating an angry *quadrille* with his boot-heels upon the deck.

To the men looking on this unfortunate incident I said, "Mr. Christian is not himself, but he is a fine officer and will be well soon. Now look lively, lads, and spruce the t'uppergallants! Lively, now! Strike the foresnocker and slack the trice-halyards! Look sharp, my chickens! We shall have a tasty surprise at supper—I have ordered a well-drenched rumcake, and after, we shall dance a jig or two!"

March 3. Otaheite. At anchor. The putting aboard of the Bread-fruit proceeds. It is good to see the men so happy. The Native girls are exceeding generous with their charms.

March 15. Otaheite. Cross with myself over incident last night. Returned to the ship after surveying the island for the Admiralty, to find Fletcher in mine own berth making exceeding merry with three Native Dollies, one of whom, a girl not twelve years of age, is the daughter of the High Priest Mahoota-ete, upon whose Good Will the success of our mission very much depends.

This rude surprise, coupled with an fierce Migraine, the result of a Malaria contracted whilst ashore harvesting Bread-fruit, the men being too occupied with fornicating to assist me, put me in no good temper, which I thereupon proceeded to lose.

I abused Fletcher most severely, calling him a "randy ram" and "disgraceful" and "unprofessional." It is with Mortification that I recall my speech. Fortunately, my expostulations went unheard, as he had passed out, either from Surfeit of Eros or my (rather good) '78 Madeira.

At anchor. This morning's muster attended only by the cabin boy, Tom, three men of the larboard watch, two of the starboard, the carpenter, and the ship's Parrot, Algernon, the rest of the crew being still ashore in pursuit of Venery.

Have resolved to sail upon the morning tide and commence our historick voyage to His Majesty's slave plantations in Guyana with our cargoe of nutritious high-fiber Bread-fruit. (Reminder to self upon return to England to mount a Campaign for the Abolition of Slavery, a most unnatural and abhorrent practice.)

The sooner we are under the discipline of the sea, the better.

April 21. At sea—finally! Men *very* sullen at having left their Toffee-darlings behind and glower at me if I so much as suggest—for I no longer bother ordering them—that they might attend to the sails.

At 7 bells espied a dark Squall approaching from SW. "Up, lads!" I called out. "Up my darlings, briskly, and douse the midforemizzen and furl the afterwanker, or we shall lose them!"

But Fletcher and the other Officers and both Watches said they could not be bothered, inasmuch as they were occupied tattooeing the names of their Otaheite Dianas on each other's chestes. Had to attend to the sails myself, with only Tom to assist me, who, being dim, is not much use aloft.

If this impertinence persists, I shall have no recourse but to write a Letter of Rebuke in their Fitnesse reports upon our return to England.

Apr. 24. Found another Native wench stowed away. Most tiresome—the fourth so far. This one they were keeping in the larboard line locker, which no doubt accounteth for the great amount of volunteering of late to fetch unneeded halyards, sheets, stays, ratlines, Etc. Gave the men a good lashing with my Tongue and threatened to cancel Friday Night Whist if I found any more Tartes in my line lockers.

Apr. 26. Awoke at 6 bells to a Commotion on deck. Found the men inebriated on taro-root beer and pelting each other with our precious Bread-fruits. To my dismay, the Officers—garishly tattooed with the most Appalling and Lewd sentiments—were taking part in this Botanicide.

I had no choice but to lash them all vigourously with my Tongue. Then ordered half grog rations until Supper. Set the Officers to conjugate Irregular Latin verbs in chalk upon their navigation slates, occasioning much grumbling.

Apr. 27. Feeling confident that Order and good Naval discipline has been restored. The men go about their business, playing Bezique and Ten-o-Whiskers, napping and smoking and fishing and holding Spitting contests.

Apr. 28. Wanting to reward this good Behaviour, at 7 bells I announced that we would heave to—which maneuver I of course offered to undertake myself—in order that we might have a nice refreshing swim before our noon-meal of Dolphin and Sharke ceviche in a lyme-cilantroe Reduction with julienned mangoes and mashed wasabi taro. (My own Recipe.)

But instead of leading the men in a chorus of "Huzzah for our Captain Bligh!" Mr. Christian became Ballistick, hopping up and down like a French who has just been denied a third helping of *foie gras pâté*. Whereat the amok Ajax unsheathed his boarding-sword and began screeching at me, "I am in hell! In *hell*, sir!"

I replied, with such composure as I was able to muster, "Well, I am most grieved to hear it, *sir*," putting an hundredweight of pig-iron into the terminal word. "But perhaps a nice swim *would* cool you off."

Whereatupon he renewed his Remonstrations, bellowing at me a litany of complaints:—my "insensitivity" in having rebuked the men for spreading the French Pox among the Otaheite Innocents;—making them eat Sour Kraute against the Scurvy;—making them dance at night to circulate the Blood;—sending them aloft in high winds to take in Sail;—making them attend prayer-service upon the Sabbath;—my "obsession" with keeping the decks clean, Etc, Etc. Moses at his Expostulations before Pharaoh was less strident.

"Enow!" I finally cried. "I have heard quite *enow*, Mister Christian! And now if you will be so kind as to order the boat lowered, and to provide me with a crust of bread and a cask of fresh water, a melon or two if you can spare them from your *food-fighting*, my quadrant and chartes, I shall no longer trouble you with my presence aboard this vessel, *sir*. For it is my plain, humble, and franke conclusion that you have Issues with Male Authority, and into the bargain are disposed to violent Humours, careening from Phlegm to Bile in the space of time it takes to furl the midspizzlejidget. So with no further Adieu, I wish you, sir, and your men—for so they now are, along with the Bread-fruit—a good *day*!"

A number of men expressed desire to accompany me in the Boat. Was most Touched.

June 12. Batavia. During our 48-day Voyage, amidst disagreeable conditions, I was able to Process my feelings toward Fletcher, assuaged by the diversion of charting the coast of New Holland (rather accurately), also with keeping my lads alive, by means of such loathsome victuals as we were able to procure—gull-feet, barnacles, jellyfish, booby eggs, sea-weedes, Etc. By the time we fetched Timor, I had exhausted my anger at him and was resolved to say nothing against him in the event of an Inquest, having no wish to put at risk his future in H.M. Navy. He is a decent fellow at heart and will make a fine Officer of the Line, if only he would purge himself of these Demons that afflicte him.

Do earnestly hope he delivered my Bread-fruit safely to West Indies.

Must go and make a Poultice for my men.

—*The Atlantic Monthly*, December 2003

GOOD EVENING AND GOOD LUCK

An Internet video newscast called the Voice of the Caliphate was broadcast for the first time on Monday, purporting to be a production of al Qaeda and featuring an anchorman who wore a black ski mask and an ammunition belt. . . . A copy of the Koran, the Muslim holy book, was placed by his right hand and a rifle affixed to a tripod was pointed at the camera.

—THE WASHINGTON POST

"In Gaza, Jews on the run—see how they squeal. Along the Gulf Coast of the Great Satan, a spectacular storm destroys the City of Homosexuals, New Orleans, and, in infidel-occupied Iraq, a car bomber drives into a supermarket, creating a fireball in the meat section, destroying the entire inventory of pork products. But there was also bad news today: A startling report on new infrared U.S. helicopter capabilities that may affect the way you commute. The Dow dips below nine thousand as traders take short-term profits. And, finally tonight, our Martyr of the Week, someone for whom the phrase 'pluck out the eyes of the crusader' is more than just a slogan. In the name of Allah, the Merciful, the Compassionate, good evening. I'm Zalwar al-Qamush.

"First, a look at the local situation. In Afghanistan, another tremendous victory. We have this live report from our correspondent Anwar bin Haz, in Kandahar. Anwar, salaam."

"Zalwar, those are poppies behind me, as far as the eye can see. Local officials—that is, the ones we have not yet thrown down wells for collaborating with the American wolves—say this year's crop will be a record, producing literally tons of base material for high-grade heroin."

"Thank you, Anwar bin Haz. In Italy tonight, an exciting plan to blow up the Vatican during Christmas Eve services—after we return."

Ali Dada. Spent his whole life struggling against Zionism and imperialism. Scrimped and saved to send all of us to madrassah and terrorist training camps. Now he's in his sixties. His arthritis doesn't allow him to sneak over the border the way he used to, to kidnap American contractors from Halliburton and Kellogg Brown and Root, though he still insists on making the improvised explosive devices himself. That's why I give him Al Advil, the non-Jewish anti-inflammatory medicine.

"In Ramallah today, a joyous celebration as hundreds of youths urinated on American flags, set tires on fire, and hurled rocks at a passing Icelandic diplomat in honor of Grandmother's Day.

"And, in Pakistan, yet more rioting to protest the lifting of a popular fatwa. The fatwa, issued last Ramadan by a Karachi imam, promised twice the number of kohl-eyed virgins in Paradise—one hundred and forty-four—to anyone who assassinated President Pervez Musharraf for his collaboration with the American crusaders. But last week the imam lifted the fatwa after taking coffee with Karen Hughes, she-devil envoy of the Salivating Hyena Little Bush. Sources tell Voice of the Caliphate that the coffee was laced with a powerful hallucinogenic drug of the type used on soldiers of the true faith by CIA and Mossad interrogators at Abu Ghraib.

"And, from Guantánamo today, still another report that Muslim prisoners there are being subjected to barbaric tortures. The report, due out tomorrow from Martyrs Without Borders, the respected humanitarian agency, says these include being made to listen to 'Purimspiel' klezmer music twenty-four hours a day and being forced to watch the Barbra Streisand movie *Yentl* while immersed up to the neck in chicken soup. Several prisoners have reportedly beheaded themselves rather than endure more of these unspeakable horrors.

"Coming up next, medical news: Could living in damp tunnels for long periods of time be affecting your sex life? We'll have a report from our medical correspondent, deep inside Tora Bora. And a report on farewell videos—is the camera you're using to record your teenage suicide bomber's final good-bye getting the full picture? We'll have that, and our Martyr of the Week, when we return."

—*The New Yorker*, October 2005

A SHORT HISTORY OF THE BILLIONAIRE

MARDUK-BEL-BABUKK

Babylon, 602 B.C. 1.2 million gold and silver pieces. Contracting. Fourteen wives, eighty-five children.

Parlayed a modest mud-and-wattle business into Babylon's premier contracting operation. One of his wives' cousins was a bridesmaid of Amytis of Media, wife of Nebuchadrezzar II. After Amytis grew homesick for her native mountain springs, Marduk cannily proposed she persuade her husband to build "drop-dead gardens around the palace." Result: the Hanging Gardens of Babylon, one of the Seven Wonders of the ancient world. Nebuchadrezzar reportedly flew into a rage when Marduk presented his final bill but eventually was mollified after feeding several hundred of Marduk's workers to his pet lions. Hobbies: making palm wine, astrology, avoiding Nebuchadrezzar at public receptions.

EFTIMIOS PANAKOUSATIS

Piraeus, 481 B.C. 4 million to 6 million glaukai (tetradrachmae). Delphic banking, yogurt. Divorced from popular Athens cabaret singer Calypso Atalanta. Three children.

Started with two goats, one of which he had to eat during the harsh Corinthian winter of '02. In his early twenties traveled to Delphi near Mount Parnassus to seek career advice from the Oracle there. Noticed that people left thanksgiving offerings for the Oracle; reportedly struck a deal with the Oracle whereby he would keep 60 percent of the offerings while the Oracle got Larry Ellison as CEO. Amassed vast real estate holdings around Mount Parnassus, where multiple "oracles" soon sprang up, advising supplicants to leave even more offerings. Scored major points with the Greek archon Themistocles when he loaned the Athenian government his yacht *Calypso*—

renamed *Anna Nicola* after a messy divorce from his singer wife—for the Battle of Salamis. Following the naval victory, he demanded the government refit the vessel with a spa, pool, and wet bar.

CASSIUS BINOCULARIUS ANTHRAX

Capri, 3 B.C. 90 million aureii. Off-circus betting, slave trading.

Nickname "Buddy" bestowed on him by Emperor Tiberius during a three-day Lupercal drinking binge. Said to have fixed the 1 B.C. chariot race at the Circus Maximus between Ben Hur and his rival Messala. Pocketed enormous winnings after Messala (favored 50–1) was trampled under Ben Hur's chariot. Parlayed windfall into franchise betting operations in Parthia, Dacia, Iberia, and Germania, using a highly controversial system of reporting Roman chariot race results. Forced to shut down Germania operations after tribes torched his betting shops (with the concessionaires inside) following years of consistent losing. Bounced back; established a slave-trading network (Jeevus Dottus Commus) that kept patrician homes from Rome to the Amalfi Coast supplied with prized Britannic butlers.

KU F'ENG

Xian, 234 B.C. 800 to 900,000 bu. Pottery. Marital status: unknown but thought to have left several thousand direct descendants.

Name translates roughly as "Maker of money from dirt." A modest potter in Xian province, F'eng convinced the thirteen-year-old emperor Qin Shi Huang—later known as "The First Emperor" after he united China—that his mausoleum should contain, among other creature comforts, eight thousand life-size terra-cotta warriors to guard him in the afterlife. Created the world's first life-size terra-cotta warrior mass-production facility (an engineering feat not much imitated since). Eleven years and 8,099 warriors later, the now twenty-four-year-old emperor had bored of the project and, on the pretext that Ku F'eng was a secret adherent of Confucianism, had him buried alive along with the vast clay army. Sometimes called "The Last Warrior."

MARCANTONIO FANTUCCI

Venice, AD 1634. 5 million to 7 million ducats. Glassblowing, telescopes.

Apprenticed under the great Venetian glassblower Finoccio Babbalucanelli, supplier of chandeliers to the Medici. Fascinated early on by Galileo's astronomical telescopic explorations. When Galileo was forced to recant his theory of heliocentrism before the Inquisition in 1633, Fantucci correctly bet the event would create a vast demand for telescopes so that, as he put it craftily, "Everyone may watch the Sun orbit around the Earth." Borrowed 1,500 florins from Vigorino (The Shrewd) di Medici; constructed a telescope factory across the border in Switzerland (just to be safe). Most of his customers being Italian, he strove to remain in the favor of Pope Urban VIII and the Inquisition by naming his telescope the "Urban 8X." The instruction manual stated the telescope was "so marvelously powerful that you can actually see God. He is the very handsome one (does he not resemble our own beloved Pope Urban?) sitting on the third ring of Saturn next to John the Baptist." The telescopes sold briskly.

ANTOINE CHARLES EDUARD MARIE-BAPTISTE HONORÉ DE SAINT-HELOÏSE MERDE-ALORS, DUC DE VAUCOMPTE-LE-GROS

Versailles, 1704. 300,000 gold écus. Versailles. Fashion design.

Trained at the Atelier of Yves Le Chat-Blanc, supplier of hosiery and undergarments to the court of Louis XIV. When Le Chat-Blanc was felled by the plague on the eve of presenting the fall line of 1694, Antoine took over, impressing *le Roi Soleil* and his mistress Louise de la Vallière with his daring presentation of intimate apparel. Louis appointed him Pourvoyeur Exclusif des Sous-Pantalons Royales, making him the overnight toast of the Continent. Immediately feuded with Colbert, the finance minister, over astronomical bills for lingerie and *jocques-strapes dorées*; quarrel eventually led to the resumption of fierce religious war, for reasons that to this day continue to elude scholars. Following Louis's death in 1715—attributed to an ill-fitting culotte—Antoine left France under a cloud, never to return. Thereafter he designed undergarments for many of the royal houses of Europe, as well as for Peter the Great of Russia, who up to then had worn only crude drawers made from monks' beards and jute. Attempts to mass-produce an early version of *le pantyhose* using silk and spiderweb failed, bankrupting him.

GILEAD (SAM) STARBUCK

Boston, 1775. 140,000 dollars to 160,000 dollars (silver). Tea.

In December 1773, Starbuck was purser on the New Bedford whaleship *Incontinent* when it put into Boston Harbor to offload. Observing a crowd of Bostonians oddly dressed as Native Americans and hurling bricks of valuable English tea into the harbor, he lowered one of *Incontinent*'s whaleboats and rescued some of the 45 tons of jettisoned tea. Opened his first tea shop in Braintree several days later, serving a beverage called "Sal-Tea." When Sal-Tea failed to catch on, he rebranded it "Patrio-Tea," which did eventually find acceptance with Boston's tea-starved public. Subsequently struck a deal with the East India Company to supply (that is, smuggle) nonsalty tea to Massachusetts. His string of tea shops prospered, but scholars argue that he made a mistake calling them "Gileads" instead of some other catchier name.

—*Forbes Magazine*, October 2007

WE REGRET THE ERROR

An article in the September issue incorrectly identified the president of the United States. The current president is George W. Bush, not Harry S Truman.

An article in the March issue about private whale hunts incorrectly identified the costs associated with the trips. The price for harpooning a sperm whale is $3,500, not $3,600. Taxidermy costs for stuffing and mounting a whale amount to $18,000, not $1,800. The cost of shipping the mounted whale by Federal Express was also incorrect. The actual cost is "a staggering" sum, not "a bunch."

The cover article in the July issue, "Now Is the Time to Load Up on Tech Stocks," incorrectly stated the actual right time. The time to buy tech stocks was July 1999, not July 2001.

A caption in the September issue incorrectly identified a man shown entering a Manhattan adult XXX peep show. It should have read, "Adult XXX peep shows have been popular among New York men since the 1680s," not "Commercial real estate broker Roscoe F. Farnsbiddle of 138 Irving Road, Pelham Manor, often spends his lunch hour at peep shows instead of the Yale Club."

An article on the new GE chairman, Jeffrey Immelt, incorrectly stated that he likes to relax by watching videos of prison electrocutions. He relaxes by reading biographies and histories, and hiking with his family.

An article in the October issue, "Fatal Shark Attacks Surge in Lake Michigan," inadvertently gave the impression that there have been fatal shark attacks in Lake Michigan. According to the Lake Michigan Shark Attack Prevention Center, there have been no fatal shark attacks in Lake Michigan thus far this year. Last year, there were also none.

An article in the April issue, "Do-It-Yourself Plastic Surgery," incorrectly represented the views of the American Association of Plastic Surgeons. It does not endorse do-it-yourself plastic surgery.

An article in the June-July issue, "How the South Won the War," misrepresented the events at the Appomattox Courthouse in April 1865. It was General Lee who surrendered to General Grant, not the other way around.

An editing error in an article on the newly opened Hotel Wakami on the Hawaiian island of Molokai gave the false impression that there had been an outbreak of leprosy among the kitchen staff. The sentence should have read, "The kitchen specializes in fresh fish baked in parsley."

Due to a computer error, the July issue was published in Tagalog. An English version is being prepared for publication.

An article in the August issue, "Prince Charles Deposes His Mother in Bloody Overnight Palace Coup as Prince Philip Flees into Exile," contained several factual errors.

1) The correct term of address for Camilla Parker-Bowles, King

Charles III's consort, is "Your Royal Consortship," and thereafter, "Chooks," not "Ducky."

2) The midnight assault on Buckingham Palace by the Coldstream Guards was led by Captain Sir Reginald Hogg-Blother, CMG, VC, KCMP, VSOP, not Col. Alistair Pimpington-Rumpworth, GCMG, ASAP.

3) Under the terms of the abdication agreement, Queen Elizabeth may appear in public, but will not be allowed a handbag.

An article in the November issue, "Polar Bear Attacks in Downtown Omaha Up 35 Percent," contained an error. According to the National Polar Bear Attack Center, there have been no polar bear attacks in downtown Omaha since the late Eocene era.

An article in the June issue, "Berkshire Hathaway Off 38,000 in One Day as Investors Flee," mistakenly gave the impression that Berkshire Hathaway stockholders engaged in panic selling following a report that CEO Warren Buffett had been eaten by a great white shark while wading in Lake Michigan off Chicago's Grant Park. Mr. Buffett was eaten by a polar bear when he stopped to fill his tank at a gas station outside Omaha.

A correction in the current issue incorrectly identified President Harry Truman's middle name as "R." His correct middle name was "Delano." We regret the error.

—*Forbes FYI*, November 2001

YOUR HOROSCOPE

VIRGO

(Aug. 23–Sept. 22)

Jupiter just passed through your fifth house and left it a mess. However, there are several good cleaning services that specialize in mopping up after large planets. If your business partner is an Aries, he's probably cheating you, but don't worry: An asteroid shower is passing through his house. However, now is not the time to run for Congress or regravel the driveway.

LIBRA

(Sept. 23–Oct. 23)

Take that shotgun barrel out of your mouth and do something positive for a change! Wash the car, tip the pizza man an extra dollar, propose to the airport security person who's just asked you to turn your belt buckle inside out. Do not appoint Pisces as your executor. He's sleeping with your girlfriend.

SCORPIO

(Oct. 24.–Nov. 21)

Scorpios love a threesome, but with Taurus in Virgo and Capricorn in Aquarius, this is no time for sex with Gemini. Instead concentrate on ridding the basement of radon and learning classical Portuguese so that you finally make good on your vow to enjoy the Lusiads of Camões in the original. Sell your remaining AOL when it hits 73 cents a share.

SAGITTARIUS

(Nov. 22–Dec. 21)

If you drive a Swedish or Japanese car, avoid oncoming sixteen-wheelers driven by amphetamine-crazed Libras. With your parents redoing their wills, this is an opportune time to tell them that it was your brother's idea, not yours, to put them in that assisted-living home that's just been cited by the state attorney general for health code violations.

CAPRICORN

(Dec. 22–Jan. 19)
Concentrate on financial matters. Now's an ideal time to "come clean" with the SEC about that $1.4 billion "loss" you reported in the second quarter, but make sure your commissioner is a Leo or Cancer, or you could find yourself sharing a cell with Michael Skakel for the next ten years. By all means treat yourself to that new yacht, but with Neptune on the rise, be on the lookout for giant sea serpents, oil spills, and rogue North Korean submarines looking to provoke an international incident.

AQUARIUS

(Jan. 20–Feb. 18)
Do not engage in any "air" element activities, such as bungee jumping, skydiving, or playing professional basketball. Instead, concentrate on indoor activities, such as baking cakes, vascular surgery, and insider trading. It's also a good time to recharge your intellectual batteries. Recite Proust out loud in pig Latin. *Emembrance-ray of Hings-tay Ast-pay* . . . But be wary of voices you hear that aren't really "there."

PISCES

(Feb. 19–March 20)
Your friends are sick and tired of hearing you complain and are plotting to kill you. Don't go to the police—they hate you, too, and are in league with your friends. Move to the Cape Verde Islands and take up whaling until they've forgotten you ever existed, then move back and act like it never happened. But no more whining about your problems!

ARIES

(March 21–April 19)

Avoid kitchen appliances and people named Jim, Nancy, or Bletherst-hwaite-Jones. Be wary of letters from shareholders whom you have bankrupted. If you encounter anyone with freckles, throw white wine on them and shout, "Fiend—you have no power here!" Tell the waiter the fish has "too much mercury" and send it back. Menace the people at the next table with the pepper grinder.

TAURUS

(April 20–May 20)

Postpone that trip to Spain, Mexico, or other Latin countries. Write Merrill Lynch and propose that they make you their new corporate logo. Do not have sex with cows until the bovine spongiform encephalitis epidemic is erased from the planet. If you find yourself in a china shop, violently smash everything in it. People expect that, and with Pisces rising, you don't want to disappoint.

GEMINI

(May 21–June 21)

We told you—didn't we?—not to tightrope-walk across Victoria Falls in Manolo Blahniks when Capricorn and Libra were in your eleventh house. But listening has never been a Gemini strong point. All you can do at this point is try to swim faster than those crocodiles and postpone making any long-term romantic commitments. If you make it to the mudbank, avoid Leos and Scorpios.

CANCER

(June 22–July 22)

Go easy on the hollandaise—your cardiologist has four kids in college and is just looking for an excuse to do a triple bypass. When taxiing for takeoff, do not stand up and shout, "Allahu akbar!" but do leave yourself open to the possibility of romance, especially with wildly attractive, scantily clad members of the opposite sex. An old friend posing as a telemarketer for a long-distance phone company is searching desperately for you with amazing news. Take the call.

LEO

(July 23–Aug. 22)
Watch out for radioactive bags of potato chips, rivers of molten lava, and people who introduce themselves only as "Turk." Keep your left arm straight and your chin down. Listen to Aries, but say you'll have to get back to him. Avoid asparagus and manatees.

—*Forbes FYI*, September 2002

Out and About

Had I been present at the Creation, I would have given some useful hints for the better ordering of the universe.

—ALFONSO THE LEARNED

RAMBLES WITH MAGGIE

"Oh, the poobs are hortin' something terrible," said the porter at the Merrion Hotel in Dublin.

There was a sly, diversionary agenda to his banter about the calamitous economic impact of the recent smoking ban on the pubs. My friend Maggie O'Moyne and I had been waiting for the rental car to arrive. This being Ireland, it was now going on two hours late. But this being Ireland, neither of us could muster more than bemused curiosity over the delay. By this point back home, we'd have been in a cold, litigious rage. Yet despite having imbibed nearly toxic amounts of caffeine in the Merrion's cozy lobby, richly hung with gleaming, important paintings, we were all at peace.

"Don't you adore Ireland?" Maggie mused rhetorically for the fifteenth time.

She has adored Ireland since she came here a quarter century ago after her disgrace with the Brazilian ambassador at the Knickerbocker Gold Cotillion. Ireland being Ireland, it took her in, no questions asked, and here for two years in her ancestral land she thrived, befriending everyone—poets, painters, players, pipers, politicians. Her memoir of that sojourn, *Rambles in Ireland*, is considered a classic.

In the fullness of time—the Good Lord be thanked—the car arrived and we could begin our sentimental journey. We would visit three notable haunts of Maggie's youth: Luggala, Glin Castle, and St. Clerans. The first is home to Ireland's last great dandy; the second, to the twenty-ninth and last Knight of Glin; the third was once the home of John Huston, the famous director. All three are open to the public, for sums ranging from impressive to quite manageable.

Though we were already running late, we had to stop at Joyce's Martello tower in Sandycove, where the opening lines of *Ulysses* are set ("Stately, plump Buck Mulligan . . ."). Brave, pink-skinned swimmers plunged into the surging, snot-green, frigid waves of the Forty

Foot Pool. Emerging from the tower thinking Joycean thoughts, we were drenched by the day's tenth or eleventh rainfall. Otherwise, it was a glorious day in May. Moistly, we drove to nearby Dalkey and warmed ourselves inside and out at Finnegan's over pints of Guinness and baked Dalkey crab.

On the way to Roundwood in County Wicklow, Maggie told a convoluted story about one of her Irish friends, someone named Roderick.

"My God," she said as we hove into Roundwood toward late afternoon, "there he is. Exactly where I left him two years ago."

Roderick was standing unsteadily on the pavement outside a pub, smoking a cigarette. The recent smoking ban has driven half the country's population onto the sidewalks. He grinned at Maggie's approach, not in the least surprised at her sudden appearance after all these years. In a country where highway projects are rerouted by town planners because they might displace notable fairy homes such as the Tree of Latoon, serendipity is taken for granted here.

He was on his fourth Irish coffee, following we guessed about as many pints, and was all congeniality. At his stage of inebriation, bar patrons in most other countries start throwing punches or shouting obscenities at the widescreen TV.

"I'm inside with a very disreputable local personage," Roderick informed us. "I warn you, he's a *serious* alcoholic."

We went inside and met his friend, who greeted us warmly, if wobbily. He turned out to be a distinguished musician who records with Van Morrison and the Chieftains and is brother to Ireland's most famous woman singer.

"You know what she's worth?" Roderick murmured as his friend staggered off toward the Gents. "A hundred and ten million euros. How much is that in pence?"

"Don't you adore Ireland?" Maggie said in the car. We were now seriously late. A spectacular vista opened to our left. It seemed familiar, though I had not been to this part of Ireland. Then the next day we passed a sign indicating that Mel Gibson filmed part of *Braveheart* here.

As Maggie drove, she told me about our host tonight, her old friend the Honorable Garech a Brún. Garech is the son of Oonagh, Lady Oranmore and Browne, one of three legendarily beautiful Guinness sisters. His brother Tara Browne was killed at age twenty-one in 1966 when he drove his Lotus Elan at lethal speed into the back of a parked van in London. Tara's friend John Lennon memorialized the event in the song "A Day in the Life" ("I heard the news today, oh boy . . .").

Garech founded Claddagh Records, which started the Irish music revival and preserved much of Ireland's musical patrimony from oblivion. He's lived at Luggala for many years and is married to an Indian princess. Really, there is nothing about him that is *not* exotic. At one point in our visit, Maggie came into accidental possession of a piece of paper containing Garech's most frequently dialed phone numbers. Among them were Bono's cell phone, a dozen maharajahs and maharanis, Chez L'Ami Louis restaurant in Paris, and the Taj Mahal.

"You've never met anyone like him," Maggie said.

We drove through a gate and descended into a long, misty valley with a river-fed lake. The road leveled as we went through a mossy glade. It felt like going through a time warp. As we emerged, I saw what looked like a small Greek temple by the shore of the lake.

"That's where the brother's buried. Look, deer."

We were in an open field planted with immense four-hundred-year-old specimen trees. And yes, there were deer.

The house loomed ahead, a low white Egyptian Gothic confection with crenellations. Luggala. It was built as a hunting lodge in the 1780s and has twice been given by a father to a daughter as a wedding present. It appears in the 2004 movie *King Arthur*. Everything here seems to have been a movie set.

Garech emerged blinking and watery-eyed from a nap to greet us. And now the illusion of being in Middle Earth was complete. Luggala's master is diminutive but dominates a room by stepping into it. I couldn't decide—man, leprechaun, hobbit . . . wizard? He carried a walking stick and had a bald pate, long gray wispy beard, hair tied in an unkempt ponytail, and was impeccably dressed in a baby-blue tweed three-piece suit. I wouldn't have been at all surprised if he'd reached into his pocket and produced either a flintlock pistol or a mandrake root. His eyes gleamed with intelligence and hospitality and a trace of sadness. Later he said to me, "I'm actually a very *shy* person." Garech looks at you with a half smile, as though daring you to blurt out whatever thought you're withholding. In my experience, aristocrats are usually cool to the touch. This one glowed like a peat fire.

His friend and Luggala's curator, a natty, polymath architectural historian with the unimprovable name of Count Randal MacDonnell of the Glens, poured champagne. Garech plunked himself down on an important-looking sofa and held court until suppertime.

Count Randal gave us a tour of the house, which has been undergoing renovation for the last five years. He showed us a 270-year-old clock that once kept time in the Irish Parliament and which plays "God Save the Queen" on the quarter hour; a horizontal harpsichord ("very rare"); a French Revolutionary cap in a Lucite case in a bathroom ("You don't see many of those, do you?"); a chair on a landing that had belonged to Napoleon; paintings by, among others, Jack Yeats, Francis Bacon, and Lucian Freud, who was a sort of godfather to Garech; and the new library, which will hold 28,000 volumes.

At dinner, as the clock repeatedly chimed "God Save the Queen," Garech read from a memoir by a member of the Bloomsbury circle, about a dinner party in this same room in the 1930s. When I got home, I found another anecdote of a dinner at Luggala in a book about the director John Huston. This one took place in the 1950s, and featured a well-and-truly-drunk Brendan Behan. Behan kept interrupting the convivial conversation, shouting, "Up the rebels!" Then, "after dessert was served, he rose unsteadily to his feet and, swaying slightly, raised his glass in the direction of our hostess. 'To her ladyship!' he roared. 'God bless her!' and fell forward onto the table, which gave way under his weight with a tinkling of breaking glass and a jingle of antique sterling silver.

"Oona [sic] said, 'Oh, dear,' as if someone had spilled a teaspoonful of salt, rose from the debris in front of her, and suggested that it was 'time for us to move back into the drawing room.' Two of the sturdier gentlemen guests lifted the eminent playwright from where he had fallen and carried him into the adjoining chamber, where they deposited him, breathing heavily, on an ancient sofa."

After dinner, sitting on that same ancient sofa with Garech, I noticed a pair of bronzed hands in front of the fire screen.

"I thought you'd notice those," he said. "They're the death hands of a very great piper named Seamus Ennis. He would stay up all night, and then after you'd finally got to sleep, wake you at five o'clock in the morning to tell you that the story he had told you at four a.m. had a detail wrong, and would tell the entire story again, which you really didn't want to hear."

The next morning, I walked to the Greek temple to pay my respects to Tara. We ate a good Irish breakfast of eggs, bacon, and sausage and prepared to depart.

"You must sign the book," Garech said. Luggala's guest book starts in 1964, the year Garech's mother gave him Luggala. It weighs as much as a Gutenberg bible and is full of drawings and photographs. Garech gave me a guided tour through it. It took almost two hours. I was in no hurry, but Maggie, who had signed the book many times over the years, was getting frantic about being late to Glin.

One early page had a photograph of a striking woman named Tessa Welborn, who designed Ursula Andress's bikini in *Dr. No*. Here, too, was John Hurt, the actor. Ronnie Fraser, the actor, who got very drunk at the races and fell down face forward on the course. John Boorman, the director (*Deliverance*, *Hope and Glory*), a near neighbor. Also Mick Jagger, a regular at Luggala. Charlotte Rampling, the actress. ("One of the Chieftains became so infatuated with her that he had to be pried off.") Tara Browne, Garech's brother, and a yellowed newspaper clipping about his fatal wreck suggesting that he'd swerved at the last second to save his passenger. He was very handsome, Tara. Ronnie Wood of the Stones. Robert Graves the poet, whose eightieth birthday party was held here. John Berryman, the poet. Marianne Faithfull. A woman with a famous German surname, an old flame of Garech, looking fiercely at the camera like combination vampire and dominatrix. ("She was *really* crazy.") Brendan Behan. Garech's wife, Purna, beautiful in her royal Indian finery. And an Irish poet whose last name I missed but who effectively ended his career by broadcasting from Berlin during the war. "His defense," Garech said, "was that an artist ought always to be on the wrong side of any issue." He continued leafing. What times this place has seen.

We said our good-byes and drove off toward the lake, past deer and stately trees on our way to Glin.

"We're going to be seriously late," Maggie said. "On the other hand, no one cares. It's Ireland."

Glin Castle sits on the Shannon River thirty-two miles west of Limerick. It was built in 1785 and is the seat of the Knight of Glin, a title that goes back seven hundred years. The current knight, Desmond FitzGerald, is the twenty-ninth and last as he and his wife produced no son, albeit three beautiful daughters.

When your family goes back seven hundred years, there are bound to be some interesting moments. Such as this, from the family history:

> *. . . Thomas FitzGerald, heir of the then Knight, was hanged, drawn and quartered by the English forces in Limerick in 1567. His mother, legend has it, seized his severed head, drank his blood, and walked, surrounded by a vast keening concourse, carrying his dismembered body to be buried at Lislaughtin Abbey.*

Or this, as the original castle was besieged by the forces of Queen Elizabeth I in 1600:

> *. . . Sir George Carew, the Lord President of Munster, captured the Knight's six-year-old son and, tying the child to the mouth of a cannon, threatened to blow him to bits if the Knight did not surrender. The reply, in Irish, was blunt: 'the Knight was virile and his wife was strong and it would be easy to produce another son.'*

So there you have the Glin parental gamut, from Mother of the Year to Dad from Hell. FitzGerald DNA runs strong.

Desmond's grandfather FitzJohn was paralyzed by a stroke and lived in the castle during the struggle against British rule. When Sinn Fein arrived one day in 1923 to torch the place, he refused to budge. He told them, "Well, you'll have to burn me in it, boys." The boys repaired to a pub and never got around to burning the castle to the ground.

Desmond is a Harvard M.A. in art history and for a decade was deputy curator of furniture at the Victoria and Albert Museum in London. He and his striking wife, Olda, have painstakingly restored Glin to a glory it never had in the first place. To pay for it all, they decided to accept guests. There are fifteen guest rooms. It's like spending the night in a museum. Every detail is flawless.

Over dinner that night, Desmond said, "Many Americans will say, 'I love Ireland,' but their entire experience of it has been staying at Ashford or Dromoland Castle and playing a few rounds of golf." A visit to Glin steeps you in Ireland like a tea bag. Glin's manager, Bob Duff, an able and amusing New Zealander, told us about a fellow from Chicago who took over the entire place for five days. He wanted a medieval feast and jousting tournament laid on. "I told him we're an eighteenth-century house, and not really organized for suckling pig and jousting."

Glin has a historic link with America: The first transatlantic flying boats landed a few miles up the Shannon, at Foynes. Desmond's mother, whose family nickname was "The Knightmare," sold fresh produce from her garden to the flying boats during the hard times of the 1930s and '40s. Veronica FitzGerald was by all accounts a demanding personality. "Battleship Britannia under full sail," Bob Duff said as he showed us her masterpiece, the gardens. That the castle survived, indeed flourished, is due to her and her son, Desmond. But with him will end seven hundred years of family history. See it while you can. Maggie and I set off the next morning in a driving rain. Late as we were, she said we had to stop at Moran's Oyster Cottage in Kilcolgan. They've been serving oysters here since 1797. On a wall is a framed poem by Seamus Heaney, one of Ireland's numerous Nobel laureates.

Our shells clacked on the plates.
My tongue was a filling estuary,

My palate hung with starlight:
As I tasted the salty Pleiades
Orion dipped his foot into the water.

It was signed "To Willie Moran, in the cool and thatch of crockery." Maggie and I sat by the fire and drank creamy Guinness and ate briny oysters and then drove to our third and last stop, St. Clerans.

There was a certain circularity to our trip. John Huston first came to Ireland in 1951 at the invitation of Garech's mother, Oonagh. One day while hunting on horseback, he saw St. Clerans looming across the fields, fell in love with it, and, in the impulsive manner of Americans, bought the place. He lived here with his fourth wife, Ricki, and their son, Anthony, and daughter, Angelica. The upkeep finally forced him to sell eighteen years later, but he always said that his happiest years were the ones spent here. His great passion was foxhunting. He became Joint Master of the Galway Blazers.

On our first night, as Maggie and I tucked into black tiger prawn tempura and Cajun roasted monkfish—typical Irish fare—I pointed to the portrait of Huston and asked our young waiter, Barry, if he was familiar with Huston films.

"I've been racking my brains," he said.

I named a few: *The Treasure of the Sierra Madre*, *The Maltese Falcon*, *Moby-Dick*, *The African Queen*, *The Man Who Would Be King*, *The Dead*.

Barry nodded. "Ah, yes. Really? Well, around here, you see, he's known for his horses. They don't know him for the other."

Famous people came to visit. One was Jean-Paul Sartre, who had rather oddly agreed to collaborate on a screenplay for Huston about Sigmund Freud. He arrived by taxi from Dublin. Huston greeted him on horseback at the gate. A description of the moment is in Peter Viertel's memoir, *Dangerous Friends*, along with the account of Brendan Behan passing out at Luggala:

It was a strange way to welcome the originator of existentialism, a man who frowned upon all personal possessions, especially those of the upper classes. Booted and spurred, Hus-

ton greeted the small, homely intellectual . . . Sartre was not impressed. To show his distaste for all the splendor . . . Sartre entered the house and made no comment whatsoever about the architecture, the art on the walls, the lavish comfort of his host's residence.

There are twelve bedrooms, all beautifully redone. The "Griffin" suite, named for St. Clerans's current owner, Merv Griffin, was Huston's bedroom. As you walk in, on either side are glass-encased alcoves in the walls. These were where he kept his Oscar statuettes. The view from Huston's old bedroom sweeps across a field where a half-dozen horses, one of them ghost white, frisk at all hours.

On the last night of our trip, Maggie and I walked out to the fountain after dinner. The house was quiet now but tomorrow would be all astir, for Griffin was helicoptering in from Shannon Airport for a visit. He would be accompanied by his pet shar-pei dog, Charlie Chan. St. Clerans's manager had been busily putting a thousand details right for the incoming lord of the manor.

I smoked my cigar, sipped my brandy, and looked at the house under the stars and thought of all that Luggala, Glin Castle, and St. Clerans had been through since the 1780s, when they were all built, within three years of one another.

Suddenly we heard a thunderous rumble coming at us and turned. It was the horses. The white one flashed as they galloped away in the night.

"Don't you adore Ireland?" Maggie said. And the answer was yes.

—*Forbes FYI*, October 2005

LEFT. NO, RIGHT. NO—STRAIGHT!

A Brief History of Directions

3297 B.C.—A Bronze Age hunter-gatherer, tired of woolly mammoth jerky and shivering, sets out from his village in what is now the Tyrolean Alps for what is now Italy, where, he has heard, the food is better and there aren't as many sabre-toothed tigers. The village shaman tells him to head due north. His body is found by hikers in 1991, clutching directions drawn on lambskin.

1275–1235 B.C.—Moses and his brother, Aaron, spend forty years leading his people from Egypt to the Dead Sea, a distance of 250 miles (San Francisco–Lake Tahoe). Moses is righteous and brave, but clueless when it comes to following directions. He misses an important exit on the Thebes–Red Sea Beltway, finding himself and his people waist-deep in water.

Moses's people eventually chafe at making only .027 miles progress per day and begin worshipping the Golden Calf (a Babylonian god of direction-giving) and practicing unsafe sex. Moses climbs Mount Sinai in what scholars consider the first recorded attempt by a male to ask directions of a higher power. The Ten Directions, later "Commandments," lead the way to the Land of Milk and Honey and usher in the start of the Three Thousand Years' Middle East Peace Process.

1184–1174 B.C.—Odysseus, king of Ithaca and master mariner, takes ten years to return home from Troy, a distance of approximately 650 miles (New York–Cincinnati). Fearing that his wife, Penelope, will hurl priceless amphorae at him upon his arrival, he commissions a sight-challenged, out-of-work poet to concoct an epic cover story based on having been given faulty directions by a vengeful sea god. Penelope, meanwhile, hoping to divert his attention from the 108 young bachelors who have been hanging around the house for a decade, draining the amphorae of his best retsina, pretends to believe her husband's so-called Odyssey, though she makes him clean up the house.

4 B.C.—Three westward-leading, still proceeding Oriental kings on their way to the annual meeting of the KOTA (Kings of Orient Trade Association) in Damascus become disoriented by a light in the sky and end up in a crowded stable in Bethlehem during the annual Christmas outbreak of violence there.

A.D. 1306—The Florentine poet Dante becomes lost in a dark wood (*selva oscura*) while trying to find an Amoco (Latin: "I love oil companies") station and accepts directions from the ghost of the Roman poet Virgil. Virgil leads him straight to Hell.

1336—The Italian poet Petrarch climbs Mount Ventoux, not, as scholars have suggested, to usher in the Renaissance, but to find the way to Milan, where he is eager to attend the first recorded runway fashion show. Pope Livid VI, disapproving of the "shameless display of ankles and wrists by the *fashionisti Milanese*," has ordered Milan to be erased from maps so that no one can find it. Petrarch's bold initiative represents the attempt by man to wrest direction-giving power away from the Church. In retaliation, Livid orders Manolo Blahnik, a cobbler, burned at the stake.

1492—The Genoese navigator Christopher Columbus buys a map ostensibly showing a "short route to the Indies" from a man he meets in a bar in Seville. After two months, Columbus's men tire of eating barnacles and licking dew off the deck. To divert them, Columbus discovers the Bahamas instead and encourages the crew to infect the local population with the many wonderful diseases they have brought with them from the Old World.

1847—The Donner Party takes a left instead of a right and spends a long winter eating bark, among other things, in what is now California. Governor Gray Davis blames the crisis on Republicans.

1964—In *A Hard Day's Night*, John Lennon tells reporters who ask how the Beatles found America, "Turn left at Greenland."

More British rock bands follow John's directions, though upon reaching Greenland, the Rolling Stone Keith Richards attempts to snort it and comes down with a severe head cold.

—*Forbes FYI*, March 2003

MACHU PICCHU

Machu Picchu had long been on my "Things to See Before I Die" list, so when my friend, boon companion, and personal physician Dr. Peaches Melocotón announced that she had reserved a suite at the Sanctuary Lodge for the full moon, I replied, "*¡Vámanos!*"

That is more or less what Pizarro's conquistadors said upon hearing that the Incan cities here were paved with gold, along with: "What an excellent time we shall have kidnapping, torturing, and burning the Incas alive, to say nothing of raping their women, looting the country, and destroying the last of a seven-thousand-year-old line of civilizations—all in the name of the One True Faith!"

This is my own gloss, admittedly, but it will be recognizable to anyone who has read William Prescott's masterpiece, *History of the Conquest of Peru*. The book was published in 1847, at a time when the United States was engaging in its own conquistadorial episode, storming the heights of Chapultepec in Mexico City and annexing California, Utah, Arizona, great swaths of Colorado and Wyoming, and just for good measure another heaping helping of Texas. Just to show what good sports we were, we named one purloined chunk of this windfall "New Mexico."

Prescott's history of Peru's tragedy is remarkable not only for its contemporaneous anti-imperialist flavor. A century and a half later, it is still authoritative, and its protein-rich nineteenth-century prose is writing to raise the hairs on your arms. ("*Thus by the death of a vile malefactor perished the last of the Incas!*") Then there's this detail: it was written by a blind man. Prescott lost vision in one eye during a food fight in a Harvard dining hall; the other the following year, due to a congenital condition. He went on to write the definitive histories of the conquests of Mexico and Peru. My dog-eared copy was the first thing I put in my overnight bag. Dr. Melocotón was in charge of altitude sickness meds.

Lima's virtues do not immediately reveal themselves to the first-time visitor. The ride from the airport to Miraflores—the city's answer to Baghdad's Green Zone—put me in mind of those movies where the arriving gringo's motorcade is suddenly blocked by a truck as men in ski masks scamper across the flanking rooftops, firing rocket-propelled grenade launchers.

It's a sprawling city of more than eight million on which less than ten millimeters of rain fall per year. The cold Humboldt Current produces a sort of dirty gray mist called *la garúa* that envelopes the city for months at a time. Miraflores's nicest residential neighborhood is a more or less continuous strand of concertina wire and spiked gates. Private security guards wear flak jackets.

Lima grew during the late 1980s and early '90s, heyday of Sendero Luminoso terrorism. Then, President Alberto Fujimori, son of Japanese immigrants, finally succeeded in capturing Shining Path's leader, Abimael Guzmán, a nasty combination of Mao Tse-Tung and Charles Manson. He and hundreds of his followers were imprisoned for life. During his ten-year reign, Fujimori also built schools, hospitals, and roads, improved services, eliminated hyperinflation, and generally brought the country back from the abyss. But this being Latin America, there was an arrest warrant out for him on charges of corruption and human rights violations. Fujimori was apprehended in Chile not long after we were there and is now awaiting extradition to the country he saved. In the meantime, Peru reelected Alan García, whose accomplishments as president in the '80s included an inflation rate of more than 7,000 percent.

Owing to a computer error, we were installed in Room 1002—one of the "Presidential" Suites—at the Miraflores Park Hotel. It has a condor's-eye view of the sea and city, a pool on the balcony, a Jacuzzi that could accommodate four—perfect for summit meetings—and a huge sauna. I proposed canceling our ten-day itinerary and remaining in Room 1002. I could always file colorful dispatches back to my editor in New York. "*The fierce jungle sun beat down unrelentingly as the anaconda slithered lethally toward our sinking dugout . . .*" I drifted off to sleep that night to the sound of the Pacific surf pounding against the coast below.

Next day, in the Cathedral of Lima we stood in front of Pizarro's tomb. A glass case atop an ornate altar encloses his rather small wooden coffin, along with a box inscribed, *Aqui yace el marquez gobernador don francisco pizarro* ("Here lies the Marquis-Governor," etc.). He brought death, destruction, and disease. In his fine book, *1491: New Revelations of the Americas Before Columbus*, Charles Mann notes that European-borne diseases may have wiped out as many as nine out of ten Peruvians in the sixteenth century. What a legacy. But as Prescott tells us, the old conquistador at least died like a cavalier. He was assassinated by a rival faction of Spaniards in 1541, just across the square from where he rests, less than a decade after he duplicitously murdered the last Inca ruler, Atahualpa. He fought his attackers with bravado and as he died, drew a cross on the floor in his own blood and bent down to kiss it.

> *A grave was hastily dug in an obscure corner [of the cathedral], the services were hurried through, and, in secrecy, and in darkness dispelled only by the feeble glimmering of a few tapers furnished by these humble menials, the remains of Pizarro, rolled in their bloody shroud, were consigned to their kindred dust. Such was the miserable end of the Conqueror of Peru—of the man who but a few hours before had lorded it over the land with as absolute a sway as was possessed by its hereditary Incas . . . he perished like a wretched outcast. "There was none, even," in the expressive language of the chronicler, "to say, God forgive him!"*

The balance of the afternoon we spent staring at 1,800-year-old ceramic depictions of . . . well, I'll let the captions speak for themselves: "Low relief scene of intercourse between the male divinity and a woman"; "Dead Man Masturbating" (Sean Penn's next movie!); "Copulating Frogs" and "Copulating Rodents." The last two specimens are rather human and amusing. All this is to be found in the "Sala Erótica" at the Rafael Larco Herrera archaeological museum, along with some 45,000 nonerotic items. We flew to Cusco early the next day, our feet tingling weirdly from altitude pills.

Cusco, Pizarro's El Dorado, nests in a valley 11,000 feet above sea level. At our hotel, the Monasterio, they'll pipe oxygen into your room for an extra $25 a day. *Sold*. The first night, I did a not-smart thing by taking a painkiller (for the altitude headache) along with my evening dose of Diamox and awoke at three a.m. to what F. Scott Fitzgerald calls the dark night of the soul.

Dawn broke to the news that a tremendous mudslide had glopped onto the railroad tracks leading to the base of Machu Picchu. This retarded our forward progress but did allow my vital organs to refresh and reboot.

Cusco was the Rome of its day, and to look on its ruins—

Qoricancha, the Temple of the Sun, or the Cyclopean-scale fortress of Sacsayhuamán on the heights above the town—is to feel something of the thrum that must have run through Shelley when he came up with "Ozymandias." I mean Rome in a literal sense.

"In 1491," Mann informs us, "the Inka ruled the greatest empire on earth. Bigger than Ming Dynasty China, bigger than Ivan the Great's expanding Russia, bigger than Songhay in the Sahel or powerful Great Zimbabwe in the West African tablelands, bigger than the cresting Ottoman empire . . . bigger by far than any European state, the Inka domination extended over a staggering 32 degrees of latitude—as if a single power held sway from St. Petersburg to Cairo."

It was also one of the shortest-lived empires in history. When the Spaniards arrived, it had flourished for less than one hundred years. But its achievements were great and in ways surpassed Europe's. The Inca erected cities on mountainsides sloping 65 degrees. (San Francisco's steepest hill is 31.5 degrees.) They built twenty thousand miles of roadways, some of which are still in use. Most impressive of all, they were the first empire in history to eradicate hunger. All this they managed without money, the wheel, writing, or the arch. Yes, there was the danger that you might qualify for human sacrifice, but otherwise, not bad by sixteenth-century standards.

It must have been something to take the breath away, Cusco. Having garrotted Atahualpa and massacred thousands of his men, Pizarro and his men entered the city on November 15, 1533. In Prescott's telling: ". . . though falling short of the El Dorado which had engaged their credulous fancies, [it] astonished the Spaniards by the beauty of its edifices, the length and regularity of its streets, and the good order and appearance of comfort, even luxury, visible in its numerous population. It far surpassed all they had yet seen in the New World."

They did not tarry with sightseeing, but instead "lost no time in plundering . . . as well as despoiling the religious edifices. The interior decorations supplied them with considerable booty. They stripped off the jewels and rich ornaments that garnished the royal mummies in the temple of Coricancha. Indignant at the concealment of their treasures, they put the inhabitants, in some instances, to the torture, and endeavored to extort from them a confession of their hiding places. They invaded the repose of the sepulchres, in which the Peruvians often deposited their valuable effects, and compelled the grave to give up its dead. No place was left unexplored by the rapacious Conquerors . . ."

There's something else I'd like to have seen: the Incan counterattack three years later. The Spaniards had steel, gunpowder, and horses, but the Inca had slings, and according to Mann, could hurl rocks with sniperlike accuracy at 100 miles per hour:

> *In a frightening innovation, the Inka heated stones in campfires until they were red-hot, wrapped them in pitch-soaked cotton, and hurled them at their targets. The cotton caught fire in midair. In a sudden onslaught the sky would rain burning missiles. During a counterattack in May 1536 an Inka army used these missiles to burn Spanish-occupied Qosqo to the ground. Unable to step outside, the conquistadors cowered in shelters beneath a relentless, weeks-long barrage of flaming stone. Rather than evacuate, the Spaniards, as brave as they were greedy, fought to the end. In a desperate, last-ditch counterattack, the Europeans eked out victory.*

As we walked to the main entrance of the cathedral, I noticed a sign: ROOM OF THE INQUISITION. Our guide, Edgard Mendivil, a deeply learned man, explained that this had formerly been a museum. "But they finally thought it was strange to have a museum showing instruments they killed people with in the name of God, so they closed it and now it's a shop."

A few years ago, a sixteenth-century papal bull was found in Seville. It officially designated Pizarro's chaplain, a Dominican friar named Vicente Valverde, leader of the expedition. So it was technically his party. Open *The Conquest of Peru* to any random page and you will find the good friar explaining the Trinity to some Inca as the flames begin to lick at his ankles. In their first encounter, the otherwise hapless emperor Atahualpa had the good sense to tell this malefic ecclesiastical busybody to go stuff his Trinity. At their last meeting, Valverde generously offered to commute Atahualpa's death sentence from immolation to strangling—provided he stopped being so obdurate about the Trinity and opted for the full conversion package. Yet another Inca, this one named Challcuchima, didn't get off so easily.

"Father Valverde accompanied the Peruvian chieftain to the stake," Prescott writes. "He seems always to have been present at this dreary moment, anxious to profit by it." (Not the sort of padre you want on the other side of the screen at Saturday afternoon confession.) Valverde was eventually slaughtered in 1541—not a windfall year for the Pizarro party, it would seem—by some apparently non-Trinitarian Indians. His cross survives. It's mounted above one of the altars in the cathedral here in Cusco. Most crucifixes put me in a reverent frame of mind. This one chilled me to the bone.

The train from Cusco to Machu Picchu runs along the Urubamba River through the Sacred Valley and into narrowing canyons. The roiling chocolate-colored water beside you eventually empties into the Atlantic Ocean thousands of miles later. None other than Jacques Cousteau figured that out.

The Peru Rail engineers hadn't yet completely deglopped the tracks, so we had to disembark, ride in a van a kilometer or so to the other side of the mudslide, and catch another train. This we did in concert with some eight hundred other people, seven hundred of whom ended up sitting on Dr. Melocotón's and my lap.

If you sit on the left side on the ride to Machu Picchu, you have bracing vistas of stupendous ravines, speckled with thousands of lush bromeliads; also wild magnolia, immense rhododendron bushes, ferns, liana vines, and Incan ruins. You're in the cloud forest now, where the Andes start to give way to jungle. It's a sight. Sit on the right side and your vista consists of hours upon hours of—rock.

We disembarked in late afternoon at Aguas Calientes, the little town that serves as a launching pad for Machu Picchu. Most people spend their nights here. But you can now spend the night up top. We boarded a bus for the final stage of the journey: a 1,500-foot climb up a switchback road. I counted fifteen turns. The view down becomes increasingly impressive, so much so that I found myself thinking of an old friend of mine whose odd hobby it was to collect newspaper clippings about bus plunges. He had dozens. No bus plunged in Pakistan or Peru without his knowing it.

We made our loud ascent, gears grinding, exhaust spewing. Perhaps noting my lack of color, or the fact that my fingernails were embedded in Dr. Melocotón's forearm, Edgard said soothingly, "Sir, there has never—*never*—been a fatality." Then suddenly a perfect rainbow appeared, and five minutes later we were checked into Room 40 (try to get this room if you can—it's got the best view, but rooms 39 and 38 will do) at the Sanctuary Lodge and furiously gobbling tea sandwiches.

There was less than an hour of light left. Edgard led us through the gates and up a trail. We came out of the bushes and there it was.

The air was soft and hushed, except for the occasional whoops of a group of teenagers. The mountains were striated with wisps of mist as in old Chinese screen paintings. Swallows dipped amid the ruins. In the distance below, a small herd of llamas, necks comic and giraffe-like above the low walls, began their daily ascent back up to their night hut. It was a scene familiar from my earliest childhood, when I had first seen it in some issue of *National Geographic*. What the Yale archaeologist Hiram Bingham thought when he first laid eyes on it on July 24, 1911, I don't know, but it must have been some variation on "Holy *s*—."

Bingham found it, as discoverers so often do, by accident. He was in search of something else, an Incan site called Vilcabamba. On his way there, he encountered a farmer who told him, "I know a place." Bingham told him, "Show me."

We sat in the gloaming as Edgard told us the story. The farmer said to Bingham, "Sir, it is a *torturous* road." (He should see the bus ride.) Bingham said he would pay well for taking him. "How much do you make in a week?" The farmer named a sum. Bingham offered two weeks pay. The farmer held out. They finally settled on five weeks.

"And so," Edgard concluded, "Melchor Arteaga, this farmer, became the first *operator* at Machu Picchu." Melchor was smarter still: The actual job of leading the gringo up the torturous road he delegated to the son of Melquiades Richarte, a neighbor, who thus become the actual first guide at Machu Picchu.

It's still not entirely clear why, exactly, the Incas built it. Theories vary. The one that makes the most sense is that it was a religious center and a depository for mummies. The Incas were crazy for mummification and treated preserved remains as living beings, much like Anthony Perkins in *Psycho*. It's logical, then, that they would have taken their dead to a mountaintop metropolis built in the shape of a condor, god of the sky. Here the spirits of the dead could be assimilated into the heavens. What tips toward this conclusion is the evidence that very few children lived at Machu Picchu.

Building all this was a staggering undertaking. Some sixty thousand workers spent seventy years on it. They lopped off the top of a mountain and built supporting terraces—8,000 feet above sea level. Not only did they have to hew the rock, they also had to lug up the topsoil. Two of the grassy plazas alone were sodded with an estimated 220 tons of clay, humped here clump by clump on aching backs from a riverbed fifty miles away. The human remains found here all show evidence of malnutrition. Why should that be, when food was abundant? The answer is—coca. They chewed the leaves to keep going. And if you've got a buzz on, hey, who needs food and drink? And all this effort to build a city for just a few hundred people.

Who only inhabited the finished city for thirty years. Why did they abandon it? Eighty percent of the mummies show evidence of smallpox. The Inca were early believers in Intelligent Design; they didn't believe disease was natural or random. "They thought," Edgard said, "that this indicated that the gods did not *like* this place." There's another theory: that they put it to the torch and buried their mummies and treasures rather than let them fall into the hands of the approaching conquistadors. Edgard, who brings clients here fifty times a year and is well versed in the scholarship, subscribes to the approaching-conquistador theory. I'd have split, too, if I heard that Friar Valverde was on his way to talk Trinity.

The next day, we climbed Huayna Picchu. ("Little Mountain,"

Machu Picchu being "Big Mountain"). Huayna Picchu is the peak you see in the photographs that looms above the ruins like a mossy, breaching whale. For any serious mountaineer, it's probably a Sunday walk in the park. For a middle-aged asthmatic gringo, it was work: 800 feet up at 65 degrees. It took us an hour, no reflection on Edgard or Dr. Melocotón. Edgard once did it in seventeen minutes, after hearing over the walkie-talkie that one of his clients had managed to fall off the top.

What a view it is from up there. Edgard pointed out a declivity carved into the summit stone. An altar. They sacrificed animals to their condor gods on it. We posed for pictures.

It began to rain. Edgard's cell phone rang. The Inca didn't have the wheel; their descendants have cell coverage at 9,000 feet. It was his five-year-old daughter, in tears with the desperate news that the bunny rabbit he had given her had died. He promised her a new one, and we started down.

—*Forbes FYI*, October 2006

DOGGED PURSUIT

It's a bit cramped in the back of the Cessna 206. The windows are frosting over, and as I scrape away the rime with the edge of a credit card what I can make out is not entirely reassuring. Fog and terrain—the latter is disturbing because it is at eye level. Nor is it reassuring that the automatic warning keeps announcing in computer deadpan voice: "Caution, terrain. Caution, terrain." At such moments one asks oneself, *What am I doing here?*

Aeronautically speaking, we are trying to find our way through the Alaska Range. That task falls to our pilot, an excellent fellow named Burke with whom we will bond tightly in the days ahead. Burke has a sweet, laid-back, Deputy Dawg manner, and a martini-dry sense of humor. He says, with a casualness that seems discordant, "Now we have the first serious obscuration ahead of us."

Burke executes a 270-degree turn in the narrowing canyon, looking for a way through the pass. The terrain is now not only eye level but quite close.

"I believe," Burke says, "we're going to have to backtrack and find a different route." He puts the plane's nose down and soon we are flying low enough to make out moose tracks. It crosses my mind that he is using these to navigate. This does not make me less nervous.

An interesting hour later, we are sitting at a bar called McGuire's Tavern in a town called McGrath, thankful that the Alaska Range is behind us. Burke drinks coffee while his three passengers self-administer restorative liquids. The bar is decorated with old boxes of blasting caps and a mastodon bone. Outside it is 10 below. Among the four of us, we are wearing a serious amount of fur: seal, moose, bear, wolf, pine marten, sea otter, and Lord only knows what else—gerbil, possibly.

The bartender hangs up the phone and announces, "Mackey's out of Anvik."

That would be Lance Mackey, a champion musher of dogs; Anvik is a hamlet roughly halfway between Anchorage and Nome, which is by way of explaining what I'm doing here. I am following the Iditarod Trail Sled Dog Race.

The Iditarod is a 1,049-mile sled dog race that honors the tradition of dog mushing generally and specifically the heroic "serum run" of 1925, when men and dogs braved the worst that nature could throw at them in order to bring diphtheria serum to icebound Nome. I grew up around New York City and many times have walked past the statue in Central Park of Balto, one of the dogs who accomplished this great feat. I now have a far better appreciation of what Balto and the other dogs and their mushers endured to save the children of Nome. After returning from this trip, I found myself quite by accident walking past Balto's statue. This time, I stopped and took off my hat.

I won't recapitulate the whole story here, other than to note, with awe and humility, that it involved among other hardships temperatures of minus 60 degrees, gales of 65 to 70 miles per hour, and a dozen other ways of dying, none of them pleasant. The frostbitten and exhausted man who mushed the last relay team (including Balto) into the streets of Nome was named Gunnar Kaasen. In their gripping account, *The Cruelest Miles*, Gay and Laney Salisbury write, "Witnesses to this drama said they saw Kaasen stagger off the sled and stumble up to Balto, where he collapsed, muttering, 'Damn fine dog.'" Diphtheria kills young children by a process of slow, agonizing suffocation. Next time you pass the Balto statue, pause in respect.

The Iditarod race is run every March. Sixty-seven teams were competing this year. Mackey, a wire-thin man with a goatee and wolf-pale eyes, had previously won two Iditarods. The record time was posted in 2002 by Martin Buser, who managed to reach Nome in 8 days, 22 hours, 46 minutes, and 2 seconds, averaging more than a hundred miles a day. The distance covered—1,049 miles—is about the same as Washington, D.C., to Miami, only this route goes over mountains, lakes, rivers, and what must seem to them an endless stretch of Alaskan winter.

We fly on from McGrath and reach Unalakleet at twilight. We tie down the Cessna. Alice, our hostess and owner of the Cessna, has made arrangements for the all-important plug-in for the engine warmer. It is essential, indeed imperative, in Alaska that you keep your plane's engine heated so that it will start. This aspect of Alaskan bush aviation will become a major theme of our trip. Plug-ins are scarce at airstrips, with the result that people go around unplugging one another's airplanes. This will happen to us, with the result that Burke and I spend the better part of one day trying to heat the Cessna's engine by means of a gas stove.

"Burke," I say, pausing before setting the match to the gas in the stove's priming cup, "is it *wise* to be doing this?"

I ask this because the idea of inserting a flaming device into an aircraft engine full of high-octane fuel feels . . . illogical, somehow.

"Yes," Burke says contemplatively.

The more immediate problem is the 30-mile-an-hour wind, which, in conjunction with the 15-below temperature, makes one's fingers less than nimble. Burke tries repeatedly to start the engine. The propeller turns—*rrruh-rrruh rrrrrrrrruh*—and then stops after a few feeble rotations. Jack London's "To Build a Fire" meets "The Flight of the Phoenix." In the end, a kindly flying cardiologist takes pity on us and lends us his super-duper engine warmer, which is like a giant hair dryer.

At Unalakleet (in the Inupiaq language, "the place where the east wind blows"), we watch Lance Mackey and his team come in. He is comfortably ahead of the field, but wastes no time. He beds down his dogs in mounds of hay and cooks them a hot meal of beaver meat, frozen salmon steaks, and high-protein pellets. The dogs get four hot meals a day, consuming 10,000 to 12,000 calories daily. The dogs are thin and not at all large: 40 to 50 pounds. I'd been expecting enormous bruisers. Alaskan sled dogs are bred for one purpose, to pull. If it is grueling work, they nonetheless seem to love it. A volunteer force of up to forty-five veterinarians from all over the world tends to them meticulously, examining them at every checkpoint for signs of illness, dehydration, and muscle sprain. Dropped dogs are picked up by the "Iditarod Air Force," a volunteer squadron of airborne pickup trucks. A musher starts out with as many as sixteen dogs and must finish with at least five. There are casualties. At the Unalakleet hangar one day I saw two notices:

> *The gross necropsy of Victor, a six-year-old male from the team of Jeff Holt, has been completed. No cause of death could be determined by the board-certified veterinary pathologist. Further testing will be conducted to complete the necropsy process.*

Nigel Is Found!

On March 10, 2009, Iditarod XXXVII musher Nancy Yoshida (Bib #3) encountered a series of events in the "Steps" on her way to Rainy Pass that forced her to scratch from the race. The impact of those events included losing one of her sled dogs, Nigel. Nancy and the rest of her team stayed put for hours hoping Nigel would return and they could move forward. When Nigel didn't return, she and the rest of her team made their way to Rainy Pass, where Yoshida officially scratched. Nancy and the Iditarod continued to search for Nigel on the ground and in the air. Today, Nigel was reunited with Nancy and his teammates after he appeared at Talvista Lodge in Skwentna.

Lance Mackey did not linger long in Unalakleet. You don't win the Iditarod by sitting around the fire reciting "The Cremation of Sam McGee." That night, we watched in foot-numbing cold (20 below) as he applied pink ointment to his dogs' paws (fifteen dogs times four paws, with bare fingers; it took over an hour), then harnessed them. The dogs did not look particularly eager to be setting off. But off they went in the crunching cold in the direction of Shaktoolik.

A promontory that juts into the frozen Norton Sound, Shaktoolik means in the Inuit language: "the feeling that you have when you have been going toward a place for so long that it seems that you will never get there." Every child in the backseat of a car instinctively grasps the concept of Shaktoolik.

The next day, after Burke and I spend hours trying to warm the Cessna engine, we set off for Nome, into pink twilight, toward the United States' westernmost parts. I swigged from a bottle of port. My face showed signs of frostbite and my hands were claws, so the port was very welcome and warming.

I looked through the windshield at Norton Sound, a forbidding stretch of ice water. Back in 1925 one of the serum runners, a famous musher named Leonhard Seppala, risked crossing Norton Sound rather than take the longer, coastal route. In Alaska, even today, people speak of Seppala in reverential tones.

At this stage of the 1925 serum rum, the entire world was watching. A headline read: NOME SITUATION CRITICAL; ALL HOPE RESTS IN DOGS.

Off to our right, the dying sun cast shadows over snow-covered mountains that looked like enormous dunes of white desert sand. We landed at Nome and to our enormous delight found that it was an oasis of plug-ins. We hitchhiked a ride into town, whose main street was being decorated to greet the front-runner.

The next day we stood on Front Street along with two thousand other people, nostrils steaming vapor in the sun-bright cold. We heard a helicopter—a news chopper—buzzing above Mackey. A booming voice over a loudspeaker announced the news in ritual wording: "We have a dog team on the street of Nome, Alaska!"

And suddenly there was Lance Mackey and his dogs, led by a phalanx of Iditarod trailbreakers on snow machines. The cheer went up, and stayed up. I am not a sports person, but this was thrilling.

He finished in 9 days, 21 hours, 38 minutes, and 46 seconds. A day longer than Martin Buser's record, but Mackey finished with all fifteen of his dogs, a record in itself. The last person to finish this year would be Timothy Hunt, who would pull into Nome six days later. Of the original sixty-seven starters, fourteen teams scratched and one withdrew.

Governor Sarah Palin telephoned Mackey. We listened in on their conversation over the loudspeakers.

"We love ya!" said the governor. Mackey said, "Say hi to Todd for me."

Mackey was presented with a check for $69,000 and a cherry-red pickup truck. I looked at the dogs. They were pawing the ground, barking and howling, oblivious to all the fuss. They wanted to keep going.

The next day, as we were boarding a plane a bit larger than our Cessna, passengers were talking about how Mackey had spent his victory night. Not soaking in a hot tub or being massaged but arm wrestling at the Breakers Bar.

"He won the middleweight," someone said. "Then he won the women's. What a guy."

—*Forbes Life*, December 2009

THE HISTORY OF THE HOTEL MINIBAR

Volume II: Rome to the Present Day

78 B.C.—Hiltonus, an innkeeper weary of being rudely woken in the middle of the night by Roman legionnaires demanding wine and salted nuts, creates the concept of the minibar by installing in each room a chest containing miniature bottles of wine and salted nuts. Guests are asked to write down what they consume on a slate, but instead write taunting sentiments—"We came, we saw, we ate your cashews"—causing Hiltonus to abandon his experiment and ushering in a thousand-year hiatus in further attempts at in-room hospitality.

A.D. 1096—Crusaders passing through Malta en route to demonstrating their Christianity by slaughtering Muslims overwhelm island hotel keepers with middle-of-the-night requests for armor repair kits (forerunner of the modern sewing kit) and yew tree bark (forerunner of modern aspirin tablets). When checkout clerks attempt to charge the crusaders for the items, they are beheaded. Pope Suburban II issues a bull excommunicating "any who pilfer salted almonds and beverages without just recompense," but Antipope Inclement III counterasserts a divine right to free snacking (*Jus Pretzelonis*) by anyone engaged in the holy work of killing Muslims. The issue becomes mired in canonical courts and is not resolved until 1922.

1400—The proprietor of London's Tabard Inn, a gathering place for Chaucer's pilgrims, installs "minny barres" in the rooms. Inside are miniature bottles of holy water "Personally blest by St. Thomas" (actually unblessed Thames water), pints of ale, and capon drumsticks. Ingeniously, the drumsticks are tied to strings that ring a bell at the front desk, signaling clerks with clubs to burst into the room and beat the guest until payment is tendered.

1570—The Hamburg clockmaker Johannes Gluck devises his famous "Honor Bar" for the local hotelmeister Adolphus Kempinski. Something of a misnomer, the Honor Bar contains a hidden steel trap similar to those used to snare beavers and water rats that clamps down violently on the hand of anyone reaching for cocktail wieners or beer, unless they have first inserted coins into a slot.

1772—The manager of Paris's famed Hotel de Luxe stocks his *bars-de-minuit* with prophylactic sheepskin "envelopes" for the convenience of his male customers wishing to avoid *le syph* or *le clappe*.

1861—On the eve of his inauguration, a thirsty Abraham Lincoln attempts to open the minibar in his room at the Willard Hotel, only to find that the key will not fit. His bodyguard, Pinkerton, offers to shoot off the lock, but Lincoln demurs on the grounds that this might further divide the nation. Lincoln's gaunt and drawn appearance during his inauguration is attributed to his lack of refreshment the night before, but the incident, widely commented upon, enhances his aura of selflessness and nobility. An early sketch for the Lincoln Memorial by the sculptor Daniel Chester French depicts the president philosophically contemplating a locked minibar.

1905—Senator Robert "Fighting Bob" Smollett of Wisconsin denounces hotel minibars that require keys to open them as "un-American" and campaigns for president on a platform of outlawing them. His campaign fizzles, however, when it is pointed out to him that there is no presidential election in 1905.

1924—F. Scott Fitzgerald publishes his roman à clef *A Minibar as Big as the Ritz*, about the Princeton man Biff Billington, whose beautiful, crazed Southern-beauty wife, Zouella, ruins him financially by opening a sealed jar of macadamia nuts.

1975—Minibar fraud reaches a crisis as more and more hotels report that guests are emptying the contents and refilling bottles of scotch with iced tea and bags of M&Ms with gravel. Hotel owners petition the government to make minibar abuse a federal crime. During heated Senate hearings, Democrats assail the high prices of items, which they say drives normally honest guests to "desperate acts." Republicans counter that hotels have the right to charge what the market will bear, "and then some." The issue becomes key in the 1972 presidential election, but unfortunately "Fighting Bob" Smollett died in 1921 and is ineligible to run, except in Chicago.

1995—The luxurious Encomium Hotel in Bangkok becomes the first to stock its minibars with live prostitutes.

—*Forbes FYI*, March 2002

TWO IN THE BUSH

Africa is a place that people fall for hard. And a place that sometimes falls on them hard. One friend of mine got trampled nearly to death by a bull elephant and returned with a shattered rib cage. Another friend was blown up by Osama bin Laden in Dar es Salaam. (He survived.) Another had an AK-47 pointed at him by a twelve-year-old. But one day my friend Peaches announced, "We're going. Here are your malaria pills." And so I found myself at the Royal Livingstone Hotel in Zambia, watching the sun set over the Zambezi River at Victoria Falls and listening to the honk and snort of hippo, a sound I had known only from zoos.

Normally, countries that begin with "Z" make me a bit nervous, and this was the second Z-country in one day (we'd entered through Zimbabwe). But I was all at peace. The only discordant sound in that first, dreamy African twilight was the abrupt shatter of glass: my Pimm's cocktail being knocked over by a vervet monkey with the alacrity of a Times Square pickpocket. He wanted the cucumber. Next morning at breakfast Peaches had her bread roll snatched off her plate. But as African dangers go, these were manageable. At the river's edge there's a two-foot-wide Maginot Line of jagged rocks and an electrified fence, to keep out hippos and crocodiles. The previous April, the Zambezi rose and crocodiles came swarming onto the lawn. That must have made for a lively happy hour.

We dined that night by candlelight, with bats flitting overhead, on roasted sweetwater langoustines, Zambezi bream, and rabbit pot stickers. After, we drank brandy and smoked in the bar, one of the most splendid I've seen on any continent. It was deserted except for us. On the wall, in large letters, are the words:

> *... Commend me to the merry midnight frogs ...*
>
> —*DR. LIVINGSTONE*

Livingstone was the Scottish missionary-explorer who opened southern Africa to exploration in the process of attempting to abolish the local slave trade. He was possibly the last person to be disappointed by the spectacular falls here. He came upon them in 1855 while trying to establish a commercial river route. He loyally named the 1,860-yard-long, 355-foot-deep falls after his queen. The local word for the falls was Mosi-oa-Tunya, "the smoke that thunders" which is more accurate than "Victoria Falls." The cataract sends up plumes of mist and vapor. As you walk along opposite the falls it appears to be raining *up*. This was January: The water was low and we could see the rocks in detail. From March to May, when the water is high, all you see is a wall of furious white froth.

Hours later we were in a six-seater Cessna 3,000 feet up, looking down on the intersection of four countries: Zimbabwe, Namibia, Botswana, and Zambia. Peaches pointed, and there below I saw my first elephants in the wild, a thrilling sight.

Our home for the next two nights was Chobe Chilwero, a very cool fifteen-"chalet" lodge on a height above the Chobe River, about ten miles from where it joins the Zambezi. It was hot and unusually dry for the time of year, but ideal for game viewing because, lacking rain puddles, the animals must go to the river to drink.

Our host said, "If you leave your room, please call us and we'll escort you to the lodge."

"Why?"

"We do get elephants and buffalo inside the electric fence. And lions."

"Lions?"

"Yes."

"What do you do if you're . . . confronted by a lion?"

"Make as much sound as you can."

"That would probably happen automatically in my case."

"Actually, the tendency is to become very quiet."

I perused a book showing photos of an actual lion charge. The caption said, "If you run, you die."

I read to Peaches from *Out of Africa*, Isak Dinesen's memoir.

Thunderstorms rumbled in the distance. At four, surfeited on scones, clotted cream, and iced coffee, we set off with our guide, Chika.

We drove through teak woodland and saw an elephant within five minutes: a thirty-year-old bull with two broken-off tusks. Chika switched off the engine. The elephant approached, and for the first of several times that afternoon, I found myself trying to roll up a window that did not exist.

Someone in the vehicle leaned forward with a camera, causing the elephant to flare his ears. This is arresting when it occurs six feet from your face.

"Don't move," Chika said. The elephant lumbered off.

We saw marabou stork, comical, professorial-looking birds that like to perch in dead acacia trees. Also francolin and guinea fowl; Egyptian geese and yellow-billed stork; vultures; and baboons, creatures for which I developed no liking.

We emerged from the woodland into the wide river's grassy savannah. Everywhere there were hippos and elephants, hosing themselves down with mud, their version of combination SPF 30 and insect repellent. Also snake eagles; tawny eagles; puku antelope; spoonbills; blue-cheeked bee-eaters; impala.

Toward sundown, Chika pulled over at a bend in the river called Puku Flats. We drank gin and tonics and ginger lemonade to the ferocious roar of baboons. "Male dominance," Chika said with a smile. The women in our group rolled their eyes in a knowing way. The baboon din and the incipient feasting of the mosquitoes made me grateful to be spending the night behind electric fencing and insect netting.

On the way back we saw our first lion. Doubtless she saw us before we saw her. She was difficult to make out even with binoculars, but I was grateful for the distance separating us. Chika circled around, and minutes later we came up behind her. She was on the go. Someone in the vehicle shifted abruptly. Chika said with distinct urgency, "Don't move."

It was late now. Chika raced back to the park gates. He arrived ten minutes late and got a stern scolding from the rangers, who take the 7:00 p.m. closing time seriously. At night the Peaceable Kingdom becomes Nature Red in Tooth and Claw. It's a jungle out there.

We dined that night on spatchcock chicken and venison meatballs ("kudu, impala, and a bit of whatever's on hand," said chef). The merry midnight frogs kept up a steady chorus. We played anagrams by lantern light, which attracted impressively large beetles. The distinguished British biologist J. B. S. Haldane was asked what a lifetime of science had taught him about God. He replied, "An inordinate fondness for beetles."

We went out the next morning for five hours. It was hot. What had seemed remarkable the day before now seemed almost commonplace.

But the evening lingers in memory. Chika took us for a cocktail cruise on the river. We passed a beach teeming with hundreds of baboons, and nudged up against sleeping crocodiles and an immense scrum of hippos. There were three dozen or so butting up against one another, by my rough calculation an aggregate of fifty tons of hippo. (What *was* God thinking the day he invented the hippo? "Let's have some fun"?) "Very dangerous," Chika said, backing away. "They have killed more people than any other animal in Africa."

The sky blazed red and orange. We drank cold white wine and nibbled on dried mango and jerky strips. Chika opened the throttle and pointed the bow over the glass-smooth surface toward home. A warthog was waiting for us at the dock.

To judge from the omnipresent signs warning of armed response, Johannesburg is more dangerous than the bush. It leaves a confused twin impression of bougainvillea and concertina wire. We drove past Nelson Mandela's house. The day before, he had buried his son.

Our hotel was the Westcliff, overlooking the zoo. As we took high tea on the terrace amid smart-looking ladies, we listened to the animals below settling in for the night. These were by now familiar sounds to us, now dissonantly mixed with the electric yelp of ambulance and police sirens.

The porter expressed satisfaction over the fact that our room (406) had recently been vacated by Brad Pitt. The view from Mr. Pitt's bathtub might just be the best in all Johannesburg. We drank martinis in a room festooned with trophy heads, zebra-skin armchairs, and fading photographs of the queen bestowing silver cups on hunky polo players and dined on baked oysters and springbok osso buco.

At nine the next morning we were at the station in Pretoria to board the Blue Train. It takes up to eighty-two passengers three times a week between Pretoria and Cape Town. There are eighteen cars, forty-one cabins, also bar, dining, and smoking cars. We had a double bed and a bathtub. The train rides on air-spring cushions, and all the cars are air-sealed to one another, producing a smooth, whisper-quiet ride. The interior is polished brass and Italian birch wood with blue inlay. A twenty-seven-hour train ride during which the main activity is being stuffed with rich food and copious drink is not an aerobic experience, but certainly a pleasant one.

The scenery coming out of Pretoria consists of shantytowns and prisons. This is sobering and gratitude inspiring. You count your blessings. By night we were crossing the great Karoo Desert to the flash of lightning and streak of rain through the windows. It was cozy inside the dining car. We sat under a mural of Victoria Falls and ate Cape Malay mussels and duck Mpumalanga and rock lobster and drank lemony sauvignon blanc. The next morning we came out of a long tunnel into the drama of the Hex River Valley and saw our first vineyards. We arrived in Cape Town at noon.

The Mount Nelson Hotel is an opulent pink pile nestled between the city gardens and the foot of Table Mountain. It was baking hot—January is high summer—so we sought the pool, which we shared with thirsty red-eye pigeons who resemble hungover doves. That night we ate at a harbor-front restaurant called Bahia, where a 25-knot wind knocked over wineglasses and created mayhem.

Next morning we took the cable car up Table Mountain. From 3,500 feet up you see it all: the perfect harbor that the Dutch found in 1652, where they could water and provision their India-bound ships. The aboriginal Khoi name for Cape Town was Camissa—"place of sweet waters." Only a handful of cities can match it for topographical drama: San Francisco, Rio, Vancouver, Hong Kong.

Robben Island is seven miles from the harbor. We arrived in midafternoon. It is essential to visit Robben Island. It was here between 1961 and 1991 that political prisoners under apartheid were incarcerated. You're taken to a limestone quarry where prisoners were made to break rocks for eight hours a day in furnace heat, scorching their eyes and lungs. One day in 1995, 1,200 former prisoners returned here. Nelson Mandela, now president, was among them. He placed a small stone on the ground in the pit, and one by one the others did the same. The cairn is there.

You're shown Room 5 in B Sektion, Mandela's cell from 1964 to 1982. Our guide had been a prisoner here himself for seven years. "The thing that kept us going," he said, "was that we were convinced that we were right."

A half hour from Cape Town, on the other side of Table Mountain, is the microclimate of Constantia, where the first wine grapes in Africa were planted hundreds of years ago. At Klein (Little) Constantia vineyard, we tasted wine that had comforted Napoleon on St. Helena. A few minutes drive down a road lined with agapanthus and eucalyptus, we came to the vineyard and restaurant of Buitenverwachting ("Beyond Expectation"). It's well named.

We lunched with its owner, Lars Maack, a transplant from Hamburg, on a perfect meal of quail saltimbocca and grilled yellowtail and blesbok. It must be the finest restaurant in South Africa and is dreamily situated. You look at vineyards crawling up the sides of a mountain whose top is swept every day by clouds. Lars's wines win prizes. He has problems that would be considered unusual in Bordeaux or Napa: baboons.

"Last night they were barking so loud you couldn't sleep." One of his vineyards, he said, should produce five tons of grapes. "We're lucky if we get a half ton. But if you shoot the leader, they break into splinter groups and cause even more trouble. The electric fence won't stop them. Before long they know which wire is electrified and step over. Hippos? We have hippos three kilometers from here—and don't try running from them. They can outrun a golden retriever." There are the snakes, too. But for all these problems, Lars seemed the happiest man in Africa. "I would *hate* to go back to Germany," he said.

We drove along False Bay, a vast expanse of green, whitecapped shark water, turned northeast, and a half hour later drove up the oak-lined road to Lanzerac Manor. The porter was named Nimrod; the bartender Goodwill. We took supper on the terrace under the stars: crème de langoustine soup, slow-cooked lamb, and ostrich with a silky merlot made on the premises.

We visited two vineyards the next day, De Toren and Mulderbosch, and that night had our last dinner in South Africa at Tokara, a restaurant in the hills overlooking Stellenbosch. It's striking, architecturally. We got there an hour before the sun set and drank a bottle of exquisite Steenberg sauvignon blanc, the most expensive wine on the menu at thirty dollars.

The evening was soft. The vineyards below darkened to purple. In the distance we could see the Cape. As the sun set it turned a low-lying layer of mauve fog. I remarked on it, and the waitress said, "It's smoke, from the fires. Twelve thousand people lost their homes." A shantytown had burned. Seven geese loudly rose out of the vineyard and made off toward the vanishing sun.

On our last morning we stood atop Cape Point, looking down on the end of Africa. On one side is the Atlantic, on the other the Indian Ocean. I'd been here before—in 1971, as an eighteen-year-old seaman on a long passage aboard a freighter bound from Ceylon to New York City. It was night when we transited the Cape. I had the watch and it was my duty to report the movements of the many other ships around us. I was terrified.

But now all was peace. We saw kelp gulls, rock kestrels, oystercatchers, terns, and gannets, and not a baboon in sight. Someone had warned us, "If you make a picnic on the Cape the baboons will come and eat your food and then you'll *have* no picnic."

We lingered, being in no hurry to begin the long journey home. A boat rounded the Cape, crossing from one ocean to another. A huge tail rose out of the water and disappeared back into it with a loud *plop*, our last African creature.

—*Forbes FYI*, May 2005

GOOD MORNING, HANOI

On my first day in Hanoi I awoke at four a.m., but for once was grateful for circadian disrhythmia, otherwise known as jet lag. I'd been told that if you want to see "the real Hanoi," you must stroll around Hoan Kiem Lake as the city is waking up. There are a hundred reasons to stay at the Metropole Hotel, as I did; one of them certainly is its proximity to Hoan Kiem.

It was dark but already steamy. Boom boxes blared tinny sounds of exercise music. Women and men did calisthenics and tai chi in groups along the shore. Some men fished. Another group of men, wearing what appeared to be underwear, were setting up weight-lifting equipment on the sidewalk outside a temple. Hadn't seen that before, but by the time I left, a week later, I decided that I hadn't seen anything quite like Hanoi before.

Walking around that first morning, I came across another temple and the smell of incense drifting from a small shrine atop some rocks. A woman appeared out of the darkness to sell me joss sticks. I paid 10,000 dong (about 60 cents) and she led me up irregular steps to the shrine so that I could light the incense. She shook her head and in sign language conveyed that I must light an odd number. In the Buddhist-Taoist-Confucian tradition even numbers are bad joss. I held out five and the old woman nodded. I made my orisons to whatever spirits inhabited the shrine, descended the tricky stairs, and crossed the bridge—appropriately called the Bridge of the Rising Sun—to the Temple of the Jade Mountain.

Stop me if you've heard this one before, but: during the Ming domination of Vietnam, a fisherman on this lake discovered a magic sword one day in his net. It had been sent by the Emperor of the Waters, to help the king end the Chinese occupation. With the sword's help, the king drove out the occupiers. A year later, while the king was boating on the lake, a tortoise appeared and asked him to return the magic sword. Hoan Kiem is thus the "Lake of the Returned Sword." There are about twenty lakes in Hanoi, each with its own legend. In 1967, Lieutenant Commander John McCain parachuted into one of them.

It was growing light, and hot. I completed my circumnavigation of Hoan Kiem and proceeded west and found my destination without difficulty. Its name is painted above the forbidding main entrance: *Maison Centrale 1896–1954.* In fact, it was in use as a prison after 1954, when Hoa Lo became known in the United States as the "Hanoi Hilton." After being fished out of the lake, John McCain spent five and a half years inside these walls.

I spent an hour inside, shuddering in silence at dungeons, shackles, torture cells, death cells, and its once busy guillotine. I will never again think of it in connection with the name "Hilton." The display about the American inmates of Hoa Lo makes it out to have been a mildly uncomfortable guest home for naughty imperialist pilots. Photos show them smiling, playing basketball, and even happily receiving "souvenirs" before they went home on March 29, 1973. Reading their memoirs tells a somewhat different story.

I made my way back to the Metropole. It's a storied place. It was built in 1901, at the height of the French colonization of *l'Indochine*. The contours of the recently installed swimming pool had to be determined by the bomb shelter beneath. Charlie Chaplin and Paulette Goddard spent their honeymoon here in 1936. Graham Greene drank vermouth cassis here. Michael Caine and Brendan Fraser stayed here a half century later while filming Greene's *The Quiet American*. (The Graham Greene suite is number 228.)

I had my first meal in Hanoi at one of the hotel's four restaurants, Le Beaulieu. I was hungry after my morning ramble, and did not hold back. I started—as you must in Vietnam—with *pho*. (To pronounce it correctly, imagine you are Inspector Clouseau.) It's the national dish: noodles in broth with meat or chicken, vegetables, and spices. I slurped down two bowls and then tucked into a plate of fried rice with bok choy and chili sauce. Then had at the croissants. I was tempted by the pancakes, the omelet station, full Japanese breakfast, cheeses, cold cuts, crème caramel, yogurts. Le Beaulieu's breakfast buffet is the sort that makes you think, *Well, I could always just spend the day* here.

Though Hanoi seemed generally laid-back, authoritywise, every day, at about the same time, loudspeakers blared outside my window. I made inquiries. A local rolled his eyes and shrugged: "The Party." I asked what the loudspeakers said. "Oh, they're either denouncing someone, or telling everyone to do something. Yesterday it was 'Have your dog or cat vaccinated by three o'clock tomorrow.'" He shook his head. "F— communism."

The hotel arranged for me and a guide to be driven around in their 1953 blue Citroën limousine. It was a pleasant, but strange sensation to drive around rainy, busy Hanoi in a car manufactured the year before Dien Bien Phu. Mr. Anh, the driver, was in full chauffeur's livery; Mr. Tuan, the guide, sat beside him in front. As we pulled into Hanoi's chaotic traffic flow (more on this later) I felt colonial, and uneasy, as if someone on a passing *cyclo* might toss a grenade through the window. We made our way to Ho Chi Minh's mausoleum and house.

The mausoleum—monumental and grim in the Soviet style—was closed for its annual renovation. Ho Chi Minh's body is preserved, as are many Communist gods, and must go annually to a sort of spa for "refreshment." I'll spare you the details. The mausoleum is sited on the spot where, on September 2, 1945, Ho declared independence from France, inaugurating nine years of war.

The house, where he conducted much of the war with the United States and the South, is near the mausoleum and stands in a peaceful, leafy precinct of grapefruit, bamboo, willow, almond, and Buddha trees alive with bird-chirp. There's a large fishpond full of carp. The house is teak and on stilts, in the manner of Vietnamese village houses. Ho's air raid helmet is there under glass, next to his three telephones, one of which is crank operated. With these modest devices he won a war against the most powerful nation on earth.

I wanted to see the "B-52 Museum" indicated on the map. It is something that an American should see. So Mr. Anh, shifting—*rrrr-unk*—gears, drove down frenetically crowded streets. Driving through Hanoi is an experience second only to walking in Hanoi. It is a city of two million motorbikes, and I saw them every single one of them, up close. On the way to the B-52, one motorbike passed us, its rear rack heaped high with boiled carcasses.

"Pigs?"

Mr. Tuan and Mr. Anh laughed. The Vietnamese laugh easily, an endearing quality along with courtesy, friendliness, and generosity.

"Dog!" Mr. Tuan corrected.

The streets grew narrower and narrower until finally we came to a lake, not much more than an acre, surrounded by city houses. The water was the color of bright jade. From the middle protruded the tail section of a B-52. It fell to earth here just before midnight on December 27, 1972, during the so-called Christmas bombing that forced the North back to the negotiating table in Paris. A plaque refers to the wreckage as evidence of the "Dien Bien Phu of the air." I said a silent prayer for the crew and we left.

We proceeded to the Temple of Literature, a thousand-year-old university where the mandarins took their exams. These were tests you wanted to pass, as mandarins ruled the country.

My tourist receptors began to flag. It was past noon. I was hungry. We went to a place in the old quarter called Cha Ca La Vong. It's been there since 1871 and it serves only one dish. If you guessed that the dish is called *cha ca*, you are correct. It was one of the best meals I've ever eaten: chunks of perch dusted in turmeric, grilled atop a wooden brazier set on the table. While it cooks you drink cold Bia Ha Noi (Hanoi beer). You add green onion, dill, fish sauce, peanuts, shrimp sauce (*not* for the faint of heart), herbs, and hot chilies, all heaped onto rice noodles. Cost of meal for three: $25. (395,000 dong. Dealing with dong takes some getting used to.)

The next day I set off on foot to see a bit of the city on my own. This turned out to be a pedestrian adventure, quite literally.

Kai Speth, the Metropole's genial general manager, had given me advice on how to negotiate Hanoi's streets: "Just walk out, and keep walking slowly. If you stop, you die. If you run, you die. And whatever you do, don't look into their eyes. It only confuses things."

My first moment of truth was Dinh Tien Hoang, the street that runs along Hoan Kiem Lake's eastern shore. When I crossed it that first morning, before five, there had been only minimal traffic. Now, as I stood sweatily on the curb, it was a continuous onrush of motorcycles, with cars and trucks thrown in. No stoplights, no cops, just Hanoi's two million motorbikes, all of them beeping.

I stood for perhaps fifteen minutes frozen, trying to muster the courage to cross. My mouth went dry. Finally I said, "Well, are you a man?" A voice replied, "No, you are not. Go back to the hotel. Have another breakfast." I took a deep breath and stepped off the curb.

Keep going, I told myself. *Do. Not. Stop. Do. Not. Run.*

Hundreds of vehicles threaded their way around me. Somehow, I made it to the far curb and collapsed against a tree, breathing heavily. Emboldened by my thrilling accomplishment, I walked for four hours. Here are some redacted notes:

> *A new and interesting challenge as I make my way down Trang Thi St: a woman driving her motorcycle at me* on the sidewalk.

> *Heart soars as I encounter an intersection with an actual traffic light! Bliss! Resolve to spend rest of day here.*

> *Turns out there is not much difference in Hanoi between intersections with lights and intersections* without *lights.*

> *A new strategy—wait until pregnant woman (plentiful) appears and cross using her as a shield.*

Some peripatetic hours later, I found myself in an open-air market a few blocks north of Hoan Kiem Lake. It's off Hang Be Street; you can't miss it. Drenched in sweat, I walked amid the most concentrated commerce I've ever seen. Everything Vietnam had to offer by way of foodstuffs was here, along with a thousand pungent smells. I made notes as I strolled:

> *Flowers, live eels, snakes, catfish, meats, spices, snails, sweets herbs, watercress, live crabs tied with vines, noodles, cooked ducks, live ducks, live shrimp in tubs, squid, giant shrimp,*

periwinkles, nuts, live sturgeon, carp, duck eggs, quail eggs, cakes, ribs, limes, cilantro, coriander, ginger, nutmeg, cinnamon, curry, coffee, chilies, ginseng, vermicelli, incense, moon cakes, live rabbits, dead chicken feet, green dragon lychee . . .

I wanted to prolong the visit, but I was due back at the Metropole for a lunch of Nha Trang lobsters and *fines de claires* from Brittany. I braced myself for one more assault on Dinh Tien Hoang Street with the thought that the five joss sticks I lit the first morning would surely see me safely across.

—*ForbesLife*, June 2010

AUSCHWITZ

You go through the visitors center and there it is. You've seen it in photographs a hundred times, the famous gate: "Arbeit Macht Frei." Work will set you free. The idea was to be reassuring, unlike the slogan Dante hung over the entrance to his hell, "Abandon hope all ye who enter here." Put in an honest day and everything will be all right. It would be counterproductive to panic the arrivals. Here, and up the road, in Birkenau, they thought through all the details, down to the numbered hooks in the dressing rooms outside the gas chambers. The SS jollied you along. Remember which hook you hang your clothes on so you'll be able to find them after the shower. And don't forget to put your shoes underneath so you'll be able to get them, too. You're a shoemaker? Great, we need shoemakers. At Auschwitz, they even had a prisoner orchestra playing inside the gate.

It helped keep order. Good for morale, too. How bad could it be, if they greeted you with music?

It's February and gray. The poplar trees that line the avenues between the cell blocks are bare. The swimming pool—See? We even have a swimming pool.—that was to impress the Red Cross is covered with dirty ice. Crows, gallows. It's hands-in-the-pockets cold, but would you want to see this in springtime, with blossoms and sweet earth smells?

Our guide is Jarek. Midforties, fluent English, dark mustache, knit cap. He grew up in Oswiecim. He speaks precisely, in a low, clear voice without emotion for nearly six hours, except for twice, once outside Block 10 and inside Block 11. We pass under *Arbeit Macht Frei*. He indicates a grassy strip. "Here is where they gave the welcome speech. They said, 'You dirty Poles, this isn't a sanitorium. There's only one way out—through the chimney of the crematorium. Jews, you have three weeks. Priests, one month. Three months for the rest of you.'"

Sixty thousand, out of about one and a half million, survived Auschwitz. If you made it through the first weeks, you stood a chance of making it. Some even managed to survive five years, from 1940 to 1945. By contrast, out of six hundred thousand at Belzec, three people survived.

It feels colder inside the cell blocks, where the exhibits are. There is a blown-up photograph of Himmler viewing Auschwitz's first inmates, Soviet POWs. Polish political prisoners, the intelligentsia, priests followed. Two years later, with the construction of the much larger Birkenau three kilometers away, the camp became ground zero for the "Final Solution to the Jewish Question."

Between October 1941 and March 1942, some ten thousand Soviet prisoners died here. Jarek as well as the exhibits use the word *murder* instead of die, or kill, or exterminate. It takes some time before the ear, accustomed to modern euphemisms, adjusts to the straightforward terminology.

"The method for murdering the Soviets was in many cases simple," Jarek says. "Put them in a field, surround them with barbed wire, and leave them." Some became so resigned from hunger that they would climb themselves onto the wagons of corpses. There was cannibalism. In Tadeusz Borowski's short story "The Supper," a group of Russians who have tried to escape are lined up, arms tied behind them with barbed wire, and shot point-blank through the back of the head in front of a crowd of starving prisoners. The prisoners clamor and rush forward and must be dispersed with clubs. "The following day . . . a Jew from Estonia who was helping me haul steel bars tried to convince me all day that human brains are, in fact, so tender you can eat them raw." Borowski was at Auschwitz. He survived and later put his head in a gas stove at the age of twenty-nine.

More exhibits. The Nazis kept meticulous records, which in the end meant that there was a vast amount to destroy as the Red Army approached in January 1945. Every death—murder—was written down. Jarek points to a photocopy of a ledger that survived. "The reason given was never 'bullet' or 'gas,' but instead 'heart attack' or 'kidney function.'" Deaths are listed in intervals of minutes.

In the next case are photocopies of transit passes for the trucks that brought the cannisters of Zyklon B pellets. The contents are listed as "material for the displacement of Jews." Here are the minutes from the Wannsee Conference outside Berlin on January 20, 1942, the meeting of the board of directors of the corporation in charge of the Final Solution. These are free of euphemism. One page shows the goal: a column of numbers, country-by-country tallies, with a bottom line of eleven million.

Up a flight of stairs, around a corner. No more paperwork. Now it becomes vivid: two tons of human hair behind glass. Mounds upon mounds, amorphous and hard to take in at first, until you focus and see the pigtails and braids. Jarek remarks that they were going to send some of this to the Holocaust Museum in Washington, but in the end it was declined as "too much." The hair was shorn after the gassings, then efficiently dried in the crematoria so it could be industrially spun into carpeting.

Here is a large pile of spectacles, a spidery mass of rusted wireframes and dusty lenses. These were left with the clothing in the dressing rooms, so the last things seen through these glasses would have been nervous kapos and Death's-Head guards.

Behind another wall of glass is a jumble of rusted artificial limbs, canes, crutches, braces. Like the hair, it blurs into abstraction until the eye settles on a child's fake leg. Now it's into another room and the suitcases, piles and piles of shriveled leather suitcases. They wrote their names on them in large white letters. Jarek points out the word for "orphan" in Dutch. Hundreds of names. I write down one: PETR EISLER 1942 KIND. The year of his birth and his child—*kinder*—status. In the next room comes the display of children's clothing, pacifiers, rattles, hairbrushes. Then the shoes, a mountain of them. Finally the empty canisters of Zyklon B, perhaps a hundred or more, in a pile. By the calculations of Rudolph Hoss, Auschwitz's first commandant, it required seven kilos of Zyklon to murder—not the word he used—1,500 people, so this pile here might have sufficed for perhaps 75,000 or 100,000 human beings. It appears from the tops that they refined the process of opening the cans. Some are jagged, others have been smoothly cut, as if in one motion by a machine. Across from this display is a clay diorama of a gas chamber in action. Once everyone was inside, between 700 and 1,500, depending on which of the five gas chambers it was, the doors and windows were sealed tight. The bluish pellets of diatomite soaked in hydrocyanic acid were poured through chutes. Exposed to oxygen, the pellets gave off prussic acid, blocking the exchange of oxygen in the blood. Those close to the chutes died instantly, the ones farther away took longer. Hoss watched one gassing through a peephole. In his *Reminiscences* before he was hanged in 1947 he describes clinically that it took two or more minutes before the screams turned to moans. Still they didn't open the doors for half an hour, just in case. After that it was safe for the *Sonderkommando*, the prisoner work crews, to wade into the tangle of bodies, vomit, and excrement to get the hair and the gold teeth and drag the bodies next door to the crematorium. The work paid well and was competed for: one-fifth liter of vodka, five cigarettes, a hundred grams of sausage for each job.

It's gotten colder outside. We're approaching Block 10 now, where Professor Doctor Carl Clauberg, a university professor of gynecology described by Borowski as "a man in a green hunting outfit and a gay little Tyrolian hat decorated with many brightly shining sports emblems, a man with the face of a kindly satyr," sterilized women and men with chemicals and roentgens and infected children with disease, for science. He was released from prison by the Soviets in 1956. Jarek says, "He went back to Germany and took out an advertisement in the newspaper saying, 'Dr. Clauberg is seeking an assistant.' He did not even change his name." A trace of a smile. "He was arrested and died the same year, of poor health." Elsewhere at Auschwitz-Birkenau, Dr. Josef Mengele performed his experiments on twins and dwarves.

In the courtyard between Block 10 and Block 11 is the Wall of Death. There is a sign urging quiet, so you approach slowly and reverently, as you might an important tomb. Visitors have placed six bouquets of flowers at its base. A woman is crouching, trying to get a red votive candle lit. People have left pebbles in every inch of the creases in the wall, in the Jewish manner of mourning. Jarek tells what happened here. Prisoners who had been tried by the SS, for trying to escape, taking food, for whatever reason, were taken out into the courtyard naked, in twos. A strong kapo, who before he came here had worked in the circus, held them face to the wall. An SS man shot them at the base of the skull, with a short air pistol if there were a lot of executions to be done, so that the camp would not ring with incessant gunshots.

A former prisoner, a Dr. Boleslaw Zbozien, described what he witnessed here one day:

> *Sometime, I cannot remember the exact date, we encountered [SS sergeant-major Gerhard] Palitzsch on the streets of the camp at Auschwitz. Before him, he was driving a man and a woman. The woman was carrying a small child in her arms, and two larger children, around four and seven years old, walked next to her. The entire group was walking in the direction of Block 11. I made it with some colleagues to Block 21 in time. From a window in a room on the ground floor, we gazed out at the courtyard to Block 11, standing on a table*

in the room. As long as I live, the scene that played out before my eyes will be engraved in my memory. The man and woman did not resist when Palitzsch stood them before the Wall of Death. It all took place in the greatest calm. The man held the hand of the child who stood on his left side. The second child stood between them; they both held his hand. The mother clasped the youngest to her breast. Palitzsch first shot the baby through the head. The shot to the back of the head exploded its skull . . . and induced massive bleeding. The baby struggled like a fish, but the mother only held him more firmly to herself. Palitzsch next shot the child standing in the middle. The man and woman . . . continued to stand without moving, like statues. Later, Palitzch struggled with the oldest child, who would not allow himself to be shot. He threw him to the ground and shot him at the base of the head while standing on his shoulders. He then shot the woman, and at the very last, the man. This was the greatest monstrosity . . . After that, although many executions were carried out, I did not watch them.

We place our pebbles. Jarek says, "Between five thousand and twenty thousand people were shot here."

We go into Block 11. The faded sign above the door reads, BLOK SMIERCI.

Block of Death. Just inside the door on the left is the room where they held the proceedings. Jarek remarks that the SS officer who sentenced five thousand Poles here to die was still alive last year, living in Germany, age ninety-two. We ask why. He shrugs. At the far end on the corridor, on the left, looking out into the courtyard, is the room where the condemned were stripped and held. An illustration depicts a naked girl holding on to her mother's legs as the SS guard comes for them. High on the wall, a prisoner scratched graffiti, a name and the date and the words, "Sentenced to die." Beneath that is the date of the next day and the words, "I'm still here."

In the basement of Block 11, the first gassing with Zyklon B took place. Six hundred Soviet POWs and two hundred and fifty Poles were locked in. They poured in the pellets. It took twenty hours to kill—murder—them all. This is how they learned the correct dosage.

Cell 18 was the "Starvation Cell." If a prisoner escaped, the *Lagerfuhrer*, or commandant, would select ten prisoners from the escapee's block. They would be shut in this cell without food or water and left to die. Generally this took a week.

In August of 1941 there was an escape. One of the prisoners, Father Maximilian Kolbe, a Franciscan missionary, asked the commandant to let him take the place of one of the ten men selected to starve. Father Kolbe was still alive in the cell two weeks later, after the others had all died. They finished him off with an injection of carbolic acid. He was canonized as a Roman Catholic saint by Pope John Paul II in 1981. Candles burn in the cell for him and the others who were murdered here.

In another room in the basement of Block 11 are the four "Standing Cells." Each measures about a yard square, with a small hole for ventilation. Four prisoners were crammed in at a time and left all night, sent out to work in the morning, and returned here at night. This punishment might last three days, or two weeks. The sign says that it produced "extreme emaciation and a slow, agonising death."

In the hall as we leave the basement I ask what the pipes are. Jarek explains that it's the only cell block in Auschwitz with central heating. "Because it was officially a Gestapo prison, it had to be heated." The second and last smile of the day. "Rules."

We walk past Cell Block 21, where Doctor Zbozien witnessed the murder of the Polish family, past a memorial stone left by President Chaim Herzog of Israel with a quote from Psalms 38:18, "My sorrow is continually before me." We walk past the gallows where they hanged prisoners twelve at a time, past the cell block where the whorehouse was on the second floor. "It was Himmler's idea, to give incentive to the non-Jewish prisoners." Borowski wrote about this in one of his stories. The prisoners' name for it was "Puff."

Outside the barbed wire you come to Gas Chamber and Crematorium Number I, Auschwitz's first functional one after the initial experiment in the basement of Block 11. Seventy thousand were murdered here. It's the only intact crematorium out of five at Auschwitz.

The SS dynamited the other four at Birkenau as the Red Army was closing in.

We stand inside and look up through the opening where SS men in gas masks poured the pellets. Through the door at the end are the ovens. These could incinerate 340 bodies a day. Jarek shows how the slide worked. It still does. A bouquet of roses has been left on one. The German company that made these, he says, finally went bankrupt in the 1960s.

A short lunch in the cafeteria, borscht and croquettes and nonalcoholic beer, since they don't serve alcohol at Auschwitz, no matter how much you could use a drink. Soup for the prisoners consisted of nettles and water. Morning tea was brewed from oak leaves. For dinner, wormy bread with a smear of lard. Some of the survivors weighed sixty pounds.

Birkenau is a five-minute car ride. This is Konzentrationlager Auschwitz II, Auschwitz concentration camp number two, built in 1942 in pursuance of the Wannsee Conference goals. "Compared to Birkenau," Jarek remarks, "Auschwitz was a Hilton." Birkenau is how the Germans said Brezinzka, which means Birch Wood, the name of the Polish village that was here. Auschwitz was how they said Oswiecim. Oz-vee-chim. The town once had a sizable Jewish population of its own.

The rail line that approaches Birkenau runs through a red brick guard tower and this is familiar from photographs and documentaries. The prisoners called it the Gate of Death. From May to October 1944, 600,000 Hungarian Jews—a line of numbers in the Wannsee document—came through here. In the spring of 1944, at the height of Auschwitz's efficiency, ten thousand arrived here each day.

We go up into the tower. Jarek opens a window and stands back and says quietly, "Birkenau." It's here, rather than at the Wall of Death or Cell Block 11, that many visitors break down and weep. Perhaps it's because of vastness that confronts them. You're looking out on an area 3,000 feet wide by 2,100 feet deep: 174 barracks, 4 crematoria, surrounded by double fences of barbed wire and guard towers. The crematoria could handle only about five thousand bodies a day, so at times to keep up they had to burn bodies in the fields by the woods in the distance. The stench from that, and from the early mass graves of Soviet POWs, is described in the literature.

Jarek gets a key to the gate and we drive to the rail platform where the arrivals got off Eichmann's transports after journeys of sometimes three or more days, no food or water, packed in so tightly that in summers water from the humidity ran off the ceilings. About 80 percent of the arrivals, those unfit for work, the older men and women, women with babies, children under fourteen, were immediately murdered in the gas chambers. Borowski's book of stories is titled *This Way for the Gas, Ladies and Gentlemen*.

We stand where the families were separated. Jarek points. We look and see a dozen deer on the other side of the barbed wire, running down an alley between barracks, white tails going up and down in the ruins as they leap.

On one side of the rail platform was the women's camp. "When the trains came," Jarek says, "women would shout to the women arriving, 'Give the baby to the granny.' That way you might not be selected for the gas chamber. This was the choice."

We drive past a small pond of foamy water where they dumped the ashes, to Gas Chamber and Crematorium II. On the maps, these are designated KI, KII, KII, and so on. KII is larger that the one at Auschwitz. Jarek's uncle lived six kilometers away and told him about the smell. We stand on the ruins of KII, which is more or less as it was after the dynamiting, collapsed onto itself, but the foundations still clear. Jarek points, "Mengele's laboratory."

Between KII and KIII is the memorial, a raised terrace of moss-lined granite bricks, a low stone sculpture, and nineteen plaques, one for each language of the people murdered here, French, Greek, Norwegian, Italian, all the rest. The one in English says,

FOR EVER LET THIS PLACE BE
A CRY OF DESPAIR
AND A WARNING TO HUMANITY,
WHERE THE NAZIS MURDERED

ABOUT ONE AND A HALF
MILLION
MEN, WOMEN, AND CHILDREN,
MAINLY JEWS
FROM VARIOUS COUNTRIES
OF EUROPE.
AUSCHWITZ-BIRKENAU
1940–1945

Jarek explains that they changed the wording after Communist rule ended in Poland. Originally, the plaques made no specific mention of Jews. "In Poland then the idea was officially that you didn't point out one group above the other." After communism, it was no longer politically incorrect. Ninety percent of Auschwitz's victims were Jews. Next came Poles, 70,000, then Gypsies, 23,000.

On the drive back to Cracow we don't say much, my father and I. It leaves you quiet, Auschwitz, even as it impels you not to be quiet about it, to witness what you saw, no matter that it is all by now so well known and documented and familiar. At the airport in Zurich, the front page of the local Sunday paper has a photo from a recent rally in Switzerland, hundreds of shaved-head neo-Nazis, giving the salute.

—*The Daily Beast*, January 2009

LONDON, REMEMBRANCE DAY

I arrived in London a bit after noon, having gotten off the *Queen Mary 2* in Southampton a few hours earlier, so I missed the eleven o'clock two-minute moment of silence. On the way in, I wondered if the cars on the M3 motorway might pull over in observance and would not have been surprised if they had.

But in Trafalgar Square and at Whitehall and Westminster and St. Paul's, everything did come to a stop. The British observe this sacred ritual every November 11, commemorating the armistice that began on the eleventh hour of the eleventh day of the eleventh month of 1918.

Walking in the rain to the Cenotaph in Whitehall, I saw that practically everyone in London was wearing the traditional red paper poppy. As you surely know, the symbol derives from a poem written in 1915 by a Canadian military doctor. The occasion was the funeral service for a friend who'd been killed by an exploding shell. The chaplain was unavailable, so McCrae scribbled a few lines, which begin:

In Flanders fields the poppies blow
Between the crosses, row on row.

And conclude two stanzas later:

If ye break faith with us who die
We shall not sleep, though poppies grow
In Flanders fields.

The Great War ended nine decades ago, but seems fresh in memory. When I reached the Cenotaph, with its problematic inscription "The Glorious Dead," I found the roadway around it entirely with wreathes of paper poppies, many of them personally inscribed. There were tiny wooden crucifixes, with names inscribed in ink now runny from the rain. If it wasn't as lavish a floral display as the one outside Princess Diana's residence in 1997, it was still impressive. I made my belated two-minute observance.

I say "problematic" above because there was so little glory in their terrible deaths. They left us extraordinary and moving literature, most indelibly in the poetry that came from the trenches. The day's *The Independent* had a moving article by Robert Fisk titled "Language of the Lost," in which he quoted his own father, a veteran of the war, telling him that it had all been "just one great waste." A year into the war, Kaiser Wilhelm was asked what the war was about. He's said to have responded, "I wish to God I knew."

I had lunch the next day with Sir Alistair Horne, one of Britain's preeminent military historians. Among his many books is one on the Battle of Verdun, *The Price of Glory*. (That word again.) I remember reading in it the arresting statistic that the ten-month battle was fought on ground not larger than Manhattan's Central Park, at a cost of 700,000 casualties.

Paul Fussell wrote in *The Great War and Modern Memory* that World War I continues even now to define and determine. Germany was defeated and then driven to humiliation and despair by the draconian terms of the Versailles Treaty. From that toxic soil rose Adolf Hitler, whose Jew-hatred wrought the Holocaust, producing a diaspora and Israel. So the bullet that Gavrilo Princip fired into Archduke Ferdinand in Sarajevo still ricochets.

The front page of *The Independent* was not entirely given over to Armistice Day, but shared a sad and moving photograph of hearses bearing the bodies of six British soldiers killed in Afghanistan. Beneath the photo was a headline: AFGHAN WAR IS BAD FOR SECURITY, VOTERS SAY.

Nearly half the British electorate now believes that keeping British troops in the same country that humbled Victorian England increases, rather than decreases, the threat of terrorism.

And there was this, just in from our British Prime Minister Gordon Brown Desk. (Mr. Brown seems to get so many things wrong these days that one reflexively inserts "Poor" in front of his name.)

The latest kerfuffle concerns a letter that he wrote, by hand, to the mother of a slain British soldier. Mr. Brown is no doubt a genuinely sympathetic man. He has written two hundred of these letters. The problem was that he told the soldier's mother that he felt her pain, being himself the father of a child who died at the age of ten days. The loss of a child is a tragedy whenever it occurs. But the mother in question did not apparently feel that the prime minister's allusion to his own loss was appropriate.

Then there were the misspellings. He got the soldier's name slightly wrong. His name was "Jamie," not "Janie." And either the PM's handwriting or spelling needs work to judge from the words "cumfort" and "cuntry."

—*The Daily Beast*, November 2009

EASTER ISLAND

Easter Island is—well, put it this way: its closest neighbor is Pitcairn Island. Pitcairn Island, as in *Mutiny on the Bounty*. Which is to say, Easter Island is not near much at all.

To get to Easter Island, or as its inhabitants call it, Rapa Nui, you must go via Tahiti or Santiago, Chile. If you go through Santiago, voyager, beware: Don't even think of bringing along something to eat. That includes, as one of my unhappy traveling companions found out, trail mix (nuts and dried fruit, notorious purveyors of contagion and plague). She spent two hours in detention filling out paperwork and forking over a two-hundred-dollar fine. A woman in line with her was reduced to tears as she explained to an implacable bureaucrat that the dried lentils the dogs had sniffed in her bag were for a favorite dish she had come to Chile to cook for her dying mother. She finally exploded: "We got rid of Pinochet—for this?"

It was a longish trip, twenty-eight hours door-to-door. Oddly, for all that time spent in the air and in airports, I crossed only two time zones. I started in Washington, D.C.; Easter Island shares about the same longitude with Salt Lake City. By the time you arrive, weary, sticky, your trail mix forfeit, you really do have a sense of being . . . out there. But also of exhilaration, because you finally made it to Easter Island, home of those strange monoliths called *moai*, the ones you first saw a half century ago on the cover of a book by a Norwegian explorer.

The place to stay is the recently opened explora Rapa Nui (the small e is intentional), also called the Posada de Mike Rapu. The architect is a Chilean who trained in Barcelona, and it shows. I found myself staring up at the ceiling, all bright pine and intersecting planes. (Or maybe it was the martini.)

We clomped off the next morning with our engaging guide Sam, in a light drizzle that soon cleared to a bright, cool day. It's small, Easter Island, just sixty-three square miles, triangular, and volcanic. Thor Heyerdahl made his fame in the 1950s with his book *Kon-Tiki*, in which he postulated that the island was first settled by aboriginal South Americans. That thesis has since crumbled, and Mr. Heyerdahl is not held in esteem in Rapa Nui. When I asked Sam about him, his handsome face creased into an exclamation of disdain. "Thor Heyerdahl?!" he said. "He wrote so many things that are not true!"

More recently anthropologists have determined that the island's settlers arrived from Polynesia, perhaps as early as A.D. 450. The earliest *moai*, those distinctive, indeed, unique, Easter Island statuary, date to about 1100.

We hiked through rain-wet brush and eucalyptus groves. Everywhere, there was bright yellow lupine and purple grass. And there in the distance was the "quarry," Rano Raraku, the volcano cone where the Rapanui carved their *moai*.

As we approached, you could see them: improbable figures protruding from the earth along the slope of the volcano. Sam asserted that the word *moai* means "face alive of the ancestor." I liked that, though there are other translations. There are some 887 *moai* on Easter Island, 397 of them at the quarry. The Rapanui carved them over perhaps eight hundred years. Overpopulation and dwindling resources eventually brought civil wars, at which point they stopped erecting *moai* and started knocking them over. Since each clan and tribe put up its own *moai*, they became collateral targets in the wars. By the time Heyerdahl arrived, most of the statues were lying on their backs or faces. Many still are, and walking past them, seeing them so forlorn, you think of Shelley: "My name is Ozymandias, king of kings / Look on my works, ye mighty and despair."

Along a beach not far from the quarry is Ahu Tongariki, a sight to give you a shiver: fifteen immense *moai* standing on a long plinth (the *ahu*), looking like pieces in a titanic chess game. In the 1960s, a tsunami triggered by an earthquake in Chile swept through here and knocked over the entire site. A Japanese company contributed funds to restore the site in the 1990s. It's haunting, all the more so for Sam's casual mention that "Rapanui people also practiced cannibalism." He showed us a petroglyph of a tuna, along with hundreds of carved dots beneath. "Each one," he said, "represents a dead child." I didn't have the heart to ask how they died.

Our days fell into a pleasant routine. We hiked in the morning, then returned to explora for lunch. One day, the staff arranged a picnic under a coconut grove on a beautiful white-sand beach. (Oddly, there are only two beaches on the island.) Afternoons, we did another archaeological-themed hike. By day's end our muscles felt nicely tired.

They saved the best for the fifth and last day. Our guide was Terry, half American, half Rapanui. If that sounds exotic, another of our guides, Niko, is half Rapanui and half Croatian.

We started at the edge of the island's single runway. It is more than three kilometers long. Why? It's leased by NASA for use as an emergency landing strip for the Space Shuttle. It's never been used for that purpose, but there it is, making Easter Island the ultimate cargo cult, awaiting the great bird that now will never come.

There was a stiff wind blowing from the west as we hiked up the side of Rano Kau, hearts and lungs pumping. We rested overlooking over a fierce cliff with great ocean swells breaking at its base and exploding into foam. We continued to a cypress grove, then a fragrant eucalyptus grove, and finally emerged 1,063 feet above the ocean, on the rim of the volcanic crater. Below we saw three small rocky islands, furiously assaulted by the sea.

It was here starting about 1600 that the Rapanui held their annual "Bird Man" contests to pick tribal leaders. These were the ultimate in Ironman Triathlons. Contestants from as many as fifty-four tribes or clans would gather. On the appointed days, they would climb down the cliffs from the volcano's lip, plunge into the sea, swim through shark-water to the islands, then climb—somehow—through the boiling surf and razor-sharp rocks, to the nests of the migrating sooty tern. The object was to return through the water and back up the cliff with the egg intact. You try it.

You can see the petroglyph depictions of Bird Men who actually made it carved into the rocks. They are stirring sights and ones to make you glad that your own life is differently ordered. Bird Man contests continued until 1867, when Catholic missionaries arrived with alternative suggestions for choosing tribal leaders.

On the other end of the island is Ana o Keke, the Cave of the Virgins. Here, young girls were kept out of the sun to "whiten"—as our guide put it with amusement. These pale virgins were the Bird Man's prize. A kilometer or so from their cave is a porous, resonant stone that was used to signal the keepers of the virgins that a new Bird Man had been crowned. Niko demonstrated, putting his lips to a hole in the stone and blowing with all his strength, producing an eerie blast.

The spell Easter Island cast was slightly altered for me on my return, when a publisher friend told me that Dan Aykroyd went there in the 1970s along with a writer for *Saturday Night Live*. They dropped acid and, inspired by the *moai*, came up with the Coneheads.

—*ForbesLife*, November 2009

A SHORT HISTORY OF THE HOTEL ALARM CLOCK

Volume IV: Ancient Egypt to the 1980s

1340 B.C.—The desk clerk of the Luxor Suites Hotel fails to waken Alexandrian grain merchant Memhotep, who is consequently tardy for his important meeting with Rekmos, grand vizier to Pharaoh Thott III. The fastidious Rekmos expresses his displeasure by forcing Memhotep to eat dung beetles while being suspended upside down over a pool of Nile crocodiles. Memhotep twitches for the rest of his life and exhibits a morbid fear of dung beetles. On his deathbed, he continually asks the time. His son Shephotep ("The Punctual") continues in the family trade, taking with him on business trips caged roosters to wake him up. Innkeepers take note and begin offering rooms with caged bedside cocks at premium prices.

212 B.C.—Emperor Shi Tzu tasks his court with devising a means of waking him one hour before sunrise so that he might get a good start on pleasuring his six hundred concubines. For the next twenty-three years, an estimated fourteen thousand engineers labor to invent a fail-proof emperor-waking instrument, but fail, despite impressive contemporaneous advances in the fields of astronomy, mathematics, medicine, and wonton, in the process bankrupting the imperial treasury and encouraging invasion by Mongolian warlords, who look upon Shi Tzu's obsession as a sign that he is *wufen nuxi* ("one brick shy of a load"). The Great Waking-Up ensues, precipitating centuries of unrest.

A.D. 197—Timex, a Greek slave in the household of the Roman general Drusus Nervus, is tasked by his master with devising a foolproof means of waking him during the ill-fated Fourth Germanic Campaign before hordes of howling Allemani tribesmen do it by crushing his skull. Timex experiments with candles placed on the heads of goats and sheep, but abandons the scheme when animal rights advocates complain to the emperor in Rome. Instead, he installs candles on top of beehives. The bees become annoyed when the flame burns down and sets fire to their abode, which encourages them to sting the soundly sleeping general, thus rousing him from his slumbers. A contemporary account of the death of Nervus ("swatting and scratching himself, howling mightily for mud packs and cursing his servant"—Livy) persuades historians that he may have died of anaphylactic shock and not from an ax in his skull. The method catches on throughout the Roman empire, making Timex—who at Nervus's dying command was placed alive on his master's funeral pyre—originator of the buzzing-type alarm now prevalent in hotels throughout the world.

500–875—Irish monks introduce the concept of the "alarm" clock during their missionary travels through heathen Europe, banging spoons on pots over their heads every morning precisely at 5:45 a.m., while simultaneously shouting biblical passages in Greek and Latin. The monks are able to reckon the time accurately by the morning steam rising off cow pies. This practice of "rude awakening" (*exsomnolentia molestias*) is not broadly popular among their converts and results in a number of on-the-spot martyrdoms.

1065—The first Norman conquest fails when Norway's Harald Hardraade, who is to join forces with Tostig of Northumbria and William of Normandy against Harold II of England, sleeps through his primitive alarm at the Stavanger Odin Inn. Harald dismembers the staff and threatens to decapitate the Odin Group chairman, Ragnar Mintpillow. Mintpillow sends Harald a written apology but gently suggests that Harald was "pig-drunk" on honey wine and "would not have woken up if Thor himself had tattooed the theme from Pippi Longstocking on [Harald's] forehead with walrus tusks"—and then cc's everyone involved in the invasion. Under pressure from Tostig and William, who are eager to get on with the Norman conquest, Harald backs off his threat to pursue the matter in the courts, but he remains rancorous, and at the victory celebration in Hastings one year later, beheads two Norman knights who tease him by calling him Harald Haardetowakeup.

1791—Louis XVI, fleeing the Revolution with his family, stops at an inn in the town of Varennes-en-Argonne. His chamberlain urges the monarch to press on, but the king insists that he is so hungry he could eat a horse (*cheval*) and orders an eight-course meal that causes him to fall asleep. He sets the alarm clock in his room to wake him at "V" (Latin for five), but neglects to wind it, since as king he is accustomed to other people doing that for him. He is arrested at Vxx.

1919—President Woodrow Wilson, staying at the Crillon Hotel in Paris for the Versailles Peace Conference, sets his bedside alarm clock to wake him in time for his speech at the opening session. But anarcho-syndicalists, hoping to sabotage the conference and precipitate World War II, sneak into the president's suite and depress the ALARM button so that it will not go off. Wilson sleeps until late morning, when maids force open the door and vehemently demand to change his sheets. Wilson returns to the United States and has a stroke. Fourteen years later, Hitler rises to power on a platform of rearmament, Aryanism, and hotel alarm clocks that will "make the world tremble."

1927—The Waldorf-Astoria Hotel in New York installs electric alarm clocks in every room. Juan Trippe inaugurates Pan American World Airways.

1928—Pan American World Airways nearly goes under as vast numbers of passengers staying at the Waldorf-Astoria fail to show up on time for their flights. President Coolidge asks Congress to appropriate money for the development of a reliable hotel alarm clock that can be operated by an "average American simpleton." The effort fails.

1957—The Soviet Union launches *Sputnik*. President Eisenhower is handed a top-secret CIA report revealing that *Sputnik*'s real mission is to jam electric hotel alarm clocks so that American businessmen will sleep through important meetings, thereby giving the Russians the edge in competing for hydroelectric, tractor-building, and steroid-manufacturing contracts. Congress steps up the pace of hotel alarm clock R&D.

1961—President Kennedy vows to "put a functioning alarm clock on the moon so that our astronauts will know when it is time to return to earth."

1972—The Hilton Hotel chain installs "easy-to-use" AM/FM clock radios in their rooms. Cumbersome, boxy, hard-to-use, and in some cases radioactive, they malfunction and, no matter what music station they are programmed to play, jolt guests awake in the middle of the night with a fierce buzzing that causes them to dream that they are being electrocuted and to wet their beds.

1974—The Confraternité Internationale des Hôteliers commissions master Swiss watchmaker Dieter Zeitz to design a hotel alarm clock so simple that it can be programmed "even by drugged rock 'n' roll musicians in the dark." Zeitz produces the Dum-Klock (later renamed EZ Clock). It is a triumph of simplicity, but still requires the user to distinguish between "am," "pm," and "FM," resulting in a failure rate of 67 percent. Despondent, Zeitz pens a scathing indictment of human intelligence and gives up clock-making for the study of eugenics.

1984—Hotels worldwide introduce the "digital" alarm clock. Slightly more complicated than its "analog" predecessor, it features a SNOOZE button. It is hailed as a breakthrough, but unless it is precisely programmed in combination with the MUSIC, SLEEP, GMT SYNCH., ELEV., and LAT/LONG switches, the alarm goes off every five minutes starting at 2:30 a.m. Because of the high number of smashed alarm clocks, an impact-resistant titanium outer shell is subsequently added, along with half-inch bulletproof plastic facing and backup battery-operated power plant. The clocks are then heat mounted on the bedside tables, which in turn are bolted to the floor, making it necessary for guests wanting to silence the clocks to smash them repeatedly with the steam iron or toilet seat.

1986—To stem the flood of requests for wake-up calls resulting from the introduction of the digital alarm clocks, hotels install WAKE UP buttons on the room telephones. The buttons are not connected to the switchboard, but to a sixteen-minute-long recording of a ringing telephone, followed by a recorded announcement that the hotel has been hit by an earthquake. The system is designed to encourage guests to study the 23-page alarm clock user's manual chained to the clock, entitled, "Please to Pushing the Ante-Meridien Function/Preference Switch, While Bewaring of Electrical Shock!" as well as the *Malay-English Dictionary of Technical Terms*, provided for guests attempting to program their clocks to wake them with soft classical FM music within one quarter hour of the desired rising time.

—*Forbes FYI*, April 2001

PLAQUE TRACKING

I spent this winter in London, specifically in Chelsea, near the Thames embankment. The first day, on my way up Tite Street to the corner grocery, I noticed three contiguous Victorian row houses, each sporting a gleaming blue-and-white enamel plaque.

The first indicated that the house had been the residence of a medical and political eminence named Lord Haden-Guest; the second, of Oscar Wilde; and the third of a composer with the quaint pseudonym of Peter Warlock. The name Guest you might recognize from his grandson Christopher's movies, most conspicuously *This Is Spinal Tap*. Oscar Wilde you know all about. He lived in this house but clearly didn't spend enough time there with his wife and children. Maestro Warlock was new to me.

The next day, a block north, I turned the corner and was arrested in my tracks by another plaque. Mark Twain ("American Writer") had lived here 1896–7. Twain would have been here when he received the dreadful cable that his beloved daughter Susy had died in Hartford; an event all the more heartrending as Twain's wife, Livy, was incommunicado in the mid-Atlantic, rushing to her stricken daughter's side.

Trying to clear my mind of that gloomy meditation, and now in need of a pint, I walked on toward the pub and three blocks later came upon the home of Bram Stoker, author of *Dracula*.

Interesting 'hood, I thought. And so I became a plaque collector, a pastime I heartily commend in London. It's free and the exercise will do you good.

In a book appropriately titled *London Plaques* (Shire Publications, 2010), I learned that there are some 1,800 of them in the Greater London area. Charles Dickens leads, with ten plaques; Churchill has only five, but then he got a statue facing Big Ben and an immense floor tablet at the threshold of Westminster Abbey—in effect, England's leading floor mat. The first person to be plaqued was the notorious Lord Byron; and—hmm—his is no longer there. Leafing through the book inclines you to agree with its author that this abundance of lustrous plaquery supports London's claim to be truly the coolest city in the world.

I decided that trying to collect all 1,800 was futile, so I confined myself to Chelsea. The fun was in connecting them like dots. This turned out to be strangely easy. On my way to meet friends at the Cadogan Hotel, where Wilde was arrested on the charge of gross indecency, I spotted a plaque a few yards from the hotel's front door indicating the former home of Sir Herbert Beerbohm Tree, actor, theatre manager, and Wilde's great friend. Leaving the Cadogan and rounding the corner onto Pont Street, I saw another noting that Lillie Langtry had lived there. It's said that it was her close friend Oscar Wilde who suggested to her that she try her hand at acting. She made her debut at the Haymarket Theatre, managed by Herbert Beerbohm Tree.

Continuing down Pont Street, I got even luckier. There in a grimy doorway was a plaque dedicated to Sir George Alexander. The name rang familiar, and what do you know: He inaugurated the role of John Worthing on February 14, 1895, the opening night of *The Importance of Being Earnest*.

Next to Chelsea Old Church is a little square of quiet greenery called Roper's Garden, once the site of St. Thomas More's orchard. (More himself lived a bit up the street.) In Roper's Garden, you'll find a relief sculpture by Sir Jacob Epstein, commemorating his studio, which stood here 1909–14. If you've visited Wilde's grave in Père-Lachaise in Paris, you already know that his tomb was carved by Jacob Epstein, between 1909 and 1912. Thus did I learn the strange coincidence that Oscar's gravestone was carved only a few blocks from where he lived.

—*ForbesLife*, May 2011

SMALL AIRCRAFT ADVISORY

BEFORE YOU GO

The longer the flight number, the smaller the plane.

Reconfirm your reservation every fifteen minutes, beginning two months before date of departure. Increase frequency to every six minutes forty-eight hours prior to departure.

Send baggage on ahead by FedEx. If feasible, have yourself sent on ahead by FedEx.

Reserve a room at the hotel airport for three days on either side of theoretical departure date.

AT THE AIRPORT

Arrive at least three days prior to departure. (See above.)

When they ask how much you weigh, do not lie.

Carry on no more than can comfortably fit in a dental cavity. The overhead compartments on most small planes were designed for pressing wildflowers—and apple cider—though they can, in a pinch, be used for crushing expensive cameras, computers, hats, etc.

When you are told that the flight is overbooked and you have no seat, remain calm. This is a test to see if you have "the right stuff" and are worthy of the seat you booked to Bangor eight months ago. Screaming at the gate agent that you are extremely important, a close friend of the president of the airline, or a cardinal (in plainclothes) of the Catholic Church, etc., is a sign that you have "the wrong stuff." So is telling the agent that he is a baboon.

Instead, dress in surgical scrubs with hemostats clipped everywhere. These will look more impressive than a cashmere blazer and Italian loafers when you attempt to convey to the agent that it is critical that you be in Bangor by noon. For added emphasis, carry a small beach cooler prominently labeled HUMAN ORGAN.

ON THE BUS FROM THE GATE TO THE PLANE

Congratulations—you are one of the "chosen." But this is no time for complacency. Here is your first chance to size up your fellow passengers and to see, from the boarding passes clutched in their hands, how many of them have also been assigned your seat. It's also a chance to see the "Quartier Latin" of the airport (where they keep the smaller, quainter aircraft), and to get on the plane for Manchester, New Hampshire, instead of the one for Bangor.

WELCOME ABOARD!

Get on first, regardless of row number. Once seated, permanently fasten yourself to your seat with chain, steel cable, or bicycle lock and heavy padlock to discourage the five other people who have also been assigned Seat 8A.

YOU AND YOUR FLIGHT CREW

The pilot and copilot are every bit as competent as the people who fly planes with engines that don't resemble food processors. They don't want to be here any more than you do. Like you, they would rather be in a Boeing 767 instead of a plane made by a company that mostly makes lawn mowers.

Pilots of small planes generally fall into one of the following categories: those who (a) don't have enough experience yet to fly planes with bathrooms you can stand up in; (b) kept crashing during the tests in the flight simulator; (c) cannot distinguish between interstate highways and runways; (d) have "attitude problems"; or (e) experience violent flashbacks involving aerial combat in Vietnam.

AFTER TAKEOFF

If you are a "nervous flier," immediately swallow enough Valium to induce hibernation in a polar bear. (Be sure to attach somewhere to your person a highly visible note indicating your final destination, contact numbers, blood type, etc., in the event that they cannot revive you when it is time to deplane.)

If you are susceptible to motion sickness, color-coordinate your clothing with the meal you eat beforehand.

To take your mind off the fact that it now looks as though the pilot will have to go *through* the thunderstorm, close your eyes and try to imagine that you are Charles Lindbergh and that this is the adventure of a lifetime. Soon you will land at Le Bourget field and be carried off by hordes of adoring French people shouting nice things about America. (Far-fetched, admittedly.) Keep repeating to yourself, in the voice of Jimmy Stewart—silently, so as not to put the already distressed person next to you over the edge—"G-Gosh, there's the Eiffel Tower!"

—*The New Yorker*, October 1996

Statecraft

Power corrupts. Absolute power is kind of neat.

—SECRETARY OF THE NAVY JOHN LEHMAN

THE VISHNU

Those of us who worked for Mr. Bush when he was vice president had a nickname for him: "The Vishnu." It was his own coinage. He had recently been to India on a state visit, where he was presented, amid great ceremony, with a statue of the four-armed Vedic deity Vishnu, its plaque describing Vishnu's many godly qualities, among them omniscience, omnipotence, and the title "Preserver of the Universe."

Mr. Bush immediately recognized a kindred godhead and began referring to himself in staff memos and on Air Force Two's p.a. system as "The Vishnu." (In more intimate settings, he was "The Vish.") There I'd be on the plane, a lowly speechwriter banging away at some arrival statement, when over the speakers would come in grave tones, "This is . . . the *Vishnu* speaking." After the visit, had it gone well, upon takeoff we would hear, "This . . . is the Vishnu. The Vishnu is well pleased . . ." It had a certain Oz-ness, which of course was the intended effect.

When the Vishnu became president in 1989, we stopped calling him that. It was only a few years ago that I was able to relax back into calling him by his old nickname. I got the sense that he'd missed being called by it.

Mr. Bush was, to be sure, an ur-Yankee blueblood establishmentarian, but he was always winking at you, even in the midst of some very formal ceremony. He took a boyish delight in kicking his own pedestal out from underneath him. After he left the White House and started using e-mail, I asked his secretary what on earth the "flfw" part of it portended. The answer was: former leader of the free world. And why not?

On the first foreign trip I made with him, in 1981, I watched him charm the staff of a U.S. embassy with a story about a visit he had made to President Reagan after his shooting. Mr. Bush was shown into the president's hospital room only to find it—empty. At a loss, he finally crouched down to look under the bed to see if perchance the current leader of the free world might (for some reason) be curled up there. At which point he heard a voice from the bathroom: "George, I'm in here. Come on in." With some reticence, Mr. Bush peered in. There was the president, on his hands and knees, wiping the floor with paper towels.

"Mr. President. What are you . . . doing?"

"Well, you see," Reagan said, "I spilled some water and I don't want the nurses to have to wipe it up."

Mr. Bush loved that story for the volumes it spoke about the profound decency and humility of Ronald Reagan. He told it again and again until we, his staff, were heartily tired of hearing about the profound decency and humility of the president. But the moral was not lost, even on cocky, self-important young politicos such as ourselves. On reflection, it could just as well have been a story about George Bush. I have no difficulty imagining him down on all fours in a hospital room, mopping up a water spill to spare the nurses. Moreover, had Mr. Bush been hospitalized after being shot by a deranged young man, I can quite easily imagine him getting back into bed after mopping the floor and handwriting his assailant's parents a note of sympathy, expressing his concern for what *they* must be going through. For a multiarmed, omniscient, and omnipotent deity, the Vish was the most considerate man I have ever known.

Which could be maddening in a politician. My boss, his press secretary Pete Teeley, would shake his head and roll his eyes and mutter frustrated imprecations over the Vishnu's steadfast refusal in those days (the early 1980s) to talk about his World War II record. One reporter, having serially failed to entice Mr. Bush into providing a dramatic account of being shot down over Chi-chi Jima by the Japanese, remonstrated afterward with Teeley. "For God's sake, your guy's a [expletive] war hero. Why won't he *talk* about it? It's like drawing water from a [expletive] rock." Teels could only shrug.

Then came the '88 campaign and the era of Lee Atwater and the other high-velocity spinners. From then on Mr. Bush pretty much had to talk about it. But you could see him wincing. He recoiled from chest thumping (the "Introspection Thing," as he called it). This was, after all, a man who had been brought up short by his own mother at the Thanksgiving dinner table in 1980. He had been regaling the family with his adventures on the presidential campaign trail. Dorothy Bush said to him sharply, "George, stop it. You're talking about yourself too much." And he did.

As a boy, one of his nicknames was "Have-Half," after his habit of always sharing half his sandwich with whoever was there. George H. W. Bush had a kind of valence: he seemed to attract nicknames. His childhood nickname was "Poppy." His namesake son famously had the converse habit of bestowing nicknames. But "Have-Half" fit him, even later on in life. When he was vice president, Mr. Bush would stay over in Washington for Christmas rather than go home to Houston, so that his Secret Service detail could spend the day with their families.

There are dozens, scores, hundreds such stories about George Herbert Walker Bush. He had noblesse oblige—or as he once called it—"noblesse noblige." Who but George Bush would have had the grace—and wit—to invite his impudent *Saturday Night Live* doppelganger Dana Carvey to spend a night at White House. This was after Mr. Bush was defeated for reelection. Carvey didn't quite believe it when the invitation arrived; but it was genuine, and he went, and was charmed by his host.

For a speechwriter, putting words in Mr. Bush's mouth could at times be a challenge. Mr. Bush was a natural storyteller, and a natural listener—a quality not generally in surplus among politicians. He was usually better off without a written text. And without props, as I learned the hard way.

The Soviets had invaded Afghanistan and as occupiers were engaged in atrocities. Among these was the usage of a device they were dropping from helicopters: "butterfly bombs," as they were labeled by NATO. Plastic, packed with high explosives, they looked like harmless toys. They fluttered gently to earth—hence the name—and when picked up by curious children, exploded. The *intent* was to maim, not kill. Psy-war, red in tooth and claw.

I proposed that we anathematize this gruesome weapon by having Mr. Bush hold one up during the speech he would deliver on Sunday at the Kennedy Center on the occasion of "Afghanistan Day." It would certainly make for a dramatic photograph. After staff discussion, Mr. Bush said he agreed.

A man from the CIA arrived in my office on Friday morning. He informed me that great pains had been gone to to provide us with the (deactivated, naturally) butterfly bomb. He would return to my office on Monday to collect it. Its custody, he emphasized, was *my* responsibility. You can see where this is going.

Mr. Bush and I rehearsed his speech. I told him it was critical that he hold the thing aloft in his hand during the reference in the speech to the device, and that he hold it there long enough for the photographers to get their shot. I suggested that he take it home with him over the weekend and practice.

The speech was at noon. Sunday morning my phone rang at seven. The Vishnu. "Say," he said, "do you have it? You know, the . . . thing."

"Sir," I said nervously, "by 'thing,' do you mean the butterfly bomb?" *That is to say, sir, the centerpiece of the speech you'll be giving in a few hours. At the Kennedy Center. In front of thousands of dignitaries.*

"Yes. Well," he said blithely, "it doesn't seem to be here anywhere." But then why should he worry? It wasn't his fingernails the CIA would remove on Monday morning.

I immediately phoned Ed Pollard, head of his Secret Service detail. You will not be surprised to hear that Secret Service agents, especially those at the supervisory level, do not brim with glee when told that you have given their principal a device associated with the word *explosives*, and without bothering to mention the fact to them. A rime of frost instantly formed over the phone line. Ed hung up without further pleasantries and ordered his men to fan out to find the bomb that I had given the vice president. Oh, Ed was just thrilled.

Several anxious hours later, Mr. Bush and I were reunited backstage at the Kennedy Center prior to the speech. He grinned sheepishly and produced from his trench coat the cherished item. I sighed with relief—and then stared.

It was punctured through and through by what appeared to be canine dentition. The vice presidential cocker spaniel, Fred C. Bush, had purloined it on the limo ride from the White House to the residence. Eventually tiring of it, Fred had deposited it in Mrs. Bush's dahlia bed. Thus a device made in Soviet Russia for the purpose of maiming Afghan children ended up as a chew toy for the dog of the vice president of the United States. Monday morning, the little gray man from Langley listened impassively to my variation on the theme of "the dog ate the homework."

During my time at the White House, I found myself, once or twice, the only other person in the room with Mr. Bush and President Reagan. Mr. Bush was unfailingly courteous in any situation, with anyone, from kings to cleaning ladies. Courtly and respectful—what we used to call "gentlemanly."

With Reagan, even in a casual atmosphere, he was especially deferential; not obsequious, but extra attentive, as one might be with, say, a grandfather. This attitude struck me as filial, and entirely without affect.

Back then, the general attitude of the Georgetown cognoscenti—the "cave-dwellers," and other bluebloods of Permanent Washington Society—were the kind of people Bush mixed with easily, for he, too, was of bluish blood. The Georgetown set, however, looked on Reagan with ill-disguised hauteur: in the now-ironic phrasing of the Establishmentarian Clark Clifford, an "amiable dunce." (Reagan, who looms larger and larger, had the last laugh; Clifford ended his career mired in a tawdry banking scandal.)

I thought then, and think still, that in a way George H. W. Bush was the real Ronald Reagan. I mean this with no disrespect for Mr. Reagan, whom I admired and loved. But George Bush had gone to war; Mr. Reagan had played war heroes in movies. George Bush was a devoted father; Reagan was perhaps devoted to his children, but in a very different way. This perception of mine jarred as I observed the two of them together up close, for it was Reagan who gave the impression of being the tougher guy. No one would fault his physical courage. After all, he'd insisted on walking into the emergency room with Hinckley's bullet in his lung, and had cracked jokes on the operating table, saying he hoped they were all Republicans. His heroic aura was genuine. Bush's was submerged beneath the genial preppy exterior: the Cowboy and Dink Stover.

Mr. Bush's critics were constantly yapping at him for being preppy. Then, memorably, when the '88 campaign got under way, the decorated war hero who had been shot down while flying his torpedo bomber into a maelstrom of Japanese flak found himself on the cover of *Newsweek*, ridiculed for "the wimp factor." Is this a great country, or what?

I never once heard Mr. Bush chafe at the preposterous notion that he lacked walnuts. He was entirely serene about his manhood. And why shouldn't he have been? If you've been to war as a young man, seen death face-to-face; cradled your dying six-year-old daughter in your arms; drilled for oil in Texas; raised a family; been elected to Congress; headed the Republican Party—during Watergate! Thanks, Dick—opened the first U.S. liaison office in China; run the CIA; and got yourself elected vice president of the United States, maybe you don't need to have your manhood validated by smartass magazine editors and other soft-faced thumb-suckers of the punditariat.

For someone who seemed gangly or physically awkward, he was quite comfortable in his own skin, as the French say. A later speechwriter of his who put into his mouth many golden words—as well as one problematical pledge involving lips—hit exactly the right note in his 1988 convention speech when she had him say, "I may be awkward at times, but there is nothing awkward about my love of country."

Being comfortable in his manhood may in fact have been one of his greatest assets as president. When the Soviet Union collapsed—on his watch—Mr. Bush took pains not to bang the drum and thump the national chest, lest it provoke a rump element of the Red Army. He was criticized for that, but history has since vindicated the wisdom of that reticence.

He was criticized, too, after the Tiananmen Square massacre, for not publicly excoriating the Chinese Politburo and demanding heads on pikes. But he understood the Chinese mind, and that grandstanding would only be counterproductive. He undertook quieter measures, and history has since vindicated those, as well.

Mr. Bush conducted what may have been America's most efficient war, against a desert despot, assembling a historic coalition of twenty-six countries including Syria. And when that war was swiftly consummated, he withdrew—mission accomplished, to deploy a phrase that would haunt another Bush in later years. The senior Bush was criticized by a great many armchair warriors in 1991—notably by the neocons—for not "going all the way." But he understood the terrible prospects involved in door-to-door warfare in Baghdad.

To be sure, he and his advisors made a tragic miscalculation when he encouraged Iraqis to rise up against Saddam. Those who did rise up were mercilessly cut down by Saddam, whose helicopters had been inexplicably given permission to continue flying. This mistake gnawed at Mr. Bush. But his wisdom in not "going all the way" has been ratified. In time, George Bush 41 may be well regarded by historians, as Eisenhower now increasingly is, as much for what he did not do, as for what he did.

For all his physical grace as an athlete—captain of the Yale baseball team; formidable doubles partner at tennis—Mr. Bush was on occasion thwarted by his own physical karma. There was the time he "vomited copiously"—as the news reports insisted on putting it—on his host, the premier of Japan, at that dinner. Years later, Mr. Bush was still shaking his head and blushing. How ironic that this should happen to the most polite person on earth.

Then there was the pro-am tournament at Pebble Beach after he retired from the presidency. Mr. Bush sliced his drive off the tee at a murderous velocity, into the skull of an unfortunate lady spectator. He rushed over to apologize and comfort her as the medics applied pressure bandages. Hours later, lining up his putt on the final hole, he saw a woman spectator in a wheelchair with her head bandaged. Remortified, he rushed over to renew his apologies, only to be informed that it was a different woman, who had been hit by Clint Eastwood's ball.

One dimension the historians surely will be wrestling with is his relationship with his son the second President George Bush. Bob Woodward has provided the indelible moment when he asked Bush 43 in the Oval Office if he had consulted with his father prior to going into Iraq. Forty-three replied that he had "consulted a higher father." What can his earthly father have thought upon reading that? I never mustered the courage to ask him.

Interviewing Bush 41 onstage, just as his son's Iraq war was revealing itself to be something far different from a "slam dunk," I asked him what it was like, watching his son take hit after hit.

Mr. Bush shrugged, unperturbed by the question. He replied simply that your children are your children, whatever their age. "When they're kids and they come home from the schoolyard after getting beat, you hug them. It doesn't change. You're still their father." He said he was proud of his son; and then immediately added that he was proud of all his children. That was George Bush, Have-Half.

I would never have traded my own father for any other, but I've always thought that George Bush is the father we all wish we'd had. His love was unconditional and total. He embodied Shakespeare's admonition that "Love is not love which alters when it alteration finds." His soul was always visible on his sleeve. And in his pocket there was always a handkerchief, usually damp.

I was present in 2004 at the National Cathedral in Washington when Mr. Bush, struggling through his eulogy to Reagan, came close to breaking down. I'd seen him do that so many times. He'd get choked up during a playing of the National Anthem. As for the Navy Hymn—forget it. Cataracts. For a flinty New England blueblood, Mr. Bush had the tear ducts of a Sicilian grandmother.

In November 1992, I phoned him at Camp David, a few days after his mother, Dorothy, passed away. A few weeks before, he had lost the presidency to a governor of Arkansas. Into the bargain, a hurricane was on its way to ravage his beloved house on the coast of Maine. Talk about a Melvillean "damp, drizzly November of the soul."

Mrs. Bush's funeral was the next day. I asked if he was going to give a eulogy.

"God no," he said. "I couldn't do it. I would choke up. I would be permanently ensconced as a member of the Bawl Brigade."

The Bawl Brigade is the Bush family term for members who cry easily; by my count, it constitutes a majority of Bushes.

He explained: "I've had trouble paying my respects to the fallen soldiers on the *Iowa*, or the dead out of Desert Storm, without getting emotional. I'd love to, but I know my limitations. I even choked up here at Camp David last night. We had our choir singing. We had a little vespers program with Amy Grant. It was so beautiful, and I found myself choking up. We had a bunch of friends up here and 'Oh God,' I said, 'please hold back the floods.'"

THE NEW YORKER POLITICAL CARTOONS

Most people have an absolute-all-time-favorite *New Yorker* cartoon that they came across at some crucial moment in their lives, bearing with it the reassurance that they were not alone in the universe. I still have mine, from twenty years ago. It's faded from sunlight, the back is torn and sticky from a dozen applications of Scotch tape, the top is perforated from pushpins as it moved with me from house to house, bulletin board to bulletin board.

I was a White House speechwriter at the time, with an office that looked out unimportantly on a sun-deprived courtyard that seemed permanently under construction. My most enduring memory of my time in the fabled corridors of power is that of jackhammers.

The chief of staff in my department was a retired four-star admiral, who, though a fine and decent man and a genuine patriot, remained every bit a four-star admiral. Which is to say, he looked upon New York writer types (always in need of a haircut, tie always loosened, shoes always unpolished, always ten minutes late) with a military despair that he was at pains to suppress. And come to think of it, did not suppress. Our relationship was similar to the one I now have with my twelve-year-old daughter, who when I ask her to clean her room, replies, "Whatever." So in retrospect, my heart goes out to Admiral Daniel J. Murphy. At last I feel his pain.

It fell to Admiral Murphy to vet my prose. Any relationship between editor and writer is a minefield. Ours was a federal disaster area. Once in a speech I quoted the Greek historian Thucydides, which ended up causing the vice president of the United States to become so tongue-tied when he got to the name that he sounded like John Hurt in the movie *Alien* just before that dreadful alien thing burst from his rib cage. Admiral Murphy came up to me afterward, glowering—I was cowering under the table in a fetal position—and jabbed me in the chest and said, "Next time say Plato!"

A week or so later, still rubbing the bruise in my sternum, I found my treasured cartoon in that week's *New Yorker*. What a 700-volt shock of recognition it gave me! The cartoon was of a politician and his speechwriter going over a draft of a speech. The Capitol Building is in the background, so we know we're in Washington. The speechwriter has that thousand-yard stare of a wretch with artistic pretensions who knows—*knows*—that his exquisite couplets are about to be turned into road kill. The politician is telling the writer: *"O.K., but change 'Her tawny body glistened beneath the azure sky' to 'National problems demand national solutions.'"*

I clipped it and taped it to my lamp. I would look at it and sigh whenever my gorgeous arpeggios on foreign policy came back from the committee looking like a blacked-out Freedom of Information request document, along with comments like "Put more here re: historic *synergy* betw. U.S. and Brazil." The cartoon spoke to me. It whispered: *It's all right. I understand.*

What a surprise, then, not to find it here. [*The New Yorker Book of Political Cartoons*] But how nice to find more than a half dozen cartoons on the theme of speechwriters and speeches, making it by my count the fourth-largest category here. The next largest is Republicans, about which, more in a moment. The second-largest number of cartoons are about spin. The biggest, consisting of twenty-three cartoons, is campaigning.

Whatever high absurdities and low syllogisms are foisted upon us every four years in the name of getting our votes, it is highly—*highly*—unlikely that they will be as funny, or as uplifting, or enduring as the moments depicted by *The New Yorker*'s cartoonists.

We live, happily and paradoxically, at a time when it is more or less safe not to pay too much attention to politicians. (Such a bold statement must surely tempt the gods. Let me explain.) Surely this is why the television show *Who Wants to Be a Millionaire* attracts 23 million viewers while the presidential debate on another channel attracts one-tenth as many.

We can indulge ourselves in this fashion—even to the extent of not voting on Election Day, as indeed 51 percent of us chose not to in the last general election, confident that we will not wake up on the first Wednesday in November to find armored tanks in the street and someone with sunglasses and a mustache standing on the Truman balcony at the White House giving a three-hour-long speech in which he refers to us as "my children."

True, we might wake up to find that Congress has approved $217 billion for a four-lane-wide tunnel connecting North Carolina and Bermuda. Or that we now have soldiers stationed in a country no one—even the CIA—can locate on a map. Or that Arnold Schwarzenegger has been elected governor of California. Dire as these eventualities might be, they're nothing, really, that we couldn't handle. One way or the other, we've already been there and done that.

This note of preternatural calm is the voice, or, if you want to put a fancy word to it, the ethos—*Say Plato, damnit!*—of *New Yorker* political cartoons. They are to the noise and bruit of daily political life what a Zen fountain is to a roaring tsunami. They soothe. They make us all—liberal, conservative, libertarian, vegetarian—smile in recognition. Yes, that's *us* they're talking about. How—sigh—ridiculous we must seem sometimes. And yet . . . and yet . . .

. . . we do *care* about politics. We must. Politics is—also—fanatics flying planes into our buildings. We may have learned to turn the channel in search of a more soothing reality (show), but in an election year, politicians are hard to avoid. We become agitated. We argue with each other—even with our loved ones. We fume, we hurl our napkins down on the dinner table like characters in Henry James novels. We pronounce each other invincibly ignorant.

But in *New Yorker* cartoon land, such asperity is banished. *Sturm* becomes a bright summer day. *Drang* is defanged, a junkyard dog turned Pekingese; pomposity is deflated and even the Orwellian machinations of spin doctors—so awful in real life—appear for what they are: posturings from commedia dell'arte. Here we find a man pleading his case at the Pearly Gates before an unamused-looking St. Peter: "*Wait, those weren't lies. That was spin!*" Distilling all this fury into a tone of gentle wit and piquancy is no mean achievement, considering the antecedents in American political cartooning. The ur-political American cartoonist was of course Thomas Nast (1840–1902), whose scathing depictions of William Marcy "Boss" Tweed of New York City's Tammany Hall and of his cronies Peter "Brains" Sweeny and Richard "Slippery Dick" Connolly—why can't our politicians have nicknames like that?—helped to bring down Tweed. Tweed is (apocryphally) said to have ordered one of his associates to "Stop them damned pictures . . . I don't care what the papers say about me. My constituents can't read. But, damn it, they can see pictures!" Not to press the point, but according to polls, significant numbers of people today get their *only* political information from our late-night comic hosts.

The Bavarian-born Nast was himself no lovely piece of work. He was fiercely bigoted, a virulent anti-Catholic and Irish-baiter—among his *other* prejudices. Many of his most celebrated cartoons would stand no chance of being published today in the mainstream press. The Nast-iness that characterized his work was prevalent in much of the other cartooning of the day, which depicted Negroes and Jews and Native Americans in racist caricature that would today arouse gasps and contumely. Those days are happily behind us, but the anger of the American cartoonist lives on. *The Washington Post*'s Herblock was capable of pretty rough stuff. Professor Roger A. Fischer's *Them Damned Pictures* is a catalogue of nineteenth- and twentieth-century visual invective. He quotes *The Chicago Tribune*'s

Jeff MacNelly's revealing comment that "Many cartoonists would be hired assassins if they couldn't draw."

New Yorker cartoonists may too, deep down, be spitting mad, but they do a good job of channeling their anger and ontological disappointment into exquisite generic commentary on the old human condition. The events of the past several years, for instance (the Clinton years), have been harrowing and very nearly cataclysmic. And yet I could find only one cartoon out of 118 that specifically referred to the whole mess, and even then it managed to do so with an obliqueness and deftness utterly sublime. A White House aide is knocking on a door emblazoned with the enormous, great seal of the president of the United States, asking, "*Are you decent?*" Fifty years from now this cartoon may be more relevant and—to use that inelegant word—accessible than the hundreds of sputtering editorial cartoons that appeared during the years of Clinton scandal.

If a newspaper editorial cartoon shouts its opinion at you over the scrambled eggs, *The New Yorker* cartoon hands you a Scotch and nudges you toward whatever truth it has in its sights. A candidate for office sticks his head out the phone booth and tells the line of anxious people waiting to use it: "*I may be awhile. I'm soliciting funds for my re-election campaign.*" While most of the cartoons here are timeless and general, this particular one may require a little context years from now. But for the time being, it's a nice gloss on Vice President Gore's violation of the Pendleton Act of 1883. Another cartoon might also require some explaining years from now. A crowd has gathered around an ambulance at the scene of an accident. "*Let me through,*" declares a businesslike-looking man holding a briefcase, "*I'm a compassionate conservative.*" What's in that briefcase? A health insurance waiver? Or a legally concealed handgun with which to finish off the poor victim?

Which brings us to the critical question: Why do Republican-oriented cartoons here outnumber Democrat ones by five to one? I have a good guess as to the politics of *New Yorker* cartoonists, but somehow it's hard to think of them as agents of the vast left-wing conspiracy.

I remember two other *New Yorker* cartoons from the Reagan era that still bring me joy every time I see them. One shows two mild, balding men in suits presenting themselves at the White House gate. *"We're from the far right. We're here to be mollified."* The other is a fierce Mongolian-type warlord sitting on a throne made of human skulls and bones. In the foreground, one courtier is whispering to the other, *"I, too, was alarmed when he took over, but I think events will inevitably push him back into the political mainstream."* I don't care how they vote—give those two cartoonists a Pulitzer.

The bottom line is, really, so plain that anyone with a C average from Yale—or Harvard, for that matter—could figure it out. As objects of fun, Republicans make better targets than Democrats; as do conservatives than liberals. What was it Oscar Wilde said about the trouble with socialism? "Takes too many evenings." Perhaps someday Democrats will be as funny as Republicans.

Meanwhile, it's the *New Yorker* cartoonists, not the nattering talking heads and pundits and spin doctors, who are the true gnostics of American politics, the keepers and revealers of its deepest truths. To our candidates for office high, middle, and low, I can only say: After your death you were better have a bad epitaph than their ill report while you live. (No, that's not ungrammatical, it's *Hamlet*.)

Let us close with a few greatest hits:

The candidate standing at the podium, grinning with open arms: *"People of North Dakota! Or possibly South Dakota!"*

The angry congressman standing at his desk in the chamber, replying to his distinguished colleague: *"Listen, pal! I didn't spend seven million bucks to get here so I could yield the floor to you."*

The two aides looking on in horror as their candidate addresses a large crowd of distinctly displeased-looking people. *"Good God! He's giving the white-collar voters' speech to the blue-collars!"*

One more for the road: the senator at his desk, scowling at the secretary who is approaching holding a coat: *"No, no, Miss Clark! I asked you to bring in the Mantle of Greatness, not the Cloak of Secrecy."*

Feel better? See, it's still a great country.

—from the Introduction to *The New Yorker Book of Political Cartoons*, 2000

VP QUESTIONNAIRE

As vice president, my highest priority would be to:

A. Support the president's agenda.
B. Quietly leak to leading columnists that I completely disagree with the president's less popular policies.
C. Attend as many funerals of foreign leaders as possible.
D. Position myself to run for president in four years.

Complete John Nance Gardner's famous sentence: "The vice presidency is not worth . . ."

A. A bucket of warm piss.
B. A bucket of warm spit.
C. A bucket of live worms.
D. A bucket of dead tarantulas.

The quality I most admire in the presidential nominee is his:

A. Vision for America's future.
B. Willingness to work across party lines for the common good.
C. Personal hygiene.
D. Willingness to reverse his long-held positions on fundamental issues for the sake of marginal electoral votes.

If the president were incapacitated and I had to assume executive responsibility under the provisions of the 25th Amendment, the first thing I would do is:

A. Emphasize "continuity."
B. Party down!
C. Have the president declared legally dead and quietly bury him at Arlington.
D. Redecorate the Oval Office to match my coloring.

In my capacity as president of the Senate, in the event of a tie vote, I would:

A. Seek instructions from the president.
B. Announce that the issue will be decided by a coin toss.
C. Dress in tights and recite Hamlet's "To be or not to be" soliloquy from the rostrum.
D. Quietly put out word to the interested competing lobbies that my vacation home is in need of extensive renovation.

The vice president I most identify with is:

A. Dan Quayle.
B. Dick Cheney.
C. Andrew Johnson.
D. Hillary Clinton.

In my acceptance speech at the convention, I would pledge to:

A. Restore dignity to the office of the vice presidency.
B. Work tirelessly to advance the president's agenda.
C. Have lunch every Wednesday with the president.
D. Not tell Senator Leahy to go f— himself.
E. Tell Senator Leahy to go f— himself every chance I get.

As vice president, I would see my role primarily as:

A. A member of the team.
B. Next in line.
C. Eddie Haskell.
D. Iago.

If the president said to me, "I need you to take the fall for the administration on this one," I would tell him:

A. "Of course, sir. That's what I'm here for."
B. "You said that last week."
C. "You give and you give and it's take, take, take."
D. "For this I went to law school?"

In the event my chief of staff leaked to the media sensitive national security information in an attempt to make me look good, I would immediately:

A. Express outrage.
B. Tearfully announce that "he was like a son to me" and throw him under the bus.
C. Make damn well sure I was protected.
D. Start searching for a new chief of staff just like the old one.

If it were leaked that my name is on the short list of vice-presidential possibilities, I would issue a statement saying that I am:

A. Not worthy to fasten the sandal strap of the presidential nominee.
B. Not worthy to touch the hem of the garment of the presidential nominee.
C. Twice the man the presidential nominee is.
D. Kind of busy right now, but might be able to find a hole in my fall schedule.

—*National Review*, August 2008

LANGELLA/NIXON

It seems somehow logical that an actor who became famous for playing Dracula should have his greatest success playing Richard Nixon—no disrespect to Dracula intended.

Frank Langella has been on stage and screen now for almost a half century. He has taken on roles from Antonio Salieri to Sherlock Holmes, the *Daily Planet* editor Perry White, the Lolita-loving Clare Quilty, the CBS chief executive William Paley in *Good Night, and Good Luck*, Cyrano de Bergerac, and a White House chief of staff in Ivan Reitman's *Dave*. Moving laterally—and vertically—from one room in the West Wing to the Oval Office, he has now received an Oscar nomination for best actor in *Frost/Nixon*.

Watching Langella become Richard Nixon during the course of Ron Howard's movie adaptation of the Peter Morgan play, I thought it fitting that this performance should come at this late stage in his career. As Langella has remarked, his leading-man days are over; he's a character actor now, and Nixon is, you might say, the ultimate character.

I saw *Frost/Nixon* on Broadway, with Langella as Nixon, and admired it greatly, but onstage, Langella's Nixon was half the show, along with Michael Sheen's David Frost. With all due kudos to Sheen, this is Langella's movie. When he's not onscreen, you're waiting for him to come back on. I reflect that I spent a good part of my youth wanting Richard Nixon to go away. Langella has managed to make me want more of him.

He told Charlie Rose, "I just didn't think it was in my bag of tricks," but he threw himself into the research as he never had before. He visited Nixon's boyhood home in Yorba Linda, California, and spent an entire hour in the tiny bedroom Nixon shared with his brothers, soaking up the humiliation and inadequacy that Nixon grew up with. He talked to everyone, watched the tapes, and "then flung it all away and said, it has to be my Nixon. It has to be the essence of the man rather than an imitation."

Several scenes into the movie, I thought, *Incredible—he's playing it as comedy.*

Explaining who Irving Lazar is to his aide Jack Brennan: "This is my literary agent from Hollywood. Hygiene-obsessed."

Coyly admiring Frost's Italian loafers: "You don't find them too effeminate? I guess someone in your field can get away with it."

More:

"I wouldn't want to be a Russian leader. They never know when they're being taped."

"You're probably aware of my history with perspiration."

"Two million?" he says when Frost tells him what the production is costing. "I didn't realize we were making *Ben-Hur*."

What makes these lines so desperately funny is that they're spoken by one of the twentieth century's most tragic figures. As another president might put it, you feel the man's pain. But then—*finita la commedia*, in the (entirely fictional) scene in which a tipsy Nixon phones Frost to rage at the people who have looked down on him all his life and to tell him that in the final interview, he's going to come after him with everything he's got, and only one of them will survive.

In the movie's climactic scene, the April 22, 1977, interview, Frost nails Nixon to his own, handmade cross and extracts the famous apologia. "I gave them a sword, and they stuck it in and twisted it with relish." Nixon is as helpless, pathetic, and broken as Bogart's Captain Queeg, unraveling under José Ferrer's cross-examination.

There is an almost Pinocchio effect, as some have observed: Nixon's ski-jump nose seems to grow during the movie. In interviews, Langella has refuted the suggestion that his prosthetic proboscis increases over the course of the drama. It just seems that way, which in itself is proxy tribute to the inner transformation that Langella is illuminating.

Nixon has been played by a number of actors over the years. Anthony Hopkins earned an Oscar nomination for his Nixon in 1995, and Lane Smith turned in a memorable Nixon in *The Final Days*, alongside Theodore Bikel's Henry Kissinger. But Frank Langella now owns Nixon, as surely as Gielgud, whose Shakespeare recordings Langella listened to as a young actor in order to shed his Bayonne, New Jersey, accent, owned Hamlet for a time.

In the movie, Frost decides, as a gamble, to start off the first of the four ninety-minute interviews by asking Nixon, "Why didn't you burn the tapes?" It fails, as a trap. Wily—rather, Tricky Dick—Nixon ties him up in videotape by prattling on endlessly about how all the presidents before him taped, and how essential it was to have accurate recordings of high-level blah, blah, blah. We never get the answer.

I met Nixon only once, about a year after the "Nixon-Frost" (as they were then called) interviews were shown on TV. I asked him that same question.

Nixon paused, nodded pensively, averting his eyes, then said, slowly, "Well . . . there were those at the time who said that would be . . ."—I thought, *Is he actually going to say "wrong"?*—". . . for the best. But we didn't and . . ."—a rueful, pained smile played across his face—"here we are."

That moment has stuck vividly in my mind for more than thirty years. But now, as I summon it from memory, it's Frank Langella sitting in that armchair in a suite at the Waldorf-Astoria, smiling at me sadly, wishing it had been otherwise.

—*The New York Times*, February 2009

TRUMP: THE INAUGURAL

Donald Trump says he is seriously thinking about a presidential bid.

—*THE CHRISTIAN SCIENCE MONITOR*

My fellow Americans,

This is a great day for me personally. You're very smart to have voted for me because I'm going to do positive things for this country, starting with this mall I'm looking out over.

For starters, I don't know why this is called a "mall." Where I come from, New York City—which happens to be the greatest city in the world, and the reason I say that is that I built most of it, and I only build quality, so I think I know what I'm talking about—a mall doesn't look like this. Where are the shops? I see grass, ponds—and what's that, an obelisk? This is not Cairo. I don't know how much the government paid for the Washington Monument—and I have no problem with George Washington, but he wasn't a businessman—they overpaid. You've got a 560 foot-tall structure sitting on some of the most prime real estate in the country, incredible views, including of my new home. People would pay a lot for a duplex co-op in a building like that. I would charge $1,500 to $2,000 a square foot, and I'd get it. No wonder this government is trillions in debt.

Everywhere I look I see wasted opportunities, and I've only been president for five minutes. At the end of this so-called mall is the Lincoln Memorial. Lincoln was an okay president, but I would have freed the slaves, too. And I would have given them something more useful than forty acres and a mule, incidentally. But if you want to make a statement about Lincoln, you could do much better than this. White marble? Columns? This is not Greece. And that statue, he looks like he's having a difficult bowel movement. This is no way to say thank you for saving the Union. And I know about unions, believe me. Ask around. Don't try offering *them* forty acres and a mule. So with respect to Lincoln, I would make a statement: pink marble, gold, mirrors, maybe some hanging gardens, fountains with water coming out the breasts. People love that stuff. A restaurant on the roof that would serve first-rate food, because that's the only kind of food I'm interested in. Mediocre food does not interest me. You know what people like? Jumbo shrimp. It's not rocket science.

So what do you think of your new first lady? I picked Moronia—what's your name, honey? Melania, right. Great name. I just picked Melania here from a very wide selection of possibilities—not just because the sex is incredible but because this nation wants and deserves a trophy first lady. When everyone sees our first lady standing next to some other first lady of another country, the wife of a premier or whatever, they'll want to go to bed with our first lady, not the other one. So the American people no longer have to worry on that score. And if they get tired of her, not a problem, because chances are I'll be tired of her before they are. And we'll get a new first lady. Trying to keep North Korea from getting the bomb, maybe that's a problem. Finding a new first lady? Trust me, not a problem.

Policy-wise? I'm going to be very hands-on. If a situation comes up, like inflation, or a union beef, or Mike Tyson beats up another motorist, I'm going to be on it. It's going to be fixed. There was a skating rink in New York City in Central Park. There were problems with it. Then I got involved. Now people can skate on it. Again, it's not rocket science.

Foreign-policy-wise? Same. I'm a businessman. Other countries want to do business with us, I'm all for it. Trade, great. I have no problems with people trading with us. But it's going to be fair trade, by which I mean *we* come out on top. They have a problem with that, they can sell their TVs and cheese and whatever to someone else. Maybe North Korea. It's just not complicated. Missiles? Very simple—you aim one at us, I fire a hundred at you. So don't go there. Turning a country into a radioactive parking lot does not bother me. I sleep fine. Ask Melanomia. And finally on the foreign front, I have something to say to Fidel Castro. *Adios*, pal. This time, we're going to nationalize *your* hotels and casinos.

That about covers it. I have to go, because important senators and congressmen are giving me a lavish luncheon in the Rotunda behind me here. I understand they're serving a lot of jumbo shrimp. Basically they're trying to impress me so I won't cancel their highway projects and ethanol subsidies. I know how they do things. Now they're going to find out how I do things.

By the way, I've directed the Treasury to issue a couple billion extra in hundred-dollar chips. Enjoy yourselves. This is the dawn of a great, great era.

—*The Wall Street Journal*

MR. LINCOLN'S WASHINGTON

On the 137th anniversary of the day Mr. Lincoln was shot, I joined a tour in Lafayette Square, on Pennsylvania Avenue across from the White House, conducted by Anthony Pitch, a spry man wearing a floppy hat and carrying a MiniVox loudspeaker. Pitch is a former British subject, and the author of an informative book, *The Burning of Washington*, about the British torching of the city on August 24, 1814. Pitch has seen, in the basement of the White House, the scorch marks left over from the incident. But for a thunderstorm that must have seemed heaven-sent, many of the city's public buildings might have burned completely to the ground. It's often said the presidential residence was first painted to cover up the charred exterior, but official White House historians say that isn't so, and point out that the building of pinkish sandstone was first whitewashed in 1798 and was known informally as "the White House" before the British ever set it aflame. Theodore Roosevelt made the name official in 1901 when he put "The White House" on the stationery.

But today Pitch's theme is Lincoln. His enthusiasm is little short of idolatrous. "He was one of the most amazing people who ever walked the earth," he says. "He was self-taught and never took umbrage at insults. That such a man was shot in the back of the head is one of the most monstrous insults that ever happened."

We crossed the street and peered through the White House fence at the North Portico. He pointed out the center window on the second floor. (You can see it on a twenty-dollar bill.) On April 11, 1865, he said, Abraham Lincoln appeared there and gave a speech.

"It was the first time he had said in public that blacks should get the vote," Pitch explained. A twenty-six-year-old actor named John Wilkes Booth was in the crowd outside, along with a man named Lewis Paine (born Powell). Booth had been stalking Lincoln for weeks. Booth growled, "That means nigger citizenship. That is the last speech he will ever make. . . . By God, I'll put him through."

Another man in the crowd that day was a twenty-three-year-old physician, Charles Leale, who a few days later would be the first to come to the aid of the mortally wounded president. Pitch pointed out another window, three over to the right. "That room was called the Prince of Wales Room. That's where they did the autopsy and the embalming."

My mind went back twenty years, when I was a speech writer for then Vice President George H. W. Bush, to a night I dined in that room seated at a small table with President Reagan and two authentic royal princesses, both of them daughters of American actresses (Rita Hayworth and Grace Kelly). I mention this for a reason. At one point during the meal, President Reagan turned to one of the princesses and remarked that his Cavalier King Charles spaniel, Rex, would always start to bark whenever he came into this room. There was no explaining it, Reagan said. Then he told about Lincoln being embalmed here, and suddenly the president of the United States and the two princesses were swapping personal ghost stories.

For two years, I had a White House pass that allowed me to wander about freely. One day I heard that Jimmy Cagney was about to get the Medal of Freedom in the East Room, where Abigail Adams once hung out her wash to dry and where Lincoln's body lay in state. Another time, I sat in that room behind Joan Collins of *Dynasty* fame as she and her husband (number four, I think it was) groped each other voraciously while Andy Williams crooned "Moon River." I rushed over from my office in the Old Executive Office Building just in time to see President Reagan pin the medal on the man who had tap-danced "Yankee Doodle Dandy." Mr. Cagney was now a crumpled, speechless figure in a wheelchair. Reagan put his hand on Cagney's shoulder and said how generous he had been "many years ago to a young contract player on the Warner Brothers lot."

During the administration of George H. W. Bush, I was invited to the State Dining Room for a talk about Lincoln's time at the White House by Professor David Herbert Donald, author of a much-praised biography *Lincoln*. I sat directly behind Colin Powell, then chairman of the Joint Chiefs of Staff, and remember that for an hour General Powell did not move one centimeter. What I also remember of the evening was Professor Donald's stories about Mary Todd Lincoln's extravagances. Mrs. Lincoln was the Imelda Marcos of her day. This woman *shopped.* Among her purchases was the enormous rosewood bed known as the Lincoln Bed, even though her husband never spent a night in it. By 1864, Mary Todd Lincoln had run up a monumental bill. While Civil War commanders were shouting "Charge!" Mrs. Lincoln was saying, "Charge it!"

Professor Donald ended his quite riveting talk by looking rather wistfully at the front door. He noted that Mr. Lincoln hadn't wanted to go to the theater that night, but the newspaper had said he would, so he felt he had to attend *Our American Cousin.*

"And so," said Professor Donald, "they left the White House together for the last time."

We're standing in Lafayette Square in front of a red brick building, 712 Jackson Place. The plaque notes that it's now the President's Commission on White House Fellowships, the one-year government internship program. But in April 1865 it was the residence of a young Army major named Henry Rathbone, who was engaged to his stepsister Clara, daughter of a New York senator.

As Professor Donald recounts in his biography, April 14, 1865, was Good Friday, not a big night to go out, traditionally. It's hard to imagine today, when an invitation from the president of the United States is tantamount to a subpoena, but the Lincolns had a hard time finding anyone to join them at the theater that night.

His own secretary of war, Edwin Stanton, declined. (Mrs. Stanton couldn't stand Mrs. Lincoln.) General Grant also begged off. (Mrs. Grant couldn't stand Mrs. Lincoln, either.) Lincoln was subsequently turned down by a governor, another general, the Detroit postmaster, another governor (of the Idaho Territory), and the chief of the telegraph bureau at the War Department, an Army major named Thomas Eckert.

Finally the president turned to another Army major, Henry

Rathbone, who accepted. The image of the president pleading with an Army major to sit in the president's box is perhaps the final tragicomic vignette we have of Lincoln, of a piece with his humanity and humility.

After Booth shot Lincoln, Rathbone lunged for Booth. Booth sank a viciously sharp seven-inch blade into his arm, opening a wound from elbow to shoulder. Rathbone survived, but the emotional wound went deeper. One day eighteen years later, now U.S. consul general in Hanover, Germany, he shot his wife dead. Rathbone himself died in 1911 in an asylum for the criminally insane. "He was one of the many people," Pitch said, "whose lives were broken that night."

I'd last been to Ford's Theatre two decades before, to see a play. It was a comedy, but even as I chuckled, I kept looking up at Lincoln's box. I don't know how any actor can manage to get through a play here. The negative energy didn't end with April 14, 1865. Ford's Theater later became a government office building, and one day in 1893, all three floors collapsed, killing twenty-two people.

You can walk up the narrow passageway to the box and see with your own eyes what Booth saw. It's an impressive leap he made after shooting Lincoln, nearly twelve feet. He caught the spur of his boot on one of the flags draped beneath the box and broke his leg when he hit the stage. Donald quotes a witness who described Booth's motion across the stage as "like the hopping of a bull frog."

In the basement of Ford's is a museum with artifacts: Booth's .44-caliber single-shot derringer pistol; the knife curators believe is the one Booth plunged into Rathbone's arm; the Brooks Brothers coat that had been made for Lincoln's second inauguration, the left sleeve torn away by relic hunters; the boots, size 14, he wore that night; a small bloodstained towel.

Members of a New York cavalry unit tracked down Booth twelve days later and shot him dead. Four of Booth's co-conspirators, including Mary Surratt, proprietress of the boardinghouse where they plotted the assassination, were hanged on July 7. The military tribunal that presided over their trial requested a lighter sentence for Surratt, but the request went unheeded.

Also displayed are the manacles the conspirators wore in prison while awaiting execution. And a replica of the white canvas hoods they were made to wear to prevent them from communicating with one another. Inevitably, one thinks of the Washington summer heat. Next to the hood is a letter from Brevet Major General John F. Hartranft, commandant of the military prison, dated June 6, 1865: "The prisoners are suffering very much from the padded hoods and I would respectfully request that they be removed from all the prisoners, except 195." That was the number of Lewis Paine, who while Booth was shooting Lincoln attacked Secretary of State William Seward at his home on Lafayette Square, stabbing him terribly in the throat and face. There's a photograph of Paine in manacles, staring coldly and remorselessly at the photographer. Perhaps it was this stare that made Major General Hartranft decline to remove Paine's hood.

We left Ford's Theatre and crossed the street to the House Where Lincoln Died, now run by the National Park Service. I had been here as a child, and remembered with a child's morbid fascination the blood-drenched pillow. It is gone now. I asked a ranger what happened to it. "It's been removed to a secure location," she said.

The air inside the house is close and musty. A little sign on a table says simply, "President Lincoln died in this room at 7:22 a.m. on April 15, 1865." Lincoln was six-foot-four. They had to lay him down on the bed diagonally, with his knees slightly bent. He lived for nine hours.

I went back outside. Pitch was telling the story of Leale, the young Army surgeon. The first doctor to reach the Ford's Theater box, Leale knew right away the wound was mortal. He removed the clot that had formed, to relieve pressure on the president's brain. Leale said the ride back to the White House would surely kill him, so Leale, two other physicians, and several soldiers carried him across the street, to the house of William Petersen, a tailor. According to the historian Shelby Foote, Mrs. Lincoln was escorted from the room after she shrieked when she saw Lincoln's face twitch and an injured eye bulge from its socket.

Secretary of War Stanton arrived and set up in the adjoining parlor and took statements from witnesses. A man named James Tanner, who was in the crowd outside, volunteered to take notes in shorthand. Tanner had lost both legs at the Second Battle of Manassas in 1862 but, wanting to go on contributing to the war effort, had taken up stenography. He worked through the night. Later he recalled: "In fifteen minutes I had enough down to hang John Wilkes Booth."

Mrs. Lincoln, having returned to the bedside, kept wailing, "Is he dead? Oh, is he dead?" She shrieked and fainted after the unconscious Lincoln released a loud exhalation when she was by his face. Stanton shouted, "Take that woman out and do not let her in again!"

Leale, who'd seen many gunshot wounds, knew that a man sometimes regained consciousness just before dying. He held the president's hand. Lincoln never regained consciousness. When it was over, Stanton said, "Now he belongs to the ages." (Some thought he had said, "to the angels.")

Mrs. Surratt's boardinghouse, where the conspirators hatched their plot, is not far away, near the corner of H and Sixth Streets. It's now a Chinese-Japanese restaurant called Wok and Roll.

Only a few blocks from the House Where Lincoln Died is the Smithsonian National Museum of American History. There you'll find a plaster cast of Lincoln's hands made in 1860, after he won his party's nomination. A caption notes, "Lincoln's right hand was still swollen from shaking hands with congratulating supporters." Then there's one of the museum's "most treasured icons," Lincoln's top hat, worn to the theater the night he was assassinated. Here, too, is the bloodstained sleeve cuff of Laura Keene, star of *Our American Cousin*, who, according to legend, cradled Lincoln's head after he was shot.

No tour of Lincoln's Washington is complete without his memorial, on the Potomac River about a mile west of the museum. It wasn't finished until 1922, built over a filled-in swamp in an area so desolate that it seemed an insult to put it there. In the early 1900s, the Speaker of the House, "Uncle Joe" Cannon, harrumphed, "I'll never let a memorial to Abraham Lincoln be erected in that God damned swamp." There's something reassuring about thwarted congressional asseverations.

Lincoln's son Robert Todd Lincoln, who had witnessed Lee's surrender to Grant at Appomattox on April 9, 1865, and who was at his father's side when he died six days later, attended the memorial's dedication. Robert was seventy-eight now, looking distinguished in spectacles and white whiskers. You can see from a photograph of the occasion that he had his father's signature large ears. (He served as ambassador to Great Britain and died a successful businessman in 1926.)

Also present at the memorial's dedication was Dr. Robert Moton, president of the Tuskegee Institute, who delivered the commemorative speech but who still was required nonetheless to sit in the "Colored" section of the segregated audience. The karma in this insult to the memory of Abraham Lincoln was finally exorcised forty-one years later when Dr. Martin Luther King, Jr., stood on the memorial steps in front of 200,000 people and said, "I have a dream."

Inside the memorial, graven on the walls, are the only two speeches in American history that surpass in magnificence Dr. King's: the Gettysburg Address and the Second Inaugural. It takes only about seven minutes to recite both of these. Edward Everett, who also spoke at Gettysburg that day, wrote Lincoln afterward to say, "I should flatter myself if I could come to the heart of the occasion in two hours in what you did in two minutes."

Daniel Chester French, who sculpted the statue of Lincoln that stares out on the Reflecting Pool, studied a cast of Lincoln's life mask. You can see it in the basement of the memorial, and it is hard to look upon the serenity of Lincoln's features without being moved. Embarking from Springfield, Illinois, in 1861 to begin his first term as president, Lincoln said, "I now leave, not knowing when, or whether ever, I may return, with a task before me greater than that which rested upon Washington." When I first read that speech as a schoolboy, I thought that it sounded immodest. I don't now.

—*Smithsonian*, April 2003

GET OUT THE PITCHFORKS

You can't turn on the TV these days without being sprayed with spittle by someone outraged over (a) vampire AIG executives, (b) Wall Street hyena-jackals, (c) capitalism in general, and (d) office-redecorating bankers. If my computer didn't give the current year as 2009, I'd swear it was 1789. (See "Revolution, French.")

A few weeks ago, the villain du jour was John Thaine—he of the relatively modest $1 million office redo. Now we have Vikram Pandit "the Bandit" and his $10 million office renovation. It's enough to make you yearn for the good old days of Dennis Kozlowski and his relatively monastic $6,000 shower curtain.

The current issue of *ForbesLife* carries an article about Plumber Manor, the charming English manor-resort where last fall the notorious American International Group executives threw themselves a bang-up pheasant shooting party just as the U.S. taxpayer was being asked to bail out their company. (Good timing, boys.)

As the author of the article, I worried that the outrage over AIG might have dissipated by the time it appeared. Not a problem, as it turned out. No, the bonus fiasco at AIG—as opposed to the pheasant-shoot fiasco—has kept public outrage piping hot. The last time the word *bonus* caused this much trouble was in 1932 when the World War I veterans marched on Washington.

There is anger in the land. If you are (a) an AIG employee, (b) a banker, (c) a capitalist, look out your window. See all those shiny metallic things glinting in the sunlight? Those, my friends, are the tines of a thousand pitchforks. A thousand points of spite. Now you know what it felt like to be Dr. Frankenstein.

In the midst of this fury, the one relatively calm voice, oddly, is the president's. His normal modulated tone became borderline snippy only when a reporter pressed him as to why he had not ordered Seal Team Six summarily to execute the AIG bonus bandits. Mr. Obama replied rather coolly that he generally prefers to know what he's talking about before he sounds off on an issue. You could almost hear the reporters in the East Room going, *Woooo—Dad's mad!*

Outrage is cardio-aerobics for the soul. It's fun, lets off steam, and leaves you nice and sweaty afterward and wanting a hot shower. This is different from asserting that it is wise and productive. Outrage run amok leads to the kind of spectacle we saw in the U.S. Congress—328 Captain Renaults shouting, *We're shocked, shocked!*—while passing an almost certainly unconstitutional 90 percent tax bill intended to confiscate the toxic bonuses. Congress did this, mind, even as it was merrily assenting to Mr. Obama's spendthrift budget. To paraphrase Churchill, seldom in human history have so many people given so little thought to so much.

One of my personal favorite historical figures is Alexandre Ledru-Rollin, a leader of the French Revolution of 1848 (whatever it was about). One evening, hearing a mob outside his window, he looked out and hurriedly began dressing. Asked what he was doing, he relied, "There go the people. I must follow them. I am their leader."

Today, his words echo through the corridors of the Congress, as our own "leaders" fall over one another to get in front of the mob. The voice of the people—*vox populi*—must be heard and obeyed. The phrase, which is at the very heart of the concept of "populism," is erroneously attributed to the twelfth-century William of Malmesbury. ("The voice of the people [is] the voice of God.") In fact, it goes back further, to the scholar and theologian Alcuin of York, who in 789 wrote to Charlemagne: "And those people should *not* [emphasis mine] be listened to who keep saying the voice of the people is the voice of God, since the riotousness of the crowd is always very close to madness."

To be a card-carrying "populist" is perforce to be "anti-elitist." A recent *New Yorker* cartoon depicts the king looking out over the parapets at a sea of pitchforks and torches. A courtier tells him, "I think, Your Majesty, that you are perceived as an elitist."

Anti-elitism is deeply rooted in American DNA. Our system of government was born of revolution, but many if not most of our founders were themselves very much among the "elite" of their day. (Thank God.) America has always had a love-hate relationship with its elites: equal parts fascination, envy, and contempt. The dichotomous American icons are the heroic cowboy and the villainous railroad baron.

The phrase "The Best and the Brightest" has been pejorative since 1972, when David Halberstam published his trenchant book about the very smart Harvard and Yale and other elite academy graduates who got us into Vietnam. Our adventure in Iraq was brought to us by Bush (Yale/Harvard), Rumsfeld (Princeton), Paul Bremer (Yale/Harvard). Bush and Bremer share another shiny credential: Andover.

What is the solution, other than not letting Andover graduates near foreign policy? But Bush's father, George Herbert Walker Bush, also went to Andover, so scratch that idea.

As I head to the garden shed to retrieve my pitchfork, seething with righteous indignation over the deflation of my 401(k) and stock portfolio, I pause to reflect that, as the president told those bankers on Friday, "We are all in this together."

I took that to mean *We are all complicit*. We—the People—did not complain when we were offered no-money-down mortgages, a plethora of credit cards, unbelievable returns on our hedge funds as we watched the national deficit skyrocket into the ionosphere. American capitalism has become a Tom Wolfe novel minus the satire. And now the satire is asserting itself, and the laughs are on us, elitist and populist alike.

Now where *did* I put the pitchfork?

—*Forbes*, April 2009

THE SECRETARY OF HISTORY

(And Other Desperately Needed New Cabinet Positions)

As I was chomping on a truly superb BLT sandwich at the old Knickerbocker, the waitress swung by and said with excitement, "Did you hear the news?" I thought in a Dorothy Parker vein: *What fresh hell is this?* Whereupon she announced, in a stop-the-presses tone of voice: "Dashley's in at Health and Urban Services."

A number of things made Tammy's remark delightful. First, that it took place in Greenwich Village, where appointments to the less sexy cabinet agencies are typically not of the *Are you sitting down?* variety. Second, her charming mispronunciation of Mr. Daschle's admittedly tricky surname. And finally, her elision of the Department of Health and Human Services and the Department of Housing and Urban Development. (But come to think of it, why *not* merge them?) I thought it wonderful that a waitress in lower Manhattan should be so excited about a cabinet appointment.

It was odd that neither of the presidential candidates proposed a new cabinet-level agency during the campaign. They almost always do, since a new cabinet-level agency is assumed to be the answer to an intractable problem. Whereas appointing a "czar"—energy, Iraq, whatever—is now generally conceded to be an admission that there is absolutely nothing to be done about it.

During the 2004 campaign, Senator Kerry boldly proposed that he would create a "Department of Wellness." (Really. I wrote it down.) This would mean having a secretary of wellness. Secretary of wellness. *What* a great title!

I see the secretary of wellness sitting at the cabinet table, probably well past the salt, toking on medical marijuana. The president would ask, "Mr. Secretary, is the nation well?" And the SOW (unfortunate acronym) would reply, "Phhhhhuppp, *very* well, sir. Everything is—phhhhupp—totally excellent."

The only part that worries me is where would the secretary of wellness rank in the presidential line of succession? If Washington, D.C., were reduced to rubble in a spectacular, Tom Clancy thermonuclear wet dream, and it fell to the secretary of wellness to lead the nation . . . well, you see the problem.

Ever since Mr. Bush took us into our adventures in Afghanistan and Iraq, I've thought that what we really need is a secretary of history. If there had been one in 2003, when Mr. Bush announced his nation-building intentions in Mesopotamia, the secretary of history, sitting at the cabinet table, would have coughed softly, like Jeeves.

"Yes, Mr. Secretary?"

"If I might, sir?"

"Go ahead."

"The British tried that, in the nineteenth century and in the 1920s."

"Yeah? And?"

"It did not meet with what could be called an unqualified success, sir."

If it did come to a Tom Clancy Armageddon scenario, the secretary of history would be qualified to show us the way back to the future. He or she would have perspective. We'd certainly better off with a secretary of history than with a secretary of wellness, who'd still be shaking his head, going, "Whoa. What was *that* about?"

Some further cabinet-level agencies for our times:

SECRETARY OF INDIGNATION

Job description: To register indignation—righteously, should the occasion require—on behalf of the American people. The SOI would speak for the nation when the price of oil goes above $100 a barrel or the Dow Jones falls below 10,000, or when a CEO receives an $18 million bonus for bankrupting the shareholders. He/she would speak from a podium with a "Department of Indignation—Washington" sign behind.

Requirements: Ability to pound the podium while shouting, "This will not stand!"

Ideal physical type: Dr. Everett Koop, President Reagan's surgeon general and scariest-looking high government official in memory.

SECRETARY OF BAILOUT

Job description: SOB to coordinate ongoing nationalization of U.S. industries, as Adam Smith's "invisible hand" continues to bitch-slap the U.S. economy.

Requirements: Ability to shrug, rub forehead, sigh, occasionally groan, and quote Gresham's Law; evince spluttering fury over CEOs flying into Washington aboard lavish corporate jets to plead for public money. Denunciations to be coordinated with Department of Indignation.

SECRETARY OF WIND

Job description: T. Boone Pickens.

Requirements: Texan accent, trophy wife, and ability to stand up to National Audubon Society and other candy-ass bird-hugging groups who claim that giant wind turbines have only one purpose, namely to puree rare, migratory birds.

Finally, and most pressingly, it is time that we had a

SECRETARY OF HYSTERIA

Job description: To make matters worse.

Requirements: Ability to crawl under the cabinet table during meetings and bite the ankles of others while shrieking, "We're all going to die! We're all going to die!"

Rank in presidential line of succession: Probably best near the bottom.

—*The Daily Beast,* November 2008

Farewells

Life does not cease to be funny when people die any more than it ceases to be serious when people laugh.

—GEORGE BERNARD SHAW

TOM CONGDON

I was having the second cup of coffee and reading the *Times* and planning a leisurely December 23 when the phone rang. My old friend and first book editor, Tom Congdon, was dead.

As John Lennon said in one of the last songs he ever recorded, just before he was killed, about this time of year, "Life is what happens to you when you're busy making other plans."

I'd last talked to Tom's widow, Connie, in August, when I phoned her to say that our friend in common Rust Hills, another great editor, had died. So many phone calls these days seem to bring such news. All the grown-ups are leaving.

Tom published my first book, but he is slightly more famous for having published another book about the sea, called *Jaws*. He was a gentleman, and a lovely, gentle man. He graduated from Yale and served as a deck officer in the U.S. Navy. How dashing he looked in his uniform, which still fit him twenty years later when he wore it at his annual Christmas party. In those days, he and his beautiful, Philadelphia-born wife and their pretty, enchanting daughters lived in a brownstone in Manhattan's West Eighties. I mention this otherwise unremarkable detail because Tom had the distinction of being Manhattan's only beekeeper.

His literary career was distinguished and varied. In the mid-'70s, his Nantucket friend Peter Benchley hatched an idea for a book about a vengeful shark that terrorizes an island rather like Nantucket. Tom had become fascinated with sharks when one day he and Connie and the girls were picnicking beneath the cliffs at Siasconset on Nantucket's eastern shore. They looked up from their cucumber sandwiches and saw, twenty-five yards off, an enormous fin slicing the water. Tom leapt into his dinghy and began rowing out to investigate, Connie shrieking at him, "Tom Congdon, you come back here! You have two small daughters!"

After *Jaws*, and the second splash of Steven Spielberg's movie, Tom could pretty much write his own ticket. His next great success was *Maxwell Perkins: Editor of Genius*, by a fresh-out-of-Princeton talent named A. Scott Berg. Scott went on from Perkins to winning the Pulitzer Prize for his biography of Charles Lindbergh. Tom published more or less everyone over the years, but he took special delight in publishing first-time authors.

My own experience with him was a two-year-long seminar titled "How to Write a Book." I triumphantly handed him a first draft of 680 pages, with serene expectation of being told I had written the greatest book about the sea since *Moby-Dick*. No, *The Odyssey*.

He called me a week or so later, purring. His voice was all velvet.

"It's just *wonderful*," he said. "Wonderful. It's even better than I had dared hope it would be."

Two weeks later arrived a memo outlining what he thought the book needed. It was 50 pages long. Single-spaced. Among his suggestions was that Part One, consisting of 150 pages that had taken me three months to write, be cut to one and a half pages.

I phoned him. "But . . . I thought you said it was wonderful?"

"It *is*," Tom said. "It's *so* good. And it will be even better!" The best editors have a way of making you want to please them.

Our friendship lasted more than three decades. He and Connie eventually sold the brownstone and moved to Nantucket, to a house that had belonged to a whale-ship captain. In time he endured a succession of cruel maladies, including a form of epilepsy that robbed him of long-term memory. He was delighted when you told him stories that he had told you years ago which he had forgotten. I reminded him of a key moment in his life that the epilepsy had removed from his hard drive.

His ship was anchored in Piraeus harbor. He was mustering out of the Navy. He'd spent of lot of his time based in Japan and had fallen in love with the country. He'd decided that he would make his life and career there. He would become a Buddhist.

Then, as he was packing his duffel, his ship swung at anchor. He looked up and there through the porthole, perfectly framed, was the Acropolis. Epiphany. "It said, 'Choose the West.' So I went to New York."

Telling the story, his lidded eyes creased into a warm, delighted look and you felt his joy. I'm one of many writers fortunate that Tom's ship swung at anchor that day.

—*The Daily Beast*, December 2008

DEAR JOE

The call came while I was hunched over a pile of quotation books, researching an article for this magazine on the topic of "The Perfect Day." Joseph Heller had died. Five minutes before, I'd stumbled across this extract from his 1986 book, *No Laughing Matter*.

> *Mario [Puzo] had called George Mandel to say he'd heard Joe [Heller] was paralyzed. "No, Mario. . . . He's got something called Guillain-Barré." "My God," Mario blurted out. "That's terrible!" A surprised George murmured, "Hey, Mario, you know about Guillain-Barré?" "No, I never heard nothing about it," Mario replied. "But when they name any disease after two guys, it's got to be terrible!"*

I called his wife, Valerie, the lovely and fine woman Joe Heller had met when she became his nurse at Mount Sinai Hospital during his gruesome months there, and whom he had subsequently married. She was in tears. It had been a long night. Joe had come up to bed earlier than usual, complaining of indigestion. When he felt no better after taking medicine, her nurse's instincts took over. Moments later she was dialing 911 and forcing her own breath into his lungs.

I fumbled out some words. I wouldn't find the better ones until I composed my letter to her that night. I wrote that if, back then, someone had told Second Lieutenant Joseph Heller, as his B-25 lifted into the air on one of those harrowing sixty bombing missions over Italy and France, that he would survive the war and die more than half a century later, one of the most celebrated writers in American history, at the age of seventy-six, in his own bed, in the arms of the woman he loved, he'd probably have said, "What's the catch?"

We had become friends five years ago, after *The New Yorker* published a review I wrote of his novel *Closing Time*, his sequel to *Catch-22*. It was a respectful but not altogether enthusiastic review. A few days later, the mail brought a cream-colored envelope with the name Joseph Heller and an East Hampton, New York, address embossed on the back. I opened it with trepidation. My experience with elder literary lions is that they do not enjoy being told by literary hamsters such as myself that their latest book has fallen short of masterpiece status.

October 7, 1994.

Dear Christopher Buckley,
I really do like the way you write, now more than ever. I think you know me, and my novel, better than I do myself, and I was touched in more ways than you might expect by the time I came to your concluding paragraph. Valerie, my wife, was also moved nearly to tears of gratitude. Thank you from both of us. Most sincerely, Joe Heller

Within weeks we were writing to each other with such regularity that we switched over to faxing. Soon our numbers were programmed into each other's speed dials.

After I spoke with Valerie on the day of his death, I reached into the cabinet for my "Joe" file. It was thick. Over the five years, we'd exchanged several hundred letters.

It was not any remarkable literary correspondence about weighty matters. Joe's letters are entertaining, wise, avuncular, acerbic, often uncomfortably direct, charmingly and self-consciously boastful, and—no surprise—funny; mine are inconsequential, the overall tone that of an ingenue continually amazed that Joseph Heller, author of *Catch-22*, was trifling to maintain the correspondence.

But maintain it he did, and the friendship became deep and affectionate. It was conducted mostly through the letters—in five years I don't think we spoke on the phone more than five times—and over a dozen or so lunches and dinners at restaurants that I knew Joe, an exigent and delighted gourmand, would approve.

At the beginning, my plan was to try to coax him into writing for this magazine. I knew it would take some doing. It is my experience with elder literary lions that they do not deign to mere "magazine work," unless enormous sums are first deposited in numbered accounts in offshore banks. My boss, Bob Forbes, enthusiastically endorsed the plan, even knowing that it would inflict some damage on my T&E report. Despite Bob's Scottish DNA, he never flinched.

Within a few weeks of our first lunch, over which Joe announced that the eighty-dollar risotto with white truffles was not bad, but that Valerie made much better, I had managed to wheedle an article out of him, as it happens, "Five Meals That Changed History." And so I found myself editing Joseph Heller, author of the great comic novel of the twentieth century. As someone who writes comic novels (of one thousandth the quality), let me be perfectly up front here. I thought: *Cool.*

One assignment he accepted from us, to revisit the Rome of his World War II years, to seek out his old haunts, particularly the restaurants, and write an article titled "What Did You Eat in the War, Daddy?" led to his memoir, *Now and Then.* The book appeared in 1998 with a black-and-white cover photograph of him as a dashing young airman in bomber jacket. It received admiring reviews.

"So, Joe," I faxed, "still averse to magazine work?"

These excerpts are published in remembrance of a beloved and generous friend, in the pages of the magazine that he occasionally stooped to adorn.

I had proposed that he write for the magazine.

December 1, 1994

Dear Christopher,

Have you taken leave of your senses? I can't write good prose—that's why I do novels that don't require much. If I could, I would have found happiness 40 years ago writing anonymous columns for "The Talk of the Town."

I proposed that he write about five historically interesting meals.

December 4, 1994

Into my mind jump . . . that snack in the Garden of Eden, the first seder and the rebellion against Moses over that incessant manna, the Last Supper (which itself changed nothing but the tourist flow in Milan), the pastry felling Napoleon before the battle of Waterloo, Marco Polo's taste of pasta in Asia, the invention of the steak by Chateaubriand at the insistence of the French official who dreaded having another meal of boiled beef with the British, and Bush [vomiting] in Japan. None but the first, an historian might argue, had any true effect upon the history of the world, but the historians can be ignored.

We'll see you for lunch. Valerie loved the idea [for the article] from the moment she read your suggestion, and why wouldn't she, since she does not have to do the work.

Joe went to work and sent in his article. I was delayed in responding for a day or two, being out of town when it arrived.

January 6, 1995

Good to get the good response. I was about to go into that petulant sulk epidemic among authors, from which I'm sure you have suffered.

I wrote to tell him that Ronald Searle, the famous illustrator, would be doing the illustrations accompanying his article.

January 15, 1995

Heartiest congratulations on landing Ronald Searle. The next time a Forbes directs you to buy me a meal to talk about my next piece—maybe at Grenouille—perhaps you'll disclose how you've been able to get people like Searle and Heller to work for a magazine nobody they know reads yet or perhaps has even heard of.

I replied: "Simple. We pay them large sums of money."

January 26, 1995

[I've been] off into the city again for a few days in hungry search of more freelance work to help me sustain the higher standard of living I've been enjoying since working for you.

In the novel you are doing now, try to put in a Britisher, a German, a Swede and an Italian, to start with, in order to improve your chances of being invited with your family to those countries for more literary festivals and foreign-publication events. If I may present myself as a model of opportunism, this coming March, Valerie and I will be away for nearly all the month in England, Sweden, Holland, and Denmark. We will have a good and . . . inexpensive time.

He had written to say that parts of his revisiting Rome piece were bound to offend. I wrote back: "Don't worry, we offend more or less everyone."

September 15, 1995

All decisions are yours, of course . . . but I want you to know that I know all magazines have their proprieties and sacred cows, and that I am already deferring to yours and FYI. If Kissinger is one of your cows, change [his name] to Agazzi or Schwarzeneger, or even Dershowitz.

September 26, 1995

You've no idea how much pleasure awaits you in my Rome piece. The only change you'll want to make is to substitute "oral sex" for "fellatio." The latter sounds sinister, while the former, of course, is by now familiar even in advertising [circles].

I think that you and I have a rather nice thing going in FYI and I don't want to see us lose it.

I suspect by this Joe meant: You'd better not change one word of it.

October 7, 1995

Put aside your optimism [about the Rome piece] because I don't think you're going to be as free to deal with all your problems with your work until you've coped with a few of mine.

Into each soup a little rain must fall, and I think a bit has begun to fall into mine. To begin with, Valerie and I are not going to be able to leave for Italy as early as planned, because of a herniated disc, mine, and something called spinal stenosis . . . Neither, I'm given to understand, is serious medically; both I tell you from experience can be cripplingly painful. For . . . four weeks now I have been reminding myself of those two characters in that one play by Beckett whose names I won't look up, but one is unable to sit and the other is unable to stand. I bob up and down as I type these amusing words. By the beginning of next week the neurosurgeon will decide what to do . . . I'll let you know.

As a result of his back problems, Joe and Valerie missed the magazine's fifth-anniversary party on the Forbes yacht, *Highlander*. I wrote him that upon debarking that night, I noticed the name of the bar on West Twenty-second Street, near the ship's pier: Catch 22.

October 11, 1995

Between codeine and Valium I feel pretty good when I lie on my back. Walking hurts; sitting does too. Although slumping back on a couch with a whiskey in my hand can feel kind of good.

October 26, 1995

Hospital was neat. It's the recuperation at home that's a torment—disabled, weak, dependent, uncomfortable, out-of-action . . .

My hands shake from codeine, coffee or terror.

I love Valerie.

I hate visitors!

I wrote to him on the first anniversary of our correspondence.

October 1995

And a very happy anniversary to you too. We also mark the occasion of our friendship and I'm sure will continue to do so. I am still somewhat subdued with awe at the thought of all the time you must have put into preparing . . . the review [of Closing Time]. I doubt you were paid enough. I hope you've been making more per hour since.

Joe began to take an almost proprietary interest in the magazine, which delighted and amused us.

Over one lunch, he'd told me that a friend of his, the author William Manchester, had recently discovered that a fragment of a Japanese World War II bullet was still lodged near his heart, setting off airport metal detectors. I asked Manchester to write about his unusual heart problems, and to my delight, he did. But Joe was not happy.

November 5, 1995

. . . Do more if you can in layout and table of contents to direct attention to your distinguished contributors. William Manchester is a man of very large reputation. Yet I had to go through your latest issue a second time before I even noticed his piece was there.

He managed to write his Rome piece for us in the midst of his spinal problems. I wrote to say we were thrilled to have it. He replied in spidery, opiated handwriting.

November 20, 1995

Good news—great news! I was in fear I might fail you. Neither my ego nor my back is as strong as you might think.

February 15, 1996

Christopher, still there? We're both still here and doing well—so well that I, as patronizing head of the family, indulged Valerie finally and allowed her to drive me up to Vermont to go skiing the past few days. She went to the slopes, I lounged about lazily indoors at the heated pool, dabbling at writing, expanding and adjusting the FYI piece with the thought of possibly having it work as the opening chapter of a book of trenchant reminiscence.

Joe's Rome piece appeared in the March '96 issue.

March 10, 1996

The issue is stunning, and so am I. . . . The only thing that might have please[d] me more was my photo on the cover.

I'm pleased to see how much the magazine has improved since I took over.

If you're in Paris for the book fair later this month, you will see us there. I don't want to come to D.C. [where I live]. Nothing ever happens there.

I offered lunch at the Notre Dame of Parisian restaurants, the flawless Taillevent, if he would write a brief review of it. Amazingly—for a man who treasured good food and wine the way Joe did—he resisted, to Valerie's fierce consternation.

March 12, 1996

It's [Taillevent] the kind of intimidating place I dread going into unless as the guest of someone known by the management. . . . George Plimpton would be better off for the assignment . . . Like many—make that all—writers, Joe's idea of heaven was traveling on someone else's dime.

May 7, 1996

If you have a couple of days in London at a hotel and have a choice, choose Claridge's. And at least one breakfast, have, after the customary health foods, an egg-white omelette with a side of smoked salmon.

His friend Mario Puzo had just brought out a new novel.

Summer 1996

Puzo is . . . very happy indeed. So are his five children and constant companion. And so are all his friends. He is as easy, generous, undemanding, and kind a person as one would ever hope to come across. And so am I. The only fly in his ointment I know about, and it was disturbing only momentarily, were the unkind remarks in The New Yorker by your colleague Anthony Lane (whom he has admired very much as a critic and still will), but he has gotten used to hostile reviews—to the extent one ever completely does.

I'd asked him if he would write a blurb for a collection of essays of mine that was being published.

Fall 1996

Don't concern yourself about the blurb. . . . I will even let you write it for me, really, at least the first draft. . . .

Is your collection all reprints or will there be much that is new? If the former, don't expect to sell as many copies as Mario Puzo, or even Joseph Heller.

It didn't. I'd stumbled across a first edition of his second novel, *Something Happened*, in a bookstore in Key West. Robert Gottlieb, who edited both *Catch-22* and *Something Happened*, considers the latter book Heller's finest novel. It remains to be seen if *Something Happened*, published in 1974, will, like its predecessor, sell more than 20 million copies, be made into a movie, and be translated into more than fifty languages.

February 1997

Something Happened? You've got a daughter and a son and you may find yourself one of those readers who are touched very deeply.

I have the new Odyssey translation on cassettes—Ian McKellen reading. It is thrilling to hear!

Joe had read a version of *The Iliad* when he was ten years old. That experience made him decide to be a writer.

April 3, 1997

Good to hear from you again finally; sorry to hear you're still out on the book tour. I tried to warn you, but you young people refuse to listen.

We're fine. I've completed the writing and editing of a new book, and Bob Gottlieb is now working very hard on its production details to make sure it looks good. It was a work inspired by FYI and the article I did on Rome, but I'm not going to dedicate it to you or FYI. A sister takes precedence, and when and if you read it (after Something Happened, *which I'm sure you've still not read), you'll understand why.*

May 21, 1997

No dice on another food or travel piece from Rome, Capri, Naples, Venice, Como, Milan, N.Y. or East Hampton. I will fax you the rest of Prague from one of those places.

The Pope confides there is no such thing as sin and expects you to know that.

After some cajoling, Joe was persuaded to write a piece for us on a recent trip he made to Prague. He also agreed to do another piece for us, on a famous Italian hotel. He was now getting to be adept at the art of handling magazine editors.

July 11, 1997

When you send me the check for Prague, I'll fax the text for "Sunrise at Villa D'Este."

July 16, 1997

Things working out as well as they seem to be doing, if you make me an offer I can't refuse for one piece on Capri and one on Venice later this year, I might let Valerie talk me into doing them.

If you read Something Happened, *I'll read* Wet Work *[a ten-year-old novel of mine].*

He sent us his article on Prague. We titled it, "Czech, Please."

July 1997

Just what I wanted to hear—that the piece was acceptable, not that you had fallen sick. The illness you describe was just Nature's way of saying you're a putz for doing so many things that take you away too often. Give them up and devote yourself to what's important: absorbing Something Happened.

Summer 1997

Have you seen a page of photos in the current issue of a magazine called W? *One of the pictures looks like me, and one looks exactly like you. The one of me is better-looking.*

Fall 1997

Very good to hear from you again. I've been struck by the uncharacteristic silence . . .

Mine has been a lackluster and mainly tedious summer, spent on nothing more important than—a good title for a book—Waiting for Galleys. Because Bob Gottlieb works so swiftly and because there was no hurry to publish, the wait for galleys has been, and still is, a long one. In case you've forgotten [I had not], the book is a reminiscence with a Coney Island background of a childhood and career that has been very much different from your own . . .

I will go to Pritikin in California . . . to lose about ten of the pounds I've been putting on. Valerie refuses to believe I will be going there. . . . She suspects, I suspect, I will be going there to tryst, and thus far she insists on going to California too and seeing me for dinner every night.

November 14, 1997

Your new issue is a lovely one, even without any contribution from me . . . For your next novel, try something scandalous in one way or another.

He'd sent me the galleys of his memoir.

December 7, 1997

*I'm glad you found the book [*Now and Then*] enjoyable; I knew you'd find it informative. . . . Knopf finds it a little difficult to believe that I truly would prefer not to sit in a Barnes & Noble bookstore in New York for an hour and sign books. The U.K. [book tour] schedule, on the other hand, is as pleasurable and luxurious as I have ever enjoyed, beginning with three nights in Dublin, where we already have some close and boisterous friends.*

December 14, 1997

Valerie is bedded with a bad cold and it appears that I will remain out here until Christmas Day (a holiday probably instituted by Jews, I'm sure you'll agree). And shortly after that, we'll be headed for Paris for New Year's Eve, a holiday of some sentimental importance to Valerie, it seems, so it does not look like I will see you for a while.

Unless your job and total future income depend on it, I'd really rather not think about another piece for FYI or anywhere else. I feel it's time now to begin thinking about another book, and since in my lifetime I've never been able to come up with more than one idea at a time, I'd like the idea I do come up with to be for that one.

December 18, 1997

On Page 309 of a scholarly book recently published by Wayne State University Press titled Tilting with Mortality *is a bibliographical reference to Forbes FYI.*

Celebrations are in order, along with a huge promotion in title and a huge increase in remuneration. You have breached the wall between Capitalist Cool [FYI's motto] and serious literary scholarship.

February 28, 1998

In case you ever feel yourself running short of BIG money, there are collectors out there who are now hungry from the FYI issue with the Rome piece. I've been advertising it [on his book tour], even in the L.A. Times, *as the first true chapter of* Now and Then.

Joe's article in the magazine on the Villa D'Este Hotel on Lake Como generated a thrilled letter from the hotel management, offering him and Valerie a complimentary return visit.

March 21, 1998

There are undiscovered fringe benefits writing for FYI, as you'll see for yourself if you can decipher the enclosed fax. We will extend our May Italian trip three or four days to take advantage of them.

Perhaps I should be editing FYI and you should be writing for me as a roving reporter . . .

I'd written to express solidarity and outrage over an allegation contained in a letter to the editor of *The Times* of London that Joe had plagiarized elements of *Catch-22* from an obscure 1950 novel. The charge was subsequently acknowledged to be baseless.

April 29, 1998

Stop grieving—there is a much better piece for me in today's N.Y. Times. Absurdly, I find myself in a rage against a man I never knew who died a few years [ago] and was the author of a novel I never heard of!

The new issue is stunning—even without me. And swollen beautifully with ads! Tell Forbes you deserve a raise.

Joe was soon playing all the angles of a seasoned magazine travel writer.

May 9, 1998

At a local book event last night, a man doing PR for the French islands in the Caribbean offered to send me and a companion to all four if I would do a piece for your magazine. I'm tempted to encourage this . . . I'll bet I could induce him to pay for you and your wife too. My idea there is to have you do the piece eventually and for me and a companion of my choice to be along for the free ride.

The fear in his temptation is that my next and final novel will be about a spent novelist who spends the final of his golden years writing travel articles read by few people he knows for a younger novelist like you, in a kind of odd Faustian bargain in which Mephistopheles himself is also prey to the Capitalist Cool he serves.

I'd reported that Valerie had come up from behind and pinched me at a Norman Mailer book party. Fairly tame behavior for a Norman Mailer book party, actually.

May 1998

Valerie has long experience at grabbing attractive men by the crotch of their trousers . . .

What does someone like you and I do at a lavish book party in which crowds of people there seem more important to us than we know they are?

"You're equivocating like a Clinton!" he wrote after I tried to hedge on a bet we had made over the number of casualties on D-day. I finally conceded defeat, and owed him another lunch at the restaurant of his choosing.

May 28, 1998

Of course I'm right! When you know me better, as my closest friends do, you'll realize that I'm always right. With my innate modesty, I never push a point unless I'm absolutely sure I'm right.

Mr. Chow's?

Spring 1998

Another piece for FYI is tempting but ought to be avoided by me at this time—but we will see.

It won't happen to you, but if you're ever stuck for a book idea, I have a wonderful opening line for a novel that is outside my capabilities, but probably well within yours. Don't ask for it now.

Just after the Monica Lewinsky story broke:

Spring 1998

Great news about Clinton, right? I haven't had so much fun since I read Lolita, *the first time . . . With Clinton there's a catch (22?). I'd rather be appalled and titillated by him than bored by Gore.*

June 24, 1998

Good to hear from you at last. I was beginning to fear you might have plummeted into one of my depressions. I think you're thinking clearly about future work. But keep in mind it is possible to be both humorous and mordantly serious. Haven't you read the novels of Joseph Heller? If you've not read God Knows, *do so right now. Also, the non-Catholic novels of Evelyn Waugh are worth stealing from.*

I had written to confide misgivings that the novel I'd just finished writing had once again fallen catastrophically short of the Great American Novel.

September 5, 1998

I'm exhausted too and I've been doing nothing all summer but resting . . . If you have finished, as you said, one f—ing book, sold it to the movies, and have started writing another f—ing comic novel, you've been doing fine. Stop thinking about "the GAN" and begin thinking of it as "a GAN." "The" GAN has already been written, perhaps even twice, and you know by whom.

A newspaper in England reported that Joe might be appointed master of a college at Oxford. I addressed him as M'lud.

December 13, 1998

Should I receive and accept the offer to succeed Lord Plante as the next Master of St. Catherine's College, Oxford University, the formal mode for addressing me in letters and speech will be Lord Heller. On informal occasions when we are dining alone or with wives, our own or other men's, you may call me Master. On truly informal, drunken occasions, if you call me Sire, I will call you Squire.

December 18, 1998

This Xmas I am being generous: I will go with Valerie up to Poughkeepsie (a colorless place, no matter how it's spelled) and have a few meals with families there. . . . Normally I dislike holidays, including birthdays, including my own, and prefer to spend them doing exactly what I would be doing if it was not a holiday, but culturally that often proves impossible. And my God—there is still that New Year's Eve to face.

Joe wrote a generous blurb for my new novel. A few months before publication, I faxed him the decidedly mixed review it received in *Publishers Weekly*, the book trade journal. He crossed out the decidedly mixed parts and sent it back.

January 25, 1999

This way, it's a total rave.

In the midst of a ten-city, ten-day book tour for the novel, I wrote him the kind of letter that writers write to other writers in the middle of ten-day, ten-city book tours. He wrote back:

April 1999

The life of a novelist is almost inevitably destined for anguish, humiliations, and disappointment—when you get to read the two chapters in my new novel I've just finished you will recognize why.

Spring 1999

Where the hell have you gone to this time?
We leave for Italy Sunday. Is there anything there worth seeing?

Fall 1999

I may be getting soft, but the new FYI *is a beauty. Even the ads are gorgeous. We had planned to have dinner in New York City around Christmas.*

Then I wrote to beg a postponement until January, pleading a busy December. Among other things, my father was retiring from his television show, *Firing Line*, after a record thirty-four-year run, and there was a big dinner to mark the occasion. I mentioned to Joe how proud I was.

Earlier in the summer, Joe had asked me to read his son, Ted's first novel, *Slab Rat*, a delightful black comedy about a young magazine editor. I thought it brilliant, and said so in an enthusiastic blurb.

This, the last fax I got from Joe, arrived the day before he died, accompanied by a rave review of Ted's novel.

December 11, 1999

Dear Chris, Good gracious—34 years? You have very good reason to be proud of your father—that must be the longest-running show on television. And he, of course, has very much good reason to be proud of you, and does show it on the rare occasions we see him.

And next, we both may have reason to be proud for backing what thus far looks like a winner of sorts with Ted's novel. As another proud father, I'm taking the liberty of sending you a couple of good pre-pub reviews.

I hope that someday I will do as good—and that you do too.

Dinner definitely as soon as possible next year . . .

Valerie misses you, and I do too.

Love, Joe

—*Forbes FYI*, March 2000

JFK, JR.

I never met him, but a few months before he died, I experienced a nanosecond of what it must have been like for him. I was walking out of the Washington Hilton lobby after the White House Correspondents' dinner, a big, black tie, celebrity-rich (*-laden* might be a better term) environment. Tourists and gawkers were lined up behind ropes on either side as we exited.

Suddenly, the crowd began to make this *noise*. I'd never heard anything like it. A collective groan of wonderment, curiosity, and awe. Cameras flashed. Female squeaks.

"It's him!" . . . "There!" . . . "Oh, *God*, it's *him*!"

As it turned out, it wasn't "him," but him's look-alike, Jamie Rubin, the State Department spokesman. But as Rubin was walking with Carolyn Bessette-Kennedy on his arm, he was, if only for a brief, shining moment, a perfect simulacrum of JFK, Jr.

It must have been a thrill, as much as it must have been a bore for the real him, who had to live with this mob response nearly every minute of his short life. No wonder he liked flying. Up there are no photographers, no gawking passersby. When I read that three top-secret KH-11 spy satellites had been retasked to scan the waters off Martha's Vineyard, it seemed weirdly, sadly appropriate—the ultimate paparazzi, 250 miles above, taking the final snapshots.

Some years ago, in the building in New York where I then worked, I sensed palpable amps of electricity humming through the corridors one morning. Secretaries were talking to each other in excited whispers. Actually, middle-aged males were also buzzing. Strange. Celebrities are regular droppers-in at the Forbes Building: Reagan, Gorbachev, Mrs. Thatcher, Bill Gates have all been to lunch. What was causing such collective water-cooler tachycardia?

The answer turned out to be that John Kennedy was coming, to try to get Forbes to invest in his prospective magazine, called *George*.

The Forbes executive whom he was coming to visit, told that Mr. Kennedy was in the lobby, asked his secretary to escort him up, thinking that it would give her a fun story to tell.

"Oh, no," she said. "I couldn't." She didn't trust herself not to swoon in the elevator riding up with the prince.

JFK, Jr., handled this burden with grace, modesty, and humor. It's ironic then, and poor tribute to him, that his death, like that death of his counterpart Princess Diana, has been the occasion for such infantilizing and trivializing sentiment.

A colleague at work remarked that while he was showering the morning after the news broke, the radio referred to "John F. Kennedy, American hero," not once but three times. It's a truism that the word has lost most of its meaning, but as my friend observed, until now he had not heard it applied so promiscuously to someone whose recklessness resulted in the death of two young women.

In other news, the Coast Guard was claiming that it would undertake a search of such magnitude for "anyone, not just John Kennedy." Really? So we'll all qualify for a National Oceanographic Administration vessel with side-scanning sonar and KH-11 satellites? Why should the Coast Guard feel compelled to assert such nonsense? What American taxpayer would begrudge any government effort to find the son of President John F. Kennedy? But all sorts of people were saying all sorts of things.

The historian Douglas Brinkley wrote in *Newsweek*, "My job as friend was to play the historian, and at a recent lunch I compared him to John Quincy Adams, the son of the second U.S. president, a fellow Massachusettsean whose entire political career was centered on escaping his father's shadow, on proving his own worth in the political arena."

He mentioned that JFK, Jr. had declared that the boxer Michael Tyson, recently rejailed for attacking motorists while on probation, had been persecuted because of "racism . . . pure and simple." This only served to remind us that Mr. Kennedy was capable of other lapses of judgment: his friendship, for instance, with the pornographer Larry Flynt; or, more grotesquely, commissioning an article for his magazine by Oliver Stone, whose movie *JFK* asserts that Mr. Kennedy's father was assassinated by his own government. There was at least this satisfaction: in his article for *George*, Stone alluded to King Henry VIII's imprisoning Thomas à Beckett for opposing his marriage to Anne Boleyn.

Norman Mailer wrote an article once in which he described escorting Jackie Onassis to some event and being overwhelmed by the flashbulbs. Reaching as usual for the Big Thought (bless him), Mailer whispered to Jackie, "It's these lights that make idiots of us all." That quote has been on my mind this sad week. To his credit, those lights did not make an idiot of young John Kennedy. It's the rest of us I'm worried about.

—*National Review*, July 1999

SOLZHENITSYN

The headline in the *Times*—SOLZHENITSYN, LITERARY GIANT WHO DEFIED SOVIETS, DIES AT 89—seemed discrepant. Hadn't he already died? Near as I could recall, the last headline about this, yes, giant, was that his TV show had been canceled for bad ratings, as if the pope had been reduced to teaching Sunday school. How did Emerson put it? Every hero becomes at last a bore.

It was hardly boring, reading his obituary, to which the *Times* devoted two entire pages, the kind of acreage typically given to statesmen, or for that matter, popes. His life reads like a Russian novel, and a long one at that. Ironic to consider that he became famous in 1962 for a novel, *One Day in the Life of Ivan Denisovich*, of only 160 pages. Tolstoy and Dostoyevsky took that many to clear their throats.

He was born one year after the Russian Revolution and outlived the Soviet Union by almost twenty years. Jailed by Stalin, rehabilitated by Krushchev, reexiled by Brezhnev, welcomed back by Yeltsin, bemedaled by the former KGB officer Vladimir Putin. That's some arc. Only Churchill, another erstwhile bricklayer, lived through such a panoramic sweep.

I fell for Solzhenitsyn as a teenager when my father introduced me to *Ivan Denisovich*. I read it, amazed and horrified. You come away from the book as you do Primo Levi's account of Auschwitz, numb and vaguely ashamed of yourself for having enjoyed the myriad benisons of a twentieth-century American birthright.

I went on to his other books, but admit to having given up about halfway through the 300,000 words of *The Gulag Archipelago*, when the account—perhaps more accurate to say accounting—of horrors reached the point of surfeit. *Gulag* is among other things a work of meticulous reporting. Solzhenitsyn interviewed 227 other survivors of the prison system, and seems to have left nothing out. The sheer math of it is monstrous: An estimated sixty million human beings went through the Gulag. Sixty million, the combined populations of California and Texas.

Reading about Solzhenitsyn puts one in mind of another giant of the Cold War era, Whittaker Chambers, author of the classic *Witness*. Solzhenitsyn was preeminently a witness. As he notes in *The Oak and the Calf*, published a year after the KGB arrested him and sent him toward exile in Vermont, "I must write simply to ensure that it was not all forgotten, that posterity might someday come to know of it."

Ill with almost certainly mortal cancer in the early 1950s, and living a wretched existence in internal exile, his main concern was that his record of Soviet-wrought human misery might be lost. So he wrote it all down on small strips of paper which he inserted into an empty champagne bottle that he buried. The ultimate message in a bottle. He did not die of the cancer, and was convinced that this was the result of "a divine miracle." Another giant of the Cold War, Pope John Paul II, was also convinced that he had been spared by Providence when Mehmet Ali Aga's five bullets failed to kill him.

If Solzhenitsyn had not endured such ordeals—world war, the camps, cancer, exile—it might be easier to tut-tut over his being so gosh-darned inconsiderate to the 1978 graduating class of Harvard. As you'll recall, he had the temerity to tell them: "After the suffering of decades of violence and oppression, the human soul longs for things higher, warmer, and purer than those offered by today's mass living habits, introduced by the revolting invasion of publicity, by TV stupor, and by intolerable music." This elicited from the graduates a collective groan of *Dude, chill!* Chill Solzhenitsyn did, at a penal camp in Kazakhstan—a place more recognizable to today's college gen as the fictional home of Borat.

While he was writing *The Gulag Archipelago*, his typewriter kept giving out. He had to solder it back together and jury-rig repairs. It was as if the machine itself were collapsing beneath the weight of all the horror stories. He worked fast, looking over his shoulder. "If the KGB descended," he wrote in *The Oak and the Calf*, "the many-throated groan, the dying whisper of millions, the unspoken testament of those who had perished, would all be in their hands, and I would never be able to reconstruct it all, my brain would never be capable of it again."

If in the end *Gulag* is too much for Western eyes and one looks up from its stark pages, wondering if there's something a bit less bleak on TV, pause and think on that "many-throated groan, the dying whisper of millions" and reflect not only on our blessings but on the nobility of the man who came through hellfire to tell the story.

—*National Review*, September 2008

GORE VIDAL

My father, the late William F. Buckley, Jr., had a bit of history with the now-late Gore Vidal. In what might be the quintessential unscripted TV exchange, Vidal called him a "crypto-Nazi." WFB returned the compliment by calling him a "queer" and threatening to sock him. This amid the tear gas and rioting of the 1968 Chicago Democratic convention.

Harold Hayes, the legendary editor of *Esquire*, asked both gents to write about the episode. Their articles are included in the anthology *Smiling Through the Apocalypse* and are worth reading. Hayes transgressed on the arrangement whereby each had mutual right of veto over items in the other's essay, resulting in a long lawsuit by WFB against *Esquire*, and an ultimately victorious out-of-court settlement. When WFB died in 2008, I found in his study—more cluttered than King Tut's tomb—a file cabinet bursting to the seams labeled "Vidal Legal." I heaved it into the Dumpster and felt lighter.

WFB's body was still warm (I exaggerate only slightly) when Vidal rendered his public obsequies: "RIP WFB—in hell." What a thorny wreath indeed he laid on Pup's grave. He called him "a world-class liar" and "a hysterical queen." I got the hell and liar bits but am still scratching my head over "hysterical queen." But as my college-age son would say, Whatever.

Vidal also took pains in that valedictory to call me personally "creepy" and "brain-dead." Who am I to disagree? *De gustibus, non disputandum est.* But it was piquant to remember that the first line of Vidal's most recent memoir was "As I move—I hope gracefully—toward the door marked Exit." Ahem.

I was left to ponder what it was within him that animated such hatred after so much time, and at such a late stage of life. I suspected that it might have to do with envy at the outpouring of respect and admiration for WFB, from almost every corner of the ideological map.

WFB had long since ceased even to mention his old adversary, even privately. I was present on a dozen occasions when he was asked for comment, and each time he demurred. Once, on someone else's TV show, he was trapped into having to watch the clip of the famous 1968 encounter. He smiled and shrugged and said, "Gore Vidal always brings out the best in me." The only time he ever mentioned Vidal was to quote, with delighted amusement, Vidal's reply to the American Academy of Arts and Letters on being offered membership: "Thanks, but I already have Diners Club." Pup thought that was about the wittiest thing he'd ever heard.

Charles McGrath's eulogy in the *Times* today quotes Vidal on the subject of Vidal's favorite topic, namely, Vidal: "I'm exactly as I appear. There is no warm, lovable person inside. Beneath my cold exterior, once you break the ice, you find cold water." And so the water remained, to the end.

My late friend Christopher Hitchens had some history with Vidal. Christopher's collection of essays, *Unacknowledged Legislation: Writers in the Public Sphere*, bears a single endorsement on the back cover: "I have been asked whether I wish to nominate a successor, an inheritor, a *dauphin* or *delfino*. I have decided to name Christopher Hitchens.—Gore Vidal."

This was truly a blurb from on high. *Dauphin!* The Sun King astride his throne, extending a silk-gloved hand to be kissed by the brightest blade in the court. I teased Christopher without mercy: "How's the *dauphin* today?" But I acknowledged then—and do still—that this was a condign *vernissage*. I've often thought of Christopher as my generation's Gore Vidal, and thought it a compliment. Vidal's mastery of the essay was supreme in his time, just as Christopher's was in mine.

Their once close relationship did not last, largely owing to 9/11. For Christopher, this was the hinge moment when Islamofascism (his coinage, I believe) revealed itself as the principal enemy of civilization. For Vidal, it was—yawn—just a chickens-coming-home-to-roost moment, well-deserved blowback against the Evil American Empire.

This languorous *what else could we expect?* of Vidal's was a bit too much for Christopher. He wrote about his former patron in *Vanity Fair*: "If it's true . . . that we were all changed by September 11, 2001, it's probably truer of Vidal that it made him more the way he already was, and accentuated a crackpot strain that gradually asserted itself as dominant."

The crackpot strain included Vidal's persistent—and rather tiresome—charge that FDR had incited the Japanese to start a war and concealed intelligence warning of the attack on Pearl Harbor. More vile in my view was Vidal's championing of Timothy McVeigh, the Oklahoma City bomber. Vidal described him as "a noble boy." Remember that phrase next time you see the photograph of the fireman cradling the dying body of the infant Baylee Almon. But allow Vidal this: he wasn't kidding when he said that under the ice was cold water.

So despite all the gorgeous essays that he left us—I have all of them on my shelves—I'm having a hard time mustering a valedictory along the lines of "Now cracks a noble heart." The tragedy of Gore Vidal is that he never opened the window to let out his demons. He takes them with him to his grave.

Footnote: If you look closely at the footage of the 1968 contretemps, you'll see WFB wince, trying to rise out of his chair at the moment of maximum heat. He seems to be physically straining, but something is holding him back. A few days before, while sailing, a Coast Guard cutter sped by too close to his boat and knocked him to the deck, breaking his collarbone. During the Chicago debates, WFB was wearing a clavicle brace. It's possible that it prevented the moment from being truly iconic.

—*The New Republic*, August 2012

CHRISTOPHER HITCHENS

We were friends for more than thirty years, which is a long time but now that he is gone seems not nearly long enough.

I was nervous when I first met him, one night in London in 1977, along with his friend Martin Amis. I'd read his journalism and was in something like awe of his brilliance and wit and couldn't think what on earth I could bring to his table. I don't know if he sensed diffidence on my part—no, of course he did; he never missed anything—but he set me instantly at ease, and so began one of the great friendships and benisons of my life. It occurs to me that *benison* is a word I first learned from Christopher Hitchens, along with so much else.

A few years later, we found ourselves living in the same city, Washington. I had come to work in an administration; he had come to undo it. Thirty years later, I was voting for Obama and Christopher had become one of the most forceful and persuasive advocates for George W. Bush's war in Iraq. How did *that* happen?

In those days, Christopher was a roaring, if not raving, Balliol Bolshevik. Oh dear, the things he said about Reagan. The things—

come to think of it—he said about my father. How *did* we become such friends?

I stopped speaking to him only once, because of a throwaway half sentence about my father-in-law in one of his *Harper's* essays. I missed his company during that six-month *froideur* (another Christopher *mot*). It was about this time that he discovered that he was Jewish, which somewhat complicated his usually fierce anti-Israel bias. When we embraced, at the bar mitzvah of Sidney Blumenthal's son, the word *Shalom* sprang naturally from my lips.

A few days ago, when I was visiting him at the M. D. Anderson Cancer Center in Houston, for what I knew would be the last time, his wife, Carol, mentioned that Sidney had recently written to Christopher. I was surprised but pleased to hear this. Christopher had caused his once very close friend Sidney enormous legal and financial grief during the Götterdämmerung of the Clinton impeachment. But now Sidney, a cancer experiencer himself, was reaching out with words of tenderness and comfort and implicit forgiveness. This was the act of a mensch. But Christopher had that effect, even on Sidney. It was hard to stay mad at him; though I rather doubt Henry Kissinger or Bill Clinton or any member of the British Royal Family will be among the eulogists at his memorial service.

I first saw his *J'accuse* in *The Nation* against—oh, *Christopher!*—Mother Teresa when my father mailed me a photocopy of it. He scrawled a note across the top, an instruction to the producer of his TV show *Firing Line*: "I never want to lay eyes on this guy again." WFB had provided Christopher with his first appearances on U.S. television. The rest is history. The time would soon arrive when you couldn't turn on a television *without* seeing Christopher, either railing against Kissinger, Mother T., Princess Diana, or Jerry Falwell.

But in the end even WFB, who tolerated pretty much anything except attacks on his beloved Catholic Church, couldn't help but forgive. "Did you see the piece on Chirac by your friend Hitchens in the *Journal* today?" he said one day, with a smile and an admiring sideways shake of the head. "Absolutely *devastating*!"

When we gathered at St. Patrick's Cathedral a few years later to see WFB off to the celestial choir, Christopher was there, having flown in from a speech in the American hinterland. (Alert: If you are reading this, Richard Dawkins, you may want to skip ahead to the next paragraph.) There he was in the pew, belting out Bunyan's "He Who Would Valiant Be." Christopher recused himself when Henry Kissinger took the lectern to give his eulogy, and went out onto rain-swept Fifth Avenue to smoke one of his ultimately fatal cigarettes.

"It's the fags that'll get me in the end, I know it," he said at one of our lunches, tossing his pack of Rothmans onto the table with an air of contempt. This was back when you could smoke in restaurants. As the Nanny State and Mayor Bloomberg extended their ruler-bearing, knuckle-rapping hand across the landscape, Christopher's smoking became an act of guerrilla warfare. Much as I wish he had never inhaled, it made for great spectator sport.

David Bradley, the owner of *The Atlantic Monthly*, to which Christopher contributed so many sparkling essays, once took him to lunch at the Four Seasons Hotel in Georgetown. It was—I think—February and the smoking ban had gone into effect. Christopher suggested that they eat outside on the terrace. David Bradley is a game soul, but even he expressed trepidation about dining al fresco in 40-degree weather. Christopher merrily countered, "Why not? It will be bracing."

Lunch—dinner, drinks, any occasion—with Christopher always was. One of our lunches at Café Milano, the Rick's Café of Washington, began at 1:00 p.m., and ended at 11:30 p.m. At about nine o'clock (though my memory is somewhat hazy), he said, "Should we order more *food*?" I somehow crawled home, where I remained under medical supervision for weeks, packed in ice on a morphine drip. Christopher probably went home that night and wrote a biography of Orwell. His stamina was as epic as his erudition and wit.

When we made a date for a meal over the phone, he would say, "It will be a feast of reason and a flow of soul." I never doubted that this rococo phraseology was an original coinage, until I chanced on it, one day, in the pages of P. G. Wodehouse,* the writer Christopher perhaps esteemed above all others. Wodehouse was "The Master."

* The phrase was actually coined by Alexander Pope.

When we met for another lunch, one that lasted a mere five hours, he was all abeam with pride as he handed me a newly minted paperback reissue of Wodehouse with an "Introduction by Christopher Hitchens." He said, "It doesn't get much better than that," and who could disagree?

The other author he and I seemed to spend most time discussing was Oscar Wilde. I remember Christopher's thrill at having adduced a key connection between Wilde and Wodehouse. It struck me as a breakthrough insight: that the first two lines of *The Importance of Being Earnest* contain within them the entire universe of Bertie Wooster and Jeeves.

Algernon is playing the piano while his butler arranges flowers. Algy asks, "Did you hear what I was playing, Lane?" Lane replies, "I didn't think it polite to listen, sir." And there you have it.

Christopher remained perplexed at the lack of any reference to Wilde in the Wodehousian oeuvre until years later when in his *Vanity Fair* column he extolled the discovery by one of his graduate students at the New School of a mention of *The Importance* somewhere in the Master's ninety-odd books.

During the last hour I spent with Christopher, in the Critical Care Unit at M. D. Anderson, he was struggling to read a new book of P. G. Wodehouse's letters. He scribbled some notes on a blank page in spidery handwriting. He wrote "Pelham Grenville." He asked me in a faint, raspy voice, "Name. What was the *name*?" I didn't quite understand at first, but recalling P.G.'s nickname, suggested "Plum?" Christopher nodded *yes*.

I took comfort that during our last time together I was able at least to provide him with that much. Intellectually speaking, ours was a teacher-student relationship, and let me tell you—Christopher was one tough grader. No matter how much he loved you, he did not shy from giving it to you with the bark off if you had disappointed him.

I once joined him on a panel at the Folger Theatre on the subject of *Henry V*. The other panelists were Dame Judi Dench, Arianna Huffington, Chris Matthews, Ken Adelman, and David Brooks. Our moderator was Walter Isaacson. Having no original insight into *Henry V*, or for that matter any Shakespeare play, I prepared a comic riff on a notional Henry the Fifteenth. Get it? Okay maybe you had to be there, but it sort of brought down the house. But when Christopher and I met up for lunch a few days later, he gave me a sour wince and tsk-tsk-y stare, chiding me for "indulging in crowd-pleasing nonsense."

I got off lightly. When Martin Amis, his closest friend on earth, published a book in which he took Christopher to task for what he viewed as inappropriate laughter at the expense of Stalin's victims, Christopher responded with a seven-thousand-word rebuttal in *The Atlantic*. But Christopher's takedown of his chum must be viewed alongside thousands of warm and affectionate words he wrote about Martin, particularly in his memoir, *Hitch-22*, which was published with terrible irony almost simultaneously with the presentation of his mortal illness.

The jacket of his next book, a collection of breathtaking essays titled *Arguably*, contains some glowing words of praise, including my own asseveration that he is—was—"the greatest living essayist in the English language." One or two reviewers called my effusion "forgivable exaggeration." To them I say: Okay, name me a better one. I would alter only one word in that blurb now.

Over the course of his heroic eighteen-month battle with the cancer, I found myself rehearsing what I might say to an obituary writer, should one ring after the news of death. Something along the lines of: the air of Byron, the steel pen of Orwell, the wit of Wilde.

A bit forced, perhaps. Still. Christopher did not write poetry, but he could recite staves, cantos, yards of it. As for Byronic aura, there were the curly locks, the unbuttoned shirt revealing a wealth of pectoral hair, and the roguish, raffish *je ne sais quoi* good looks. (Somewhere in *Hitch-22*, he writes that he had now reached the age when "only women wanted to go to bed with me.") Like Byron, Christopher put himself in harm's way in "contested territory," again and again. Here's another bit from *Hitch-22*, a chilling moment when he found himself alone in a remote and very scary town in Afghanistan,

> *in a goons' rodeo duel between two local homicidal potentates (the journalistic euphemism for this type is "warlord";*

> *the image of the goons' rodeo I have annexed from Saul Bellow). On me was not enough money, not enough food, not enough documentation, not enough medication, not enough bottled water to withstand even a two-day siege. I did not have a cell phone. Nobody in the world, I abruptly realized, knew where I was. I knew nobody in the town and nobody in the town knew (perhaps a good thing) who I was, either. As all this started to register with me, the square began to fill with those least alluring of all types: strident but illiterate young men with religious headgear, high-velocity weapons and modern jeeps.*

His journalism, in which he championed the victims of tyranny and stupidity and "Islamofascism," takes its rightful place on the shelf along with that of his paradigm, Orwell.

As for the wit: one day we were talking about Stalin. I observed that Stalin, murderer of twenty, thirty—forty?—million had trained as a priest. Not skipping a beat, Christopher remarked, "Indeed, was he not among the more promising of the Tbilisi ordinands?"

I thought—as I did a thousand times over the course of our thirty-year-long tutorial—*Wow*.

A few days later at a dinner, Stalin came up. I said to my dinner partner, "Indeed, was he not among the more promising of the Tbilisi ordinands?"

The lady to whom I proferred this thieved aperçu stopped chewing her salmon, repeated the line I had casually tossed off, and said with frank admiration, "That's brilliant." Oh, was I tempted, but I couldn't quite bear to continue the imposture, and told her that the author of this nacreous witticism was in fact none other than Christopher Hitchens. She laughed and said, "Well, *everything* he says is brilliant."

Yes, it was. It was a feast of reason and a flow of soul.

Two fragments come to mind, the first from *Brideshead Revisited*, a book Christopher loved and which he could practically quote in its entirety. Anthony Blanche, the exotic, outrageous aesthete, has been sent down from Oxford. Charles Ryder, the book's narrator, laments: "Anthony Blanche had taken something away with him when he went; he had locked a door and hung the key on his chain; and all his friends, among whom he had been a stranger, needed him now."

Christopher was never a "stranger to his friends"—*ça va sans dire*, as he would say. Among his prodigal talents, his greatest of all may have been the gift of friendship. Christopher's inner circle, Martin, Ian McEwan, Salman Rushdie, James Fenton, comprise more or less the greatest writers in the English language. That's some posse. But in leaving them—and the rest of us—for "the undiscovered country" (he could recite more or less all of *Hamlet*, too), Christopher has taken something away with him, and his friends, in whose company I am grateful to have been, will need him now. We are now, finally, without a Hitch.

The other bit is from Housman, from a poem Christopher and I would recite back and forth at each other across the table at Café Milano. I hesitate to quote it here. I see him wincing at my deplorable propensity for "crowd-pleasing." But I'm going to quote it anyway, doubting as I do that he would chafe at such consolation as I can manage over the loss of my beloved athlete, who died so young.

Smart lad to slip betimes away
From fields where glory does not stay,
And early though the laurel grows
It withers quicker than the rose.

—*The New Yorker*, December 2011

Criticism

People who like this sort of thing will find this the sort of thing they like.

—ATTRIBUTED TO A BOOK REVIEW WRITTEN BY ABRAHAM LINCOLN

FIFTY MILLION FRENCHMEN CAN'T BE WRONG

As Philip Larkin so indelibly put it,

Sexual intercourse began
In nineteen sixty-three
(Which was rather late for me)—
Between the end of the Chatterley ban
And the Beatles' first LP.

But things didn't really get going until 1972, when Dr. Alex Comfort published his groundbreaking and indeed earth-moving *Joy of Sex*. Since then it has sold in all its various editions eight million copies. If you were born after 1972, you may owe your very existence to Comfort. Now, on the occasion of the book's thirtieth anniversary, it has been revised and reissued by Comfort's son, Nicholas, and lavishly—lasciviously—reillustrated.

A lot has happened sexwise since 1972: *Roe v. Wade*; the herpes epidemic; AIDS; Attorney General Edwin Meese's doomed Commission on Pornography; ubiquitous breast implants; the rise and fall of *Penthouse* magazine; X-rated videos; triple-X-rated videos; Larry Flynt; the *Sports Illustrated* swimsuit issue industry; Victoria's Secret; cyberporn; *Boogie Nights*; RU-486; Wilt Chamberlain's 20,000th conquest; Courtney Love and her band, Hole; the Wonderbra; Monica and Bill; Ellen DeGeneres and Anne Heche; Viagra; *Maxim*; Manolo Blahnik; the Anna Nicole Smith television show. It would appear that more people are having sex than ever before.

Whether "joy" has increased apace amid all this furious exertion is debatable, but anyone seeking either initiation or a refresher course on *ars amatoria* could do worse than to peruse these mauve, titillating pages. There are some delicious giggles to be had along the way. If these are not necessarily intentional, they are no less enjoyable.

The young man featured in the illustrations in the 1972 ur-text has evolved. He is no longer hirsute and missing only a peace symbol, looking as if his day job were playing bongos with the Lovin' Spoonful. His partner in bliss is a comely raven-haired lady who just can't seem to stop smiling, and little wonder, though she's surely going to have a crick in her neck after all this.

In this 2002 edition, the emphasis on hair is—I'll just quote Comfort, whose name remains on this book's title page despite his son's revisions: "Many women shave their armpit hair, conditioned as they are by the idea that hairlessness is sexy. Opinions are divided on this one—fashion dictates armpits should be bare, but in my opinion shaving is simply ignorant vandalism." This aperçu will surely stimulate lively dinner party conversation in the months ahead.

Comfort gets quite passionate on the general subject of the armpit. Under the heading "Armpit" we find: "Classical site for kisses. Should on no account be shaved (see *Cassolette*). Can be used instead of the palm to silence your partner at climax." I know you're in a hurry to find out about *cassolette*, but please first note that "if you use your palm, rub it over your own and your partner's armpit area first." At points as these, the text seems to intersect with the script of the movie *A Fish Called Wanda*, in which Otto, the mad ex-C.I.A. assassin played to hambone perfection by Kevin Kline, takes a deep snort of his own armpits before leaping onto Jamie Lee Curtis.

Cassolette is—well, it's right there on page 33 and I think I'll just let you look it up. The book teems with French words, and why not, French being the lingua franca of love. Until now I had thought *cassolette* involved rabbit and white beans. Some of the terms are quite recherché, but I yearn to conjugate them, conjugally. There is, for instance, *pattes d'araignée*, literally "spider's legs," and it does sound like fun. On page 101: "The round-and-round and cinder-sifting motions of the woman's hips—what the French call the Lyon mail-coach (*la diligence de Lyon*)—come easily with practice if you've got the right personality." The word *postillionage* was also new to this reviewer, and you're going to have to look that one up for yourselves, too. The section on *la petite mort*—"the little death"—is an alarming prospect and basis for an entire Woody Allen movie. And the word for one particular position is *négresse*. No comment.

The other foreign terms here serve to validate French's claim to be *the* proper vocabulary of love. Take *saxonus*, a word for—never you mind. German may be the language of philosophy, but it is not the vernacular of the pillow. Shall we do the *coitus saxonus*, Liebchen?

Were you aware of *srpski jeb*? That is, we are told, "Serbian intercourse" or "mock rape." Not tonight, Slobodan, I have a headache. Or *hrvatski jeb*? Croatian intercourse, "reputed by local wiseacres to be 'exhausting.'" I'll bet, what with all those NATO jets whooshing by overhead.

The Chinese have, as does their cuisine, delicious names for such positions as Wailing Monkey Clasping a Tree and Wild Geese Flying on Their Backs. I'll have both, please, and the hot-and-sour soup. But there are English terms here, too, such as Viennese Oyster, defined as "a woman who can cross her feet behind her head, lying on her back, of course." (Love the "of course.") And it is nice to hear a few good words on behalf of the old missionary position: "Name given by amused Polynesians, who preferred squatting intercourse, to the European matrimonial. Libel on one of the most rewarding sex positions."

Italian terms pop up here and there, but in the end it's basically a *Larousse Érotique*. There's *flanquette*, *cuissade*, *croupade*, *ligottage*, *poire*—not your grandfather's pear, either—and you'll very definitely want to know the meaning of *pompoir*, "the most sought-after feminine sexual response of all." The nineteenth-century explorer Richard Burton, the Ernest Shackleton of sex, wrote that if a woman can perform this technique, "her husband will then value her above all women, nor would he exchange her for the most beautiful queen in the Three Worlds." Or as *Cosmopolitan* magazine would put it: ONE SEX TRICK THAT *WORKS*!

There are pages and pages of cautionary notes about AIDS. (Casual sex was *sooo* '70s.) Some critics have taken Comfort to task for urging complete abstinence in the matter of using an orifice not specifically designed by nature for purposes to which it is sometimes put in, say, English public schools. Also, he notes that spermicide can sometimes increase the chance of transmitting HIV. There's a useful-sounding section on something called "hair-trigger trouble," otherwise known as premature ejaculation, that income stream of a thousand sex clinics. And gentlemen are enjoined from blowing air into a certain part of madam, since this can be extremely injurious, to say nothing of embarrassing to explain at four a.m. in the emergency room. Meanwhile, Spanish fly can be as poisonous "as mustard gas."

This is a manual, as it were, and manuals must employ the language of precision. Occasionally, however, you wonder if you've wandered into a game of Twister refereed by Casanova and the entire Académie Française, with video conferencing by the Marquis de Sade. If you thought the section on "frontal" would be fairly straightforward, parse this: "To unscramble a complicated posture for purposes of classification, turn the partners round mentally and see if they can finish up face-to-face in a matrimonial without crossing legs. If so, it's frontal. If not, and they finish face-to-face astride one leg, it's a *flanquette*; square from behind (*croupade*); or from behind, astride a leg (*cuissade*). It's as simple as that." What could be simpler? Honey, what are you doing on the floor?

Dr. Comfort died in 2000, having done more than most for the general pursuit of happiness. He was not a proselytizer, like those tiresome Esalen types who were always urging us to do it in the road. The phrase "free love" is mercifully absent. On the other hand, he didn't see anything wrong with voyeurism or group sex. In fact, he quite enjoyed both, and the evidence suggests that he did enough research for a second Ph.D. But he doesn't make you feel like a dweeb (or dweebette) if your idea of fun doesn't include *croupade* and *flanquette* with the entire neighborhood block association. On the whole, the tone is warm, learned, and friendly, as if Marcus Welby, M.D., had disappeared to California for a few months and come back with a great big grin on his face and some nifty new ideas on stress reduction. The occasional refusal to admit irony—as when he advises wearing a hard hat during motorcycle sex—will cause guffaws, but that only shows, once again, the impotence of being earnest.

—*The New York Times*, January 2003

KISSINGER ON CHINA

Ah, warm and fuzzy China. Torturing and jailing dissidents, hacking into Gmail, cozying up to the worst regimes on earth, refusing to float the renminbi, spewing fluorocarbons into the ozone, building up its navy, and stealing military secrets—all while enabling America's fiscal incontinence by buying all our T-bills. The $1.1 trillion question at the start of what's been called "The Chinese Century" is simple: Friend or enemy? Frenemy?

While Henry Kissinger doesn't quote Mario Puzo, Don Corleone's maxim, "Keep your friends close, but keep your enemies closer," echoes throughout his grand, sweeping tutorial, *On China*. Kissinger has been the go-to China wise man since his first secret meeting there in 1971. In the intervening decades, he's made fifty-odd trips back, often carrying critical messages between leaders, defusing crises, or pleading with each side to understand the other's position. His perennial ambassadorship-at-large puts readers right in the room with Mao Zedong, Deng Xiaoping, and Hu Jintao.

It also overflows with a lifetime of privileged observations. Here's a great one: Why did China invade Vietnam in 1979? To "teach it a lesson," Kissinger writes, for its border clashes with the Cambodian Khmer Rouge. But when the Soviet Union failed to come to Vietnam's aid, China concluded it had "touched the Tiger's buttocks" with impunity. "In retrospect," Kissinger explains, "Moscow's relative passivity . . . can be seen as the first symptom of the decline of the Soviet Union. One wonders whether the Soviets' decision a year later to intervene in Afghanistan was prompted in part by an attempt to compensate for their ineffectuality in supporting Vietnam against the Chinese." As such, Kissinger concludes, the 1979 clash "can be considered a turning point of the Cold War, though it was not fully understood as such at the time." Of course. Just the proverbial game of dominoes—with the pieces very widely separated. As for the psychology behind China's extraordinary death toll in Vietnam, more on that in a minute.

While Kissinger can sometimes appear to be an apologist for—or explainer-away of—Chinese unwarm and unfuzzy behavior, he demonstrates a profound understanding of the impulses behind that behavior. And those impulses, he believes, go back many thousands of years. During a meeting in the 1990s, then President Jiang Zemin wryly remarked to Kissinger that seventy-eight generations had elapsed since Confucius died in 449 B.C. By my count, we in the United States have seen eight generations since the Declaration of Independence. Rather puts things in perspective.

According to Kissinger there are four key elements to understanding the Chinese mind: Confucianism ("a single, universal, generally applicable truth as the standard of individual conduct and social cohesion"); Sun Tzu (outsmarting: good; direct conflict: bad); an ancient board game called *wei qi* (which stresses "the protracted campaign"); and China's "century of humiliation" in the 1800s (karma's a bitch, ain't it, you Imperialists?). Actually, make that five: Wei Yuan—a nineteenth-century mid-ranking Confucian mandarin—developed the Chinese concept of "barbarian management," which was at the core of Mao's diplomacy with the United States and the Soviet Union. How one wishes China's Ministry of Foreign Affairs would change its name to Office of Barbarian Management.

No, sorry, make that six: overwhelming fear of internal disorder or chaos. The resulting gestalt is an absolute imperviousness to foreign pressure. Kissinger recounts a chilly moment when, in the wake of the Tiananmen Square massacre, Deng tells him that overreaction by the United States "could even lead to war." He meant it. Even more chilling were Mao's repeated, almost gleeful, musings about the prospect of nuclear war. "If the imperialists unleash war on us," Kissinger recalls him saying, "we may lose more than three hundred million people. So what? War is war. The years will pass, and we'll get to work producing more babies than ever before." Those grim and quite believable words sound as though they came from the last scene of *Dr. Strangelove*. But Kissinger reminds us that during the first Taiwan Strait confrontation in 1955, it was the United States that threatened to use nukes.

Several other episodes since have combined—rightly or wrongly, as Kissinger might put it—to turn Chinese popular opinion against America: Tiananmen Square; the accidental 1999 U.S. bombing of the Chinese Embassy in Belgrade; and the Hainan incident in 2001, when a Chinese fighter jet collided with a U.S. reconnaissance plane and precipitated George W. Bush's first foreign-policy crisis. Then there are more recent, obvious events, such as the collapse of the American and European financial markets in 2007 and 2008, which stripped much of the luster from our image as the global economic leader. That latter year, as the world's Olympic athletes gathered in Beijing for a proxy celebration of China's arrival on the world stage, Washington was busy coping with a distressed Wall Street, two quagmire wars, and three ailing auto companies.

Is Kissinger optimistic about future relations between the United States and China? In a word, yes and no. No, because of a disturbing, emergent "martial spirit" that envisions conflict with the United States as an inevitable consequence of China's rise—much as the Kaiser's naval buildup led to World War I. In this Chinese view, the United States is not so much Mao's famous "paper tiger" but "an old cucumber painted green." In retrospect, I think I preferred it when we were a paper tiger.

On a more upbeat note, Kissinger explains that despite its unprecedented economic ascendance, China has one or two problems of its own. Its economy has to grow annually by 7 percent—a goal that would leave any Western industrialized nation gasping—or face the dreaded internal unrest. Corruption, meanwhile, is deeply embedded in the economic culture. "It is one of history's ironies," he writes, "that Communism, advertised as bringing a classless society, tended to breed a privileged class of feudal proportions." Then there is China's rapidly aging population, which may dwarf our own impending Social Security crisis.

Yet the Chinese may be better equipped, psychologically and philosophically, to withstand the coming shocks than the rest of us. A country that has endured four thousand years of uncounted wars and upheavals, through the Taiping Rebellion of the 1850s (tens of millions killed), and man-made calamities such as Mao's Great Leap Forward (twenty million) and the Cultural Revolution, is nothing if not resilient. Sun Tzu coined a term, *shi*, which roughly translates to "the art of understanding matters in flux." Writes Kissinger: "A turbulent history has taught Chinese leaders that not every problem has a solution." The Chinese get it—*shi* happens.

It's hard to imagine a U.S. president holding such a view, much less expressing it out loud. But by the time one reaches the far shore of this essential book, there's little doubt that Henry Kissinger, historian and maker of history, Nixon consigliere, and secretary of barbarian management, also takes the long view. Perhaps, from the heights on which he perches, it may be, for better or worse, the only view.

—*Bloomberg BusinessWeek*, June 2011

HOW IT WENT: KURT VONNEGUT

Kurt Vonnegut died in 2007, but one gets the sense from Charles J. Shields's sad, often heartbreaking biography, *And So It Goes*, that he would have been happy to depart this vale of tears sooner. Indeed, he did try to flag down Charon the Ferryman and hitch a ride across the River Styx in 1984 (pills and booze), only to be yanked back to life and his marriage to the photographer Jill Krementz, which, in these dreary pages, reads like a version of hell on earth. But then Vonnegut's relations with women were vexed from the start. When he was twenty-one, his mother successfully committed suicide—on Mother's Day.

It's a truism that comic artists tend to hatch from tragic eggs. But as Vonnegut, the author of zesty, felicitous sci-fi(esque) novels such as *Cat's Cradle* and *Sirens of Titan* and *Breakfast of Champions* might put it, "So it goes."

Vonnegut's masterpiece was *Slaughterhouse-Five*, the novelistic account of being present at the destruction of Dresden by firebombing in 1945. Between that horror (his job as a POW was to stack and burn the corpses); the mother's suicide; the early death of a beloved sister, the only woman he seems truly to have loved; serial unhappy marriages; and his resentment that the literary establishment considered him (a mere) writer of juvenile and jokey pulp fiction, Vonnegut certainly earned his status as Man of Sorrows, much as Mark Twain, to whom he is often compared, earned his.

Was Kurt Vonnegut, in fact, just that—a writer one falls for in high school and college and then puts aside, like one of St. Paul's "childish things," for sterner stuff?

This vein of anxiety runs through Shields's diligent, readable, but uneven biography. But the question seems self-answering: When did you last reread *Slaughterhouse* or *God Bless You, Mr. Rosewater*? That long ago? Okay, but when did you last read *Huckleberry Finn* or *To Kill a Mockingbird*?

Or we could just crunch the numbers: in the first six months of 2005, *Cat's Cradle*, published the year JFK was assassinated, sold 34,000 copies; *Slaughterhouse* sold 66,000. Most of those are probably being read in the classroom. But so what? You want to shout across the River Styx: "It's all right! Cheer up! You're immortal!"

Vonnegut and the other great "comic" (or if you prefer, ironic or tragico-comical-ironic) novelist of World War II, Joseph Heller, are getting their biographical due, almost simultaneously. Tracy Daugherty's fine biography of Heller was recently published, in time for the fiftieth anniversary of *Catch-22*.

There are some odd synergies. The two men met years after their respective wars, onstage at a literary festival in 1968, and became great friends and eventually neighbors. Heller's war was up in the air, as a bombardier in the nose cone of a B-25. Vonnegut's was at ground level, as an infantryman in the Battle of the Bulge, and ultimately beneath ground level, in the basement of Schlachthof-Fünf during the firebombing.

Both men were profoundly, and with respect to their war novels, specifically influenced by the French author Louis-Ferdinand Céline. Both their novels were numerically titled—Heller had to retitle his original *Catch-18* when Leon Uris brought out *Mila 18*.

In a detail that struck me as, well, weird, Vonnegut's breakthrough moment while he was trying to get a handle on how to write his novel came during a visit to a war buddy—in Hellertown, Pennsylvania. But perhaps most ironic of all is that both their World War II novels ended up being Vietnam novels.

Heller's appeared in 1961, just as American pacificists were starting to ask, What exactly are we *doing* there? Didn't the French try this? *Catch-22* became an existential field manual for the antiwar movement, and a must-read for the grunts and soldiers doing the fighting. Vonnegut's novel came out in March 1969, by which time the question had pretty much been answered. It made him famous—the proverbial "voice of a generation" (always a problematic title)—and a Pied Piper to disaffected American kids. It also made him rich.

Vonnegut was born in Indianapolis in 1922 into squarely bourgeois circumstances. His father, an architect, lost his money in the Depression; his mother, unable to cope without the luxuries to which she had become accustomed, killed herself. (Thanks, Mom.) Kurt's older brother, Bernard, was the star; he became a physicist and climatologist, experimenting with ways to supercool water, a detail that perhaps seeped into his brother's fourth novel, *Cat's Cradle*, in the form of "ice-nine," the substance that turns all moisture on Earth into a supersolid.

Kurt dropped out of several colleges, but worked while he was there on school or local newspapers, where he learned to write clear, concise, punchy, and often very funny sentences. "Writing that was easy to scan," Shields tells us, "would become one of the hallmarks of his fiction." He worked as a reporter at a news bureau in Chicago, covering a city beat, and later as a publicist at General Electric.

"A lot of critics," Vonnegut would say later with some asperity, "think I'm stupid because my sentences are so simple and my method is so direct: they think these are defects. No. The point is to write as much as you know as quickly as possible."

He did, cranking out short stories, some of which he sold to "slicks" like *The Saturday Evening Post*; in those years, a single story could earn him the equivalent of six weeks salary at G.E. An editor and old college friend named Knox Burger (to whom Shields dedicates this biography) took him on, publishing him first at *Collier's* magazine and then at Dell paperbacks before trying to become his agent in 1970. One of Vonnegut's less admirable traits was his tendency to throw his mentors—decisively—under the bus. He did this not only to Burger, backing out of their representation agreement, but also to the legendary editor Seymour Lawrence.

This, as much else here, does not make for pleasant reading. Vonnegut was Whitmanesque, contradictory, containing multitudes. As a parent, he could be sweet and generous but also aloof, and even, according to one nephew, "cruel" and "scary." When his sister died of cancer within a day of her husband's ghastly death in a train wreck, Vonnegut and his wife took in and raised three of their four orphaned children. But the domestic scenes do not read like *Cheaper by the Dozen*.

Shields has a deep affection for his subject and does what he can to rebut charges of hypocrisy, but in this he is not entirely convincing. Vonnegut the staunch anti–Vietnam War spokesman couldn't be bothered to help his wife campaign for Eugene McCarthy; more disconcerting is the revelation that as an avid purchaser of stocks, he had no qualms about investing in Dow Chemical, maker of napalm. At the least, it seems an odd buy for a survivor of the Dresden firebombing. The champion of saving the planet and the Common Man also, we learn, owned shares in strip-mining companies, malls, and corporations with antiunion views. So it went.

As a writer of science fiction—a label he tried strenuously to shed, lest his books be shelved in the genre ghetto—he was curiously blasé, even antagonistic, about the moon landing on July 20, 1969. On a broadcast with Walter Cronkite, Gloria Steinem, and others, he dissed the entire enterprise and reiterated his view that the $33 billion should have been spent "cleaning up our filthy colonies here on Earth." The avuncular Cronkite let it go, but CBS was swamped with furious letters. (For the record, many of the writers felt that Steinem, too, had been "un-American.")

But this was *echt* Vonnegut: not with a bang or a whimper but with a shrug. If he, like Twain, was angry at the universe—and had every reason to be—he wasn't going to yell himself hoarse or make himself a spectacle in the process. He possessed more ambivalence than passion; odd, perhaps, in someone of German ancestry. (Seems more . . . French, somehow.) But then the line with which he will always be remembered, from *Slaughterhouse-Five*, is "So it goes," as close an English-language phrase as there is to denote hunching shoulders.

As to whether he wrote for the kids, or for—pardon—kids of all ages, and for the ages, perhaps that's more definitively answered by the Library of America's recent publication of *Kurt Vonnegut: Novels and Stories 1963–1973*, ably edited by Sidney Offit. Turn to the first sentences of *Slaughterhouse-Five*:

"All this happened, more or less. The war parts, anyway, are pretty much true. One guy I knew really *was* shot in Dresden for taking a teapot that wasn't his. Another guy I knew really *did* threaten to have his personal enemies killed by hired gunmen after the war. And so on. I've changed all the names."

There's an echo there of another voice—Holden Caulfield's, and didn't the guy who came up with him also have a reputation for writing for kids?

—*The New York Times*, November 2011

APOCALYPSE SOON

As annus mirabilis 2000 approaches, we'd best start dealing with the fact that there will be Elijahs on every street corner, and cable channels and Web sites urging us to repent—repent!—for the end is at hand. There's just something about an impending millennium that brings out the gloom and doom.

The year 999 was a boom year for monasteries. Penitents flocked in, hysterically bearing jewels, coins, and earthly possessions by the oxcartful, hoping to cadge a little last-minute grace before Judgment Day. The year 1999 may turn out to be a similarly good one for the coffers of fundamentalist Christian churches—especially if Pat Robertson's apocalyptic novel, *The End of the Age*, is any indication of what the faithful think is going to happen when the ball atop the Times Square tower plunges into triple zeros.

Mr. Robertson is no ordinary street-corner Elijah. He's a graduate of the Yale Law School and chairman of both the Christian Broadcasting Network and International Family Entertainment (the Family Channel). He has his own daily television show, *The 700 Club*, and is the author of nine previous books. In 1988, he ran for president in the Republican primaries, giving the non-fire-breathing Episcopalian George Bush a brief case of the heebie-jeebies during the Iowa caucuses and establishing the Christian Right as an electoral force to be reckoned with. So when he ventures forth into pop-fictional eschatology, attention must be paid—if only for the pleasure of hearing a president of the United States tell the nation in a televised address, "We are the world," and to watch as an advertising executive is transformed into an angel.

It's hard to define *The End of the Age* exactly. It's a sort of cross between *Seven Days in May* and *The Omen*, with the prose style of a Hallmark card. The good guys are a born-again advertising executive and his wife, a black pro basketball player and a Hispanic television technician, all led by one Pastor Jack, a descendant of the eighteenth-century American preacher Jonathan Edwards. They tend to sound like a bunch of Stepford wives who have wandered onto the set of *The 700 Club*, eerily polite and constantly telling one another to please turn to the book of Revelation:

> *"That's right, Manuel. Every bit of it is in the Bible. As a matter of fact, whole books have been written about a diabolical world dictator called the Antichrist. He got that name because he will try to perform for Satan what Christ performed for God."*
>
> *"Wow, I hope he fails," Cathy said.*

The bad guys tend to sound like the villains in a Charlie Chan movie being simultaneously translated from some sinister Indo-Iranian tongue:

"Panchal, sorry to wake you. Get your people ready. Tonight the gods have given America into our hands."

That "sorry to wake you" is one of the many hilarious moments that relieve the general tedium. For all the apocalyptic pyrotechnics, the book leaves the eyeballs as glazed as a Christmas ham. But just when you start wondering if there's something more interesting on C-SPAN 2, there's a reason to go on:

"The Antichrist raged within his palace. . . . The final battle was coming. He would march on Jerusalem at the head of his armies. 'Then,' he said to Joyce Cumberland Wong, 'I will win! At last I will have my revenge!'"

The book begins with a bang in the form of a 300-billion-pound meteor that lands in the Pacific Ocean with the force of five thousand nuclear bombs, setting off a three-thousand-foot tsunami, earthquakes, fires, nuclear plant meltdowns, volcano eruptions, ash in the atmosphere, floods, and food shortages. All in all, a bad hair day for Mother Earth, sending the Antichrist ouching toward Bethlehem to be born. Meanwhile, at 1600 Pennsylvania Avenue, things are getting a bit sticky:

"Well, here's the story," the secretary of defense explains to his top general over lime and sodas while the world burns. "As you know, we had one president commit suicide. The next was killed by a snakebite, and then the man who left the cobra on the president's desk was murdered. They say he committed suicide, but don't you believe it."

At this point, if I were the general, I'd have asked for some scotch to go with my soda, but in evangelical literature the good guys don't drink.

"Now," the secretary continues, "we've got this ex–campus radical in the White House, and if you heard the speech tonight, you know he's got some mighty big plans."

That would be the aforementioned "We are the world" speech, and, yes, President Mark Beaulieu (as in "mark of the beast") does indeed have big plans: a one-world government with its own currency and a police force in United Nations–ish uniforms, a grand new $25 billion world headquarters palace in Babylon (natch) with some positively kinky special effects, computer-tattoo ID markings for everyone, drugs and orgies for schoolchildren, vintage wines for the grown-ups.

Your basic liberal agenda, right down to the chardonnay. President Mark of the Beast's cabinet would certainly provide for memorable nomination hearings:

"For secretary of education, the president had selected a Buddhist monk who shaved his head and dressed in a saffron robe and sandals. For secretary of agriculture, he asked for a shepherd from Nevada who lived alone in the hills and spoke broken English. The man's only known 'credential' was that he had once played jai alai in Las Vegas. For secretary of energy, he named a Lebanese Shiite Muslim who was a member of the terrorist group Hezbollah and ran a filling station in Dearborn, Michigan.

"For drug czar, he picked a man who had spent his life crusading for the legalization of all narcotics. For secretary of state, a professor of Eastern religions from Harvard University"—a Yale man just can't help himself—"who had close ties to Shoko Asahara, the leader of the Japanese cult of Shiva worshipers known as Aum Shinri Kyo, or Supreme Truth. They had been linked with a poisonous gas attack in a Tokyo subway in 1995. And he chose for attorney general a militant black feminist attorney who advocated abolishing the death penalty and closing all prisons."

And you know, I'd bet not one of them paid Social Security tax on the nanny.

The End of the Age is to Dante what Sterno is to *The Inferno*. When you have a hard time keeping a straight face while reading a novel about the death of a billion human beings, something is probably amiss.

But lest we be smug, bear in mind two recent events:

In March 1989, a large asteroid passed within 450,000 miles of Earth. Had it landed in an ocean, according to scientists quite genuinely rattled by 1989FC's sudden appearance, it would have created three-hundred-foot tidal waves. If you think 450,000 miles is a country mile, consider that Earth had been in the asteroid's path just six hours earlier.

Then there was Hurricane Gloria. In September 1985, this violent storm was working its way up the Atlantic, headed for Virginia Beach, headquarters of the Christian Broadcasting Network, with murderous force. Mr. Robertson went on the air and prayed, commanding the storm to stay at sea. It did—and came ashore at Fire Island, demolishing the summer house of Calvin Klein.

—*The New York Times*, February 1996

THE NEW YORKER MONEY CARTOONS

One of the first Latin quotations schoolchildren of my generation were given to translate—and indeed meditate upon for the good of our souls—was the Chaucerian chestnut *Radix malorum est cupiditas*. Greed is the root of all evil. Greed, of course, being synonymous with "money."

The sentiment sounded plausible enough back in the fifth grade. Now that I have a fifth grader of my own, I would translate it differently: "Money is the root of all tuition." It would be preposterous, not to say downright idiotic, in the context of *New Yorker* cartoons on this subject, to attempt to strike a more high-minded pose.

Money has certainly always been the root of humor at the magazine that since 1925 has published more than sixty thousand cartoons. In the beginning, its founding editor, Harold Ross, scraped together a meager operating budget, which did not provide the staff with a working environment that could be called lavish. Certainly none of them ever accused it of that. The late Brendan Gill, an aboriginal *New Yorker* staffer, used to regale listeners with a hilarious description of how he had to walk over the desks of three other staffers in order to reach his own. One day, Ross demanded of Dorothy Parker why she had not handed in the article that was due. She replied, "Someone else was using the pencil."

The root of all evil continued to be the root of great mirth among *The New Yorker*'s legendary staff. After James Thurber's short story "The Secret Life of Walter Mitty" was turned into a big box-office movie success starring Danny Kaye, Samuel Goldwyn tried to hire Thurber away from the magazine to be one of his studio contract writers. Goldwyn offered him $500 a week, a princely salary that in 1947 would have weakened the knees of most *New Yorker*—or for that matter, New York—writers. But Thurber cabled back: "Mr. Ross has met the increase."

Goldwyn knew Hollywood, but he clearly did not know Harold Ross, who would no more have paid a writer $500 a week than he would have bought another pencil. He cabled back, offering Thurber $1,000 dollars a week. Thurber wired back that again Mr. Ross had met the increase. Goldwyn upped his offer to $1,500. Again Thurber sent an identical cable. Finally Goldwyn offered $2,500. (That's almost $25,000 a week in today's dollars.) Still Thurber wouldn't budge.

Goldwyn gave up. But then later, he renewed his siren-singing, this time offering Thurber $1,500, apparently forgetting his previous offer of $2,500.

"I'm sorry," Thurber cabled back, "but Mr. Ross has met the decrease."

Twentieth-century literature and culture are the better off for Thurber's remarkable resistance. However, a number of *New Yorker* staffers did succumb to the lure of Hollywood. As John McNulty headed west, Ross's valedictory comment to him was, "Well, God bless you, McNulty, goddamn it."

Robert Mankoff, cartoon editor of *The New Yorker* since 1986, estimates that of the thirteen thousand cartoons the magazine has run since that year, about a quarter of them have been on the subjects of business and money. Most *New Yorker* cartoonists, he points out wryly, have never gotten *near* business. This obdurate reality no doubt accounts for their tone of—shall we say—ironic detachment. As Sydney Smith wrote, "I read Seneca's *On the Contempt of Wealth*. What intolerable nonsense!"

Twenty-five percent seems like a lot when you consider the other available themes, such as, say, Love, Death, Lawyers, and Cats. But Mr. Mankoff explains that, until fairly recently (1992 and the arrival of Tina Brown as editor), *The New Yorker*'s cartoons never touched on another of life's truly major themes. (Sex.) He attributes the cartoonists' obsession with business and money as a "sublimation" of this forbidden territory. One grasps his point. If you can't have sex, you might as well make do with money. As Hillaire Belloc put it:

I'm tired of Love; I'm still more tired of Rhyme,
But money gives me pleasure all the time.

Or as Jack Benny, in his signature skit, says to the impatient mugger who has given him the choice of his money or his life: "I'm *thinking* . . ."

The 1980s was all about Wall Street money. The 1990s have been about—money. According to *The Wall Street Journal*, over the last five years, U.S. households have created $13 trillion of net new wealth. If that strikes you as a lot, or to put it as Alan Greenspan would say, a "s—load" of money, you are in fact correct. Thirteen trillion equals the entire U.S. bond market. Or put it this way: the entire U.S. Gross Domestic Product (that is, the value of the work performed by maids, butlers, cooks, gardeners, nannies, etc.) in 1998 was $8.5 trillion.

There is more money now than ever. Ten years ago, the richest person on the Forbes 400 was John Kluge, with a net worth of about $2.5 billion. In 1999, the richest person on the list was Bill Gates, with a net worth of $58 billion. It's been a while since I took Econ 101, but I think this is called exponential growth.

One of my favorite *New Yorker* cartoons is John Agee's pastiche on the National Debt Clock near Times Square in New York City. This one is called "Bill Gates' Wealth." Beneath the display of continuously increasing mind-boggling numbers, is a subcategory labeled, as in the original, "Your Family's Contribution."

It's not that the rich have gotten richer. Everyone has gotten richer. (Okay, except for you and me.) That dorky guy you went to high school with now has his own Gulfstream. One of the longest-running books on *The New York Times* best-seller list is called *The Millionaire Next Door*. According to its authors, that guy next to you in the supermarket looking for a bargain on jumbo boxes of generic raisin bran, wearing a ripped, grease-stained, eight-year-old sweater from the Lands' End catalogue and driving a rusty twelve-year-old Corolla is . . . rich. He just isn't into looking rich.

When I was growing up in the sixties, one of the coolest shows on TV was called *The Millionaire*, about an old money-buckets named John Beresford Tipton, Jr., who gave away a million dollars at a pop to people in distress. And what do you know—their lives were often *not* bettered by the hailstorm of manna. But the name of the show alone was exotic and alluring and unattainable. Your parents would whisper of someone, "He's a *millionaire.*" Today, only Austin Powers is impressed by *one . . . million . . . dollars.* Once upon a time, the rich would cluster in places like Gatsby's East Egg, "where they could be rich together." Now they're next door. They'd no longer all fit in East Egg. Even Seattle is getting cramped.

As a result of this efflorescence of moola, the stuff has become a ubiquitous theme of modern life. At this point, a three-year-old would probably recognize the letters IPO. Not a day goes by without the newspapers informing us of the cost or amount of something. Having just sent in my tax returns, I now know exactly what portion I contributed to the cost of one of those Tomahawk missiles we lobbed into Belgrade during the recent unpleasantness. They cost $1.4 million apiece. A cruise missile goes for $1.5 million. To some, this seems like a lot just to take out an enemy truck—or a friendly embassy, for that matter. But since a single B-2 bomber costs $2.2 billion, who's to say? (Bill Gates could afford twenty-six B-2 bombers. Should we be concerned?)

In the midst of all the expensive bombing and peacemaking, an Air Force general sallied forth to point out that JDAMs, that is, Joint Direct Attack Munitions, the type of bomb that drops from the pricey B-2, cost only $20,000 each, or $10 per pound. As he gamely put it, "about the same as prime ground beef."

In the fifties and sixties, it was considered impolite to ask someone how much they made. Now magazines devote entire issues to "Who Made What." I never had the remotest idea, or really cared, how much Walt Disney made from his Magic Kingdom. But last week we were all informed that Disney's chairman, Michael Eisner, made—jumpin' Jehoshaphat—$547 million. (Having two children who are heavy Disney consumers, I could probably calculate My Family's Contribution.)

But how come *I* didn't make $547 million last year? Obviously, I need one of Roz Chast's Wonderwallets: "I know there's only seven dollars in here, but it looks like seven hundred!" The genius of a *New Yorker* cartoonist is, to paraphrase Emerson, they know exactly what we're thinking.

Money, money, money. Most people today could tell you the opening weekend box office gross of the *Phantom Menace* Star Wars movie, or the new Austin Powers sequel. I could tell you the Gross Net Product of Pamela Lee Anderson. I didn't even know such a thing existed, until I read it in a magazine last week. I knew she existed, but I didn't know she had a Gross Net Product ($77 million). So now I know, and my life is fuller. The good news is that some *New Yorker* cartoonist is out there also mulling this important issue and preparing to reduce it to laughter.

It is good to have this book as we near the end of "The American Century" and this money-mad decade. What can better distill the *zeitgeist*—German for "wish we had a word like that in English for 'spirit of the times'"—than a *New Yorker* cartoon?

One of Gahan Wilson's shows a prison inmate in the upper bunk exclaiming cheerfully to a gloomy one in the bunk below, *"Well, anyhow, it sure is handy having my broker right here in my cell!"* At a time when everything is for sale, Ed Frascino's cartoon says it all: the tooth fairy hovers over an elderly gent in bed, announcing: *"Hi, I'm the tooth fairy. Want to buy back some of your teeth?"*

We spent a lot of time in the nineties thinking about health—and "managed" care. Frank Cotham gives us a doctor outside the Intensive Care Unit consoling the bereaved relative of the deceased: *"His final wish was that all his medical bills be paid promptly."* And there's a warning, as well as a laugh, in Bernard Schoenbaum's two world-weary dogs walking along, one saying to the other, *"Let's face it—man's best friend is money."* Mick Stevens gives us a man standing at the Pearly Gates before a scowling Saint Peter: *"You had more money than God. That's a big no-no."* And here's Mort Gerberg's Leonardo da Vinci, interrupting his work on a portrait of a woman with an inscrutable smile, to paint an even larger canvas entitled *Production Expenses: Project—Mona Lisa.* Two oppressed working stiffs stare philosophically at something going on offstage, one saying to the other, *"There, there it is again—the invisible hand of the marketplace giving us the finger."* That could have run in 1929 or during the last recession. Or Mick Stevens's of a wife demanding of her newspaper-reading husband, *"I married you for your money, Leonard. Where is it?"* Or Henry Martin's two businessmen strolling down a street where every sign, every ad, every awning, flag, and license plate displays the same word: "Money." Says one to the other, *"Remember a few years ago when everything was sex, sex, sex?"*

Sort of. Or has it always been money, money, money? You could look it up in Chaucer.

—from the introduction to *The New Yorker Book of Money Cartoons*, 1999

CATCH-22 AT FIFTY

> *There was only one catch and that was Catch-22, which specified that a concern for one's own safety in the face of dangers that were real and immediate was the process of a rational mind. Orr was crazy and he could be grounded. All he had to do was ask: and as soon as he did he would no longer be crazy and would have to fly more missions. Or be crazy to fly more missions and sane if he didn't, but if he was sane he had to fly them. If he flew them he was crazy, and didn't have to; but if he didn't want to he was sane and had to. Yossarian was moved very deeply by the absolute simplicity of Catch-22 and let out a respectful whistle.*
>
> *"That's some catch, that Catch-22," he observed.*
>
> *"It's the best there is," Doc Daneeka agreed.*

The phrase "Catch-22" has so permeated the American language—or embedded itself, to put it in Desert Storm terminology—that we deploy it almost every day, usually to describe an encounter with the Department of Motor Vehicles. It's common usage is so common that it's right there in the dictionary. Not many book titles end up being (sorry, unavoidable) catchphrases. My own *American Heritage Dictionary* defines it as: "1.a A situation in which a desired outcome or solution is impossible to attain because of a set of inherently illogical rules or conditions. *In the Catch-22 of a close repertoire, only music that is already familiar is thought to deserve familiarity. (Joseph McLennan).*"

Joseph . . . who? But it's possible, even likely in fact, that the other Joseph would be amused at not being mentioned until the very bottom of the entry. I can hear him chuckling, "And how many copies of the *American Heritage Dictionary* have they sold so far?" I don't know, but my guess is, not as many as *Catch-22*, which in the fifty years since it first appeared in October 1961 has sold more than ten million.

In his memoir *Now and Then*, published the year he died, Heller tells us that he wrote the first chapter of his masterpiece in longhand on a yellow legal pad in 1953. It was published two years later in the quarterly *New American Writing* 7, under the title *Catch-18*. Also in that number were stories by A. A. Alvarez, Dylan Thomas, Heinrich Böll, and someone calling himself "Jean-Louis"—Jack Kerouac, a piece from a book he was writing called *On the Road. Catch-22* and *On the Road*? Not a bad issue of *New American Writing*, that.

The full story of how *Catch-22* came about is told in Tracy Daugherty's fascinating new biography, *Just One Catch*. Briefly: the novel grew out of Heller's experiences as a bombardier in World War II, flying missions out of Corsica over Italy. It was seven years in the writing, while its author worked in the promotional departments of *McCall's* and *Time* magazines. Just before being published, the novel had to be retitled, when it was learned that Leon Uris was about to bring out a World War II novel called *Mila 18*. Which is why you didn't have a Catch-18 experience today at the Department of Motor Vehicles.

The novel got some good reviews, some mixed reviews, and some pretty nasty reviews. *The New Yorker*'s was literary waterboarding: ". . . doesn't even seem to have been written; instead it gives the impression of having been shouted onto paper . . . what remains is a debris of sour jokes." Heller dwells on that particular review in his memoir: "I am tempted to drown in my own gloating laughter even as I set this down. What restrains me is the knowledge that the lashings still smart, even after so many years, and if I ever pretend to be a jolly good sport about them, as I am doing now, I am only pretending." (That was Joe Heller. Whatever flaws he may have had as a writer and human being, he was absolutely disposed of what Hemingway called the writer's most essential tool: a first-class s— detector.) Evelyn Waugh, one of Heller's literary heroes, pointedly declined to provide a blurb for the hardcover jacket. *Catch-22* never won a literary prize and never made the *New York Times* best-seller list.

But a number of people fell for it—hard. To paraphrase the novel's first line, "It was love at first sight." They took it up as a cause, not just a book, with evangelical ardor. Among these were S. J. Perelman, Art Buchwald, and the TV newsman John Chancellor, who printed up YOSSARIAN LIVES bumper stickers. (The phrase eventually became an antiwar slogan, the "Kilroy Was Here" of the Vietnam era.) Word spread: *You have to read this book*! In Britain, it went straight to the top of the best-seller lists. A reviewer there called it "*The Naked and the Dead* scripted for the Marx Brothers, a kind of *From Here to Insanity*."

Back on native soil, the novel took off after it was published in paperback. By April 1963, it had sold more than a million copies, and by the end of the decade, had gone through thirty printings. Heller's biographer Tracy Daugherty concludes his *Catch-22* chapter with an arresting quote from a letter Heller received a few months after the hardcover came out: "For sixteen years, I have been waiting for the great anti-war book which I knew WWII must produce. I rather doubted, however, that it would come out of America; I would have guessed Germany. I am happy to have been wrong . . . thank you." The writer was the historian Stephen Ambrose.

Joe Heller began work on his World War II novel about the time the Korean War was winding down and published it just as another

American war, in Vietnam, was getting under way. He was not the first twentieth-century author to find dark humor in war. Jaroslav Hasek's unfinished classic *The Good Soldier Schweik*—a book Heller knew well—got there first. But *Catch-22*'s tone of outraged bewilderment in the midst of carnage and a deranged military mentality set the tone for the satires against the arms race and Vietnam. *Dr. Strangelove* appeared in 1964. Robert Altman's 1970 *M*A*S*H*, with its Osterizer blend of black humor and stark horror, is a direct descendant of *Catch-22*. Ironically, that movie appeared the same year as Mike Nichols's film version of *Catch-22*. *M*A*S*H* is the better movie by far, but in a nice bit of irony, it propelled the novel—finally!—onto American best-seller lists.

When Heller died in December 1999, James Webb, the highly decorated Marine platoon leader, novelist (*Fields of Fire*), journalist, moviemaker, and now United States senator for Virginia, wrote an appreciation in *The Wall Street Journal*. Webb, a self-described Air Force brat, had first read and liked the novel as a teenager growing up on a Nebraska air base. He reread it in a foxhole in Vietnam in 1969, during a lull in fierce combat that took the lives of many of his men. One day, as he lay there feverish, insides crawling with hookworm from bad water, one of Webb's men began laughing "uncontrollably, waving a book in the air. He crawled underneath my poncho hooch and held the book in front of me, open at a favorite page.

"'Read this!' he said, unable to stop laughing. 'Read it!'"

Webb wrote, "In the next few days I devoured the book again. It mattered not to me that Joseph Heller was then protesting the war in which I was fighting, and it matters not a whit to me today. In his book, from that lonely place of blood and misery and disease, I found a soul mate who helped me face the next day and all the days and months that followed."

Soul mate. *Catch-22*'s admirers cross boundaries, ideological, generational, geographical. Daugherty relates a very funny anecdote about Bertrand Russell, the pacifist and philosopher. He had praised the book in print and invited Heller to visit him while in England. (Russell was then in his nineties.) When Heller presented himself at the door, Russell flew into a rage, screaming, "Go away, damn you!

Never come back here again!" A perplexed Heller fled, only to be intercepted by Russell's manservant, who explained, "Mr. Russell thought you said 'Edward Teller.'" The ideological distance between Jim Webb and Bertrand Russell can be measured in light-years. An author who reached both of them exerted something like universal appeal.

Returning to a favorite book, one approaches with trepidation. Will it be as good as one remembers it? Has it dated? As Heller's friend and fan Christopher Hitchens would say, "Has it time-traveled?" Any answer is subjective, but a fifty-year-old book that continues to sell 85,000 copies a year must be doing something right, time-travel-wise—even discounting the number assigned in the classroom.

I asked Salman Rushdie, another friend and admirer of Heller's, what he thought about the book all these years later.

"I think *Catch-22* stands the test of time pretty well," he replied, "because Heller's language-comedy, the twisted-sane logic of his twisted-insane world, is as funny now as it was when the book came out. The bits of *Catch-22* that survive best are the craziest bits: Milo Minderbinder's chocolate-coated cotton-wool, Major Major Major Major's name, and of course the immortal Catch itself ("it's the best there is"). The only storyline that now seems sentimental, even mawkish, is the one about 'Nately's whore.' Oh well. As Joe E. Brown said to Jack Lemmon, nobody's perfect."

A book resonates along different bandwidths as it ages. *Catch-22*'s first readers were largely of the generation that went through World War II. For them, it provided a startlingly fresh take, a much-needed, much-delayed laugh at the terror and madness they endured. To the Vietnam generation, enduring its own terror and madness, crawling through malarial rice paddies while pacifying hamlets with napalm and Zippo lighters, the book amounted to existential comfort and the knowledge that they were not alone. (Note, too, that *Catch-22* ends with Yossarian setting off AWOL for Sweden, which before becoming famous for IKEA and girls with dragon tattoos, was a haven for Vietnam-era draft evaders.)

As for *Catch*'s current readers, it's not hard to imagine a brave but frustrated American marine huddling in his Afghan foxhole, drawing sustenance and companionship from these pages in the midst of fighting an unwinnable war against stone-age fanatics.

Daugherty tells how Heller was required to take a barrage of psychological tests for a magazine job. (Fodder, surely, for an episode of *Mad Men.*) The color cards he was shown conjured in his mind terrible images of gore and amputated limbs. He mentioned to one of his examiners that he was working on a novel. One of them asked, *Oh, what's it about?* Joe wrote in his memoir forty years later, "'That question still makes me squirm."

There's a certain numerology about *Catch-22*: Yossarian, helpless and furious as the brass keep raising the number of missions he has to fly before he can go home. He's Sisyphus, with attitude. Then there's the title itself, a sort of algorithm expressing the predicament of the soldier up against an implacable, martial bureaucracy. For us civilians, the algorithm describes a more prosaic conundrum, that of standing before the soft-faced functionary telling us that he cannot register the car until we produce a document that *does not exist*. Bureaucracy, as Hannah Arendt defined it: the rule of nobody.

Roll credits. *Catch-22* is Joe Heller's book, but it did not arrive on the shelves all by itself. His literary agent Candida Donadio got the first chapter into the hands of Arabel Porter, editor of *New American Writing*; and then into the all-important hands of Robert Gottlieb at Simon and Schuster. Gottlieb, one of the great book editors of his day—he later became head of Alfred Knopf—played a critical role shaping the text. Daugherty describes how the two of them pieced together a jigsaw puzzle from a total of nine separate manuscripts; *Catch-22* seems to have been stitched together with no less care and effort than the Bayeux Tapestry. Their collaboration was astonishingly devoid of friction. Gottlieb is a genius, but Heller was an editor's dream, that rare thing—an author without proprietary sensitivity, willing to make any change, to (in Scott Fitzgerald's great phrase) murder any darling. As the work proceeded, it took on within the offices of Simon and Schuster "the aura of a Manhattan Project."

Nina Bourne at S&S was passionate about the book and promoted it relentlessly after it initially faltered, with a zeal that would induce a sigh of envy in any author's breast. The jacket design with the red soldier dangling like a marionette against a blue background became iconic. It was the work of Paul Bacon, himself another World War II veteran, who also designed the original covers for *Slaughterhouse-Five*, *Rosemary's Baby*, *One Flew Over the Cuckoo's Nest*, *Ragtime*, and *Shogun*.

It was a fertile time for letters. While Heller was conjuring Yossarian and Major Major Major and Milo Minderbinder and Chaplain Chapman and the other members of the 488 Bomb Squadron, J. P. Donleavy was writing *The Ginger Man*, Ken Kesey was at work on *Cuckoo's Nest*, Thomas Pynchon on *V*. Heller's good friend Kurt Vonnegut was banging away at *Cat's Cradle*.

Joseph Heller will forever be known as the author of *Catch-22*—and who wouldn't be happy to wear that laurel? But in the opinion of some, including Bob Gottlieb, it is not his best novel. According to this view, that garland belongs to *Something Happened*, Heller's dark and brilliant 1974 novel about the tragic office worker and family man Bob Slocum. The reviewer for *The New York Times* wryly observed that to film *Catch-22*, Mike Nichols assembled a fleet of eighteen B-25 bombers—in effect the world's twelfth-largest air force. To turn *Something Happened* into a movie, the reviewer ventured, would cost roughly nothing.

I put it to Joe once, after a martini or two: So, did he think *Something Happened* was a better book?

He smiled and shrugged. "Who can choose?"

American literature is deplorably replete with books that secured fame for their authors, but little fortune. Think of poor old Melville schlepping about the streets of Manhattan as a Customs inspector, having earned a lifetime profit of about $500 for *his* hyphenated masterpiece, *Moby-Dick*.

Joe made out rather better. Simon and Schuster paid him an advance of $1,500 (about $11,000 today). If the paperback royalties didn't make him rich, they certainly made him comfortable. The movie rights went for a tidy price, and larger paychecks lay ahead. Not bad for a kid who grew up poor in Coney Island. In fact, one might ask, *What's the catch?*

We became friends in his final years. I loved him. For someone who had flown sixty missions in a world war, who had endured a devastating, near-fatal illness (Guillain-Barré), who had gone through a rough and somewhat public divorce, Joe seemed to me a surprisingly joyous person. He sought joy, and seemed to find it often enough—in his myriad and devoted friends; in good food and dry martinis; in his wife, Valerie, his son, Ted, and his daughter, Erica, who has written a touching and frank account of growing up as an Eloise of the Apthorp apartment building in Manhattan.

In that book, *Yossarian Slept Here*, she writes, "When *Catch* was finally beginning to make a real name for itself . . . my parents would often jump into a cab at night and ride around to all of the city's leading bookstores in order to see that jaunty riot of red, white and blue and the crooked little man, the covers of 'the book,' piled up in towers and pyramids, stacked in all the nighttime store windows. Was anything ever again as much fun for either of them, I wonder?"

A few months before Joe died, I wrote him from the midst of a too-long book tour, in somewhat low spirits. His tough love and sharp-elbowed humor always yanked me back from the brink of acedia. This time there were no jokes, instead something like resignation.

"The life of a novelist," he wrote me, "is almost inevitably destined for anguish, humiliations, and disappointment—when you get to read the two chapters in my new novel I've just finished you will recognize why."

That book, *Portrait of the Artist, as an Old Man*, is a sad one, about a novelist who has had great success early on, only to have less in later years. It was published after Joe died.

So perhaps in the end, there always *is* a catch. But the one Joe Heller left us remains, even after all these years, the best catch of all.

—Introduction to the 50th Anniversary Edition, 2011

YOU THIEVING PILE OF ALBINO WARTS!

The Letters of Hunter S. Thompson, Volume II

"It's been a weird night," Hunter S. Thompson wrote to the CBS News correspondent Hughes Rudd one morning in 1973 as dawn was breaking over Owl Farm, his "fortified compound" in Woody Creek, Colorado, "and I've been dealing with a head full of something rumored to be LSD-25 for the past six hours, but on the evidence I suspect it was mainly that PCP animal tranq, laced with enough speed to KEEP the arms & legs moving. The brain is another question, I think, but I keep hoping we'll have it under control before long."

A great many of the letters in this, the second volume of a projected trilogy of the letters of the *monstre sacré* of American journalism, appear to have been written under various chemical influences in the wee small hours: "Cazart! It's 5:57 a.m. now & the Aspen FM station is howling 'White Rabbit'—a good omen, eh?"; "It's 6:37 now"; "Christ, it's 5:40 a.m." Sometimes the sun is halfway to the meridian before he reaches for the off button on his I.B.M. Selectric: "It's 10:33 in the morning & this is the longest letter I've ever written. It began as a quick note to wrap up loose ends."

This makes for some pretty electric reading, and for some not-so-electric reading. During the period covered in this collection, Thompson was a vital, deliriously erratic force in journalism, covering the turbulent 1968 Democratic National Convention in Chicago, the 1968 election of Richard M. Nixon, the 1972 campaign, Watergate, the falls of Nixon and Saigon. There are letters here to Tom Wolfe; Senator Eugene McCarthy; the Chicano lawyer Oscar Acosta (the inspiration for the "300-pound Samoan attorney" character in *Fear and Loathing in Las Vegas*); Charles Kuralt; Thompson's Random House editor, Jim Silberman; Warren Hinckle (then the editor of *Ramparts* magazine); the soon-to-be-elected-congressman Allard K. Lowenstein; Paul Krassner; Jann Wenner; the illustrator Ralph Steadman; Joe Eszterhas (then a reporter for the Cleveland *Plain Dealer*); Senator George McGovern; Gary Hart (then McGovern's campaign manager); Anthony Burgess; Patrick J. Buchanan (then a Nixon speechwriter); Robert Kennedy's former campaign press secretary Frank Mankiewicz; Garry Wills; Jimmy Carter (then a presidential candidate); Thompson's then-lawyer Sandy Berger, now the national security adviser; the movie director Bob Rafelson; the political prankster Dick Tuck; and the Merry Prankster Ken Kesey. That's a pretty good sampling of the folks who brought you the 1960s and '70s. This being an omnium-gatherum of the Thompsonian "gonzo" archive, there are also memorandums, drafts of book-jacket copy, and movie treatment outlines.

It's not surprising that so many of these letters are about what one of Thompson's early boosters, Tom Wolfe, once declared the great subject of American writers: money—in this case, the general lack of it and the desperate need for more. Thompson is always one step ahead of the Internal Revenue Service, the Diners Club, or a hornet-mad collection agency. Yet again, one is sadly reminded that writing an American classic—in this case, *Fear and Loathing in Las Vegas*—is no guarantee of financial security.

That book, which began as a series of articles in *Rolling Stone*, sold only about 18,000 copies in hardcover when it was published in 1972. "I find myself," Thompson wrote to his mother, "getting 'famous,' but no richer than I was before people started recognizing & harassing me almost everywhere I go." On the brighter side, a quarter century later finds Thompson still alive, despite a lifestyle that, if these letters are accurate, would surely have long ago brought down a milder constitution.

One of the things that made Thompson an "outlaw" hero to this reviewer's generation was the demonic zest of his invective and contumely. The DNA of Thompson's adjectival lexicon is made up of the following, often in sequence: *vicious*, *rancid*, *savage*, *fiendish*, *filthy*, *rotten*, *demented*, *treacherous*, *heinous*, *scurvy*, *devious*, *grisly*, *hamwit*, *foetid*, *cheapjack*, and *hellish*. Favorite gerunds and other verb forms of abuse include *festering*, *stinking*, *soul-ripping*, *drooling*, *rabbit-punching*, and *knee-crawling*, to say nothing of even more piquant expressions.

"You worthless . . . bastard," begins a mock-malevolent letter to his good friend Tom Wolfe, in response to a letter Wolfe wrote to him while on a lecture tour in Italy, "I just got your letter of Feb 25 from Le Grande Hotel in Roma, you swine! Here you are running around . . . Italy in that filthy white suit at a thousand bucks a day . . . while I'm out here in the middle of these . . . frozen mountains in a death-battle with the taxman & nursing cheap wine while my dogs go hungry & my cars explode and a legion of nazi lawyers makes my life a . . . Wobbly nightmare. . . . You decadent pig . . . you thieving pile of albino warts. . . . The hammer of justice looms, and your filthy white suit will become a flaming shroud!"

Reading Hunter Thompson is like using gasoline for aftershave—bracing. "His voice is sui generis," writes David Halberstam in the foreword. "It is not to be imitated, and I can't think of anything worse than for any young journalist to try to imitate Hunter."

So true. Thompson's maniac style—and pharmacology—made him a folk hero on college campuses about the time these letters were written. Garry Trudeau made him into the character Duke in "Doonesbury." (Trudeau is referred to here in a letter to Thompson's lawyer as "that dope-addled nazi cartoonist.")

Reading these letters does make one consider how relatively pallid our own times are, compared with the stomping mad epoch in which he wrote them. Assassinations, Vietnam, Nixon. Today's big issues are prescription drugs for the elderly and whither-the-Middle-East-peace-process.* An amphetamine-crazed, Wild Turkey–swilling Hunter Thompson on the press bus today would probably be put off at the first stop, as the British writer Will Self was a few years ago when he was discovered taking heroin aboard Prime Minister John Major's press plane. It's doubtful that Thompson's antics—setting fire to the door of the Jimmy Carter aide Hamilton Jordan's New York hotel room in 1976—would be looked on as merely scamp-

* This was written in December 2000.

ish by today's PC commissars. This isn't to suggest his antics didn't eventually wear thin—as anyone who ever sat through one of his college-lecture-circuit performances will tell you—but man was it fun at the time.

The question that lingers is, how much of it was actually *true*? How much of it was journalism, as opposed to something between "new journalism" and out-and-out fiction? The historian Douglas Brinkley, who edited these letters and has written a fine introduction, concludes, "It would be a mistake to claim that *Fear and Loathing in America* answers the question of whether Thompson writes fiction or nonfiction."

Hm. We find Thompson writing frantic letters to his lawyer Sandy Berger, threatening the Washington writer Sally Quinn and *Esquire* magazine with legal action because the magazine has published an excerpt from her book in which she quotes him saying, "at least 45 percent of what I write is true." He's a bit concerned what effect this might have on his employers. A few pages later, in a letter to Quinn, he writes that he usually tells people that *Fear and Loathing in Las Vegas* was "60 percent–80 percent" true, "for reasons that should be perfectly obvious." Earlier on, in a letter to Bill Cardoso of *The Boston Globe*, who had coined the term "gonzo journalism," he calls one of his own articles for *Scanlan's Monthly* "a classic of irresponsible journalism." The clincher comes in a letter to his Random House editor, in which he admits that the book "was a very conscious attempt to simulate drug freakout. . . . I didn't really make up anything—but I did, at times, bring situations & feelings I remember from other scenes to the reality at hand." He later wrote to the same editor, "I have never had much respect or affection for journalism."

One feels Brinkley's pain, but the reasonable reader is left to infer that Thompson's reportage had an . . . impressionistic element—for which his fans, including this one, are profoundly grateful. These untidy letters are welcome, showing us as they do a great American original in his lair. But a word of advice: If one of his peacocks or Dobermans comes at you, be very, very afraid.

—*The New York Times*, December 2000

RAY BRADBURY

In an episode of the hit TV show *Mad Men*, set in 1962, one of the characters is skeptical about a planned business trip to the West Coast. He asks his boss in a smug New York City way, "What's in L.A., anyway?"

The boss, Don Draper, played by Jon Hamm, smiles coolly: "The Jet Propulsion Lab? Ray Bradbury?"

It's a throwaway line, a fleeting tip of the hat by *Mad Men*'s creator Matthew Weiner to the ultimate Writer's Writer: Ray Douglas Bradbury, who, as I type these words, is one day shy of his eighty-ninth birthday here on Planet Earth. The middle name derives from Douglas Fairbanks, an idol of a different sort, from another era.

Ray Bradbury published his first short story in 1938, which means that he has been a working author for seventy-one years. He is a self-professed "sprinter" at the short story, rather than a "marathon runner" novelist. It is hard to think of a writer who has done more with the short story form than Ray Bradbury. According to his able biographer, Sam Weller (*The Bradbury Chronicles*, 2005), he has written one every week since he started. By my math, that comes to 3,640. The "Also by" page of a recently published book of his essays, *Bradbury Speaks*, lists thirty-two titles.

Many writers are prolific. What perhaps most distinguishes Ray Bradbury is his influence on other writers, to say nothing of his readers. In the pages of Mr. Weller's book, you'll find tributes from and friendships with a diverse group: Bernard Berenson, Christopher Isherwood, Aldous Huxley, Stephen King, Federico Fellini, François Truffaut (who managed *completely* to screw up the film version of *Fahrenheit 451*), John Huston (for whom Ray wrote the screenplay to his *Moby-Dick*), R. L. Stine, Buzz Aldrin (among dozens of astronauts), Walt Disney, John Steinbeck, Charles Laughton, Rod Steiger, the legendary editor Bob Gottlieb (who helped to shape many of these stories), Sam Peckinpah, and Steve Martin. I'll stop there, other than to say this is but a partial list of Ray Bradbury's fan club.

Glittery names, to be sure, but his influence runs even deeper. Literally, it occurs to me. Whenever I'm on a subway, I'm always curious to see what books—if any—kids are reading these days. And the two books that I routinely see teenagers reading, intently at that, are *Atlas Shrugged* and *Fahrenheit 451*. The next most-often-sighted book is *Dandelion Wine* (1957), which many Bradburians insist is his finest work.

Ray Bradbury has covered the world—indeed, universe—with his themes: small-town America, Mars, fantasy, horror, and science fiction. You could even go so far as to say that we live today in a world that was prefigured by Ray Bradbury. *Fahrenheit 451*, published in 1953, anticipated an age dominated by television, wall-sized plasma-screen TV, and even Sony Walkman–like devices. One of the most chilling stories in this collection, "The Veldt," published at the start of the TV era, today reads like an Elijah-like warning against surrendering ourselves to the false Edens of the vast wasteland and its bastard offspring, video games.

There are some ironies here in being warned against all this by one of the most famous writers of science fiction. (He prefers to be known as a writer of fantasy.) But few writers have a crater on the moon named for one of their books (Dandelion Crater, named by the crew of *Apollo 15*) or have consulted on the U.S. pavilion for a World's Fair, or on an EPCOT exhibit at Disney World. You'll learn in Weller's book that Ray was also the inspiration for the design of a number of leading—brace yourself—shopping malls in America. Then, of course, there's the Ray Bradbury Park in his hometown of Waukegan, Illinois. Bradbury is that rarity in America: the writer who has made his hometown unequivocally proud.

Any appreciation of him must begin in Waukegan, where a robotic stork or Martian obstetrician dropped him down the chimney on August 22, 1920. That was the year Prohibition began, the first commercial radio broadcast was made, Harding was elected, and F. Scott Fitzgerald married (don't do it, Scott!) Zelda. Other notable births that year: Isaac Asimov, America's most graphomaniacal sci-fi writer; and Alex Comfort, author of *The Joy of Sex*, a book that, like so many of Ray's, brought a whole lotta pleasure to a whole lotta people. In 2001, Ray told *Salon*: "Why would you clone people when you can go to bed with them and make a baby?"

The town Ray Bradbury grew up in is very much the Green Town of the *Dandelion Wine* stories. The very first story, "The Night," begins, "You are a child in a small town." And there you suddenly are, in a magical and often mystical world of grandparents and pie smells and fireflies and the bang of the screen door. *And there are things in the woods beyond.* Another story, "Farewell Summer," was originally included in *Dandelion Wine* but was cut. It's haunting. It will take you back to that summer in your own youth when you realized that it *wasn't* going to last, and that there were some seriously scary things out there beyond the woods.

"Grow up?" Ray commented once, after sadly watching a boy balk at entering a toy store in Sausalito. "What does that mean? I'll tell you: It doesn't mean anything."

There's a rare note of contempt in that statement, and it's telling. Ray Bradbury is a sunny, decent, loving, gregarious, generous man, both on the page (at least when he's not scaring the bejeezus out of you) and in person. The joyousness and zest that he brings to his work—even to the darker works—seem (to me, at least) to arise out of his eternal boyishness. Bradbury has no Inner Child, only an Outer one. On the page, he's Douglas (note the Fairbanksian name) Spaulding of the *Dandelion* stories. Douglas is a Huck Finn: prototypically Midwestern, a rule-breaker, adventurer, and dreamer. (Odd, come to think of it, that nowhere in the literature about Bradbury have I found a single reference to Twain. Perhaps it's not true, as Ray's fellow Illinosian Ernest Hemingway said, that "All modern American literature comes from one book by Mark Twain called *Huckleberry Finn*.") But to paraphrase Hemingway, all literature by Bradbury certainly comes from Buck Rogers, L. Frank Baum, Edgar Rice Burroughs, H. G. Wells, Jules Verne, Edgar Allan Poe, Sherwood Anderson, Herman Melville, John Steinbeck, William Butler Yeats, and of course Giovanni Virginio Schiaparelli.

Who?

Well, okay, I hadn't heard of him either: the nineteenth-century Italian astronomer who discovered the allegedly man-made channels on Mars (permanently mistranslated into English as "canals,"), providing Ray Bradbury with the inspiration for *The Martian Chronicles*.

Bradbury is perhaps the standout autodidact of late-twentieth-century American literature. His parents couldn't afford college during the Depression, so he hit the library—three days a week, for ten years. Libraries were his—to use the Spanish word—*querencia* ("loved place"—in bullfighting, the spot in the ring where the bull feels safe). He was haunted by the destruction of the Royal Library of Alexandria, by the thought of all those books, burning. That obsessive worry, coupled with memories of Hitler-era book burnings and the excesses of the McCarthy era, ultimately inspired his best-known work, *Fahrenheit 451*, set in a future where the firemen start fires.

He wrote that book in the stacks at the UCLA library, on rented typewriters, inserting dimes into slots for a half hour of typing time. Hugh Hefner, another fellow Illinosian, liked the manuscript so much that he serialized it in issues 2, 3, and 4 of his racy new magazine, *Playboy*. A half-century later, the phrase "Fahrenheit 451" has thoroughly permeated the language. Michael Moore filched it for his documentary about the Iraq war, later apologizing to an unflattered and unamused Bradbury. The danger—now—is of another kind. As he put it in 1979, "You don't have to burn books to destroy a culture. Just get people to stop reading them."

As he approaches his ninth decade, he remains a tireless and ardent voice for reading and libraries. Recently, *The New York Times* ran a page 1 story on his fund-raising efforts on behalf of the Ventura County Library. The *Times* photo shows him holding a sign that says APPLAUSE! (*Very* Bradburian). The caption: "I don't believe in colleges and universities. I believe in libraries." A few paragraphs down one comes across this: "Bo Derek is a really good friend of mine, and I'd like to spend more time with her." The story notes that a spokesperson for Ms. Derek confirmed that the two are friends, and said that Ms. Derek "would like to see some more of Mr. Bradbury, too." Also in the story is a red-hot diatribe against the Internet. Don't get him started on *that*.

"The Internet is a big distraction," Mr. Bradbury barked from his perch in his house in Los Angeles, which is jammed with enormous stuffed animals, videos, DVDs, wooden toys, photographs, and books, and other things like the National Medal of Arts sort of tossed on a table . . .

"Yahoo called me eight weeks ago," he said, voice rising. "They wanted to put a book of mine on Yahoo! You know what I told them? 'To hell with you. To hell with you and to hell with the Internet.'

"It's distracting," he continued. "It's meaningless; it's not real. It's in the air somewhere."

This is not the voice of a crank but that of a word lover who has spent his life creating stories about worlds far more exotic and wonderful than anything dreamed up by a video-game programmer or cyberfabulist. He's amusingly scathing on the subject of the blogosphere and Internet chat rooms. "Who do you want to talk to? All those morons who are living across the world somewhere? You don't even want to talk to them at home."

In 1995, he rather bravely told a college audience: "I don't understand this whole thing about computers and the superhighway. Who wants to be in touch with all of those people?" The answer now, fifteen years later, is: more or less everyone. How it will all play out is anyone's guess. My own is that Ray Bradbury is for the ages. He has been drawing people together for decades, by telling stories.

John Updike once said that the whole publishing process—printing, distribution, reviewing, promotion—was just a way of getting a book into the stacks of a small-town library somewhere slightly west of Kansas, where a teenage boy is looking for something to read.

That wasn't quite how it worked in my case. I was twelve or thirteen, about Doug Spaulding's age, clutching an illicitly obtained copy of *Playboy*. And here you may snort with derision, as you did when Mr. Clinton told us that he didn't inhale. But God's truth and pinky swear: what caught my attention wasn't Miss Whatevermonth but the cover line saying, "New Fiction by Ray Bradbury." It was the story about the time-traveling safari where you could go back and shoot a dinosaur—*so long as you stayed on the wooden walkway and didn't disturb anything*. I can still remember getting to the last paragraph and feeling the skin prickle at the back of my neck.

I got that same prickle rereading some of the stories in here. It seems to me ironic—to say the least—that someone with Bradbury's profoundly sunny disposition should be able to induce such gooseflesh. But take it from a far better source—Stephen King—who wrote in a memoir, "Without Ray Bradbury, there would be no Stephen King, at least as he grew. Bradbury was one of my nurturing influences, first in the EC comics, then in *Weird Tales*. . . . What was striking was how far down into the viscera he was able to delve in those stories—how far beyond the prudish stopped-point of his 1940s contemporaries. In that sense, Ray was to the horror story what D. H. Lawrence was to the story of sexual love."

Here's a paragraph, from "The Next in Line," in which a husband and wife tour the catacombs of Guanajuato and walk between two rows of mummified cadavers:

> *There was an embarrassment of horror. You started with the first man on your right, hooked and wired upright against the wall, and he was not good to look upon, and you went on to the woman next to him who was unbelievable and then to a man who was horrendous and then to a woman who was very sorry she was dead and in such a place as this.*

Do you hear an echo of Hemingway in there? A few pages on, there's an unmistakable echo of the original master of American horror, Edgar Allan Poe, as the cemetery's docent shows the horrified couple a case of premature burial:

> *Believe me, señor, rigor mortis pounds upon no lids. Rigor mortis screams not like this, nor twists nor wrestles to rip free nails, señor, or prise boards loose hunting for air, señor. All these others are open of mouth, sí, because they were not in-*

jected with the fluids of embalming, but theirs is a simple screaming of muscles, señor. This señorita, here, hers is the muerte horrible.

I myself have seen these grotesques in Guanajuato. Bradbury missed nothing; or as Poe might have put it, "caught all."

Turn, then, to "The Parrot Who Met Papa," one of the most delicious, inventive, and downright funny short stories anywhere, in which he channels—canals?—Hemingway and Poe again. This is Bradbury at his most antic: "The final Hemingway novel of all time! Never written but recorded in the brain of a parrot! Holy Jesus!"

Bradbury is a master at the ending that sucks your breath away, and in this he seems very much in the Maupassant/Saki/O. Henry tradition. As I sat down to reread the stories here, I found myself wondering how many of them had been adapted for TV's *The Twilight Zone*, whose amazing twist endings left my circa 1962 generation buzzing for days.

The answer, oddly, is only one. Bradbury sold "I Sing the Body Electric!" to Rod Serling, but Serling went back on his word that he wouldn't change it, and left out a key scene. Bradbury never quite forgave him. Later, Serling admitted having lifted parts of *The Martian Chronicles*, and apologized. One speculates: if there had been no Bradbury, would Rod Serling have come up with *The Twilight Zone*?

For a man who never flew on an airplane until he was sixty-two years old, and who has never had a driver's license, Bradbury has seen a bit of the world and returned with wonderful stories, especially here in "McGillahee's Brat," a story of an encounter with a beggar woman in Dublin. Therein lies—another—tale.

One of Bradbury's most famous short stories is "The Fog Horn." It came to the attention of the director John Huston, who invited him to come to Ireland with his family for seven months to write the screenplay for his adaptation of *Moby-Dick*. That tumultuous, not exactly fun experience is related in Ray's novel *Green Shadows, White Whale* (1992). Rereading "The Fog Horn," with the Huston–*Moby-Dick* connection in mind, one comes across an almost eerie number of Melvillian tropes within two paragraphs: "a cold November evening" . . . the ocean "rolls and swells a thousand shapes" . . . "the God-light flashing out from [the lighthouse]" . . . "They never came back, those fish, but don't you think for a while they thought they were in the Presence?"

Another fan of Ray Bradbury was Christopher Isherwood, the British expat lover of W. H. Auden, and L.A.-based mystic. Isherwood was a friend of Aldous Huxley and Gerald Heard; the three of them were early experimenters with LSD and mescaline. Weller's biography tells the story of Bradbury receiving a glowing, highbrow review of *The Martian Chronicles* from Isherwood. It was a welcome signal from the world of Serious Lit that they considered him no mere writer of pulp fiction.

Bradbury formed a friendship with Isherwood and Heard, and through them with Huxley, author of *Brave New World* and *The Doors of Perception* (the title, from William Blake, would later become the name of Jim Morrison's rock band). Heard was especially complimentary, telling Bradbury, "You're not a writer, you're a poet." Huxley and the others were at this point deeply into mescaline—under a doctor's supervision (personally, I always found it more fun *not* under a doctor's supervision). They tried to get the author of *The Martian Chronicles* to tune in, turn on, and drop out, dangling before him the prospect of marvelous and abundant perceptions. Bradbury demurred, telling the psychedelically inclined trio: "I don't want to have a lot of perceptions. I want to have one at a time. When I write a short story, I open the trapdoor on the top of my head, take out one lizard, shut the trapdoor, skin the lizard, and pin it up on the wall."

There are some quite amazing lizards in this collection, of every description. It's strange to consider that they all somehow sprang from the mind of a once-small boy from Waukegan, Illinois. That may be putting it a bit disingenuously. The boy from Waukegan moved to L.A. in his early teens. At the age of fourteen, he wrestled his roller skates away from Al Jolson (who'd purloined them for his onstage act). He got W. C. Fields's autograph one day outside the Paramount Studios. Fields told him, "There you are, you little son of a bitch." At about the same time, Bradbury persuaded a young and dapper George Burns to let him watch him do his radio broadcast. He sold newspapers on the street corner, got his first stories published in *Weird Tales* at half a cent a word. Years later, he was still in the same town, presenting an award to Steven Spielberg. And there in a corner of the room was George Burns. They hugged. An American story.

Spielberg said of Ray Bradbury that his "most significant contribution to our culture is showing us that the imagination has no foreseeable boundaries. . . . Today we need Ray Bradbury's gifts more than ever, and his stories have made him immortal."

Tributes from Stephen King and Steven Spielberg. One drools. As jacket quotes go, you really can't do better than that. Toward the end of Mr. Weller's biography, attempting to sum up this un-sum-upable man, he takes note of Bradbury's prodigious output. Bradbury's comment: "Every time I've completed a new short story or novel . . . I say to the mailbox, 'There, Death, again one up on you.'"

When he was twelve back in Illinois, he met at a circus a Mr. Electrico, who took the boy under his wing and told him, "Live forever!" Bradbury adopted that as a mantra, and here he is, all these years later, still living, still writing, still championing libraries and reading—leaving a little time, of course, for Bo Derek.

Literary immortality is tricky to predict. The author of *Moby-Dick* was all but forgotten until right about the time Ray Bradbury was born. But these hundred stories, only a sampling of the canon, surely amount to a miraculous legacy. Each one, whether about the young boy in Green Town or a heartbroken dinosaur or a mischievous animatronician or a man at war with his own skeleton or a homicidal infant or a grandmother who has gone up to her room quietly to die, comes from the heart of a man with a soul as big as the Mars Ritz.

"My job," he told college students in 1995, "is to help you fall in love."

So we did.

—Introduction to *The Stories of Ray Bradbury*,
Everyman's Library, 2010

TO-GA!

Has it really been almost thirty years since *Animal House* first filled the big screen? We grow old. The movie, on the other hand, hasn't aged a bit. "Double secret probation," "See if you can guess what I am now? I'm a zit! Get it?" and the immortal chant "To-ga, to-ga!" are classic, time-defying, laugh-out-loud moments encased in celluloid amber. I've watched the movie with my father, now eighty, and my son, fourteen; both were on the floor gasping for breath.

Comes now Chris Miller, Dartmouth Class of '63, who wrote the screenplay along with Harold Ramis and Douglas Kenney, to give us, as his subtitle demurely puts it, "the awesomely depraved saga" of Alpha Delta Phi, the fraternity whose bacchanals and outrages provided the inspiration for the movie, along with Ramis's and Kenney's own experiences of Greek life. (Not to be confused with Plato or Pythagoras.) Miller calls this book,* on its cover, "a mostly lucid memoir." It's unclear whether *lucid* is a typographical error. Miller may well have intended *lurid*.

His book is sophomoric, disgusting, tasteless, vile, misogynist, chauvinist, debased, and at times so unspeakably revolting that any person of decent sensibility would hurl it into the nearest Dumpster. I couldn't put it down. I make this self-indicting admission with all due trepidation, but there it is. For better or worse, this an utterly hilarious book.

Toga-wise, Miller's book is to *Animal House*, the movie, what *Caligula* is to Larry Gelbart and Burt Shevelove's *A Funny Thing Happened on the Way to the Forum*. There's enough radioactive material in here to shock everyone, and perhaps that's its strength: it's a nuclear bomb—and a dirty one at that—of political incorrectness.

It's hard to imagine this book being published in the 1980s or

* *The Real Animal House: The Awesomely Depraved Saga of the Fraternity That Inspired the Movie.*

'90s. That it's appearing now, at a time when HBO's hit series *Entourage*, a guy's version of *Sex and the City*, is playing, may indicate that some paradigm shift is under way. There seems to be some resurgent testosterone in the body cultural. Either that, or someone spilled a giant bottle of Old Spice over the country.

Animal House—the book—also manages somehow to be elegiac. How Miller accomplishes that is truly beyond me, but he does. By the end, he has you—depraved me, at any rate—almost sighing for the good old days. Polymorphously perverse it may have been, still it all sounds like it was a blast.

I seem to be digging myself in deeper. I hereby take back everything I have said so far. It's a disgusting, horrid, loathsome book. Miller should be ashamed. No—he should be executed. I issue a fatwa.

Normally, a reviewer quotes from the book. However, since there are very few sentences in these 321 pages that do not contain an obscenity or moral atrocity, we will not be quoting extensively from the text. The more's the pity, because Miller is a genuinely witty writer. He's also a crackerjack storyteller. Wince you may—and if you have any modesty, you should—but bored I guarantee you will not be.

There must be *something* quotable. How about:

"Doberman had crawled onto the hood of the hearse and licked the bugs off the windshield, explaining to Flea, who was driving, 'I just wanted to make sure you could see.'"

Or this description, right out of Jane Austen, of a fraternity brother:

"Rat's hair was short as a marine's, his belly hung over his belt, and he wore Dumptruck-type glasses, big with black rims. He'd gotten his name last week. *The Adelphian* naming thing had worked again—he resembled a big, bloated water rat, creeping out of some Amsterdam canal, dripping with stuff you didn't want to know about."

Or this touching moment, in which Pinto—I can't go into the derivation of his fraternity name—waxes nostalgic about the really good old days: "Pinto's eyes were starry, hearing about the 'oooold AD's,' as the brothers referred to their forebears. He loved these tales of a fabled, earlier time when the AD house was at some kind of crazed behavioral zenith and outrageous Adelphians strode the earth like depraved gods, doing whatever they felt like, and the good times never stopped." Given what Pinto and his brothers were doing in 1960, it beggars the imagination what deplorable antics their predecessors were up to; in fact, I don't *want* to know.

Anyone remember "norgling"? What a "double hogback growler" was? Sorry, can't explain that one, either. There are, on the other hand, a few relatively innocent terms, like the synonyms for breasts: *jehoshaphats*, *ba-boos*, *wazookies*, *ka-hogas*, and of course *gabongas*. The Inuit language contains—what?—seventeen different words for "snow"? The ADs had twice that many for "vomit." But vomiting is but one of the many bodily functions extensively, indeed, exhaustively explored in the pages of *The Real Animal House*.

Aside from drinking enough beer to fill Lake Erie, the great pursuit—indeed, holy grail—at AD house was losing one's virginity. Hard as it may be to believe today, back in the early 1960s this was still a problematic goal. These days only ten minutes elapse between "Hi, what's your name?" and "Oh God oh God oh God." When you compare the Adelphians of 1960 with the college kids in Tom Wolfe's novel *I Am Charlotte Simmons*, you realize what tremendous strides we've made in this field of endeavor.

In any event, the lucidly lurid—or luridly lucid—events depicted herein happened a long time ago, and it would be unfair to judge them by today's P.C. standards. This is a memoir, not a manifesto. Eisenhower was president, Doris Day was the cheesecake of record, and everyone was singing along to the Schaefer beer ads on TV. ("Schaefer is the one beer to have, when you're ha-ving more than one!") Up to now, I've thought of the jacket-and-narrow-tie-wearing youth of that era as "The Quiet Generation." No longer. There is nothing remotely "quiet" about Pinto, Otter, Coyote, Snot, Black Whit, Giraffe, Rat, or any of the other AD brothers, unless they're passed out facedown in the snow with the blood-alcohol content of an embalmed corpse.

However sick, depraved, and irredeemably gross, the animal house of Dartmouth 1960 produced a writer who became a leading voice at *National Lampoon*, the magazine that shaped and defined the comic sensibility of its generation. He then went on, with one of his colleagues, Douglas Kenney (who died tragically in 1980), to write a movie that accomplished the same thing cinematically, as well as to inaugurate the movie careers of John Belushi, Tom Hulce, Peter Riegert, Karen Allen, and others.

No mean feats. And to think it all began with power-booting (don't ask) in the basement and watching brother Seal—a model for the movie's Bluto Blutarsky, played by Belushi—pour a giant jar of mustard over his head and crawl around on all fours on the dance floor, biting girls on the bottom. Now we know. As the plaque on the statue of the founder of Faber College in the movie says, "Knowledge Is Good."

—*The New York Times*, November 2006

REVIEWS IN BRIEF: DIANA BOOKS

That'll Be Ten Pounds, by Earl Spencer. Diana's brother reveals that just before her death she told him that if anything happened to her he should build a gift shop at Althorp, the family estate, so he "wouldn't ever have to do an honest day's work." He writes, "We spent many happy hours together deciding how much to charge for souvenir mugs and T-shirts." He hopes to be able to accommodate three times as many visitors next year, but complains that the local council authorities "are being damned shortsighted about the need for more public loos."

First serial: Country Life; *author tour.*

Chicken Soup for the Diana-Lover's Soul: 101 Inspirational Stories to Make the Authors of the Chicken Soup Series Even Richer Than They Already Are, edited by Jack Canfield. This collection, seventy-eighth in the successful series, inclues a wide range of heartwarming stories: a teenage boy learns to channel his anger into more positive pursuits after being sent to prison for stomping on a few freesias that were lying outside Kensington Palace not doing anybody any good anyway; a rich, aimless woman finds the fulfillment that eludes her in marriage by going on "the mother of all shopping sprees"; a businessman, moments before his car plows head on into the Arc de Triomphe, hears empty Pernod bottles rattling around in the front seat next to the chauffeur and decides to buckle his seat belt.

One Spirit Book Club main selection.

Royal Warrant, by Mohammed al-Fayed. The author, father of Dodi, claims to have "solid evidence"—never quite specified—that his son and the princess were murdered by MI6, the British Secret Service, on orders from the Royal Family. Al-Fayed alleges that the Windsors wanted to avoid paying the £327 million in charges at Harrods—which he owns—that Diana accumulated during her marriage to Charles. "They are cheap, very cheap," he writes, "*always* coming in asking for reductions." The chapter about how Mossad, the Israeli intelligence agency, was responsible for the mad-cow-disease epidemic in Britain seems somehow off the point here.

Film rights to Oliver Stone.

Thanks a Bunch, Luv, by Camilla Parker Bowles. A remarkably candid memoir by the infamous third person in the marriage between Prince Charles and Diana, in which she confesses to "mixed feelings at best" about the events of last August. Parker Bowles was on the verge of being accepted by the British public as the prince's consort when the accident occurred, postponing an open liaison, perhaps indefinitely. (According to a not very nice recent poll, 90 percent of Britons wish it had been Parker Bowles in the tunnel with an Egyptian playboy instead of Diana.) Taking pains to be polite, the author notes that "Diana wasn't quite as dim as everyone said," and even compliments the late princess on her "rather neat" handwriting.

Liberté, Égalité, DNA, by Barry Scheck. Scheck, the lawyer who helped acquit O. J. Simpson, was hired by the family of Henri Paul, the chauffeur who was driving on the night Diana was killed. They were convinced that the autopsy results showing that Paul's blood-alcohol limit was three times the legal limit had been doctored to deflect blame from the real culprit: the LAPD detective Mark Fuhrman. Scheck obtained an order to exhume Paul's body from a cemetery in Brittany. His conclusion: "He didn't look drunk to me."

First Serial: Vanity Fair.

"Looking at Myself in the Mirror": Celebrities Talk About Where They Were When They Heard the News, by the editors of *US Magazine*. The title, from Donald Trump's answer, pretty much explains the basic idea. Trump calls Diana a "world-class princess," and says that he and Diana were "really, really close," despite the fact that they spent only a few minutes together, in a Plaza Hotel elevator. "The real tragedy," he says, "is that she never got to experience the Royal Suite at the Taj Mahal casino." Calista Flockhart wept because Diana would never get to see the "Baby Chacha" episode on *Ally McBeal*. And Tom Cruise fondly remembers meeting Diana after an Elton John concert and telling her "how amazing it was that so many letters of her name appeared in the word *Dianetics*," the philosophy of the Scientologist L. Ron Hubbard.

—*The New Yorker*, September 1998

YOURS EVER, PLUM

The Letters—and Life of P. G. Wodehouse

I visited Christopher Hitchens in hospital just after he'd been given a diagnosis of mortal illness. By his bed I noticed a dog-eared Jeeves and Wooster paperback. Christopher esteemed P. G. Wodehouse above all other writers as "The Master," a title originally bestowed on Wodehouse by another master of English prose, Evelyn Waugh.

Christopher looked at the novel. His face clouded. "I worried about bringing it," he said, "because I thought—*what if it doesn't work*?" The prospect of a Jeeves novel failing to work its magic was the only time in our thirty-year-long friendship that I saw him register something close to genuine alarm. The last time I saw Hitch, three days before he died in another hospital after his eighteen-month battle with cancer, he had on his lap an early British edition of this very book, Sophie Ratcliffe's *P. G. Wodehouse: A Life in Letters.*

Ratcliffe, a tutor at Christ Church, Oxford, has given us a monumental, exemplary book, excellent in every regard and indispensable to a three-dimensional understanding of one of English literature's great figures. Many of the letters are published here for the first time. It is a worthy companion to Robert McCrum's splendid 2004 biography.

It was said of Gibbon, author of *Decline and Fall of the Roman Empire*, that he lived out his sex life in his footnotes. The footnotes here are often eye-poppingly fun. We learn, among much else, that Wodehouse was descended from Anne Boleyn's sister, Lady Mary, as in *The Other Boleyn Girl*. (He was also related to Cardinal Newman.) Also that a previous recipient of the Twain medal Wodehouse is about to get went to—Benito Mussolini. (Who knew Il Duce was such a wag?) In another, we hear that in 1941 the Queen Mother ordered eighteen books for little Princess Elizabeth, the present queen, all of them by Wodehouse.

Letters are a kind of BACKSTAGE ALL ACCESS pass. We get the man—or woman—with hair down and no makeup. They often provide the ultimate in dish. One mourns the almost certain extinction of the genre. Future collections of e-mails and text messages of the great and famous aren't likely to be quite this satisfying.

Let's stipulate, too, that the bitchier the personality (Waugh, or Gore Vidal, Truman Capote, etc.), the deeper the dish. Alas, Pelham Grenville Wodehouse—his lifelong nickname was Plum or Plummie—was one of Nature's most gentle specimens: humble, self-deprecating, shy of publicity, considerate to a fault, generous, devoted to his family and friends, forgiving and deplorably lacking in bile—qualities that ought make for pretty damn dull letter reading. To be sure, some of these pages are more scintillating than others, but there's plenty of ginger and plenty of dish, and a lot of it is—no surprise—hilariously observed.

And golly, what a life! In terms of American history, Wodehouse was born in 1881, the year of the gunfight at the OK Corral, and died (on Valentine's Day) in 1975, the year the Vietnam War ended. Rather a lot went on in between.

He became world-famous by his thirties, both as a novelist and Broadway lyricist. He collaborated with, among others, Guy Bolton, Ira Gershwin, and Cole Porter. As a young hustling writer in New York, he banged out copy for the *Saturday Evening Post*, *Vanity Fair*, and *Collier's*. His signature valet, Jeeves, made his debut in the *Saturday Evening Post* in 1915 in a short story titled "Extricating Young Gussie." Jeeves's name was borrowed from a Warwickshire cricket player.

The late 1920s found him in Hollywood ("This place is loathesome"), drowning, stingless, in MGM honey, while doing hack work on a silly Marion Davies vehicle. His descriptions of reptilian studio fauna make for delicious reading. He mostly ignored them and beavered away at his own stuff, producing a novel and nine short stories.

His error was being candid in an interview with the *Los Angeles Times* in which he declared that over the past year, he'd been paid "$104,000 for loafing." (This was a fair bit of pelf: more than $1 million today.) Such frankness did not sit well with the *lares et penates* of the studio, and in due course the faucets ceased their golden gush. He couldn't have cared less. All one really needs in life, he said in one of the letters here, are two good friends, books, and a Pekingese. He might have added: his wife, Ethel, and—most of all—work.

With respect to the last item on the list, Wodehouse was graphomaniacal, churning out stories, novels, and librettos at a dizzying rate. He did boast a bit about that in his letters, but he was rightly proud of his output: 40,000 words of a novel in two weeks; an 8,000-word golf story in two days. In a letter to the satirical novelist Tom Sharpe, he reveals that he wrote the last twenty-six pages of *Thank You, Jeeves* in one day. It wasn't the money, although like, oh, 99.99 percent of writers, he certainly did care about the dough. But it was simply that he *had*—always—to be writing.

"As long as I'm working I feel all right, but in between stories it's rotten." Fortunately for him—and for us—there weren't many "in between" periods. He was the Energizer Plummie. By the 1930s he was one of the highest-earning writers in the world; only to find himself in scalding hot water with the tax man. He had unwisely entrusted his business affairs to an incompetent friend. Wodehouse's Achilles heel was naiveté, though you *could* call it innocence.

Here the story takes a rather rum turn. In 1940 he and Ethel were tax exiles living in Le Touquet, France. Wodehouse paid insufficient attention to the howling winds of war and rumble of tanks. He wasn't entirely oblivious, but there was the matter of Wonder the Peke and the other dogs, who couldn't be taken across the Channel to England, where the quarantine laws were so strict. One murmurs as one reads: *Dude—lose the Pekes!* Too late. In due course, Hitler was pounding on the front door.

Wodehouse was sent to an intern camp—formerly a lunatic asylum—in Tost, Upper Silesia. (It *would* have to be called Tost.) He remarked in a radio broadcast (about which, more anon, alas), "If this is Upper Silesia, I would hate to see Lower Silesia."

It was just Wodehouse being Wodehouse, but the japery becomes less amusing when one learns that Upper Silesia was home as well to Auschwitz. He was of course unaware of that god-awful fact, as indeed he was of most of what was going on in the world, but his naïveté—innocence—was so profound that at times it comes off as a sort of geopolitical Asperger's.

He became an unwitting pawn of the Nazi propaganda machine, agreeing to make five shortwave broadcasts to America on what might as well have been called Radio Goebbels. The unfortunate technicality for him was that the broadcasts could also be heard in Britain, which opened him up to charges of propaganda mongering. The tone and content was typically lighthearted, bemused, and nonpolitical, but the world was not laughing along, and soon the once-beloved author was a figure of revulsion and obloquy in his own country. Such was his innocence, believe it or not, that he cabled to Hollywood to alert his great friend Maureen O'Sullivan, "Jane" of Tarzan fame and later known as Mia Farrow's mom, about the impending broadcasts, just so she wouldn't miss them. Oh, *dear*.

Among those who howled for his head on a pike were A. A. Milne, creator of Pooh and Tigger, and somewhat more consequentially, Winston Churchill. Among his defenders were Dorothy Sayers, Compton MacKenzie, George Orwell, and Malcolm Muggeridge, the young British intelligence officer sent by MI6 after liberation to debrief Wodehouse and decide if he should be prosecuted for war crimes.

Muggeridge became a great and true friend. On one visit, he brought along a writer named George Orwell, who took up Wodehouse's case. Orwell pointed the finger of shame at the British left for making a whipping boy out of Wodehouse for the crime of being identified with aristocratic nincompoops. The irony there was rich indeed, for Wodehouse was singularly devoid of English snobbism and class-consciousness, a trait that made him such a natural adopted American. As Ratcliffe asserts, he was the first truly Anglo-American author.

The broadcasts scandal cast a pall over much of the remainder of his life. Mutatis mutandis, it was to Wodehouse what the Queensbury libel suit was to Oscar Wilde—ruinous and life-altering. He never again set foot on British soil for fear of prosecution; but unlike the self-doomed Wilde, he pulled up his socks, spat on both palms, and went back to work—not that he'd ever stopped. He wrote three novels and countless short stories while a guest of the Reich.

He was cleared of treason by MI5 and MI6, both of which had swiftly concluded that he was simply a political naïf whose only crime was deplorable judgment. But—damningly—the document attesting to his innocence remained under seal until 1965; and was made public only in 1980, five years after his death. Shame, Britannia!

Once his usefulness as a tool had ended, the Nazis moved him in 1943 from Berlin to occupied Paris, along with Ethel and Wonder the Peke. Paree was rather less than gay. In a letter written after the city's liberation, during which 1,500 resistance fighters were killed, he wrote: "It was all very exciting, but no good to me from a writing point of view." His aloofness can at times be frustrating.

In 1921, during the national emergency in Britain, he wrote, "This darned coal-strike is a nuisance." But as Ratcliffe avers, "Political events were marginal to his imaginative life—the imperative was to avoid disturbance of any kind." Plum. Just. Didn't. Get. It. But the twentieth century could be insistent and hard to ignore.

After liberation, he was arrested by the suspicious French, who were now in a froth of Jacobinical *épuration* (purification), rounding up and shooting collaborators and shaving the heads of women who'd dallied with *les Boches*. He was sent to a harsh transit camp outside Paris that the previous Vichy government had used to process French Jewry on their way to Auschwitz and other charnel houses. They were, *ça va sans dire*, unperturbed by this inconvenient historical detail.

They put him in detention in a—maternity ward. Thus the great comic writer began World War II in a lunatic asylum and ended it amid squalling French newborns. You can't make this stuff up. His treatment there was harsh enough that even his old nemesis Churchill was moved to suggest that "the French are overdoing things about P. G. Wodehouse."

Eventually the French did what they do so well, which is to say, shrug, and released him. He and Ethel found digs two doors down from the ghastly, celebrated Nazi sympathizers the Duke and Duchess of Windsor. Wodehouse wrote to a friend with bemusement, "no doubt [they'll] be dropping in all the time." They didn't; too bad—it might have made for a good letter or two.

His name might stink back in Old Blighty, but he was still P. G. Wodehouse, creator of Jeeves and Bertie, Lord Emsworth, the Empress of Blandings, Ukridge and Psmith, and he was still beloved. Friends and admirers from all over sent letters and packages, among them Plum's old collaborator Ira Gershwin. Wodehouse wrote to a friend:

> *There is a mysterious Arab gentleman who calls from time to time with offerings. He has just come and fixed us up with a great chunk of mutton. And a rabbit! Also a Dane (unknown to me) has sent us an enormous parcel, the only trouble being that all the contents are labeled in Danish, so we don't know what they are. There are three large tins which I hold contain bacon, but Ethel, who is in a pessimistic mood today owing to a bad night, says that they are stuff for cleaning floors. But surely even the most erratic Dane wouldn't send us stuff for cleaning floors.*

He and Ethel eventually found their way out of France to America, a process so complicated and prolonged that it makes Ingrid Bergman and Paul Henreid's escape from Casablanca seem like a whiz through the EZ Pass lane. They arrived in New York on the SS *America*, along with fellow passenger Mary Martin of future *Peter Pan* fame.

Wodehouse had fallen in in love with America on his first visit in 1904, an experience he described as "like being in heaven without having to go to all the bother and expense of dying." He became a citizen in 1955 and spent the balance of his formerly hectic life in relative peace and quiet in Remsenburg, Long Island, where he banged out novel after novel, did his Daily Dozen exercises and six-mile walk, cuddled with his Pekes, quietly despaired of the coarseness of modern culture (while writing for *Playboy*), and became addicted to soap operas. His special favorites were *The Edge of Night* and *The Secret Storm*. He declared *The Dick Van Dyke Show* "the best thing on TV."

In his final years, he received two great honors: a wax likeness in Madame Tussaud's and a knighthood from the queen, who as a young girl had steeped in his novels. The knighthood was bestowed *in absentia*. It came too late. Not that he wasn't tickled by this *vernissage*—or perhaps more bemused—but for the most part he was really past caring.

To his publisher, a chap with the—as the Hitch would surely put it—unimprovable name of J. D. Grimsdick, he wrote:

> *I am trying to decide whether I would advise a young man to become a knight. The warm feeling it gives one in the pit of the stomach is fine, but oh God those interviewers. They came round like flies, and practically all of them half-wits. I was asked by one of them what my latest book was about. "It's a Jeeves novel," I said. "And what is a Jeeves novel?" he enquired. Thank goodness they have left me now, including the one who printed, "I don't understand why authors receive knighthoods," when I said refuse knighthoods. Alters the sense a bit, what?*

Walk into any bookstore these days and one finds yard upon yard of Wodehouse, much of it in fresh editions. Why is he so imperishable, fresh as a Wooster boutonnière, when so many other writers of his generation have vanished, long since past their sell-by date? A writer with an eye to literary immortality would do well to consider the Wodehousean oeuvre.

It's not rocket science. The Master revealed the secret himself in a 1935 letter to Bill Townend, his old Dulwich school chum and the recipient of most of the letters here. It was a question, he said, of "making the thing frankly a fairy story and ignoring real life altogether." Wodehouse's admirer and defender Evelyn Waugh framed it perfectly; or as Jeeves might say, quoting Plautus, *Rem acu tetigisti*. ("You have hit the nail on the head.")

In an appreciation of Wodehouse in 1939—a year before the fateful arrival of the German army in Le Touquet—Waugh observed of Wodehouse's characters:

> *We do not concern ourselves with the economic implications of their position; we are not skeptical about their quite astonishing celibacy. We do not expect them to grow any older, like the Three Musketeers or the Forsytes. We are not interested in how they would 'react to changing social conditions' as publishers' blurbs invite us to be interested in other sagas. They are untroubled by wars [. . .] They all live, year after year, in their robust middle twenties; their only sickness is an occasional hangover. It is a world that cannot become dated because it has never existed.*

That last sentence nails it: Jeeves and Wooster, Lord Emsworth, Psmith, and the rest inhabit an alternative universe, Platonically apart from any real one. In Bertie's world, the most formidable menace is an inheritance-controlling, match-making aunt. (Not, mind you, that this species *isn't* terrifying.)

"I sometimes feel," Wodehouse wrote Townend in 1933, "as if I were a case of infantilism. I seem mentally so exactly as I was then [at school]. All my ideas and ideals are the same. I still think the Bedford [cricket] match is the most important thing in the world."

A decade later, he was writing to Townend after his release from the internment camp, where he had lost sixty pounds and where conditions were such that some of the other internees committed suicide: "Camp was really great fun." Such blitheness might just be unique in the annals of internment camp literature. And Wodehouse might just be the only English writer who appears to have enjoyed every single moment of boarding school. *That's* aloofness.

But as Ratcliffe notes, the tone of the letter, and indeed of the five fatal broadcasts, was "typically Wodehousian. From Dulwich days onwards, the notion of mentioning hardship was, for him, the ultimate in 'bad form.' In times of crisis, cheerfulness was seen as a vital, even patriotic, virtue."

That insight is well on display today on this side of the herring pond, in the recent profusion of refrigerator magnets embossed with the British war slogan: KEEP CALM AND CARRY ON. Wodehouse certainly did that. One of his greatest literary heroes—along with Kipling and Conan Doyle—was W. S. Gilbert, author of the refrain, "For he is an Englishman."

In 1960, on the occasion of Wodehouse's eightieth year, tributes poured in from the high priests of English literature: W. H. Auden, Nancy Mitford, James Thurber, Lionel Trilling, John Updike. Waugh laid a garland eloquent of Wodehouse's immortality: "Mr. Wodehouse's idyllic world can never stale. He will continue to release future generations from captivity that may be more irksome than our own. He has made a world for us to live in and delight in."

What fun, then, in light of that aperçu, to find Wodehouse in these pages writing in 1946 to Compton MacKenzie (author of *Whisky Galore*) from glum, postwar Paree, fretting over the reception of his next Jeeves novels in America: "I think they're all pretty funny, but, my gosh, how obsolete!" As Jeeves might respond after softly clearing his throat, *With all respect, sir, I might incline to an alternative view?*

In the final pages of this narrative hybrid of letters and biography, Wodehouse himself seems not entirely unaware of his future durability. One letter contains a lovely rumination on the subject of "the knut." What on earth, you ask, is a "knut"? Well, Bertie Wooster was a knut, par excellence: a second son of an earl or other nobleman, equipped with a monthly allowance providing a perfectly happy, if somewhat pointless existence.

"Like the lilies of the field," Wodehouse writes of the knut and his ilk, "they toiled not neither did they spin, they just existed beautifully . . . Then the economic factor reared its ugly head. Income tax and super tax shot up like rocketing pheasants, and . . . Algy had to go to work."

And so ended a nifty, golden era. "It is sad to reflect," he adds, "that a generation has arisen which does not know what spats were." There is not one speck, not one nanogram of irony in that statement.

He closes that letter on a hopeful, which is to say, quintessentially Wodehousian note:

But I have not altogether lost hope of a revival of knuttery . . . the heart of Young England is sound. Dangle a consignment of spats before his eyes, and the old fires will be renewed. The knut is not dead, but sleepeth. When that happens, I shall look my critics in the eye and say, "Edwardian? Where do you get that Edwardian stuff? I write about life as it is lived today."

Couldn't have put it so well myself, sir. Will there be anything else?

—*Newsweek/The Daily Beast*, December 2012

REVIEWS IN BRIEF: NEW LINCOLN BOOKS

According to the *The Washington Post*, about sixteen thousand books have been written about Abraham Lincoln, whose two hundredth birthday we celebrate this week. Several thousand more are coming out this week, among them:

Team of Weevils, by Samantha Ort. Ort, author of several revisionist books, including *Churchill the Tyrant* and *Hitler, Peacemaker*, posits that Lincoln's cabinet was actually a hotbed of back-stabbing, name-calling, and even, on one occasion, a shoving match that left Treasury Secretary Salmon P. Chase with a bloodied nose after he called War Secretary Edwin Stanton a "hemorrhoid-faced poltroon." Navy Secretary Gideon Welles broke up the fight by threatening to dispatch an ironclad to bombard Stanton's house. Ort writes: "The real civil war was taking place not on the killing fields of Virginia, but on the ground floor of the White House." Her assertion that Lincoln was "passed out drunk" during cabinet meetings may cause some grumbling in certain quarters.

Mary Quite Contrary, by Herbert Donald David. David, author of twenty-seven books of Lincolniana, now says that there is "persuasive evidence" that Mary Todd Lincoln was in fact a man. "If you look closely at the photographs," David writes, "it's *way* obvious. The face, the hands, they couldn't possibly have been those of a woman. The intriguing part is how she was able to conceal the fact from her husband all those years." Intriguing, indeed. David asserts that the Lincoln children, Tad and Willie, were actually born to a Danish housekeeper named Hagnar, whom "Mary"—whose birth name was allegedly Obadiah—was at pains to keep out of sight.

Dream of the Father, by William Smuntz. Smuntz, who was physically ejected from the American Genealogical Society in 2002 for his monograph proposing that George W. Bush is related to Albert Einstein, now says there is "overwhelming" evidence that President Barack Obama is a direct lineal descendant of Abraham Lincoln. Citing the conveniently only-recently unearthed memoirs of a White House gardener, he claims that Lincoln had an affair with "a fetching and willing" upstairs housemaid named Merrie Christmas. In this telling, Lincoln was "at a low point, both in the progress of the war and in his personal life, having just discovered that his wife was in fact a man," and thus "sought solace in the arms of the comely and willing Merrie." When Merrie became pregnant, Lincoln's secretary John Hay quietly arranged for her to be sent to Kenya, but said presciently, "I suspect this will not be the last of it."

No crop of Lincoln books would be complete without yet another version of the assassination. So comes Wilmot Dimwiddle's expansive, five-volume *Sic Semper*.

Somewhat boiled down, Dimwiddle's thesis is that Lincoln, bored "out of his gourd" by the play *Our American Cousin*, was scratching the back of his head with his own .44-caliber derringer when it went off accidentally. Dimwiddle asserts that John Wilkes Booth had snuck into Lincoln's box to congratulate him personally on winning the war and freeing the slaves. When the gun went off, Booth's "acting instincts spontaneously took hold of him, like a sudden fever." Realizing this could be "the role of a lifetime," he pulled out his knife, carved Major Rathbone "like a Thanksgiving turkey, and leapt onto the stage, spouting Latin." Dimwiddle even goes so far as to allege that Booth, "an early proponent of Method Acting, broke his leg on purpose, knowing that this would give his performance extra authenticity."

—*The Daily Beast*, February 2009

OUR MAN IN HAVANA

I first read *Our Man in Havana* in my teens and ever since have recalled it as being kind of a hoot: the hapless protagonist Wormold, recruited by the British Secret Service, sends London diagrams of the vacuum cleaners that he sells for a meager living, resulting in high-comic mayhem. Fun stuff.

So I was surprised, on returning to the novel after all these years, to find it rather darker than I had remembered. The basic premise remains hilarious, if perhaps less so in the era of "Curveball," the supposed Iraqi intelligence "asset" who managed to convince our government that there were abundant Weapons of Mass Destruction to be found in Iraq.

The novel's atmospherics are intense, the characters vividly morose or menacing. I dare you not to wince when Wormold's only friend, the forlorn Dr. Hasselbacher, reveals what happened to him in the trenches in the First World War; or not to squirm when Captain Segura (nickname: "The Red Vulture") explains the difference between the "torturable" and "untorturable" classes. So what I had remembered as comedy, one of Greene's "entertainments," turned out to be quite grim. When I came across Greene's own description of the novel as "light-hearted comedy," I wasn't sure quite what to think, but then Greene himself remains a slippery character: you never quite know when he's pulling your leg or up to mischief.

If *Our Man* seems darker now, it is almost eerily undated, no small compliment for a book first published in the waning years of the Eisenhower administration. In its adumbration of the coming conflict between the superpowers over Cuba, it was bizarrely prescient. Within three years of the book's publication, the world was nearly turned to cinders because of missile silos planted amid the Cuban verdure. Not much comedy there.

Few novels become everyday phrases. "Catch-22" has entered the language to such an extent that one uses it all the time, usually to describe an encounter with some agency of municipal government. "Our Man in [blank]" is not quite as common, but one hears it often enough. When I worked at the White House, various people in our embassies were pointed out to me—wink, wink—as "Our Man in [Moscow, Paris, etc.]." It is also one of those rare novels that went on to become a movie, an opera, *and* a play. I'm surprised that my eighteen-year-old son isn't playing an "Our Man in Havana" game on his Xbox.

If you've seen the movie, made only a year after the novel came out, you may find it impossible not to hear Alec Guinness's voice rising up at you from the pages. Guinness's quiet monotone is deceptive, for it contains a vast emotional diapason; it's like listening to tapes of whale sounds, slowed down, and discovering that enormous vocabularies are being deployed. Guinness was as perfect a Jim Wormold as Michael Caine was a Thomas Fowler in the 2002 remake of *The Quiet American*: two of England's finest actors in roles created by England's finest twentieth-century novelist (a distinction he shares with his fellow Catholic convert Evelyn Waugh).

For Americans, Greene remains problematic. To put it bluntly, he despised us. *Really* despised us. (As indeed did Waugh.) His anti-Americanism is muted here, but you can see the periscope poking through the surface. We might just as well relax and live with it. Ones doesn't read Greene to have our sense of American exceptionalism validated. We read him because he was an incomparable writer who heard the beating of the human heart like few others, and because he was possessed of what Hemingway called the writer's most indispensable tool, "a first-rate s— detector." Fowler understood that America's anti-Communist crusade in Vietnam was doomed from the start, and to boot, pernicious; in Havana, Wormold understands that America has thrown in on the wrong side. Within months of the publication of *Our Man*, the foul Batista regime and its Captain Seguras were casting off from the dock and headed to Miami in a flotilla that has held American electoral politics hostage ever since.

Toward the end of the novel, Wormold tells his secretary, Beatrice, "I don't care a damn about men who are loyal to the people who pay them, to organizations. . . . I don't think even my country means all that much. There are many countries in our blood, aren't there, but only one person. Would the world be in the mess it is if we were loyal to love and not to countries?" Fair question; still, I wonder what King Priam, whose kingdom was brought down over loyalty to love, might have to say.

Later Beatrice introduces the hoary old moral equivalence argument that we used to hear from the left during the Cold War: "But they [NATO, SEATO, and other international organizations] don't mean any more to most of us than all the other letters, U.S.A. and U.S.S.R." *All the other letters?* Really, Mr. Greene. Given his public record of discerning no moral difference between the United States and the nation that came up with the Gulag Archipelago, it's no small leap to venture that Beatrice's views are a proxy for the man who put these words in her mouth.

In real life, Greene notoriously defended Kim Philby, a traitor of Judas Iscariot dimension. Greene's championing of Fidel Castro also goes down the gullet hard. As I type these words, fifty-one years into the Castro dictatorship, the papers relate the death of Orlando Zapata Tamayo, who starved himself in prison after seven years' captivity for the crime of "disrespecting authority." If Greene were alive today, he'd be cheering on Hugo Chavez, the latest minatory clown in the Tropic of Cancer.

But I come to praise, not to bury. *Our Man in Havana* is a great book: for its plot, its characters, and, despite my cavils, for its rendering of the uncomfortable moral ambiguities that it lays on the bar before us, along with the copious daiquiris. And—yes—for its humor, which if not exactly lightheartedly comic, tickles the funny bone deep within.

Wormold's recruiter Hawthorne, played to tight-assed British perfection in the movie by Nöel Coward, provides him with a copy of *Lamb's Tales from Shakespeare*, for his code work. "It was the only book I could find in duplicate except *Uncle Tom's Cabin*." Back in London, Hawthorne's superior at MI6 tells him that he has great expectations of Wormold: "I believe we may be on to something so big that the H-bomb will become a conventional weapon."

"Is that desirable, sir?"

"Of course it's desirable. Nobody worries about conventional weapons."

This is comedy of a high order.

Finally, there's the virtuosity of language, the hauntingly perfect phrasing. This is a book to be read slowly:

"He carried with him the breath of beaches and the leathery smell of a good club."

"He had left his elegance behind in the Caribbean."

"Captain Segura squeezed out a smile. It seemed to come from the wrong place like toothpaste when the tube splits."

"The girl screamed but only in a tentative way."

"The skyscrapers of the new town stood up ahead of them like icicles in the moonlight."

"He found himself taking to truth like a tranquilizer."

"A grey stone statue of Columbus stood outside the Cathedral and looked as though it had been formed through the centuries under water, like a coral reef, by the action of insects."

"Captain Segura gleamed. His leather gleamed, his buttons gleamed, and there was fresh pomade upon his hair. He was like a well-cared-for weapon."

If you are holding this splendid new hand-bound edition of *Our Man* in your hands, it's a fair bet that you are not reading it for the first time. So fix yourself a daiquiri and turn now to Chapter One and immerse yourself in Greeneland and the ever-vivid world of Wormold and his daughter, Milly, Dr. Hasselbacher, Hawthorne, and Captain Segura. But for heaven's sake, don't spill the daiquiri on it.

—Introduction to the Arion Press edition of the novel, 2007

REAGAN'S CARD FILE

"The battle for the mind of Ronald Reagan was like the trench warfare of World War I: never have so many fought so hard for such barren terrain."

A dollar to the first reader who can identify who said that. Christopher Hitchens? Bill Maher? The editor of *Pravda*?

No, Peggy Noonan, in her otherwise fawning 1990 memoir as one of Reagan's speechwriters. That was then. Now it's 2011, centennial of the Great Man's birth. In recent years a profusion of books have put paid to the notion that our fortieth president was an "amiable dunce," in the phrase of the late Clark Clifford (as in Washington "Wise Man" and disgraced BCCI bank scandal player).

At the top of this syllabus would be the somewhat verbosely titled: *Reagan, in His Own Hand: The Writings of Ronald Reagan That Reveal His Revolutionary Vision for America* (2001). Then comes *The Age of Reagan*, by Steven Hayward, and the almost identically titled *The Age of Reagan: A History, 1974–2008*, by the left-leaning but admiring Sean Wilentz. And most recently, *The Reagan Diaries*, edited by the historian Douglas Brinkley.

Here, again, comes the indefatigable Brinkley with this fascinating addition to the No-Dummy-He subgenre of Reaganalia. As he writes in his introduction, *The Notes* consists of the collection of four-by-six-inch index cards Reagan kept over the years—his chrestomathy, or commonplace book of wit and wisdom, all of which were written in his "impeccable" scrawl. Brinkley speculates that Reagan began them between 1954 and 1962, when he traveled around the country as spokesman for General Electric, and kept amassing them after he became in 1981 the most powerful man in the world. Thankfully, the Iran-contra counsel Lawrence Walsh didn't know of their existence or he'd have subpoenaed them and they'd be still languishing in some government warehouse like the one in the final scene of *Raiders of the Lost Ark*.

Instead, amazingly, they languished for years in a cardboard box at the Ronald Reagan Library in Simi Valley, California. They were discovered only during a renovation leading up to this year's centennial. The library staff calls them "The Rosetta Stone," but their discovery puts me more in mind of the archaeologist Howard Carter's utterance in 1922, upon first peering into King Tut's tomb. Asked what he saw inside, he replied, "Wonderful things."

Indeed, these notes—which make up Reagan's own personal *Bartlett's Familiar Quotations*—are wonderful things. Witticisms, observations, apothegms, newspaper cuttings, statistics, *bon mots*—as well as some *mal mots*—from Aristophanes to Mao. In between there's a lot of Jefferson, a lot of Lincoln, FDR, and a French politician of the 1840s whom I'd never heard of, by the name of Claude-Frédéric Batiat. Also Hilaire Belloc, Whittaker Chambers, Abba Eban, Ho Chi Minh, Ibn Khaldoun (about whom, more in a moment), Lenin, Ortega y Gassett, Pascal, Seneca, and Sun Tzu. For a dunce, Reagan was a voracious pack rat of wisdom in the pre-Google era.

These notes provide a portal into the—dare one say, fertile?—mind of one of the late-twentieth-century's great leaders. Two big themes run through the notes: (a) the imperilment of individual liberty by growth of the state; and (b) the oppressive taxation that Leviathan demands. As Barry Goldwater once put it—though the quote is strangely not included here—"A government that is big enough to give you everything you want is also big enough to take it all away."

Yet for a so-called right-wing ideologue, Reagan seems to have gotten his inspiration from a diversity of sources:

"Every time we that we try to lift a problem to the govt., to the same extent we are sacrificing the liberties of the people." Irving Kristol? Actually, JFK.

"Strike for the jugular. Reduce taxes *and spending*. Keep govt. poor and remain free." Jack Kemp? No, Justice Oliver Wendell Holmes.

I'd bet an (aftertax) dollar you won't guess the provenance of this one:

"At the beginning of the dynasty taxation yields a large revenue from small assessments. At the end of the Dynasty taxation yields a small revenue from large assessments." Give up? Who knew that Ibn Khaldoun, identified by the Gipper as "Moslem Phil. 14th Century," anticipated the Laffer Curve by seven hundred years? Not me.

Reagan's delight in humor and wit, never really in doubt even among his detractors, is on full display here. The section titled "Humor" is indeed the book's longest. My favorite is the "Chinese Proverb, 400 B.C." that says, "When the music of a nation becomes fast, wild & discordant it shows the nation is in confusion." Did Reagan come across this one after his first exposure to Janis Joplin? Or the dulcet arpeggios of Meat Loaf's singing "Paradise by the Dashboard Light"?

Alas, Brinkley doesn't tell us when Reagan found this one, or for that matter, any of the notes. In fairness, it's possible there was no way of knowing, but even so, *The Notes* is somewhat lacking in footnotes. There's a glossary at the back that will tell you who Ibn Khaldoun was. (Answer: a forefather of social science in the East, and as the Gipper noted, something of a philosopher.) Or Claude-Frédéric Batiat. (An early economist known for his clever attacks on certain state policies.) But many of the notes cry out for more notes, unless you already knew why Harrison Gray Otis of the *Los Angeles Times* circa 1910 was such a stinker. (It's a long story.)

Brinkley's introduction is pleasant and informative, but is marred by sentences such as: "The reader gets the impression that Reagan is a redwood tree and these are the decorations of his own philosophy, the ammunition that he will need to survive the hustings ahead." Okay, if you insist. But surely "U.S. federal government" is tautological, and not to nitpick, but was James A. Garfield technically "assassinated on July 2, 1881" if he died on September 19? *The Notes* would have been a richer book had its editor invested more effort. Brinkley, a protégé of the late Stephen Ambrose, is a humblingly prolific historian and writer. How many historians are capable of writing a biography of Dean Acheson and editing the letters of Hunter S. Thompson? The man must sleep only one hour a night.

Still, this is a dandy little volume. And may also be an important one. Much has been said and written about Reagan's enigmatic, elusive personality. True enough, Reagan has been, and may forever remain, a puzzle to his biographers. A few recent books claim finally to have uncovered the *real* Reagan, but we might never get closer than in these scribbles, which reveal so much about a curious mind, glad soul, and warm heart. They reveal him to be a man who'd known sorrow and defeat, but who by dint of indomitable cheer, gentlemanly grace, and extraordinary energy overcame all obstacles—to say nothing of an evil empire—while always keeping his smile. As Reagan jotted to himself: "An undeveloped Nation—that's one Henry Kissinger hasn't visited yet." Or in a line that may inspire the next gusher of Reaganalia: "When a woman loves a man he can get her to do most anything she really wants to."

—*Bloomberg BusinessWeek,* May 2011

THE PATRIARCH

The Remarkable Life and Turbulent Times of Joseph Patrick Kennedy

The next time you land at Logan Airport in Boston, pause a moment to reflect that you are standing on landfill annexed to what was once Noddle's Island. Here, sometime in the late 1840s, a young escapee from the Irish potato famine named Patrick Kennedy first set foot in the New World. A cooper by trade, Patrick died of cholera in 1858 at age thirty-five. His grandson and near namesake, Joseph Patrick Kennedy, was born in 1888 in a neighborhood now known as unfashionable East Boston. The rest, as they say, is history. In the hands of his biographer David Nasaw, it is riveting history. *The Patriarch* is a book hard to put down, a garland not lightly bestowed on a cinder block numbering 787 pages of text.

Nasaw is the Arthur M. Schlesinger, Jr., professor of history at the Graduate Center of the City University of New York. Not *quite* the disinterested credential one might hope for in a Kennedy biographer, but Nasaw informs us that the family placed no restrictions on him, and allowed him unfettered access to the deepest recesses of the archive. This book is a formidable labor of six years.

Kennedyland is terrain notably susceptible to idolatry, hatemongering, whitewash, conspiracy thinking, sensationalism, and other agendas. Nasaw credibly avers that he has taken forensic pains to excise anything that could not be confirmed by primary sources. I am no historian, but the evidence appears to support his claim. His research is Robert Caro–esque; barely a paragraph is not footnoted. And he is unsparing about his subject's shortcomings, which are numerous.

Given the extraordinary sweep of Kennedy's life—banker, Wall Street speculator, real estate baron, liquor magnate (but not bootlegger), moviemaker, Washington administrator, ambassador, paterfamilias, and dynastic founder—the miracle is that Nasaw was able to tell the whole damned story in only 787 pages.

The book's subtitle, "The Remarkable Life and Turbulent Times," is if anything an understatement. Joe Kennedy was personally involved in virtually all the history of his time. There has been no dearth of books about America's royal family, but this one makes a solid case that the ur-Kennedy was the most fascinating of them all.

Fascinating, that is, as opposed to entirely admirable. Not that he wasn't in ways, but boy, was JPK one complicated boyo. To paraphrase the heavyweight Sonny Liston's manager: Joe Kennedy had his good points and his bad points. It's his bad points that weren't so good.

On the positive side of the ledger, he was an utterly devoted father. He adored his children and, when he was there—which wasn't often—was a touchy-feely, hands-on daddy. When he wasn't there, he regularly wrote them all copious letters. He superintended every aspect of their lives. And in his own highly idiosyncratic way, he was a devoted husband to his wife, Rose, a priggish, pious, humorless, and deeply boring woman, while conducting conspicuous affairs with Gloria Swanson, Clare Boothe Luce, and "hundreds" of other women.

Also on the positive side: he was a genius at management and organization; a Midas at moneymaking. He amassed his immense fortune without even seeming to break a sweat. As a Wall Street manipulator, he was involved in some shameful episodes; but he was also the first chairman of the Securities and Exchange Commission, and headed up the Maritime Commission at critical times in the nation's history. At these enormous tasks he performed tirelessly and valiantly.

As for the not-so-good part: he was a deplorable and disastrous United States ambassador to the Court of St. James's during the crucial prewar period. One ought to refrain from smug judgments on the commonplace biases of prior generations. Kennedy was culturally anti-Semitic, but over time his anti-Semitism metastasized into a grotesque and paranoid obsession.

His isolationism was formidable and adamant, but in that, too, he was hardly unique. A lot of Americans, notably Charles Lindbergh, wanted to keep America out of another European war. But Kennedy's relentless drive to appease—indeed, reward—tyranny was monomaniacal, preposterous, and dangerous. In his view, Hitler was really just another businessman with whom a deal could be struck. Here his business genius impelled him in a direction that would have led to hell.

But it was his profound defeatism, a trait seemingly contrary to his talent for rising to a challenge and getting things done, that was so—to quote from the subtitle—remarkable. At one point we see him fulminating at the Royal Air Force. Why, you may ask, is Ambassador Kennedy in such a rage? ("Yet another rage" would be more accurate, for you can open *The Patriarch* to almost any page and find him spluttering in fury, indignation, or resentment. Or all three.) Well, the answer is that he was livid at the RAF for winning the Battle of Britain and thus halting the German invasion of England. No, Nasaw is not making this up. You see, all that those brave young men in their Spitfires had really accomplished was "prolonging" Britain's inevitable defeat. One rubs one's eyes in disbelief. Next to Joe Kennedy, Cassandra was Dr. Pangloss.

As the saying goes, to be Irish is to know that sooner or later the world will break your heart. Daniel Patrick Moynihan adduced this chestnut of Hibernian *Weltschmerz* on November 22, 1963, upon the assassination of the patriarch's son. Nevertheless, for someone on whom the gods had lavished every blessing—as well as one hell of a lot of the proverbial "luck of the Irish"—Joe Kennedy was possessed of a pessimism that ran deeper than the Mariana Trench. And yet—and yet—in the end, his suspicion that the cosmic deck was stacked against him was weirdly and tragically validated. When, in 1969, this vibrantly alive man, who over a lifetime generated more energy than a nuclear reactor, died after eight years as a drooling, stroke-afflicted paralytic able to utter only one word—"No!"—he had outlived four of his beloved nine children.

His firstborn son and namesake was taken from him by the war he had so desperately tried to avert. His most cherished daughter, Kathleen, known as Kick, went down in a private plane that had no business being aloft in dangerous weather (a recurring Kennedy tragic theme). Two more sons were gruesomely murdered in public. Then there was the daughter, also much loved, whose life was permanently destroyed by a botched, if well-intentioned, lobotomy that her father had authorized.

The invalid patriarch was told about the assassinations of his sons. Nasaw does not reveal whether he was told about his remaining son's rendezvous with karma at Chappaquiddick. Probably not; and probably just as well. His devastation was already consummate. To whom the gods had given much, the gods had taken away much more.

The dominant animus in Joe Kennedy's life was his Irish Catholic identity. (Identity, as distinct from religious faith.) He was born into comfortable circumstances, went to Boston Latin and Harvard (Robert Benchley was a classmate and friend). But as a native of East Boston, he was permanently stamped as an outsider. He could never hope to aspire to the status of "proper Bostonian." This exclusion, harnessed to a brilliant mind and steel determination, fired the dynamo of his ambition.

One of the more arresting sections of the book is the betrayal—and it was certainly that, in Joe Kennedy's view—by the Roman Catholic Church when his son was trying to become the first Catholic president. The Catholic press relentlessly criticized John, while the church higher-ups sat on their cassocks, murmuring orisons for a Quaker candidate.

Nasaw cites a 1966 oral history by Cardinal Richard Cushing of Boston, an intimate Kennedy friend and beneficiary: "Some of the hierarchy . . . were not in favor of John F. Kennedy being elected president. They feared the time had not arrived when a president who was a Catholic could be elected." This reticence may remind some of the modern-day reservations expressed in quarters of the American Jewish community that a Jewish president might exacerbate and inflame anti-Semitism. Many blacks had similar reservations about Barack Obama when he first decided to run for president.

Kennedy's Irish Catholicism, his outsiderness, both paralleled and reinforced his anti-Semitism. He identified with Jews, to a degree. They, like the Irish, were an oppressed people who had also been persecuted for their religion. But in Kennedy's view the Irish had fled their holocaust in Ireland and found haven in the New World. Now, in the 1930s, the Jews were trying to draw the entire world into a war.

Kennedy was not indifferent to the plight of European Jewry. Indeed, he tried hard to achieve some international consensus on establishing new Jewish homelands somewhere in the British Empire. His motives were more tactical than humanitarian: if European Jews could be removed from the equation, then perhaps Hitler would have his *Lebensraum* and . . . chill?

Back home, Kennedy shared the extremist consensus that Franklin Roosevelt was the captive of his cabal of left-wing Jewish advisers: Felix Frankfurter, Samuel Rosenman, Bernard Baruch, Eugene Meyer, Sidney Hillman, and the whole schmear. (Brainwashed, as Mitt Romney's father might have put it.) At war's end, even as news of the Nazi death camps was emerging, Kennedy was pounding the table and railing at the overrepresentation of Jews in the government. Nasaw writes: "The more he found himself on the outside, scorned and criticized as an appeaser, a man out of touch with reality, a traitor to the Roosevelt cause, the more he blamed the Jews." None of this is pleasant to learn.

Kennedy's relationship with Franklin Roosevelt is on the other hand supremely pleasant; indeed, is the book's *pièce de résistance*. Roosevelt's supple handling of his volatile—make that combustible—ambassador and potential rival for the presidency in 1940 and 1944 constitutes political spectator sport of the highest order. Long before *The Godfather*, Roosevelt well grasped the idea of keeping one's friends close, one's enemies closer.

Roosevelt and Kennedy were "frenemies" on a grand stage, full of sound and fury, strutting and fretting, alternately cooing and hissing at each other. As president, Roosevelt held superior cards, but Kennedy played his hand craftily—up to a point. The epic poker game ended on a sad and sour note. We hear the president telling his son-in-law that all Joe really cared about deep down was preserving his vast fortune: "Sometimes I think I am two hundred years older than he is." What a tart bit of patroon *snobisme*. It would have confirmed Kennedy's worst suspicions about "proper" WASP establishmentarians. Of Roosevelt's death, Nasaw writes with Zen terseness: "The nation grieved. Joseph P. Kennedy did not."

"Isolationist" seems a barely adequate description for Kennedy's worldview. He opposed the Truman Doctrine of containing communism in Greece and Italy, the Marshall Plan, the Korean War, the creation of NATO, and congressional appropriations for military assistance overseas. Oh, and the Cold War. His foreign policy essentially boiled down to: We ought to mind our own damn business. But in fairness, this debate is still going on. (See Paul, Ron.)

Perhaps most stunningly, his pessimism could not even be assuaged by . . . victory! After the war, we find him accosting Winston Churchill, someone he abhorred: "After all, what did we accomplish by this war?" Churchill was not a man at a loss for words, but even he was momentarily flummoxed. In Kennedy's view, it was Churchill who had foxed (the Jew-controlled) Roosevelt into the war that had killed his son. Elsewhere we see him lambasting—again, Nasaw is not making this up—Dwight Eisenhower, who favored retaining American troops in Europe. Kennedy "was aggressive, relentless, without a hint of deference to the general, who was arguably the most popular and respected American on two continents." Kennedy did not know Yiddish, but he did not lack for chutzpah.

And rage. Nasaw cites an oral history—though he advises that we approach it with caution—in which Kennedy is described as browbeating Harry Truman: "Harry, what the hell are you doing campaigning for that crippled son of a bitch that killed my son?"

(A strange omission in the book: Roosevelt's son Elliott was on the bombing mission in which Joseph P. Kennedy, Jr., was killed. Elliott's plane was following behind Joe Jr.'s to photograph the operation when Joe Jr.'s bomber suddenly exploded, perhaps because of an electrical or radio signal malfunction. Surely this *Iliad*-level detail—Roosevelt's son possibly witnessing the death of Kennedy's son—was worth including?)

Kennedy was a man of uncanny abilities, but among them was a talent for snatching defeat from the jaws of victory. And here we—or rather, Kennedy's perspicacious biographer—arrive at the crux and fatal flaw:

> *Joseph P. Kennedy had battled all his life to become an insider, to get inside the Boston banking establishment, inside Hollywood, inside the Roosevelt circle of trusted advisers. But he had never been able to accept the reality that being an "insider" meant sacrificing something to the team. His sense of his own wisdom and unique talents was so overblown that he truly believed he could stake out an independent position for himself and still remain a trusted and vital part of the Roosevelt team.*

As his son indelibly put it some months before his father was struck down: "Ask not what your country can do for you—ask what you can do for your country." One wonders what was going through the mind of the patriarch, sitting a few feet away, listening to that soaring sentiment as a fourth-generation Kennedy became president of the United States. After coming to know him over the course of this brilliant, compelling book, the reader might suspect that he was thinking he had done more than enough for his country. But the gods would demand even more.

—*The New York Times*, November 2012

THE WAY YOU MOVE

We may have landed a man on the moon and invented penicillin, Paris Hilton, and the iPod, but deep down in our stem cells, we're still hairy, barely bipedal chimpanzee cousins trying to make it through the day while protecting our vital organs from attack.

This at least is the conclusion I drew from this hefty, informative, often amusing, sometimes a tad self-apparent encyclopedia of body language. The first edition of this book* was published twenty-two years ago. This one contains 50 percent new material, including lots of pictures of Bill Clinton and Marilyn Monroe. I'm sorry not to have made its acquaintance back then, since a good deal of the body-language studies seem to be devoted to the all-important question: *Is your date going to sleep with you?* How useful it would have been, back in 1984, to know that while her eyes seemed to be saying yes, her right foot, pointed toward the door, was whispering, "I'm out of here."

If the approximately one zillion studies adduced here by the authors are any indication, it seems that 90 percent of the population has been gainfully employed studying the body-language patterns of the other 10 percent. While you and I have been hunting-gathering at the office, protecting our necks and other vulnerable areas, the authors, along with legions of academics and students of evolutionary behavior, have been monitoring how often French people touch each other in outdoor cafés (142 touches per hour versus zero touches per hour for Londoners); or who opts for the end toilet stall (*that* must have been a fun project); the smiling patterns among middle-class residents of Atlanta and Memphis (more fun than watching public toilets, anyway); the hip-to-waist ratios in fifty years of *Playboy* centerfolds (significantly more fun than the toilet survey); how many among four hundred cigar exhalations at a festive event were directed upward, as opposed to downward (a toss-up between that and observing toilets); and whether larger-breasted women hitchhikers get more rides than smaller-breasted ones. This last was undertaken by "researchers at Purdue University." Care to hazard a guess as to the finding? I smell an earmark in some omnibus transportation bill.

Indeed, a number of the studies cited here have about them the aroma of sizzling appropriations pork. According to a study of handshaking at the University of Alabama—prepare to have your preconceived notions shattered—"extroverted types use firm handshakes, while shy, neurotic personalities don't." Well, thank God *that's* settled.

* *The Definitive Book of Body Language*, by Allan and Barbara Pease.

Many of the other studies, though, are rather interesting. The Gillette razor company, for instance, commissioned research that indicates that Scotsmen are Britain's vainest males, spending sixteen minutes a day preening in front of the mirror. (Presumably post-*Braveheart*; or maybe not. All that blue face paint takes time to apply.) And I was grateful to learn that "Professor William Fry at Stanford University reported that 100 laughs will give your body an aerobic workout equal to that of a 10-minute session on a rowing machine." Now, instead of working out, I'm just going to watch *Young Frankenstein* on the DVD player while eating Cheetos and drinking 36 ounces of Coke.

The authors, whose other books include *Why Men Don't Listen and Women Can't Read Maps*, have over the years advised clients ranging from politicians to rock stars to Australian Customs. This last client wanted help in identifying smugglers. (Hint: When walking through customs at JFK with a half-dozen Cuban Robustos stuffed in your underpants, smile a lot and don't sweat.) Using research in pupillometry done at the University of Chicago, they were able to help Revlon increase sales of its lipstick by enlarging the pupil size of the models in the catalogues. I'm hard pressed to think of a better example of science at the service of humanity.

In this political season, those running for office might find *The Definitive Book of Body Language* handy. If, say, you're a candidate being interviewed on TV, don't look sideways from the reporters to the camera. It will make you look shifty. (Or shiftier.) There's also some good advice on where to stand while being photographed shaking hands. The chapter titled "Evaluation and Deceit Signals" is illustrated with a photo of Bill Clinton giving his famous grand jury testimony. In that regard, our noses apparently do actually swell when we're lying. Call it the Pinocchio effect. The even worse news is that "a man's penis also swells with blood when he tells a lie." *No, really, honey, it's this damn Viagra.*

Aficionados of Stephen Potter's imperishable *Upmanship* books will appreciate some of the tips and strategies. My favorite is in the section called "The Power Gaze," on how to counter someone who is either trying to dominate you or bore you. (Hard to say which is worse.) "Imagine the person has a third eye in the center of their forehead and look in a triangular area between the person's 'three' eyes. The impact this gaze has on the other person has to be experienced to be believed." Can't wait to try it out this Thanksgiving.

Chess and poker players will profit, too—the latter probably more than the former. If while you touch your chess piece to make your next move, your opponent "steeples" his hands (as in "Here's the church, here's the steeple"), this signals he or she feels confident. If he clenches his hands, he feels threatened. If he stabs you in the chest with his bishop, he feels really threatened. The prudent poker player, meanwhile, will wear dark glasses. It's not an affectation: he's shielding his dilating pupils from signaling to the other players that he's aroused by that third king he's just drawn.

The book is amply and often wittily illustrated with celebrity photographs. There's a fetching one of Brigitte Bardot, goddess of my youth, executing the "head toss and hair flick." What's going on here—God knows how much government research went into finding this out—is that the pose "lets her expose her armpit, which allows the 'sex perfume' known as pheromones to waft across to the target man." Did Gillette participate in this study? And what book on body language would be complete without 107 photos of Marilyn Monroe, who "reputedly chopped three-quarters of an inch off the heel of her left shoe to emphasize her wiggle."

On a more sober note, Nazis during World War II were on the lookout for males sitting in what the authors call "The American Figure Four"—legs spread to reveal the crotch, with the left crossed over the right at an almost 90-degree angle. "Anyone using it was clearly not German or had spent time in the U.S.A." Our Department of Homeland Security might do well, as it strips us of our unguents, shampoos, and precious bodily moisturizers, to employ the authors to instruct them on body lingo profiling.

This is a truly fascinating book, though clearly more—much more—government funding is needed to study the hitchhiking patterns of busty women. After reading it, you'll be able to decode and analyze the signature moments of our times. The famous confrontation, for instance, between Tom Cruise and Matt Lauer on the *Today* show.

Observe as Tom sprays spittle at Lauer for having no understanding at all, Matt, of why Brooke Shields should be clubbed to death for resorting to modern medicine to help her cope with postpartum depression. Note that Tom's legs are splayed open in the classic Crotch Display. He's leaning forward toward Lauer, eyebrows lowered in the manner of our Neanderthal forbears. Note, too, that he is pointing his finger at Lauer's chest, at his heart, a signal of aggression which—listen up, guys—women find *totally* offensive. And what is Matt doing, other than wondering, Will I get rabies from Tom's saliva? He's leaning back in his chair. The wide-open eyes denote not only elation over the probable ratings jump for this episode, but also fear that he might not make it out of the studio alive. Now look at his right leg: it's crossed defensively over the left. What's with that? *He's protecting his genitals.* I'd have, too.

—*The New York Times*, September 2006

THAR HE BLOWS (AGAIN): *MOBY-DICK*

I have written a wicked book, and feel spotless as the lamb.

—HERMAN MELVILLE TO NATHANIEL HAWTHORNE

Dr. Johnson wrote of Shakespeare that it is impossible to say anything original about him, so the best one can hope for is to be wrong about him in a new way. This humbling insight tugs at my sleeve as I embark on a surely doomed task of contributing an afterword to the great masterpiece of American literature, *Moby-Dick*.

This assignment came about by accident, as a result of something I'd written for an online magazine on the topic of advice to young people, specifically, "Five Things You Really Need to Know."

I nominated: the U.S. Constitution (surely the least we can do by way of thanking the Founders); the Bible (even if you don't believe a word of it); the first stanza of "The Star-Spangled Banner" (Beyoncé didn't get that memo, apparently); *The New York Times* (even if you're a crotchety right-winger); and *Moby-Dick* (because it's, well, *Moby-Dick*).

Shortly after it went out into cyberspace, an e-mail arrived from an old friend, one of America's most distinguished literary critics. He wrote: "I re-read *Moby-Dick* for the first time since prep school, where I had hated it. This time I thought the first 100 or so pages were great but once again got totally bogged down in all that whaling s——."

There is no airtight counterargument to this familiar lament about *Moby-Dick*, and I won't attempt one here. I'd be dishonest if I myself claimed to have been riveted by the novel's whaling . . . parts. Let us stipulate that *Moby-Dick* is a challenging work. But let's also stipulate that there are challenging bits in Shakespeare as well. Nor is the Bible without its challenges. Or Joyce's *Ulysses*, or Proust's 4,300-page chef d'oeuvre. And who could forget the perfect moment in 1947 when W. H. Auden, lecturing at Harvard on *Don Quixote*, began by telling his stunned listeners that he'd never managed to get all the way through it—and for that matter, rather doubted that anyone in the audience had, either. (This frank admission may have been enabled by the martinis that the great poet had consumed prior to going on stage.)

Elmore Leonard, a modern master of American literature, was once asked the secret of his success. He beguilingly replied that it was simple—he just left out the boring parts. Why didn't Melville think of that?

The answer is: He did, but only, by and large, in his first five sea books. *Moby-Dick* is Melville's sixth. His first two, *Typee* and *Omoo*, were hugely popular fictionalized accounts of his time in the Marquesas living among the savages, including the lovely Fayaway, after jumping ship. (No boring parts there.) Those books made the author an exotic figure back home. Students from Williams and other colleges would show up at his Massachusetts farmhouse, wanting to meet the man who had lived with savages. In time, this celebrity began to chafe, as we know from a wry letter Melville wrote to a friend: "To go down to posterity is bad enough, but to go down as the 'man who lived with cannibals'!"

His sea adventure books continued with *Mardi*, *Redburn*, and *White Jacket*.* By early 1850, when he started in on the book that would become *Moby-Dick*, Melville was past his youth, thirty-one years old and intellectually ravenous. He read deeply in classic literature. Straightforward adventure no longer intrigued him. He was after bigger game now.

He absorbed Shakespeare, especially the tragedies, *Lear*, *Macbeth*, and *Antony and Cleopatra*; also Milton's *Paradise Lost*, Carlyle's *Sartor Resartus*, Dryden's translation of Virgil's *Aeneid*. And another book, as Andrew Delbanco tantalizingly informs us in his excellent biography, *Melville: His World and Work*: a novel by Mary Shelley by the name of *Frankenstein*.

Melville was given a copy of it in London by his publisher, Richard Bentley, who a few years later would fatally botch the British edition of Melville's *The Whale*.† In Shelley's novel, a deranged scientist who has created a monster pursues it into the vastness of the Arctic Sea, aboard a ship that, as Delbanco notes, he has transformed "into an instrument

* When the U.S. Senate outlawed flogging in the U.S. Navy, the author of *White Jacket* could take some credit for the reform, having brought it vividly to the public attention, along with Richard Henry Dana's *Two Years Before the Mast*, published in 1840.

† Bentley rewrote passages that he thought might offend British sensibilities; moved the introductory "Extracts" to the end; and, most ruinously, eliminated the all-important epilogue, leaving British readers to wonder how in hell Ishmael could be narrating the story if he went down with the *Pequod*. Into the bargain, the spines of the three volumes of *The Whale* were embossed with drawings of a right whale, rather than a sperm whale. All in all, a disaster. Melville published the book first in Britain in order to protect his copyright, which rights barely existed in the United States then.

of his private vengeance." Sound familiar? The speech Frankenstein delivers to his crew exhorting them not to falter in their quest is uncannily reminiscent of the "Quarter-Deck" chapter, in which Ahab, in the role of Antichrist, urges his own crew to fiendish vengeance. This extraordinary set piece of demagoguery, where Ahab incites his men into an ecstasy of hatred against a nonhuman enemy, is adduced by numerous Melville scholars, Delbanco among them, as evidence of Melville's eerily prescient anticipation of twentieth-century totalitarianism. "To borrow a phrase from one of his best readers, Walker Percy," Delbanco writes, "Melville seemed to know in advance the great secret of the twentieth century—'that only the haters seem alive.'"

Thus you can trace a rhumb line from *Moby-Dick*'s antecedents—Milton's Satan, Shakespeare's tragic king, and Mary Shelley's Frankenstein—through Melville's novel on up to the monomaniacal monsters of our own era. Small wonder the book continues resonant.

Even the brushstrokes give pause. Just five pages into the novel, Ishmael is breezily speculating that his whaling voyage "formed part of the grand programme of Providence that was drawn up a long time ago. It came in as a sort of brief interlude and solo between more extensive performances. I take it that this part of the bill must have run something like this:

'GRAND CONTESTED ELECTION FOR THE PRESIDENCY OF THE UNITED STATES.

'WHALING VOYAGE BY ONE ISHMAEL.

'BLOODY BATTLE IN AFFGHANISTAN.'"

It would be arresting to have come across those lines for the first time in, say, November 2000 or the months following 9/11. By way of footnote: Melville was born in 1819 just a stone's throw from Ground Zero, at 6 Pearl Street.

"Call me Ishmael." The narrator of *Moby-Dick* gives us the most memorable—and most parodied—first line in all American literature; and for my money, with the finest first paragraph:

> *Some years ago—never mind how long precisely—having little or no money in my purse, and nothing particular to interest me on shore, I thought I would sail about a little and*

> *see the watery part of the world. It is a way I have of driving off the spleen, and regulating the circulation . . .*

As you already knew from that other book on my must-read list, Ishmael takes his name from the illegitimate son of Abraham by the slave girl Hagar. He's an outcast—though the biblical Ishmael went on to big things as father of the Arab race. Our Ishmael, being a nomad and wanderer, is an ideal American type. His friendship with the extravagantly tattooed South Seas harpooner Queequeg is among the most poignant in any literature. Huck Finn and the runaway slave Jim may be ur-paragons of racial diversity in American literature, but Melville introduced us to Ishmael and Queequeg three and a half decades before Twain gave us Huck and Jim.

Recently, walking into a London pub, I found a menu board on the wall with this written on it in chalk: "Better to sleep with a sober cannibal than a drunken Christian." That, of course, is from the hilarious first meeting of Ishmael and his surprise bunkmate at the Spouter Inn. It was a racy sentiment in 1850s America. I mention it only to point out that *Moby-Dick* enthusiasts are everywhere, and share their continuing delight, even on crowded menu boards along with the day's specials.

If *Moby-Dick* is Ishmael's story, it is Ahab's book. Of all the archetypes in American literature—Ichabod Crane, Hester Prynne, Huck, Gatsby, Yossarian, Holden Caulfield—the captain of the *Pequod*, who "looked like a man cut away from the stake, when the fire has overrunningly wasted all the limbs without consuming them," casts the longest and most formidable shadow across the psychic landscape. One comes across Ahab almost every day, not only in reference to the novel, but also as a signifier of obsessive pursuit: the prosecutor who pursues a president over a thong-wearing intern; a mayor intent on banishing cigarettes and large servings of soda pop; a bearded Islamic fanatic waging holy war from a cave. In his biography, Delbanco amusingly lampoons the introductory "Extracts" in the novel with his own compilation of Melville and *Moby-Dick* references, including a hilarious and recherché lit-crit riff on *Billy Budd* from an episode of TV's *The Sopranos*.

Ahab is an "embed" in our national consciousness. We met him as the obsessive captain in *The Caine Mutiny*, rather coolly renamed by Herman Wouk after the first half of Queequeg; we met him as Richard Nixon; as Captain Quint of *Jaws*; and there he was, reincarnated in none other than Ricardo Montalban—he of the rich Corinthian leather—in a *Star Trek* movie, hurtling electronic harpoons and snarling death curses taken word for word from the ur-text. Ahab lives.*

I have written a wicked book. In that letter to Hawthorne, whom he befriended while he was writing *Moby-Dick*, Melville is being only half accurate. In fact, he had written two books: one nonwicked, a conventional, if fantastical, sea chase. Onto that book, he grafted a second one, quite wicked for its day: an ontological epic, a subversive, metaphysical smackdown of the Deity, so unconventional as to expose its author to accusations of sacrilege and even lunacy.

The consensus among Melville scholars is that he set out to write one book but then turned the helm hard over and steered into deeper waters. In 1947, a scholar named Charles Olson published an electric if out-there book under the title *Call Me Ishmael*. Like many Melvilleans, Olson was obsessed—*Moby-Dick* has this effect on people. He spent a good part of his life trying to reassemble Melville's library.

For him, the smoking gun was Melville's copy of Shakespeare's plays. Melville's granddaughter showed him the volumes, which contain Melville's notes in pencil on the flyleaf. From those jottings Olson concluded with an adamantine, indeed Ahab-like certainty, that Melville had started his book lacking both Ahab and the white whale, and then, having steeped in *King Lear* and the other tragedies, threw aside that book and began to write *Moby-Dick*.

It's exhilarating to read Olson, even though at points you feel that you've been collared by Elijah, the raving dockside prophet who accosts Ishmael as he boards the *Pequod*. Olson is a brilliant illuminator of the mystical aspects of *Moby-Dick*, but his Shakespearean

* By way of a very weird QED, after I wrote the paragraph above, I turned to the *Times* crossword for my daily humiliation and there was the clue: "Grand, un-godly, godlike man" of fiction. Four letters.

omphalos hypothesis starts to creak when we confront the fact that Melville's jottings in his Shakespeare folio are undated: We don't know when exactly Melville made those notations, so it is speculation that *Moby-Dick* and Ahab and the whale owe their genesis entirely to *King Lear*. Nor can we ascertain the facts from the manuscript, which has long since disappeared. (What a find *that* would be.)

Melville's biographer Lorie Robertson-Lorant describes another letter from Melville to his friend Hawthorne, this one written in the sweltering third-floor room on Lexington Avenue and Thirty-first Street where Melville was polishing the last chapters, even as the first chapters were coming off the press. He offers to send Hawthorne a "specimen fin" of his whale, but cautions him that the book has been broiled in "hell-fire." This was a reference that Hawthorne would appreciate—he described his own *The Scarlet Letter* as a "positively hell-fired story."

When Melville was getting started with his book, he wrote a very differently toned letter, rather playful, to Richard Henry Dana. He told the author of *Two Years Before the Mast* that he was well aware of the difficulty inherent in producing a book about whales:

> *Blubber is blubber you know, tho' you may get oil out if it, the poetry runs as hard as sap from a frozen maple tree;—& to cook the thing up, one must needs throw in a little fancy, which from the nature of the thing, must be as ungainly as the gambols of the whales themselves. Yet I mean to give the truth of the thing, spite of this.*

There in two letters, one to America's most famous novelist, the other to its most famous author of sea nonfiction, Melville limns his book: blubber cooked in hell-fire.

When he finished, Melville wrote to Hawthorne to admit that he knew he had created a Frankenstein monster—a book rather hard to categorize. He had thrown everything into the pot, producing a literary olla podrida. His friend and mentor, Evert Duyckinck, editor of the influential *The Literary World*, would write a two-part review of the book, by no means a rave, calling it "intellectual chowder."

That letter to Hawthorne is wrenching to read. It seems to come from the inner depths of Melville's soul. It verges on self-pity, but concludes in a valiant shrug: "Try to get a living from the Truth, and go to the Soup Societies. . . . Truth is ridiculous to men. What I feel most moved to write, that is banned—it will not pay. Yet, altogether, write the other way I cannot. So the product is a final hash, and all my books are botches." You want to reach back through time and give the poor man a hug.

Early reviews seized on the book's problematic duality. The priggish conservative critic of the London *Athenaeum* declared that it was an "ill-compounded mixture of romance and matter-of-fact" amounting to "so much trash belonging to the worst school of Bedlam literature." Was it any consolation to Melville that if they're calling you a madman, at least they're paying attention? More of this was on the way. An American journal called for a "writ of *de lunatico*" to be taken out against the author. As far as the conventionalists were concerned, Melville had—to put it in contemporary terms—jumped the shark.

Reading these fulminations against the book tempts us to speculate: What if Melville had played it safe? The idea of a vengeful sperm whale was by no means far-fetched. One way or the other, *Moby-Dick* had its beginnings in the sensational episode of the sinking of the whale ship *Essex* in 1820 by a very angry pale-hued sperm whale with the Ben and Jerry's–sounding name of "Mocha Dick."

Nathaniel Philbrick's bestseller *In the Heart of the Sea* relates the story in all its harrowing, cannibalistic detail. Charles Olson's *Call Me Ishmael* gives us the fascinating detail that Melville met Owen Chase, former mate of the *Essex*, in mid–Pacific Ocean in 1841, not far from where the *Essex* had met its fate. Stranger still, a few months later, Melville met Owen Chase's sixteen-year-old son, also at sea. The young Chase showed Melville a copy of his father's famous account of the disaster. A final detail worth mention: Olson notes the fact that the *Essex* set out on its fated voyage from Nantucket eleven days after Herman Melville was born. In a way they were coterminous.

So: What if Melville had contented himself with a fictionalized rendering of an *Essex*-like event? What would the result have been? *Moby Dick* lite?

The likeliest answer is: Had Melville played it safe, *Moby-Dick* would probably not be the classic that it is, and you would not be holding in your hands another fresh edition of a book first published a decade before the start of the U.S. Civil War.

What accounts we have of Melville while he was at work on the book indicate that he knew exactly what he was doing—that he was, to paraphrase the captain of the starship *Enterprise*, boldly going where no man had gone before. They also show that he had little idea of the ultimate cost.

When he began his book in New York City in the winter of 1850, Herman Melville was a name-brand novelist of sturdy reputation, contentedly married, looking forward to enlarging his family and to living on a pleasant farm with breathtaking views of the Berkshire Mountains, a snug harbor where he could write his ambitious book in peace, far from the noise and clamor of his native Manhattan.

Flash forward a year and a half, to the winter of 1851. The book has been published, on November 1—All Soul's Day, one notes. We find a very different Herman Melville, who indeed resembles someone who has taken on the cosmos and the Almighty. He is exhausted, spent, hollow-eyed, and stares into the embers of his fireplace. In the opinion of some Melville scholars, Delbanco included, he may be in the grip of what we now call bipolar disorder. Certainly his behavior suggests such a diagnosis: extreme mood swings between mania and depression. In a few years, his family will become so alarmed that they will ask a neighbor, Dr. Oliver Wendell Holmes, to examine him and evaluate his sanity.

But for now, November 1851, his marriage has gone cold. He broods over the reviews and the poor sales. His lifetime earnings from *Moby-Dick* will amount to $556.37; it will fail to sell out its first printing of three thousand copies. His friend Hawthorne, the only person to whom Melville ever truly opened up, has moved away and deserted him. Hawthorne is dazzled by *Moby-Dick*, but refrains from saying so publicly. In fairness, Melville has—almost masochistically—asked Hawthorne *not* to review the book in *The Literary*

World, where Melville had published his own glowing encomium to Hawthorne's *Mosses from an Old Manse*. Hawthorne accedes to his friend's wish, perhaps a bit too neatly. But his continued reticence to praise the book, to lift even a finger in its support, leaves one a bit chilled. Hawthorne's passiveness is all the more frustrating when, as quoted in Olson's *Call Me Ishmael*, one finds him writing in his journal, after seeing his old friend for the last time: "He has a very high and noble nature and is better worth immortality than most of us." Hawthorne's betrayal is compounded by Evert Duyckinck's two-part review of the book, the first tepid ("intellectual chowder"), the second adducing sacrilege. All in all, quite a "damp, drizzly November of [the] soul."

Adding to the disaster, we find Melville working out the plot of a new novel, one that he thinks will appeal to female readers and set his reputation and finances straight again—a novel titled *Pierre*. In the description of one Melville scholar, it will amount to an act of literary suicide. If you have read *Pierre*, no further explanation is necessary.

There, then, are the before and after vignettes that bookend *Moby-Dick*.

After a few more failures, Melville will become a Customs inspector in Manhattan, spending his days walking the docks of the Hudson River, not far from where he was born. His son Malcolm will die a suicide; another, Stanwix, will die alone in a hotel room. *Billy Budd*, the novella that will do much to burnish his reputation and fuel the Melville revival, will not be published until 1924, thirty-three years after his largely unnoticed death. His granddaughter will retrieve it from the tin bread box where Melville's wife stored it, and give it to Raymond Weaver, one of Melville's first biographers.

A tin bread box. The letter to Hawthorne about having written a wicked book ends on a note of mystical triumph. Melville tells his friend that he has cracked at least one major piece of the eternal puzzle. "I feel," he writes, "that the Godhead is broken like the bread at the Supper, and that we are the pieces." All of Melville's ontology is contained in that single sentence. W. H. Auden quotes it toward the end of his haunting poem "Herman Melville."

Not long ago, I found myself in the room where he wrote most of

Moby-Dick, a small corner north-facing study on the second floor of Arrowhead, his farmhouse near Pittsfield, Massachusetts.

"If they but knew it," Ishmael tells us at the end of the novel's first paragraph, "almost all men in their degree, some time or other, cherish very nearly the same feelings towards the ocean with me." For anyone who cherishes very nearly the same feelings for *Moby-Dick*, standing in that room will induce a pilgrim sensation. The kindly, informative docent goes on with his narrative, pointing out this and that detail, but his words fade as the reverential hush descends on you. A quiet but overwhelming feeling rises as you think of all those whom Melville conjured into immortality in this shabby little space: Ahab, Ishmael, Queequeg, Starbuck, Father Mapple, Elijah, Pip, all them.

You can see the whale through the window over the desk, looking out toward Mount Greylock, with its distinct whalelike hump. The windowpanes have that distorted quality of antique glass, which makes you wonder: Are these the same panes through which Melville stared when he looked up from his epic labor on his wicked book? I don't know, but I'll assert here that they are, if only so that, having failed to say anything original, I can at least claim to have been wrong about *Moby-Dick* in a new way.

—Afterword to the Signet Classics edition, 2013

THE YEAR OF LIVING DYINGLY

Christopher Hitchens began his memoir, *Hitch-22*, on a note of grim amusement at finding himself described in a British National Portrait Gallery publication as "the late Christopher Hitchens." He wrote, "So there it is in cold print, the plain unadorned phrase that will one day become unarguably true."

On June 8, 2010, several days after the memoir was published, he awoke in his New York hotel room "feeling as if I were actually shackled to my own corpse. The whole cave of my chest and thorax seemed to have been hollowed out and then refilled with slow-drying cement." And so commenced an eighteen-month odyssey through "the land of malady," culminating in his death from esophageal cancer last December, when the plain unadorned phrase that had prompted him to contemplate his own mortality became, unarguably, true. He was sixty-two.

Mortality is a slender volume—or, to use the *mot* that he loved to deploy, *feuilleton*—consisting of the seven dispatches he sent in to *Vanity Fair* magazine from "Tumorville." The first seven chapters are, like virtually everything he wrote over his long, distinguished career, diamond-hard, and brilliant. An eighth and final chapter consists, as the publisher's note informs us, of unfinished "fragmentary jottings" that he wrote in his terminal days in the critical-care unit of the M. D. Anderson Cancer Center in Houston. They're vivid, heart-wrenching and haunting—messages in a bottle tossed from the deck of a sinking ship as its captain, reeling in agony and fighting through the fog of morphine, struggles to keep his engines going:

> *My two assets my pen and my voice—and it had to be the esophagus. All along, while burning the candle at both ends, I'd been "straying into the arena of the unwell" and now "a vulgar little tumor" was evident. This alien can't want any-*

thing; if it kills me it dies but it seems very single-minded and set in its purpose. No real irony here, though. Must take absolute care not to be self-pitying or self-centered.

The alien was burrowing into me even as I wrote the jaunty words about my own prematurely announced death.

If I convert it's because it's better that a believer dies than that an atheist does.

Ordinary expressions like "expiration date" . . . will I outlive my Amex? My driver's license? People say—I'm in town on Friday: will you be around? WHAT A QUESTION!

Fans of the movie *Withnail and I* will recognize "arena of the unwell" and "vulgar little tumor." Readers of his 2007 atheist classic, *God Is Not Great*, will get the frisky "convert" bit; more than a few of the pages in *Mortality* are devoted—as it were—to a final, defiant and well-reasoned defense of his non-God-fearingness.

As for the "jaunty words," those are of course from Chapter 1 of the memoir whose promotional tour was so dramatically interrupted by the tap-tap-tap of the Reaper. Self-pity? Those of his friends (I was one) who witnessed his pluck and steel throughout his ghastly ordeal will attest that he never succumbed to any of that.

"To the dumb question 'Why me?,'" he writes, "the cosmos barely bothers to return the reply: Why not?" He was valiant to the end, a paragon of British phlegm. He became an American citizen in 2007, but the background music was always *H.M.S. Pinafore*: "He remains an Englishman."

Mortality comes with a fine foreword by his longtime *Vanity Fair* editor and friend Graydon Carter, who writes of Christopher's "saucy fearlessness," "great turbine of a mind," and "his sociable but unpredictable brand of anarchy that seriously touched kids in their 20s and early 30s in much the same way that Hunter S. Thompson had a generation before. . . . He did not mind landing outside the cozy cocoon of conventional liberal wisdom."

Christopher's wife, Carol Blue, contributes a—I've already used up my "heart-wrenching" quota—deeply moving afterword, in which she recalls the "eight-hour dinners" they hosted at their apartment in Washington, when after consuming enough booze to render the entire population of the nation's capital insensible, Christopher would rise and deliver flawless twenty-minute recitals of poetry, polemics, and jokes, capping it off saying, "How good it is to be us." The truth of that declaration was evident to all who had the good fortune to be present at those dazzling recreations. Bliss it was in those wee hours to be alive and in his company, though the next mornings were usually less blissful.

"For me," he writes in *Mortality*, "to remember friendship is to recall those conversations that it seemed a sin to break off: the ones that made the sacrifice of the following day a trivial one." In support of this, he adduces several staves of William Cory's translation of the poem by Callimachus about his beloved friend Heraclitus:

> *They told me, Heraclitus; they told me you were dead.*
> *They brought me bitter news to hear, and bitter tears to shed.*
> *I wept when I remembered how often you and I*
> *Had tired the sun with talking, and sent him down the sky.*

He was a man of abundant gifts, Christopher: erudition, wit, argument, prose style, to say nothing of a titanium constitution that, until it betrayed him in the end, allowed him to write word-perfect essays while the rest of us were groaning from epic hangovers and reaching for the ibuprofen. But his greatest gift of all may have been the gift of friendship. At his memorial service in New York City, thirty-one people, virtually all of them boldface names, rose to speak in his memory. One selection was from the introduction Christopher wrote for the paperback reissue of *Hitch-22* while gravely ill:

> *Another element of my memoir—the stupendous importance of love, friendship and solidarity—has been made immensely more vivid to me by recent experience. I can't hope to convey the full effect of the embraces and avowals, but*

> *I can perhaps offer a crumb of counsel. If there is anybody known to you who might benefit from a letter or a visit, do not on any account postpone the writing or the making of it. The difference made will almost certainly be more than you have calculated.*

One of the "fragmentary jottings" in the last chapter of *Mortality* is a brushstroke on Philip Larkin's chilling death poem "Aubade":

"Larkin good on fear in 'Aubade,' with implied reproof to Hume and Lucretius for their stoicism. Fair enough in one way: atheists ought not to be offering consolation either."

For a fuller version of that terminal *pensée*, turn to his essay on Larkin in his collection *Arguably*: "Without that synthesis of gloom and angst we could never have had his 'Aubade,' a waking meditation on extinction that unstrenuously contrives a tense, brilliant counterpoise between the stoic philosophy of Lucretius and David Hume, and his own frank terror of oblivion." The essay ends with two lines from another Larkin poem that could serve as Christopher's own epitaph:

> *Our almost-instinct almost true:*
> *What will survive of us is love.*

What discrepant parts were in him: the fierce tongue, the tender heart.

There is no "frank terror of oblivion" in *Mortality*, but there is keen and great regret at having to leave the party early. But even as he stared into the abyss, his mordant wit did not desert him:

> *The novelty of a diagnosis of malignant cancer has a tendency to wear off. The thing begins to pall, even to become banal. One can become quite used to the specter of the eternal Footman, like some lethal old bore lurking in the hallway at the end of the evening, hoping for the chance to have a word. And I don't so much object to his holding my coat in that marked manner, as if mutely reminding me that it's time to be on my way. No, it's the snickering that gets me down.*

In his first collection of essays, *Prepared for the Worst* (1988), he quoted Nadine Gordimer to the effect that "a serious person should try to write posthumously. By that I took her to mean that one should compose as if the usual constraints—of fashion, commerce, self-censorship, public and perhaps especially intellectual opinion—did not operate."

He refers back to that in *Arguably*, the introduction to which he wrote in June 2011, deep in the heart of Tumorville. He was still going at it *mano a mano* with the Footman, but by then he was at least realistic about the odds and knew that the words he was writing might very well be published posthumously. As it turned out, he lived just long enough to see *Arguably* hailed for what it is—inarguably, stunning. What a coda. What a life.

He noted there that some of the essays had been written in "the full consciousness that they might be my very last. Sobering in one way and exhilarating in another, this practice can obviously never become perfected."

Being in Christopher's company was rarely sobering but always exhilarating. It is, however, sobering and grief-inducing to read this brave and harrowing account of his "year of living dyingly" in the grip of the alien that succeeded where none of his debate opponents had in bringing him down.

In her afterword, Carol relates an anecdote about their daughter, then two years old, one day coming across a dead bumblebee on the ground. She frantically begged her parents to "make it start." On reaching the end of her father's valedictory *feuilleton*, the reader is likely to be acutely conscious of Antonia's terrible feeling of loss.

—*The New York Times*, August 2012

La Belle France

How can anyone govern a nation that has two hundred and forty-six different kinds of cheese?

—DE GAULLE

A REUSABLE FEAST

When you are in love, you go to Paris, and then you are really in love.

I am trying not to write like Hemingway, but this is not an easy thing to do, because I have spent the last four days in Paris with Peaches reading *A Moveable Feast* aloud to her in cafés and in the hotel room where Oscar Wilde died. It is a very fine book, which Papa wrote forty years after he lived in the Paris of F. Scott Fitzgerald and Gertrude Stein and Ezra Pound and Ford Madox Ford and James Joyce. It was published after he died and created a sensation not just because it was so good but because of the scene where Scott confides to Hemingway that he is worried about the size of his manhood. The restaurant where this alarming scene took place was Michaud's, at the corner of the rue Jacob and the rue des Saints-Pères. As for Peaches, this is not her real name but it seems a good name for her since she is from the American South and is very wild. Zelda would also be a good name for her, except that was the name of F. Scott Fitzgerald's wife and she was crazy technically, the kind where they come and take you away. Peaches is not crazy in that way but she is from the South and is exuberant in the way Southerners have of never wanting the day to end.

At Taillevent, which is a very great restaurant not far from where Scott and Zelda lived in those days, Peaches was so exuberant after the meal of wild boar and *foie gras de canard* with the caramelized figs and tangerines, as well as after the bottle of Nuits-St-Georges, the glasses of Maury, the sweet red wine from the southwest, and the four glasses of 1975 Armagnac, that she wanted to make love under the table. I said absolutely no because I want to come back to Taillevent and I am certain that they do not like it when patrons make love under the table, even after the other diners have gone and though the tablecloths are very long. Still she kept insisting, and finally I had to say, "All right, we're going." It was four thirty anyway, a time when decent people have finished lunch.

We walked the few blocks in the cold rain to 14 rue de Tilsitt, where Scott and Zelda lived. There is no plaque like the one outside 74 rue du Cardinal Lemoine, where Hemingway and Hadley lived in those years. That did not seem right, since Scott moved there the same month he published a very good book called *The Great Gatsby*. But we did not care about that or the cold, being very happy from the meal and the quantities of wine and Armagnac.

We walked in the rain down the Avenue de Friedland, and I stopped into a *tabac* opposite the statue of Balzac to buy a cigar, and when I came out not two minutes later, a Frenchman had stopped his car and was asking Peaches if she would like to go home with him. In the restaurant she had flirted with three elegant French businessmen in the next booth when I went to the *toilette*. They had been looking at her the whole meal, and I could not blame them, since Peaches is wonderful to look at. I was also feeling sorry for the French because George W. Bush had just won reelection, so I smiled at them when I came back and took my seat, and they smiled at me as if to say, "You are very lucky, Monsieur." In fact, the maître d' had said that exact same thing, and not just because he was angling for a big *pourboire*.

But now when I came out of the *tabac* and saw the Frenchman scurrying off in his car and Peaches grinning at me, her blond hair shining like gold leaf against the wet and the dusk of the boulevard, and her green eyes bright and her cheeks dimpling in that way they do, I took her arm and resolved not to leave her out on any French boulevards untended.

This was how it was for us during our four-day stay in Paris. We were not very young and not very poor, but we were very happy. You can be happy in Paris if you are poor, but it is as Dickens says a far, far better thing to have euros in your pockets, even thick wads of euros, because then you can eat at Taillevent and Caviar Kaspia in the Place de la Madeleine and stay in the Oscar Wilde suite at L'Hôtel on the rue des Beaux-Arts and order champagne at all hours which to judge from the bill we did. Looking over the bill and feeling the hardness in my liver and the taste of cigars in my mouth, which I cannot get rid of even after brushing my teeth dozens of times with the strong American toothpaste, I am surprised that I remember anything of our stay in Paris, but I remember being very happy.

You do not have to eat at expensive restaurants in Paris. For most lunches we had *jambon-beurre* sandwiches and drank house red wine and tap beer. We would sit outside under the mushroom-shaped propane heater and eat and drink, utterly content and thinking that the meal, which cost perhaps 20 euros, was the best that could be had in Paris. After, we walked to the Cluny Museum and looked at the tapestries of the Lady and the Unicorn that were woven about the time Columbus landed in the New World. In one tapestry the Lady is stroking the Unicorn's horn in a way that must have caused giggling, or even a serious stir at court, for you had to be careful in the fifteenth century. They were very strict about things.

From there we walked up the steep hill toward the Panthéon, past a group of drunk men who were nice about our being American despite the recent victory by Bush, until we came to the Place de la Contrescarpe, at the foot of the rue Mouffetard. Hemingway and Hadley and their baby son, Mr. Bumby, lived a few yards from here. We celebrated finding it by having a drink at the little café, and I read Peaches one of the most beautiful paragraphs in the book:

> *As I ate the oysters with their strong taste of the sea and their faint metallic taste that the cold white wine washed away, leaving only the sea taste and the succulent texture, and as I drank their cold liquid from each shell and washed it down with the crisp taste of the wine, I lost the empty feeling and began to be happy and to make plans.*

It made us want to have white wine and oysters, but that would have to wait, because now we had to find 27 rue de Fleurus, where Gertrude Stein lived with Alice B. Toklas. I did not want to do this too precisely, because one of the pleasures of Paris is getting lost. We ended up on the street where Madame Curie worked.

"Remind me," I said, "what she did that was so wonderful."

"Radium," Peaches said. "And I can't believe you asked me that."

Peaches is an M.D. and is getting her Ph.D. in public health, so she was unimpressed by my ignorance of the wonderful thing Madame Curie did, but by the time we came to the Jardin du Luxembourg, she had forgotten about it. There was a vendor of hot chestnuts by the gate, and I wanted to buy some until he blew his nose into his hand so we walked on. Hemingway wrote that he would come to the gardens to trap pigeons for dinner. Perhaps this is true, though I have read that he was not quite so poor as he said he was in those days, since Hadley, whom he would shortly dump for Pauline, had a comfortable inheritance. But it made a better story to write about how hungry and poor they were, so I tried not to dwell on this. I decided instead to dwell on the Palais du Luxembourg, where Thomas Paine was imprisoned during the Revolution and escaped beheading because the jailer didn't see the X on the door indicating that he should have his head chopped off. I also dwelt on the fact that Isadora Duncan used to come here to dance early in the morning before she was strangled by her own scarf in the wheel of her car, which could not have been fun. Before we knew it, Peaches and I had crossed the tranquil park and were standing in front of 27 rue de Fleurus, residence of Gertrude Stein and her strange but *sympathique* companion, Alice B. Toklas, who had a mustache and would sit with the wives while Miss Stein lectured young writers on what was wrong with their work. I sensed from the Stein chapters that Hemingway thought she was grouchy and full of *merde* but that is only my opinion. I once tried to read Gertrude Stein and gave up after several hours, not having understood a single word other than *rose*, but I may be wrong. At the university I attended you could study her but I did not.

We walked up the rue d'Assas past a heartbreaking plaque noting that a Jewish family had been taken from here and sent to Buchenwald. There are a depressing number of these in Paris. In 1962, de Gaulle unveiled the moving Mémorial des Martyrs de la Déportation at the eastern tip of the Île de la Cité near Notre-Dame, the monument to the 200,000 people, many of them Jews, and 30,000 of them Parisians, who were deported by the Nazis and the Vichy government. We went there the next day, and when you enter the cryptlike enclosure and see the 200,000 quartz pebbles embedded in the wall, it is hard not to be overcome. As you exit, you see above you the words *Pardonne. N'oublie pas*. Pardon. Do not forget.

We were looking for 113 rue de Notre-Dame-des-Champs, where Hemingway lived over a sawmill, but all traces of it are long gone. Ezra Pound, who ended up in the same asylum where John Hinckley now lives, lived at number 70. He and Hemingway used to box for exercise, but Hemingway could never teach him how to throw a left hook.

That night we went to the Madeleine to hear Mozart's *Requiem*. It is a humbling space, the more so because Saint-Saëns used to play the organ here and Chopin's *Marche Funèbre*, the anthem of death familiar to any five-year-old, debuted here. Josephine Baker's funeral mass was held here in 1975. The second-grandest funeral in Paris ever accorded an American was that of Myron T. Herrick, the American ambassador to France at the time of World War I, and from the photographs it resembled the funeral of a king. The French do turn out for a funeral. In 1885, Victor Hugo's cortege passed in front of two million Parisians. But what is truly impressive about the Madeleine is that it is named for a prostitute. Peaches, who is a churchgoing Episcopalian, did not appreciate this insight of mine and hit me. But then the music started and she forgot to be cross with me. After the concert we walked across the street to Caviar Kaspia and sat in the room upstairs with the oil painting of the Russian boyar coursing through the snow in his horse sleigh and ate caviar on blinis and drank iced vodka and afterward felt very poor but very happy.

—*Forbes FYI*, September 2005

PARIS TO DIE FOR

People going to Paris for the first time will ask you what they should see. I always tell them, "Père-Lachaise." And always their eyebrows furrow when I explain that it is not a hot new restaurant but a cemetery. "Cemetery?" they say. "We're not going all the way to Paris to see a *cemetery*."

"Too bad," I reply, "because then you'll miss Oscar Wilde, Héloïse and Abélard, Jim Morrison, Edith Piaf, Chopin, Balzac, Rossini, Colette, Gertrude Stein and Alice B. Toklas, Richard Wright, Modigliani, Sarah Bernhardt, Isadora Duncan, Molière, and Proust." The ultimate *Who Was Who*.

I've been there a half dozen times. A few hours in this vast, leafy necropolis and you'll emerge back into the hum and thrum of Paris feeling serene and refreshed. I first heard about Père-Lachaise a quarter century ago from Alistair Horne. He's Sir Alistair now, in recognition of his achievements as a historian. He was knighted the same day as Mick Jagger, who showed up at Buckingham Palace twenty minutes late wearing jogging shoes. The palace chamberlain looked down his long nose and said, "Ah, Sir Michael, how *very* good of you to join us." My favorite of Alistair's nineteen books is *Seven Ages of Paris*, brilliant in every respect, including his description of Père-Lachaise, which, as he writes, "contains probably more of France's past than any other 44 hectares of her soil."

Père Lachaise was Father François d'Aix de la Chaise, confessor to Louis XIV. Being the priest who heard the Sun King's confessions was, to judge from the acreage and the view from here, a very good gig to have. *Cheated on the queen, again, eh? Well, no one's perfect. How about one Hail Mary and half an Our Father?* After the Revolution, the land was sold to the city. A city in which 1,343 people got their heads chopped off in two years was bound to run out of burial space sooner rather than later.

In 1817 city administrators had a brainstorm about how to attract customers: reunite the remains of the doomed twelfth-century lovers Héloïse and Abélard and showcase them under a grand gothic marble canopy. Before long, Père-Lachaise was the chic place to be shoved six feet—rather, two meters—under. The remains beneath the ornate marble canopy are in all likelihood *not* those of the doomed twelfth-century lovers, but now there are so many famous people here that it no longer matters.

Mark Twain visited in the 1860s and reported that there were people "snuffling" over Héloïse and Abélard's tomb. Today the snuffling takes place up the hill, at Jim Morrison's grave. The first time I visited, there were a dozen young snufflers sitting around Jim's grave, channeling their grief with fragrant hand-rolled cigarettes, multiple body piercings, and graffiti. These vigils became such a nuisance that the authorities put up a chain-link fence and posted a notice warning that grave defacement is frowned on almost as much as cooperating with U.S. foreign policy. But the liminal—from the Latin *limen*, threshold—urge to leave mementos on tombs runs deep. Tombs, particularly mausoleums, are vestibules to the underworld. On a previous visit, I found Oscar Wilde's tomb covered with hundreds of lipstick kisses.

One of the pleasures of prowling about Père-Lachaise is stumbling upon the unexpected. You never know who you're going to stumble on. While looking for the grave of Nadar, the nineteenth-century photographer who took history's first aerial photographs, from hot air balloons over Paris, I came upon the inscription:

PIERRE DE CHABOULON
SECRÉTAIRE DE L'EMPEREUR
"IL ETAIT
PLEIN DE FEU
ET DE MÉRITE"
—NAPOLEON À ST-HÉLÈNE

A few feet away, my companion Peaches and I found the tomb of Dupuytren, the surgeon who performed the first successful cataract operation. He's just up the avenue from Beaumarchais, author of

The Marriage of Figaro and financier of the American Revolution. A distance from him we found Edith Piaf's simple black granite tomb piled high—as it always is—with flowers. She died in 1963. If they're still laying flowers on your grave forty years later, *that's* immortality.

As you approach the eastern wall of Père-Lachaise, a kind of silence descends that's even more still than the silence elsewhere here. This section evokes the greatest grief. It was here in the final days of May 1871, against the bullet-pocked wall, that 147 members of the Paris Commune were lined up and shot. It's become a rallying point for France's left wing.

It is also here that Père-Lachaise's most wrenching memorials are to be found: those to the dead of Auschwitz, Buchenwald, Dachau, and the other hecatombs of the Third Reich. Soil from those places was brought here and mixed with the earth beneath the sculptures.

It was November. We walked down the avenue lined by sculptures of emaciated, tortured humans. The late afternoon sun, slanting through the yellow acacia leaves, failed to warm. Here the chill goes through you. We did not speak. I looked and saw that Peaches's cheeks were streaked with tears.

We climbed from there and soon we came upon Gertrude Stein (of Allegheny, Pennsylvania) and Alice B. Toklas (of San Francisco) and our mood lightened. We turned onto the Avenue Carrette, and there waiting for us, as he has been since he was reburied here in 1909 after nine years elsewhere in a pauper's grave, was Oscar Fingal O'Flahertie Wills Wilde. Today we had a connection, since we were staying in the hotel room where he died a sad and painful death in broken exile on November 30, 1900.

The lipstick kisses were gone, but there were lots of flowers, including one bunch with a handwritten note in Italian pinned to it. I read a few lines. It was a love note. I felt as though I were prying, and stopped reading.

The tomb is striking, an Art Deco–Assyrian sphinx, executed by Jacob Epstein and paid for, anonymously, by a Mrs. Carew. Striking, but I still can't decide even after a half dozen visits whether I actually like it. According to one account, the sphinx's naked genitals offended a pair of old ladies, who knocked them off with a hammer. Poor Oscar, assaulted in death as in life. They were restored in 1992.*

On the back is a lengthy description of Wilde's accomplishments, oddly focusing on his academic career at Oxford. Beneath are two in scriptions, the first from his *The Ballad of Reading Gaol*:

AND ALIEN TEARS WILL FILL FOR HIM
PITY'S LONG BROKEN URN,
FOR HIS MOURNERS WILL BE OUTCAST MEN,
AND OUTCASTS ALWAYS MOURN.

The second is from the book of Job:

VERBIS MEIS ADDERE NIHIL
AUDEBANT ET SUPER ILLOS
STILLEBAT ELOQUIUM MEUM.
JOB CAPUT XXIX.22

My schoolboy Latin wasn't quite up to the translation, and the Oscar Wilde suite at L'Hôtel on the rue des Beaux-Arts provided no Gideon Bible, so it wasn't until I got home that I was able to look it up: "After my words they spake not again; and my speech dropped upon them." Wilde could easily have provided a translation. When he took his oral examination in Greek at Oxford, he was given a passage from the Passion of Christ to translate. He did it so fluently that the dons interrupted him and said they were satisfied. He replied, "But I want to see how it ends."

His own ending, in Paris, was as wretched as his life had been radiant when, five years earlier in London, he had two hit plays running in St. James's. Few have fallen so far so fast. He went from riches, honor, and a front table at the Café Royal to ignominy, trial, jail, exile, penury, and death in a seedy *pension*. He's celebrated for

* On my most recent visit, I found the tomb encased in plexiglass, to protect it from the smooches. The plexiglass was entirely covered in lipstick kisses, with the result that the tomb now looks like a heavily graffitied construction site.

his deathbed witticisms: "My wallpaper and I are fighting a duel to the death—one or the other of us has to go"; "I am dying as I have lived, beyond my means." But it was no way to go, dying slowly and agonizingly of a misdiagnosed ear infection possibly resulting from tertiary syphilis. Peaches and I paid our respects and left.

Down the cobblestone avenues past Balzac and Nerval and Géricault and Colette. We looked for Doctor Gachet, who had tended to another tragic artist of the time, Van Gogh, but couldn't find him.

We walked all the way back to the hotel that afternoon and early evening, stopping to refresh ourselves in the crowded Marais. As we crossed the Pont Neuf, built in 1607, you could see the whole city at once: at one end, the Eiffel Tower sparkling from twenty thousand computerized strobe lights, at the other, the softer, ancient panorama of Notre-Dame.

Somehow we ended up at a restaurant on the rue des Grands-Augustins, wearing silly feather hats given us by the waiter, drinking champagne and eating escargots and *cuisses de grenouilles* and listening to "If I Had a Hammer" sung in French to the accompaniment of accordion music. From the sacred to the profane, in one afternoon.

L'Hôtel, formerly L'Hôtel d'Alsace on the narrow rue des Beaux-Arts, would be barely recognizable to its former tenant. It is now *tout luxe* and ornate. There's a small bar adorned with black-and-white photographs of a few of its better-known visitors: Johnny Depp, Keanu Reeves, Sean Penn, Robert De Niro, Dennis Hopper, Jeanne Moreau.

The Oscar Wilde suite is number 16 on the first floor, up the narrow winding staircase. His biographer Richard Ellman recounts how one day, unable to pay for his drinks at an outdoor café in Saint-Germain, Wilde remained at the table even as the waiters, trying to drive him away, rolled back the awning, leaving him to be drenched in the rain.

Judging from the deathbed photograph taken by Maurice Gilbert, the wallpaper that annoyed him has been changed. The room is dominated now by a fantastical green-and-gold mural of peacocks. It looks similar to others done by his old friend and verbal sparring partner James McNeill Whistler. The mahogany bed looks as though it had been designed by Aubrey Beardsley, with its headboard carved with swans. A haunting period crystal chandelier hangs in the alcove that gives out onto a small balcony overlooking what used to be the courtyard. The walls are adorned with letters that he wrote in this room to his last publisher, Leonard Smithers; also, with the final bill from his kindly hotelkeeper, Dupoirier; and with caricatures by Spy and Toulouse-Lautrec, as well as a yellowing news clipping from May 19, 1897:

FREE ONCE AGAIN
OSCAR WILDE WILL RESUME
HIS CAREER AS A PLAYWRIGHT

He never did. I once owned a first edition of his masterpiece, *The Importance of Being Earnest*, published by Smithers in 1899. When it was published, the name Oscar Wilde was still so radioactive that his name did not appear. It says only "By the Author of *Lady Windermere's Fan*." In the play, Jack tells the Reverend Chasuble that his invented brother has died. "He seems to have expressed a desire to be buried in Paris."

"In Paris!" says the Reverend, shaking his head. "I fear that hardly points to any very serious state of mind at the last."

—*Forbes FYI*, December 2005

HOW FOIE GRAS WAS MY VALLEY

I try to avoid the sweeping statement, but I assert that there is surely no sight more preposterous than a busload of German tourists pulled over to the side of a road in France to take pictures of the daily 10:00 a.m. force-feeding of geese. But you have to credit their Teutonic pluck. It takes guts to go play tourist in a country you've been invading since the 1870s. We bicycled a total of 245 kilometers, and it seemed that every time you looked, there was a marker saying that here some poor twenty-four-year-old garage worker named Philippe or Marc had been *lâchement assassiné* by *soldats Allemands*. I had to look up *lâchement*. It means "cowardly." What do they think, these busloads of people from Stuttgart and Munich, when they see that through the bus windows on their way to the next *gavage* of hysterical geese?

But the Dordogne has been a misery magnet since 1337, when the Hundred Years' War began. That funfest was followed by the more grim wars between Catholics and Huguenots, when it was okay—a moral duty, even—to burn people alive for their views on the Real Presence. Then, just as the place was getting back on its feet after the Revolution and two Napoleons, phylloxera wiped out the vineyards. And then the Nazis arrived—and not for the geese. But a history of ruination and tragedy does bestow on Eden a certain depth. Henry Miller, who appreciated earthly beauty almost as much as he did women, declared this part of France "the nearest thing to Paradise this side of Greece." It did not feel remotely like paradise as I pedaled up the seven-kilometer-long hill to Rocamadour, trying vainly to keep up with my nine-year-old son. But for most of the week I agreed with Miller. The Dordogne is quite something.

I'd been hearing about "the Dordo" for years, and finally took the family there on a bike trip. It's a landscape built for kids: dramatic castles once lived in by Richard the Lionheart; caves where man created the first art; rivers for fishing and paddling; town markets redolent with lavender and statice and cheeses; starred restaurants in Relais & Châteaux hotels; hot fields of blazing sunflowers; cool forests aromatic from moss and truffles; picnics on bluffs looking down on trout-dimpled water; biking through a thunderstorm to a cozy inn offering a lunch of fresh mushroom omelets and glasses of Bergerac wine. It's not a hard sell, really.

We had our first semiserious hill the morning of Day Two. Perhaps for the best, since dinner the night before consisted of foie gras and a dessert called a chocolate volcano, which left Conor (my heir) looking like a Jackson Pollock painting. At the top of the hill, we stopped at a farmhouse for refreshments, which consisted of foie gras and white wine. I was hesitant at first, but I here declare that foie gras and wine is an excellent midmorning restorative.

The Lascaux Cave was found, as many caves are, by children and a dog. In this case, the pooch—named Robot—did not make it back out. But what an amazing feat of "Fetch!" he performed. Here in this cave seventeen thousand years ago, men and women created the first art gallery.

They closed the original Lascaux Cave in 1963 because the carbon dioxide emitted by thousands of daily visitors was causing "green and white disease"—a limestone version of gingivitis—to form on the paintings. Lascaux II is an exact copy, painstakingly re-created using the same painting techniques as in the originals: pigments mixed in the mouth and blown through marrow bones onto the walls.

A few days later, we visited a real cave, the Font-de-Gaume near Les Eyzies. As we went in, a woman was coming out holding her head, blood spurting from a gash. "*Pas sérieux!*" she cheerily exclaimed.

Our guide was a scholarly Englishwoman who stated in a fashion not inviting argument that Cro-Magnon was—I wrote it down—"more advanced than us." Surely a sweeping statement, but I could not argue with her assertion that the first evidence of "organized fire" was found in Nice, and dates back some 450,000 years.

We regained the light and pushed on to La Bugue and heavenly omelets; then pedaled back to Les Eyzies in a drenching rain, but it felt fine and carefree, as if it were a scene in a French B movie accompanied by accordion music. Later, my thirteen-year-old daughter, Caitlin, and I took a stroll over a bridge and looked down and there saw a dozen antique cars parked cheek-by-jowl next to a small by a stream. We wandered down. It was a club of English Alvis owners, on a ramble through the countryside. They were having their pints, pink-faced, jolly as could be, delighted to explain all about their marvelous cars. They were happy to be away from their damp sceptered isle, tootling and honking through paradise in their gleaming, buffed autos.

Cat and I walked back to the hotel for a dinner of foie gras on white asparagus, sole, and chocolate soufflés. The chef was in an especially fine mood, since that very afternoon he had received the Légion d'Honneur for his contributions to French cuisine.

Three days into the trip I had eaten so much foie gras that I was wondering if I ought to go on intravenous Lipitor. I decided to cut back. But every day at lunch arrived heaping bowls of warm potatoes. Boy, were they good. The bad news was that they were cooked in goose fat. Well, I thought, maybe it will be a massive heart attack and over quickly.

Beynac Castle looms 150 meters above the Dordogne River. They shoot a lot of movies there. It was owned by the same family from 1115 to 1961, except for a brief spell in the late twelfth century when Richard the Lionheart occupied it. I was taken by the baronial hall from which the barons of Beynac issued their decrees from a portal 30 meters above the courtyard below. And picked up a useful tip: clockwise ascending spiral stairways favor right-handed defenders descending with drawn swords. Be sure to mention this to your architect when planning the beach house.

We peeked into Richard the Lionheart's apartment (or so at least they claim it to be). He was killed not far from here, during the siege of Chalus. I have never been a special fan of Richard's ever since I learned about his slaughtering 2,700 Muslim captives at Acre during his crusade. It took three days to behead them all. Reading about the Crusades provides insight into our complex relationship today with the Muslim world. But my feelings about Richard were tempered when I came across James Reston, Jr.'s excellent book *Warriors of God*, which is largely about Richard and his fierce opponent Saladin.

At Chalus, Reston relates, Richard was strutting about in plain view of the defenders, and not wearing armor. A young crossbowman, one Peter Basil, let fly a bolt. It struck Richard in the arm and lodged deeply.

A butcher botched the extraction. Richard's arm turned black with gangrene; the death watch began. His forces meanwhile took Chalus. He ordered all the defenders hanged, with the exception of Peter Basil, whom he had brought before him.

"What harm have I done to you that you have killed me?" Richard demanded.

Peter replied, "With your own hand you killed my father and my two brothers, and you intended to kill me. Therefore take any revenge on me that you want, for I will endure the greatest torments you can devise, as long as you have met with your end. For you have inflicted many and great evils on the world."

Lionheart's attendant urged an especially painful and slow death for the cheeky young regicide, and God knows the medieval mind was good at coming up with horrible torture. But Richard said, "I forgive you my death" and ordered Peter released and given one hundred English shillings. "Live on," he told the surely stunned Peter. "By my bounty behold the light of day. Let the vanquished learn by my example."

The next morning, I chanced into the little church in Carsac, built on the site of a Roman temple. An old woman was cleaning cobwebs and bird nests out of the high-up stained-glass nooks with a five-meter-long branch of bamboo. There was something quietly beautiful about this simple office she was performing. We pedaled to the mill where they've been pressing oil from walnuts and chestnuts for more than four hundred years.

We had hot dogs for lunch that day—slathered with peppers and onions, tomatoes and Gruyère and then broiled. We ate them in the shade of a tall chestnut in the town square and drank cold draft beer and then pedaled on to Souillac and the old abbey there, built by returned Crusaders in the style of Hagia Sophia, which they'd seen in

Constantinople on their way to Jerusalem. Carved in stone at the entrance is a relief of the prophet Isaiah. His carvers caught him at the moment of revelation that a messiah would someday be born, and Isaiah is dancing at the news. During the Revolution, someone smashed off his nose with a hammer, but Isaiah remains joyful, his whole body and beard twisting in ecstasy at the news he has just been given. You could stand there for hours, Christian, Jew, Muslim, atheist, and watch him dance as swallows flit overhead and your nostrils fill with the centuries-old smell of incense.

We spent the last two nights in a riverside hotel called the Château de la Treyne, which in the course of its half millennium's existence was sacked and resacked by Catholics, Protestants, and Jacobins until history had run its course and it could at last become a hotel. Our room, named Cardinale, was at the very top, and in the early morning you looked out and saw ghostly mists rising up from the Dordogne.

On our last day we pedaled to Rocamadour. For centuries it was a stop on the great pilgrim route from Paris to Santiago de Compostela in Spain. It was also a destination in itself. Here in 1166 a perfectly preserved body was found; it was said to be that of the publican Zaccheus, husband of Veronica, who wiped the face of Christ as he stumbled toward Golgotha. According to legend, Veronica and Zaccheus fled Palestine and ended up here. Veronica died and Zaccheus became a hermit in these cliffs—Roc Amator, the lover of the rock.

You don't have to believe any of this, but Henry Plantagenet, later Henry II of England, husband of Eleanor of Aquitaine and the father of Lionheart, did. He came here to pray to the Black Madonna that still looks down from the wall of the little chapel housing the tomb where the hermit's body was found. Henry was cured of his sickness, or so he said he was, and so began another wave of pilgrims, including St. Dominic, St. Bernard, St. Louis, Blanche of Castile, Philip the Fair, hundreds of thousands of others. The flag of Rocamadour flew over the battle of Navas de Tolosa, when the Moors were routed by the army of Alfonso VIII of Castile.

Today Rocamadour is a crush of tourist buses. But you can steal away from that and refresh yourself in the cool and dark of the chapel beneath the Black Madonna and the lamps hung there by Crusaders and the bell that was said to ring miraculously every time storm-tossed sailors were saved by the Virgin of Rocamadour. Then you can walk down the steps and have a pleasant lunch and justify the second glass of cold Bergerac wine by virtue of having to pedal all the way back to Treyne in time for champagne cocktails on the patio and one last death-defying inhalation of foie gras.

—*Forbes FYI*, April 2002

HANGIN' WITH VAN GOGH AND DE SADE IN PROVENCE

We were a gay party that night at dinner at the hotel outside St. Rémy and slept soundly, if erratically, awaking at intervals throughout the night to the sound of—I would guess—ten thousand bullfrogs croaking symphonically. It's not an unpleasant sound. I suppose it is reassurance of sorts that global warming has not yet asphyxiated critical links in the food chain. But when next I tuck into a plate of *cuisses de grenouille*, there will be a note of revenge.

There's nothing like a thirty-seven-kilometer bicycle ride, the last six uphill and into a stiff mistral, to whet the appetite. And nothing like the Provençal landscape on a bright spring morning to squeegee eyes grimy from living amid skyscrapers. We pedaled through fields ablaze with red poppies, past lavender, herb, and melon, and orchard trees—apricot, cherry, plum, and olive—branches pendulous with ripeness. The sky seemed blue as never before, the clouds white as snow. The air shimmered. If it rained it would come down Perrier.

"This country," Van Gogh wrote from here to Emile Bernard, "seems to me as beautiful as Japan as far as the limpidity of the atmosphere and the gay color effects are concerned."

The main roads are lined with plane trees, originally planted by Henry IV. Everywhere you see straight lines of cypress trees, windbreaks against the stern mistral, which can blow so hard as to knock a man down or drive him mad. Perhaps it was a factor when a young ponytailed, spittle-spraying shepherd leapt out at me from the bushes with a knife. But first, lunch.

And what a lunch, at the Mas de la Brune near Eygalières. (*Mas* is Provençal for large farmhouse. In Paris, for some odd reason, the *s* is silent.) To the American eye, this particular *mas* seems more château than a milieu for clucking hens and mooing livestock. It was built in 1572, and into its limestone facade are carved the old French words for: MORTAL: THINK OF YOUR END IN HELL, OR PARADISE WITHOUT END. A sobering notice, but certainly on a higher plane than WELCOME TO BILL AND BETTY'S! We sat outside in the bright sunshine drinking cold pastis and watching the mistral ripple the château's ivy.

The nonbicyclists had spent the morning at market in town, buying fresh vittles for our noon feast. They and the *mas*'s resident chef then cooked them in the kitchen. Out came platters of anchovy-tangy tapenades, grilled eggplant, ragouts, sausage, duck, cheeses without end, sun-warm cherries with mascarpone.

If this groaning board sounds familiar, you're probably one of the seven billion people who read Peter Mayle's book *A Year in Provence*. He lived not far from here, in the Luberon Valley. His great success was not without cost: If you make a place sound this wonderful, can busloads of tourists be far behind? His neighbors, the ones he wrote about so charmingly, were not thrilled by the resulting barbarian invasion. Mr. Mayle had to sell his house and flee. He entered the Author Protection Program and lives at an undisclosed location somewhere in Nebraska near an ICBM silo.

My encounter with the deranged knife-wielding *berger* took place after lunch, a mile or so northwest of the *mas*. Walking on ahead of the group, I found the road completely blocked by two hundred or so sheep. I clapped my hands to shoo a path through them. This is apparently a serious faux pas in this part of Provence. To paraphrase Dr. Johnson, nothing so concentrates the mind as to have a knife held to one's throat. But the rest of the walk was delightful, and by six in the evening I had reached St. Rémy and drank a cold *pression* beer on a terrace named for Michel de Nostradame, born here in 1503.

Having spent many a hour over the years being bored comatose by people who maintain—insist—that Nostradamus predicted the Great Fire of London, World War II, the Kennedy assassination, and the 1986 *Challenger* shuttle disaster, I was prepared to detest the man. But standing outside his house and reading the plaque I learned that he was a medical doctor, highly educated, greatly respected, and moreover, devoted much of his life to treating the plague with herbal medicines rather than with the ghastly "cures" favored by the more butcherly of his brethren. He so impressed Catherine de Médicis—albeit because of his prophecies—that he was installed as "King's Doctor." Too late to help her husband, Henry II, who took the tip of a jousting lance through the eye socket, but no blame can attach to Nostradamus for the king's demise ten painful days later.

I walked the last kilometer back to the hotel in the gloaming, to the squeak and flutter of bats. Back at the château—words I hope to type many more times before I die—we gathered over cocktails to share the day's gossip and adventures.

The Maison de Santé de Saint-Paul de Mausole has been a sanitarium on and off for four centuries. It was here that Vincent van Gogh came in May 1889 to find peace after the quarrels with his friend Paul Gauguin in Arles and cutting off part of his left ear and presenting it to a prostitute for safekeeping.

It's peaceful here on a hot day, in the cool cloister filled with purple pansies and red and yellow roses. Poor Vincent was tormented by epileptic fits and probably by what we now call bipolar disorder: periods of manic intensity and abysmal depression. Upstairs above the cloister is a replica of his room. You can look out through the iron-barred windows and imagine a swirling starry night looming above the field. He said that when he was painting, he never noticed the bars.

Vincent wrote eight hundred letters (in four languages) over his lifetime, mostly to his brother, Theo, the art dealer. During the fifty-three weeks he spent here at the asylum, before going north and shooting himself mortally in a wheat field at the age of thirty-seven, he produced 189 paintings—including the irises that would eventually set the record for the highest price fetched at auction at the time. He also managed to turn out a hundred drawings. It works out to about one work of art per day. He wrote to Theo: "As for me, I'm working like someone possessed . . ."

When he lived in nearby Arles, he fueled himself mostly on coffee and alcohol. To Theo: "I admit all that, but all the same it is true that to attain the high yellow note . . . I really had to be pretty well keyed up." Coffee and absinthe—just what a doctor would prescribe for epilepsy and bipolar disorder. The calmer routine and the hydrotherapy baths at the asylum, along with Roman ruins, cypress groves, olive fields, and abundant irises, must have been a benison. He lived in terror of his fits and the frightening hallucinations. But without them, we would not have his *Starry Night*. Van Gogh is the artist who most elicits empathy, even as you sense, a bit guiltily, that you would probably have crossed the street to avoid him.

Before he left Arles for St. Rémy, he wrote to his sister: "As for myself, I am going to an asylum . . . not far from here, for three months. . . . Every day I take the remedy which the incomparable Dickens prescribes against suicide. It consists of a glass of wine, a piece of bread with cheese, and a pipe of tobacco. This is not complicated, you will tell me, and you will hardly be able to believe that this is the limit to which melancholy will take me; all the same, at some moments—oh dear me . . ."

One day we bicycled up a steep incline to the twelfth-century walled town of Bonnieux, where we ate lunch on a shady veranda and drank rosé and smoked cigars. From there we hiked through a valley of cherry and olive trees and up another steep hill to the ruins of the castle that was once home to the Marquis de Sade.

The odd part—well, there were many odd parts to the Marquis—is that he emerged after thirteen years in the insane asylum at Charenton adamantly denying that he was the author of *Justine* and *The 120 Days of Sodom*. Those very naughty books—the *50 Shades of Gray* of their day—he published anonymously, whereas according to his biographer Francine du Plessix Gray, he published "more than twenty excruciatingly chaste, excruciatingly boring plays, and a few equally chaste and tedious prose fictions, of which he was immensely fond." *Figurez-vous.*

He loved his château here at Lacoste, and he had some pretty good times in it, too. There were forty-two rooms, including a private theater—the home entertainment center of its day—that could seat eighty. At a time when hygiene did not rank high on any nobleman's agenda, there were fifteen portable toilets and six bidets. The Marquise, Mrs. de Sade, even had a bathtub with a copper water heater. But then if you threw the kind of parties he did, innovative plumbing would have been de rigueur.

Between de Sade and Van Gogh, a lot of folks around here seem to have ended up in mental asylums. The shepherd who wanted to cut my throat for disturbing his sheep could use a week or two of anger-management therapy and hydrotherapy; or even a full frontal lobotomy. The afternoon's de Sadean theme continued back at the château, when one of our party, a jovial but mischievous fellow, produced a bottle of absinthe.

Absinthe, after being mixed with iced, sugary water, tastes like molten Good & Plenty. Delicious. It is also 140-proof and distilled from wormwood, whose molecular structure bears an interesting resemblance to that of tetrahydrocannabinol, the active ingredient in marijuana. In Belle Epoque Paris, happy hour in the boulevard cafés was known as *l'heure verte*. How pleasantly we all chatted that night as our absinthe dispenser repeatedly refilled our glasses.

The next morning, lying sticky-mouthed in my bed of pain, the frogs beating a vicious tattoo in my eustachian tubes, I prayed for death; and for the death of the purveyor of the absinthe. It was a pretty grisly twelve-kilometer hike over the Alpilles to Alphonse Daudet's windmill. Someday I will return to pay proper homage to that writer of gentle, humorous tales. What Van Gogh felt like in the morning after four or five glasses of absinthe, with epilepsy and mania coming on . . . I'm no art historian, but is it possible the poor man intended to cut off not his ear but his entire head?

—*Forbes FYI*, April 2006

ZAGAT SURVEY

L Lighting	J Japanese Tourists	S Seating Available	U Uplift	(Scale: 0–30)

2001
LOUVRE MUSEUM, edited by Christopher Buckley

The Mona Lisa
Leonardo da Vinci (1452–1519)

L	J	S	U
12	29	0	20

"Enigmatic" but "accessible," this Florentine "dish" has been packing them in "like sardines" since da Vinci (no relation to DiCaprio) "humped" it from Italy into France over the Dolomites on muleback in a burlap sack. Prepare to "be crushed" "to death" by a "camera-toting" "tsunami." But those who "shoulder" their way through the crowds say they "mona" with delight, even though some ask "what's the deal" "anyway" with the tilting background landscape.

Victory of Samothrace

L	J	S	U
23	29	0	29

This "Kate Winslet" of 190 B.C. standing on the prow of an ancient galley still looks like the "Queen of the World," even if some think she would look "a whole lot" "better" with "her head on." Viewers hail the "ineffable grandeur" of this "Rhodian ex-voto" commemorating a sea victory at the beginning of the second century B.C. But some quibble: "If this is supposed to be Nike, where are her sneakers?" and "What's the big deal? I got one of these on my Rolls."

Napoleon Bonaparte Visiting the Plague-Stricken at Jaffa (March 11, 1799)

Antoine-Jean Gros (1772–1835)

L	J	S	U
14	21	0	27

"Kind of a downer" and "a real Gros-out" say some, but most "kind of" "like" this 17-by-23-foot "nineteenth-century Imax" "celebration" of Napoleon's "humanity" and "noix" (nuts) when he visited his dying soldiers during the Syrian campaign—without latex gloves or face mask. Other viewers say Gros, who studied under David, liked his art "big" and "naturalistic," and is here seeking "to fuse" the "contemporary" with "traditional elements" of "High Romanticism."

Venus de Milo
(Circa 100 B.C.)

L	J	S	U
23	30	0	31

"Disarming," "great hooters," and "characteristic of the late Hellenistic, reviving classical themes while innovating," say Venusians. Fans divide, insisting she is "Aphrodite" or "Amphitrite." Whether she's goddess of love or the sea, all agree that the "slipping drapery" on the hips "entails a closed stance" and "imparts an instancy" to the figure. "Whatever," say self-declared "philistines" just looking to spend some "quality eyeball time" with a "babe-alicious" "piece" "of marble."

The Consecration of Emperor Napoleon and the Coronation of Empress Josephine
Louis David (1748–1825)

L	J	S	U
14	20	0	24

"Whoa!" and "Check it out!" and "How did they manage to get this in here?" are typical reactions to David's "money shot" of Bonaparte's ("What, him again?") self-coronation on December 2, 1804, in Notre Dame. Some puzzle why the French emperor had himself crowned in South Bend, Indiana, but savvier viewers "get a big kick" out of the "oy vey" expression on Pope Pius VII's face while General Murat looks like he can't wait to "pork" Josephine's ladies-in-waiting, "preferably three" "at a time."

Young Neapolitan Fisherboy Playing with a Tortoise
François Rude (1784–1855)

L	J	S	U
14	2	5	12

"Refreshing," especially after a "jillion" "goddamn" "gods and goddesses," and "This would look great in the garden back in Palm Beach," are the verdicts on François Rude's 1833 "marmoreal jeu d'esprit." Rude, the Dijon native who came up with the "flag-waving" "hog-stomping" "derriere-kicking" Marseillaise, here offers a "genre scene" in which, most agree, the classical is "mischievously subverted" by a "new sense of freedom." (Sans doute.) Don't miss the expression of "unbridled joy" on the face of the "cute-as-a-button" "bugger" as he blocks the turtle's escape with a reed, though animal rightists find it "appalling" and "sad" that a "supposedly great" museum "condones" "reptile abuse."

Christ on the Cross Adored by Donors

El Greco (1541–1614)

L	J	S	U
18	11	0	29

"Sublime" even if you're "not in the mood" for "rigorously symmetrical composition" accompanied by "austere" color schemes and "sculptural depth" in a depiction of Christ's body. Some were so "totally" "blown away" that they say Crete-born Domenicos Theotocopoulos should have changed his name to "El Fabuloso" and moved to Toledo, Ohio, "instead of Spain," where he really could have "sunk his teeth" into some "industrial-quality" "mystic" "s—." Others feel that the two "idealized" donors praying at the foot of the Cross dramatically underline El Greco's "ardent" "if subtle" support for campaign finance reform in Philip II's Spain. Don't tell the Inquisition. Meanwhile, check out those "trippy" skies.

The God Horus

Circa 800–700 B.C.

L	J	S	U
27	17	0	22

"Stunning example of Third Intermediate Period Cire-Perdue Bronze" and "Like something out of *The Mummy Returns*" is the consensus here. Still, most find a "majestic serenity" in this "anthropomorphized hawk," one half of the Horus-Thot "divine duo" that used to purify Pharoah's drinking water prior to "major league" "ceremonial occasions." On the quibble front, some insist "your average Central Park pigeon" is "way more numinous" than this "Bronze Foghorn Leghorn." Thot so?

Self-Portrait
Albrecht Dürer (1471–1528)

L	J	S	U
14	2	0	6

The only picture by Dürer in France, "thank God!" say natives still "en colère" at what the Germans have been doing to them since 1870. But foreign visitors love arguing over whether the thistle ("eryngium") in the artist's hands is a symbol of "conjugal fidelity" or "an allusion to Christ's passion." "Du-uh!" counter scholars. Some call Dürer "eine kleine narcissist" for doing so many self-portraits ("Enough already!") while others give him "high Marks" for "fusing the Gothic traditions of the North" with the "plasticism" of the South.

Reliquary of St. Henry
Hildesheim, Lower Saxony
Around 1175

L	J	S	U
16	2	30	15

Kids "dig" "old saints' toes" and "fingernails" "and dried up organs and stuff." "Totally sick"—a high compliment, coming from fourteen-year-old viewers. Grown-ups find the "subdued coloring" of the "quadriform" reliquary "characteristic" of Hildesheim enameling around the time of Henry "le Lion," "Duke" of Saxony (1142–1181). Of the four sides, the one depicting the "wet and wild" Empress Cunégonde seems most popular.

—*Forbes FYI*, September 2001

Continuing Education

What'll they think of next?

—SAMUEL GOLDWYN, ON BEING SHOWN A SUNDIAL

TEACH YOUR FOUR-YEAR-OLD TO SKI

Set alarm for 4:00 a.m. in order to begin dressing process of child. (Note: Allow at least a half hour for locating left mitten, which child does not remember having used for toy soldier's sleeping bag the night before.)

Drop child off at resort's Ski Bunny program. Banter cheerfully with staff as you attempt to pry hysterical child from your legs. Affect bemusement over his insistence that he does not *want* to be enrolled in Ski Bunny program. Tell staff that child "actually loves" skiing and is really adorable once he stops screaming. Slip staff twenty-dollar bills for "treats."

Head off with wife, teary over "abandoning" child.

Stand in thirty-minute-long lift line. Attempt to console wife by remarking how impressed you were by the "professionalism" of the Ski Bunny program's staff. Also remark that you had forgotten how cold it sometimes gets in Vermont, and how windy, with today's nippy, gale-force wind blowing down from Baffin Island. Impress her by calculating that the wind-chill factor comes out to thirteen degrees below zero.

As you reach the head of lift line, remain calm as public-address-system loudspeaker announces: "Will the parents of [your child's name] please report to the Ski Bunny program immediately."

Arrive to find child physically intact but hyperventilatingly adamant that he will not remain another minute in Ski Bunny program. Despite their "professionalism," staff members eagerly concur.

Agree to wife's proposal that you have "fun bonding" experience by teaching child to ski yourself, as she disappears in search of chemical "warmers" to counteract numbness in extremities.

Fasten harness around child and, using reins, repeatedly pull delighted child a hundred yards up baby slope, until your knees begin to make crunching sound similar to snapping stalks of celery, audible even through thickly insulated ski pants.

Convince child that he is "ready" to go with you on ski lift. Emphasize how much "fun" it will be.

Attempt to reassure child as gusts of Canadian air rock the ski lift wildly from side to side, a hundred feet above the slopes. Explain, too, that it is "normal" for the ski lift to stop every three minutes for long periods. Tell him that you cannot feel your nose, either.

Slowly but surely accept the fact that you have erroneously got on a lift to the summit, thereby committing yourselves to a bonding experience you'll both remember for years and years.

As end of lift approaches, attempt to persuade panicking child that the machinery was not expressly invented for purpose of mangling him.

With dubious child held firmly between your legs, begin snow-plowing down several thousand yards of ice covered with a thin veneer of artificial snow. This is Vermont, after all—but think of how much money you saved by not going to one of those expensive places out west!

Try to ignore acute shooting pains in your lumbar region by focusing on interesting new pain on insides of your knees. Remind yourself that with recent advances in arthroscopic surgical technique you'll be walking normally in weeks.

Whoopsie daisy! Apologize to child for falling on top of him. Try to make him laugh by pointing out that tip of his ski is embedded in your left eye.

When lumbar pain increases to unignorable level of intensity, tell child your are going to have "even more fun" by hooking yourselves together with the "kiddie harness."

Fall on ice and, spinning like a wildly thrown Argentine bola, cartwheel down the mountain. Reassure child that death is not imminent by shouting "Whee!" and "Isn't this neat?"

Attempt to stop by grabbing on to leg of passing skier. Profusely apologize to skier, who, it turns out, is a successful negligence lawyer from Manhattan.

Continue bola-like descent. At bottom, hand over frozen, traumatized child to furious wife, who, having stuffed her clothing with two hundred dollars' worth of chemical warmers, resembles a scarecrow.

Remain flat on back for duration of scathing lecture on your incompetence as a ski instructor. (Note: Your wife does not care that you have no feeling in your legs.)

—*The New Yorker*, March 1997

IT IS WITH REGRET

As someone who has received his fair share of rejection letters over the years, let me extend a collegial hug to the many fine and talented high school students who will be receiving college rejection letters this spring.

This year's classic *Oops* award goes to U.C. San Diego, whose admissions department (by the way, why do they call them "admissions" departments when their primary focus is really more on "rejections"?) sent out an e-mail to 47,000 high school seniors, congratulating them on being admitted. The only problem was that 28,000 of them had already been rejected earlier in the month. The admissions director quite properly accepted all responsibility but, in a clear ethical lapse, did not publicly disembowel herself on the front quad.

On occasion, colleges even manage to screw up acceptance letters. Some years ago, Arizona State University famously sent out a letter that began:

To the parent or guardian of Truman Bradley

Dear Parent or Guardian:

Congratulations on 987-65-4321's admission to Arizona State University! We commend you for the significant role that you have played in helping him to prepare for this exciting and critically important time. A.S.U. is committed to providing an outstanding collegiate experience, and we are pleased that he has chosen to take advantage of this tremendous opportunity. We are fully prepared to assist 987-65-4321 in making a successful transition from high school to college.

At least they got Truman's Social Security Number right. His father had the wit to respond:

Dear ____:

Thank you for offering our son, 987-65-4321, or as we affectionately refer to him around the house—987—a position in the A.S.U. class of 2003. His mother, 123-45-6MOM and I are very happy that such a prestigious institution of higher education such as A.S.U. has extended this offer.

In selecting a college for 987, we are looking for a place that will prepare him for the technological challenges of the 21st century.

Patrick Mattimore of Examiner.com wrote a funny and sadly informative piece two years ago about students who award prizes for best and worst rejection letters. That year, Harvard won in the category of "most obsequious while maintaining utter insincerity." As he described it:

"Harvard lets students know how 'very sorry' they are to reject them. They then bestow three wishes, none of which they grant. First, Harvard wishes that they were writing with a different decision. Second, they wish that it was possible to admit the rejectee. Finally, they hope the student they deny will accept their best wishes."

Another category was concision. Normally, it takes at least two words to introduce the dismal theme ("We regret"). But Northwestern improved on that. Its rejection letter began, "After . . ."

In the category of "Most Emphatic," Cornell was the clear winner. It sent out an e-mail informing the rejectee to piss off, and then added that he would be getting a follow-up letter *confirming* his/her unworthiness.

The "grand prize for total insensitivity" went to Reed College. When a student wrote its admissions department to ask if they'd received all his application materials, they sent him back "what was apparently intended to be an interoffice memo." It read: "He's a deny."

A nifty site called www.collegiatechoice.com contains a few primo examples of these, among them the ASU's letter accepting 987-65-4321. It was all too much, apparently, for a young man named Paul Devlin. After getting the heave-ho from one too many colleges, he wrote a letter that was published in *The New York Times*. It began:

Dear Admissions Committee:

Having reviewed the many rejection letters I have received in the last few weeks, it is with great regret that I must inform you I am unable to accept your rejection at this time.

This year, after applying to a great many colleges and universities, I received an especially fine crop of rejection letters. Unfortunately, the number of rejections that I can accept is limited.

All I can say is, any "admissions" department that would turn down someone who can write a letter like that is in the wrong business.

Seeking consolation for young people who will endure these terrible letters this spring, I went to a site called—literally enough—collegedropoutshalloffame.com. What better solace than knowing who among the rich and famous flunked out, dropped out, or never went at all.

To name a few, in more or less alphabetical order:

Edward Albee, playwright. Trinity College, three semesters.

Woody Allen. A double dropout! (NYU and City College.) Mr.

Allen wrote somewhere that he was "thrown out of college for cheating on the metaphysics final. I looked into the soul of the boy sitting next to me."

Kevin Bacon, actor. Dropped out of high school. Wait—wasn't his first big role playing the really smart, screwup kid in the movie *Diner*? The one who knows all the answers on *Jeopardy*? But come to think of it, wasn't he a Bernard Madoff victim? Hm.

Warren Beatty. Northwestern, one semester. Comforting to know that a college dropout can end up with a classy lady like Annette Bening.

Carl Bernstein. His fellow reporter Bob Woodward went to Yale. Is there a moral here?

Yogi Berra. The most quotable American philosopher in history. Beside him, Socrates was a hack metaphysician.

James Cameron, director of *Titantic* and *Terminator*. QED.

George Carlin, the smartest comedian since Lenny Bruce.

Andrew Carnegie. Became one of the richest human beings in history and endowed more than three hundred public libraries.

Scott Carpenter, Mercury astronaut. Whoa—an *astronaut*? Are astronauts *allowed* to flunk out? (He missed the final exam at U.C. Boulder on heat transfer. If he'd been smart, like Teddy Kennedy at Harvard, he could have hired someone to take the test for him. But wait a minute—Teddy got caught. Never mind.)

Winston Churchill never attended a day of college and won World War II. (With a little help from a Harvard man.)

So, parents, if your wonderful, smart, and generally deserving sons and daughters get a "he's a deny" letter or its equivalent, give them a printout of this. It will give them audacity of hope.

Audacity of hope . . . isn't that the title of a book by that guy who started out at Occidental, transferred to Columbia, and finished up Law Review at Harvard?

—*The Daily Beast*, April 2009

AS YOU GO FORWARD

Members of the graduating class:

On my way in from the airport, as I was composing my thoughts for my talk to you, a phrase kept coming back to me. I believe it was a great American, La Rochefoucauld, who first said, "*Ou est la plume de ma tante?*" These immortal words—or, as the first Americans would say, *mots*—seem to me to sum up the very spirit of your generation.

When La Rochefoucauld said that, during the cold winter at Valley Forge when vastly outnumbered Americans assisted only by Guatemalan mercenaries faced the overwhelming forces of Genghis Khan, knowing where your aunt's pen was could mean the difference between having something to write with and trying to make yourself understood to an impatient Mongol warrior by scratching "I surrender" in the dirt with a stick. We lost a lot of *plumes* at Valley Forge, and even more aunts, but then, as Herodotus says, "History is worth a few dead aunts." How true.

Your future, however, is much brighter than it was for the aunts of Valley Forge. As I look out on your faces, a veritable pointillist pageant of diversity, I am reminded of what Descartes, the father of contract bridge, once said, namely, "If you want to get to know someone really well, you must first smell his mocassins after he has walked a mile in them."

Descartes was, of course, speaking metaphorically. And yet, in a larger sense, he was echoing the sentiments of Lao-tse, breeder of the malaria-carrying African dipterous insect that bears his name twice, who so memorably said, "If you want to get to Hang-chou before Fang Li, feed gravel to his ox."

I vividly recall the speaker at my own graduation, so many years ago now. He—or she—said to us, "You stand on the shoulder of people who came before you, so don't jiggle." Wise words indeed. And isn't that what education is all about?

Great changes have taken place during your short lifetime. You no longer have to hunt woolly mastodons with rocks and spears if you want a late-night snack. If you want something to eat, you simply say, "Hey, waiter." If it's money you want, you no longer have to stick a gun in the teller's face and say, "Give me all your money." You just hack into their mainframes. Things really aren't so bad, when you come right down to it.

It has been said that those to whom much has been given will want even more. Someday, not in my lifetime, perhaps, but maybe in yours, human beings will be able to eat all they want without putting on weight. Someday they may be able to avoid jury duty by simply sending in a postcard saying, "No way!" Someday, computers may not only be able to beat human beings at chess, but also at tennis and ice hockey and volleyball. Someday, computers may be able to marry Brooke Shields.

Whether all this comes to pass is now up to you. It is your turn now. My generation is tired. Soon we will take the money you are paying into Social Security and move to gated communities in places where it does not snow and we can start drinking before five o'clock. Or even earlier. In fact, I've already started, not that you would notice.

Yours will be an era of great change. But, as George Harrison put it with the piquancy that is uniquely his, "You know it don't come easy." You will spend hours stuck in traffic listening to cabdrivers explain their proposals for peace in the Middle East. Your flights will be delayed—or, yes, even canceled. Your frequent-flier miles will expire, and the microwaved bean burrito, hot as molten lava on the outside, will still be frozen on the inside. You will be tested, perhaps as no generation before has ever been tested. At such times, try to remember—to paraphrase the words of another Beatles song, "Hey Dude"—that it is a fool who takes his world and tries to make it cooler by inhaling freon.

In one of the last letters he ever wrote to Dorothy Parker, inventor of the fountain pen that bears her name even today, the prince formerly known as Niccolò Machiavelli declared, "If all the *pappardelle* in the world were laid end to end, I wouldn't be a bit surprised."

It may be daunting to you to imagine twenty-five thousand miles of bow-shaped pasta girdling the globe, but let me today say to you, on behalf of my generation, "You can do it!" We certainly hope you can, anyway. It cost a lot of money to educate you people, you know.

—*The New Yorker*, June 1997

NASA ASTRONAUT SCREENING, REVISED AND UPDATED

Which of the following do you most resemble?

A. John Glenn
B. Scott Glenn
C. Glen Campbell
D. Glenn Close

Which of the following do you enjoy watching?

A. *I Dream of Jeannie*
B. *CSI: Orlando*
C. *Desperate Housewives*
D. *Dog the Bounty Hunter*
E. *Three's Company*

Which of the following items would you *not* bring on a road trip?

A. Brass knuckles
B. Teddy bear
C. Nunchuck sticks
D. Throwing stars
E. IED

Which of the following statements best describe the correct relationship between astronauts?

A. More than a working relationship but less than a romantic one.
B. More than a not-romantic relationship, but less than a bodily-fluid-exchanging one.
C. More than a purely physical relationship, but less than one where we don't give each other enough space.
D. More than having hot, steaming, bare-assed, mind-blowing sex while orbiting the earth 250 miles above, but less than doing it on the surface of the moon.

At the end of the movie *2001: A Space Odyssey*, the space ship piloted by Keir Dullea has apparently landed in a lavishly decorated parlor. Which of the following scenarios best describes to you what has happened?

A. The parlor represents the decorative ideal that the apes in the first scene were striving to articulate by clubbing each other with the jawbone.
B. The director, Stanley Kubrick, went totally off his nut.
C. What kind of astronaut name is "Keir Dullea" anyway? These are stupid questions. I don't have to talk to you. Leave me alone.
D. I *said* leave me alone.
E. Won't listen, huh? Here, have some pepper spray.

When you hear the words "Houston, we have a problem," what is the first thing that comes to mind?

A. Malfunction in the retro-fire OMS rockets.
B. Loss of ceramic heat-shield tiles on takeoff.
C. Thruster malfunction in the Reaction Control System.
D. Shuttle commander is attempting to boil crew member's bunny rabbit.

A space shuttle travels at approximately 15,000 mph. A BB pellet has a velocity of about 50 feet per second. If a space shuttle were launched from Houston and a BB gun were fired simultaneously, which would hit the boyfriend-thieving bitch in the Orlando airport satellite parking lot first?

Complete the following sentence: "Three-two-one . . ."

A. Ignition.
B. Ready or not, here I come!
C. Oh God, oh God, oh *GOD, give it to me—now!*
D. Roll down the window, Colleen.

—*Slate*, February 2007

POST-TALIBAN AFGHANISTAN: A GUIDE TO THE KEY PLAYERS

Bulnadir Glubglubaddin, 46. Pashtun. Warlord. Ruled Afghanistan for five hours (1992) until he was overthrown by his cousin **Abdulnadir.** Since '92, has lived in London but has been unable to find full-time employment as warlord. A self-styled "liberal," he allows his four wives to speak to one another twice a year on feast days, and even allows them to walk ahead of him, though his political rivals suggest that this is due to his fear of land mines.

Rasheed Haq, 42. Pushtun. Warlord-producer-director. Son of 1970s-era government minister, he attended Beverly Hills High

School. Recruited by CIA to document Soviet occupation, but disappointed by making "art" films (*My Dinner with Achmed*, *Bamiyan Mon Amour*) instead of videotaping Russian atrocities. However, has extensive contacts within Pakistani Intelligence, whom he has cultivated with addresses of movie actresses taken from outdated "Maps to the Hollywood Stars' Homes."

Nugud Attal, 52. Pishtun. Warlord–grief counselor. Wealthiest of the warlords, maintains villas in Montreux, Cap-Ferrat, and Majorca. Built fortune by "offering" grief counseling to relatives of his tribe's victims at above-market prices. Is said not to be on cordial terms with fellow warlord **Badman Shah** (see below), whose turban he set on fire during a theological discussion in 1984.

Affal Zir, 24. Hazara. Warlord trainee. Entered the Warlord Baccalaureate program at Kunduz University, where he was a member of the Glee, AK-47, and Heroin Smuggling Clubs. Took junior year off to be warlord intern under **Bludrunnin Haq** but never returned to college. Popular among Gen-X warlords for not summarily executing those caught listening to rock music. But his widely quoted remark—"Pashtuns have brains softer than figs"—has not endeared him to some, who have threatened to cut out his tongue.

Malak Alak Mir, 64. Uzbek. Warlord emeritus. The "Grand Old Man" of the Northern Alliance, has been fighting continuously since his fourteenth birthday. Told the BBC that he hopes to be fighting "someone—anyone!—when I am 164, God willing." May be the one man with enough authority to pull together the so-called Rainbow Coalition from Hell: Pashtun-Pushtun-Pishtun-Hazara-Huzara-Tajik-Uzbek-Methodist. A colorful character, he is apt to slaughter goats in the middle of press interviews and offer the blood to squeamish Western reporters.

Badman Shah, 32. Tajik. Warlord consultant. Prefers to operate behind the scenes. Since 1992, has consulted not only with Afghanistan's leading warlords, but all over the world. Offices in Burma, Nigeria, Somalia, and Calgary. His fee structure, a monthly retainer plus hourly rates and first-class air travel as well as east-facing hotel suites, has caused client grumbling, but J. D. Powers Associates named him "#1 Warlord Consultant" in 1997. Motto: "Being a successful warlord today means not just killing the people, but terrifying them 24/7."

Yur Al Tost, 36. Shiite minority, non-Hazara. Warlord-Starbucks franchisee. Cultivated valuable contacts through his six Starbucks locations, all within one block in downtown Jalalabad. Disseminated anti-Taliban political statements through sales of CDs, deceptively labeled *Tunes to Beat Women To*, and *Be-lightful, Be-lovely, Beheaded*. Rumored to have eliminated rivals by poisoning their Mocha Frappucinos.

Abdulrash Azhol, 37. Huzara. The "Warlord's Warlord." Sent letter to U.N. Secretary General Kofi Annan vowing to kill him if he attempts to impose peace on Afghanistan. Hobbies: harshly interpreting Holy Koran, instigating trouble between other warlords, firing on convoys of trucks carrying humanitarian aid. An avid practical joker, he once put C-4 explosive inside his "unamused" fellow warlord **Gulbaddin Hekmatyar's** toothpaste.

Mohammed Zahir Shah, 87. Ex-king. Has lived in Rome since being deposed by his cousin in 1973. Might unify Afghan tribes at a *loya jirga* ("Grand Kaffeklatch"), but the U.S. State Department is reported concerned by his lack of a warlord credential. Also, his habit of calling everyone he meets "Sweetie" may not sit well with the sterner tribal leaders.

—*The New Yorker*

THE DEBT OF SOCRATES

I went down yesterday to the Piraeus with Glaucon, that I might offer up my prayers to the goddesses Brussels and Euro. There we chanced to find among other companions Polemarchus, who was sorely vexed.

Why the long face? I asked.

He replied that his wife, a hairdresser, had just been informed by the Assembly that because of the recent calamities in the Treasury, the state will no longer recompense her an additional sum on top of her regular fee for dying her ladies' locks with Egyptian henna.

It leaves her hands much stained, he said. Is this the action of a just state, that it should abrogate the Handling of Possibly Dangerous Substances clause in the Hairdressers Guild Contract—said to date to the time of the Titans?

Amid the general murmuring, Cephalus, a Retiree, began to curse so vehemently as to make Hera turn the color of pomegranate, saying that he, too, had been ill used by the Assembly.

Now they tell me, he said, that I may no longer have free passage aboard the state interisland trireme for my visits to Mykonos, where I make sacrifice to Apollo Suntan Oil. Am I to pay for transport out of my own purse? Did I not give Athens a lifetime of service, a full ten years, licensing and dispensing the monthly bonuses to Thessalonian olive inspectors?

Indeed you did, I replied, but did the Assembly not recompense you an additional portion for knowing how to operate the bonus-tabulating counting apparatus, and another portion for speaking Phoenician?

Why should I not receive a little extra? he hotly replied. Are the foresters not paid an extra portion for working in the forest?

Very well, I said, but let me ask you, Should a fisherman be paid extra for fishing?

Glaucon replied, Yes, that would be only fair inasmuch as fish, though beloved of Poseidon, are slimy and often stink. Nor is catching them a pleasant business, for one must rise and take to the boat even before Helios's chariot has climbed in the East.

Mischievous Adeimantus interjected, I suppose, Socrates, you will now ask if a philosopher should be paid extra to corrupt the youth of Athens? This occasioned a great slapping of thighs.

I replied, Before you would increase the philosopher's salary, Adeimantus, you must first *give* him a salary. Look at my cloak. It is not nearly as fine as that of our companion Niceratus, who as collector of fees at the Temple of Athena on the Acropolis is paid a higher hourly wage than Herakles received for cleaning out the Augean Stables. And he gets an extra portion merely for showing up on time. No wonder the state money-house looks as though it has been visited by the Furies. Tell me this, Did brave Achilles demand extra compensation for slaying Hector?

He should have, asserted Cleitophon. Under Rule 17 of the Warriors' Guild Standard Contract, anyone volunteering for single combat during a siege more than a hundred miles from Athens and lasting not less than one year is eligible for triple pay, plus retirement on full salary with payments to be continued after one's death to female descendants up to and including the third generation. To say nothing of lifetime trireme privileges, and thrice-annual consultations with the Oracle at Delphi.

A pretty package indeed, I said. I may volunteer for single combat myself. But let me ask you, Glaucon, Polemarchus, and you other wise fellows: Who shall pay for all these handsome emoluments, while the wind howls through the emptied Siphnian Treasury?

They murmured among themselves. At length Thrasymachus said, Let us ask the gods. Surely they would not leave us to the mercies of austere Brussels and flighty Euro.

By all means, I said, make your entreaties to Olympus. But remember—Whom the gods would destroy, first they make pensioners at forty.

—*The New York Times*, May 2010

AFTER SADDAM: A BRIEFER

Ali al-Qastani. Chairman, Iraqi Expatriate Congress. Close to the Pentagon but distrusted by the State Department and the CIA. Deputy Secretary of Defense Paul Wolfowitz's favorite "good Iraqi," though privately viewed by others in the Pentagon as a merely okay Iraqi. In a speech to the Council of Terrific Iraqis, al-Qastani called for a "democratic pluralistic Iraq," administered by himself and members of his immediate family. Did not endear himself to Jordan's King Abdullah when he challenged him to arm-wrestle during a recent Pan-Arab conference.

Ismail bin Aziz. Director, Coalition of Very Good Iraqis. Soft-spoken, moderate, a favorite of Colin Powell, but viewed suspiciously by Pentagon "neoconservatives"—the Zionist cabal directing U.S. foreign policy on behalf of Ariel Sharon—for admitting to the *Financial Times* that he still has to look up "Sunni" and "Shiite" in his copy of *Jane's Inter-Denominational Hatreds*. But, with his contacts, he might be given a second-tier government department to run, such as the Ministry of Dromedary Emissions.

Mansour al-Shazz. Director, Association of Excellent Iraqis. Favored by the CIA director George Tenet, who in 1997 had an electronic bug and tracking device secretly implanted in al-Shazz's lower GI during a routine colonoscopy at the Mayo Clinic. Attracted considerable following among expatriate Iraqis after promising each of them 10 percent of the country's oil revenues once he is installed as leader.

Mohammad bin Bashir. Executive director, Coalition of Perfectly Fine Iraqis. Favored by the Defense Policy Board member Richard

Perle, whom he met in 1993 at a French cooking school in Provence. Popular among gastronomically sophisticated Iraqi expatriates, but could face U.S. congressional opposition for his support of Strom Thurmond for president in 1948.

Anwar Karam. President, Friends of Anwar Karam. Favored by Exxon Mobil for his "Whatever" attitude to U.S. investment in post-Saddam Iraq. Gave a widely noticed speech at the Council on Foreign Relations denouncing President Jacques Chirac and Foreign Minister Dominique de Villepin of France as "despicable amphibians who have seen their last drop of Iraqi oil."

Omar bad Karmah. President, Coalition of Recovering Bad Iraqis. Favored by no one, really, but has made himself useful by acting as liaison to the very worst elements of the former regime, who, though truly awful, may be needed to perform some of the unpleasant work of nation rebuilding, such as WMD (Weapons of Mass Destruction) disposal and replacing the heads on the statues of Saddam Hussein with likenesses of the new leader.

Said Hassan. Executive director, League of Rapidly Improving Iraqis. Charismatic. Nicknamed "Scooter" for his habit of driving a Vespa from table to table at Pan-Arab conferences. Well liked by Powell and Tenet, but may have damaged his chances of being taken seriously again by referring to Geraldo Rivera during an on-camera interview as "a latter-day Alexander the Great."

Salim al-Wolfowitz. Chairman, Association of Iraqis Who Have Changed Their Last Names, formerly the Association of Could Be Much Worse Iraqis. Widely viewed as opportunistic and self-promoting but seen as "inflexible" for waiting too long to change his previous name, Salim al-Gore.

Omar Sharif. Honorary chairman, Association of Still Dashing Egyptian Actors Who Look Iraqi Enough to Play the Part. Commands strong following pretty much everywhere, though Wolfowitz, stung by recent celebrity protests against the war, is said to harbor reservations about putting an actor, no matter how Middle Eastern–looking, in charge of the new Iraq. Rumored to be the top candidate of Laura, Barbara, and Lauren Bush.

—*The New Yorker*, April 2003

THE NEW JAPANESE SAT

TOKYO, April 5—The Education Ministry on Tuesday approved a controversial new series of school textbooks that critics say whitewash Japan's militaristic past . . . Some schoolbook publishers and government officials have argued that it is time to remove "self-deprecating" historical references.

—*THE WASHINGTON POST*

MULTIPLE CHOICE

1. What historically significant event occurred on December 7?
   A. Woodrow Wilson declared war on Austria, in 1917.
   B. Admiral William Bligh, of HMS *Bounty* fame, died in 1817, regretting that he never had the opportunity to visit Japan.

C. Charles Brooks, Jr., became the first American to be executed by lethal injection, in Texas, in 1982.
D. U.S. Secretary of State Cordell Hull flouted diplomatic protocol by speaking in a rude and disrespectful manner to Japanese imperial ambassadors in Washington, in 1941.

2. The cry "Tora! Tora! Tora!" is heard at:
   A. Pamplona, Spain, to warn runners that a female bull is approaching.
   B. Ascot, England, to compliment ladies on their hats.
   C. Synagogues during bat- and bar-mitzvah ceremonies.
   D. Japanese baseball games when Toshimura Tora (no. 39) steps up to bat.

3. Which of the following statements most accurately describes America's President Franklin Roosevelt?
   A. A fanatical, Supreme Court–packing bigot intent on ending the Depression by fomenting war with Japan.
   B. A philandering, wheelchair-bound, stamp-collecting tyrant.
   C. Invited Imperial Japanese Navy to participate in a "friendship mission" by flying over Hawaii, and then perfidiously ordered U.S. Navy to open fire.
   D. All of the above.

4. What was the main objective of the Divine Wind squadron in 1944 and 1945?
   A. To bring oboe and clarinet concerti to remote areas of the Pacific.
   B. To entertain the emperor and his court with works by the French fin-de-siècle performance artist Le Petomane.
   C. To win the America's Cup for Japan, despite the New York Yacht Club's disqualifying Japan's boat for allegedly concealing a Kaiten-type "human torpedo" in its keel.
   D. Parts of all of the above.

5. Historians agree that Japan's doctrine of "preemption" in Hawaii was directly responsible for:
   A. The long-overdue emergence of America as a benign hegemon.
   B. The development of nuclear power as a promising new energy source.
   C. The story line of the award-winning *Snow Falling on Cedars*.
   D. The drafting of Hideki Matsui by the New York Yankees.

6. The term "comfort women" refers to:
   A. 200,000 Chinese and Korean females invited to Japan between 1939 and 1945, as honored guests with all expenses paid, for the purpose of experiencing Japanese culture and customs and promoting friendship and understanding.
   B. Prostitutes in the southern United States.
   C. Female interns in the White House.
   D. Wives of Donald Trump.

7. "Bataan Death March" refers to:
   A. A Seattle grunge band.
   B. Hole no. 5 at Osaka Golf and Country Club.
   C. A badly maintained highway west of Manila Bay.
   D. A lesser-known funereal composition by F. Chopin.

8. What took place at Los Alamos?
   A. A handful of Americans briefly held off the entire Mexican Army.
   B. American scientists unearthed prehistoric winged monsters with which to attack an unsuspecting Japan.
   C. American scientists devised an inexpensive car-rental agency.
   D. The "good" American Robert Oppenheimer was overcome with remorse after unleashing supernatural evil and was persecuted by the U.S. government for the rest of his life.

FOR EXTRA CREDIT

1. Hirohito : Roosevelt ~
   A. Jupiter : Pluto
   B. Joan of Arc : Joan Collins
   C. Gold : Lead
   D. Chrysanthemum : Ragweed

—*The Atlantic Monthly*, November 2005

THE HIGGS BOSON PARTICLE AND YOU: Q & A

Q. *What exactly is a Higgs boson, and why all this fuss?*

A Essentially, it's an eentsy-teensy-weensy particle—we're talking *small* here—that contains the answers to how the universe came about, including whether God was involved. As for the "fuss," the CERN laboratory in Geneva, where the particle was discovered, spent $10 billion on its Large Hadron Collider. Over the last two years, 800 trillion (give or take) proton-proton collisions have been performed, which works out to—what?—maybe not so much per collision, but $10 billion is still $10 billion. For that kind of dough, you expect more bang for your buck than, "Ja, ja, we're working on it, go away!" Physicists—spare me.

Q. *How did they discover it?*

A. It's not rocket science. Basically, two guys with Ph.D.s, one Swiss and one from some other country—they don't have to speak the same language or even get along—stand in this really long tunnel near Geneva and fire protons at each other. When the little bell on top of the Large Hadron Collider goes *ding-a-ling*, presto, there's your Higgs boson in the in-box. But then you need this totally ginormous magnifying glass to find the little bugger. Anyway, they did. *Finally*.

Q. Why is it so expensive?

A. The bell is handmade. And the magnifying glass must be made out of melted diamonds or something. They nearly fainted when they got the bill for that. Then there's the tunnel, which wasn't cheap. Then there's the tanning salon bills for the Ph.D.s, who have to spend their lives in tunnels, like moles. Then there was this huge kerfuffle a few years ago, with these whack-job groups suing CERN, saying it was going to create a black hole that would suck the entire solar system into it. Endo-finito, human life, as we know it. (What jerks.) So CERN had to go to court to get that thrown out, and if you think lawyers in the United States are expensive, try Swiss particle-physics lawyers. Talk about black holes. So it all adds up, and pretty soon you're talking real money.

Q. According to the news reports, all the scientists involved were drinking champagne when the Higgs boson particle was found, leading to jokes that it should be called the "Hic boson." Does drinking help in particle physics?

A. Up to a point. CERN was embarrassed a while back by news reports that the two Ph.D. dudes were firing champagne corks at each other instead of protons. Some scientists defended the practice, saying that champagne corks are a lot more practical—and more fun—to shoot than protons. But who knows? Who cares? Bottom line—they found the sucker. Everyone's happy.

Q. Will there be "spin-offs" from the discovery, as there were with the space program?

A. CERN will soon announce a Higgs boson–flavored powdered breakfast drink. But historically, the Food and Drug Administration has been wary of drinks derived from the debris of primordial fireballs left after proton collisions, so don't expect it at a supermarket near you anytime soon.

Q. Will the discovery affect everyday life?

A. Well, duh.

Q. Hey, I'm not a science-y person, okay?

A. Sorry. The answer is absolutely. Sort of. Well, yes and no.

Q. Can you be like a little more specific?

A. For starters, you're going to be hearing the phrase "Higgs boson" about 800 trillion times. You'll be at a cocktail party talking about the Kardashians and someone will say, "OMG, Higgs boson!" and you'll go, "No, no, no—*please* no more with the Higgs boson." So there's that. Plus this Halloween, every other trick-or-treater is going to be dressed as—guess what? So yes, it's going to affect your everyday life. My advice? Deal with it.

—*The New York Times*, July 2012

Essays

Drawing on my fine command of the English language, I said nothing.

—ROBERT BENCHLEY

HOOF IN MOUTH

"Good to see you again," I greeted the gentleman, a family friend, important businessman and former cabinet secretary. "How's Carol?" The friendly grin remained, but I caught the suppressed wince.

"She died three years ago," he said.

Where *does* one go from there? "Gosh, well . . . seen any good movies, lately?" I made my way to the men's room to bash my head against the wall in private. The Japanese are so much more efficient about this: you chop off the little finger and present it neatly wrapped in a pocket handkerchief to the offended party. If you really screw up, use a bigger knife and disembowel yourself. You have to admire a culture that has ritualized shame into performance art.

Our own phrase for these horrible moments is *faux pas*, "the false step," from the French, language of courtiers, diplomats, and arbiters of elegance *par excellence*. The phrase first turns up in English literature in 1676, in Wycherley's satirical Restoration play *The Plain-Dealer*. The *Oxford English Dictionary* defines it as "a slip, a trip; an act which compromises one's reputation, esp. a woman's lapse from virtue."

It's not a phrase one hears much anymore, and the more's the pity. "I made a faux pas" sounds better than "Man, did I just step in it."

The word *gaffe* gets a pretty good workout. The *OED* cites modern French—*une gaffe*, "a remark by which one 'puts one's foot into it.'" (In screwup etymology, the French seem to rule.) But "gaffe" covers only the spoken word; and who's to say what constitutes a gaffe, in our mendacious age? Pundit Michael Kinsley's lapidary definition of a gaffe is "when a politician accidentally speaks the truth."

During Watergate, the president's men were constantly having to announce that he had "misspoke himself," an odd neologism that somehow made it sound as though Nixon had wet his pants. Just once it would be nice to hear a White House press secretary say, "The president made a faux pas."

There's Dr. Freud's eponymous "slip of the tongue," that awkward moment when the id crawls up your esophagus, grabs you by the uvula, and shouts your secret out your mouth and onto the dinner table. When this happens all the time, it's called Tourette's syndrome. I have a mild case of Tourette's that causes me to blink; on more than one occasion this has been embarrassingly misinterpreted by various women as making a pass.

American presidents have kept us entertained with tongue slips. Jimmy Carter perhaps set the standard at the 1980 Democratic Convention when he extolled the former vice president as "Hubert Horatio Hornblower." Vice President Hubert Horatio Humphrey made a beaut of a slip himself when he remarked, "No sane person in the country likes the war in Vietnam, and neither does President Johnson." Ronald Reagan said in a speech, "Facts are stupid things." (He meant "stubborn.")

My favorite Freudian slip story is the man telling his friend about what happened when he went to the train station to buy two tickets to Pittsburgh.

"The ticket agent," he says, "was a woman with an amazing figure and when I got to the counter, I asked her for two pickets to Tittsburgh."

"That's nothing," his friend replies. "I took my mother out to dinner last night and told her, 'You've ruined my life, you hideous bitch.' It just slipped out."

But gaffes, misspeakings, and Freudian slips are fairly low on the scale compared with true faux pas. Arthur Caldwell, an Australian member of parliament, memorably said, apropos an immigration issue involving Asians, "Two Wongs don't make a white." (His remark doesn't technically qualify as a faux pas, because it was intentional. A faux pas by definition is accidental.)

Faux pas perform a valuable, indeed essential service. Ontologically speaking, they keep us in our place by reminding us that however much the human race may dress itself up, you still cannot take it out. The French philosopher Henri Bergson defined laughter as the self-assuring response of the herd to the behavior of nonconforming members. Faux pas thus provide amusement of the most primal kind. What could be more satisfying than the high and mighty brought low by acts of inadvertent self-immolation? Such at any rate was the balm I applied after my own disaster, as I set out to collect faux pas.

They abound. Not for nothing did Aquinas call man "the risible animal." The moment *homo* became *erectus* he started stepping in it and has been at it ever since. In the old days, putting your foot wrong often meant forfeiting another extremity, like your head. But with the general decline of manners, faux pas became less important. Still, we know that as recently as the seventeenth century it was considered rude to break wind loudly in the presence of the English monarch. Edward de Vere, seventeenth earl of Oxford (believed by some insistent folks to have been the real author of Shakespeare's plays), once embarrassed himself in this way in front of Queen Elizabeth I. He blushingly retreated to his estate for several years. When he finally presented himself in court again, the queen greeted him with "My lord, we had forgot the fart."

The current Queen Elizabeth has in her day had to put up with more than mere colonic trumpet involuntaries. Last year, she was forced to endure some well-phrased abuse in the form of a eulogy by the brother of her former daughter-in-law. Though Earl "Champagne Charlie" Spencer was instantly hailed as the new Mark Antony, his speech qualified as lèse-majesté, a faux pas of the highest sort. Whatever one's views on the monarchy, is it appropriate to dis the queen in her own church in the middle of a funeral? But then the occasion was itself a national gathering to canonize a woman whose entire life had been a series of faux pas—marching up the wedding aisle with the wrong man, throwing herself down those stairs, giving all those self-pitying interviews, getting into bed with a treacherous lover, and finally getting in that car outside the Ritz in Paris—so it was perhaps fitting that she should be laid to rest with one.

On a lighter note, one of the queen's subjects recently made screaming tabloid headlines by not curtsying to her. The offender was one of the Spice Girls, Ginger, to be precise. But she had a reason. Ginger is—like the aforementioned railroad ticket agent—amply endowed. On this occasion, she was also scantily clad, and afraid that genuflection before Her Majesty might cause a truly eye-popping faux pas. This was not the first Spice faux pas. Previously, another grabbed the bottom of the Prince of Wales, causing him to blush. This is what happens when you do away with beheading. The people get *ideas.*

Prince Charles is himself capable of faux pas. A friend of mine was at a wedding lunch at Hampton House outside London for Prince Pavlos of Greece and Marie-Chantal. Prince Charles approached my friend, who was standing next to his wife, whom the prince had not met.

"I hear you're a very good friend of ________," said HRH, referring to a female cousin of my friend's wife. Wink wink, nudge nudge, continued his Royal Highness. "Yes, I hear you're having a *very* good time together."

All my friend could do was croak, "Sir, may I present my *wife* to you?"

"Oh my *God,*" said Prince Charles, "I've really put my foot in it again."

I'm struck by that "again." Does Prince Charles do this *all* the time? Public service alert to all adulterous acquaintances of Prince Charles: think twice before presenting your wife to him at Royal Ascot.

The queen herself is known to be tolerant of faux pas. When the Polish leader Lech Walesa visited Buckingham Palace, he was served artichokes. Never having encountered one, he began to eat the spiny leaves. Her Majesty deftly stepped in and said, "Why don't you eat the bottom part? It takes so long to eat the leaves." *That's* noblesse oblige.

During the Edwardian era, the shah of Persia visited London. At dinner he was served asparagus, a legume unknown to the occupant of the Peacock Throne. After eating the tip of each spear, he tossed the stalk over his shoulder onto the floor. Consternation ensued. Finally everyone else began tossing their stalks onto the floor. *That's* diplomacy.

Buckingham Palace is the scene of my all-time favorite mispronunciation faux pas. President and Madame De Gaulle came to lunch. It was near the end of his term. Her Majesty asked Madame De Gaulle what she was most looking forward to in retirement. Madame De Gaulle's English was thickly accented. Her answer sounded like, "A penis." Her husband leapt to clarify. "Yes, we are looking forward to *happiness.*" One hopes Madame got her wish.

Runner-up in the Department of Unfortunate Mispronunciations goes to Mrs. Stuyvesant Fish, who was attending a fancy dress ball in Newport. At the door, she whispered to the *embayeur*—the guy with the pole who bangs it on the floor and shouts out your name—the theme of her costume: "A Norman peasant." The majordomo banged his stick and thundered aloud to all assembled: "Mrs. Stuyvesant Fish. An enormous pheasant."

Uniforms can lead to confusion. Robert Benchley, bibulously leaving the "21" Club one night, saw a man adorned with gold braid, assumed he was the doorman, and instructed him to call a cab. The man replied somewhat starchily, "I am an admiral."

"In that case," said Benchley, "call me a battleship."

Some years ago in London at a white-tie ball, Claus von Bulow good-naturedly teased a fellow guest who was dressed in black tie. The man shot back, "At least I didn't kill my wife."

The British foreign minister George Brown attended a state dinner in Vienna in 1966. He had enjoyed his wine, and upon hearing the orchestra strike up a tune, turned to an exquisite creature in violet beside him and said, "Madame, you look ravishing. May we dance?"

The exquisite creature in violet said to him, "No, Mr. Brown, for three reasons. First, this is a state dinner, not a ball. Second, that is the Austrian state anthem, not a waltz. And third, I am the cardinal archbishop of Vienna."

How appearances deceive. In the 1930s a woman was seated at a banquet next to Wellington Koo, Chiang Kai-shek's foreign minister. Koo was a superbly erudite man who spoke many languages. The woman began the conversation with, "Chin-ee man, you come far on boat-ee?" Koo nodded politely. She went on like this all evening. Finally it was time for the speeches. Koo rose and gave a stunningly brilliant speech on the larger questions of the day. He sat down and said to the woman, "You lik-ee speech-ee?"

State protocol is to faux pas what a highwire is to a misplaced foot—spectacularly noticeable. Prime Minister Harold Wilson visited Washington in the 1960s, at a time when it looked as though the sun really was starting to set on the British Empire: post-Suez, colonies everywhere clamoring for independence, labor strikes, a free-falling pound. On arriving at the White House for the formal welcoming ceremonies, Wilson pointed out to the U.S. chief of protocol, James Symington, that two of the Union Jacks were flying upside down, the international sign of distress. Next day *The Washington Post* ran a huge picture of the flags over the caption "Oops!"

Symington's phone rang at six a.m.: an unhappy Lyndon Johnson. A formidable thing at any hour. Symington did what he could to assuage LBJ (whose own history of faux pas would fill several volumes), only to arrive at the White House that night for the state dinner to find the following three songs listed on the postdinner musical entertainment program: "I've Got Plenty of Nothing," "On the Road to Mandalay" and "You'll Never Walk Alone." It was, Mr. Symington remembers vividly, that kind of day.

In 1981 his successor in the post, Leonore Annenberg, wife of the publishing giant Walter Annenberg, created a sensation with a literal faux pas—she curtsied to Prince Charles while welcoming him to the United States at Andrews Air Force Base. Mrs. Annenberg, a gracious woman and admired hostess, was only trying to be courteous. The problem was that America had fought a war two hundred years earlier for the republican privilege of not bowing or scraping before royalty. In a way, every American's proudest birthright. Mrs. Annenberg returned to private life shortly after.

Americans and royalty don't necessarily agree on what constitutes a faux pas. Alfonso XIII of Spain, grandfather to the current king, Juan Carlos, visited Hollywood in 1926, where he was accorded a royal welcome. After a while he declared, "I have not met my hero, Fatty Arbuckle."

Embarrassed looks were exchanged between his hosts.

"Well, Your Most Catholic Majesty," one ventured, "Fatty Arbuckle is not really 'seen around' much in Hollywood these days."

"Why ever not?"

"Well, Your Most Catholic Majesty, there was a, um, party."

"Yes?"

"And there was a young woman."

"Yes?"

"And she was, um, penetrated by a jeroboam of champagne. And died. Of peritonitis."

"And?"

"And you see, Your Majesty, after that, he is not received."

"Are you telling me," said Alfonso XIII, growing angry and red-faced, "that this great artist is not *received*? Why, it could have happened to any of us!"

Perhaps the most visual international faux pas occurred in 1992 when President George H. W. Bush experienced sudden, violent gastric distress during a state dinner in Tokyo and vomited "copiously"—as the news report insisted—onto the lap of Prime Minister Miyazawa. Mr. Bush is a model of gentlemanliness, manners, and Episcopalian propriety, a true Yankee aristo. His mortification the next day on reading the newspapers can only be imagined.

But he is not the only president to cover himself—and his dinner partner—in fluid glory. José Mara Velasco Ibarra was five times president of Ecuador. He was constantly being deposed. On one occasion, he turned up at an embassy reception. Accounts vary. He either urinated in the punch bowl or upchucked onto the West German ambassador. (According to one version, he managed to accomplish both feats.) The army immediately deposed him for having compromised the dignity of the republic.

Should this happen to you, consider the presence of mind evinced by Herman Mankiewicz, author and screenwriter (*Citizen Kane*), who once threw up at a dinner party. "It's all right, Arthur," he said to his host, "the white wine came up with the fish."

Can a newspaper typo be considered a faux pas? You decide: In 1915, *The Washington Post* ran an item about President Woodrow Wilson escorting his fiancée, Edith Galt, to the theater. Wilson was so attentive to her that he barely paid any attention to the play. The reporter from the *Post* noted the president's attentiveness to Mrs. Galt, but a typesetting error resulted in people reading the next morning that the president had "spent most of his time entering Mrs. Galt." Could a typo this exquisite really be accidental? Shortly after she became queen, Elizabeth II made a royal tour of London. One of the newspapers reported that at one vista, she got out of her car and "peed down upon her city."

One of the more impressive faux pas of the Gilded Age was committed by James Gordon Bennett, Jr., the very wealthy newspaper magnate. He got gloriously drunk on New Year's Day 1877 and climbed in through the window of his fiancée's Fifth Avenue mansion. Here he became a bit confused and, mistaking the fireplace for a toilet, emptied his bladder into it in full view of his prospective in-laws. The marriage did not go forward. Bennett went off to live in Paris for a while. What a shame Edith Wharton never included this incident in any of her novels. Madame Olenska exiled herself to Paris for less.

A clever recovery can void a faux pas. The Duc de Richelieu, First Gentleman of the Bedchamber, and close friend to Louis XV, one day opened the door and found his wife in bed with a count. He immediately closed the door.

Later, he said to his wife, "*Madame, quel honte! Si ça aurait été quelqu'un d'autre?*" ("Shame, Madame! What if it had been someone else?") Only a Frenchman could have handled the situation with such aplomb. But then only the French could have produced the Duchesse de Noailles.

My friend Timothy Dickinson tells the story:

> *Poor old woman, crazy as a bedbug. She was known as "Madame L'ettiquette" because she was always upset about some lapse in etiquette, if you can imagine someone having a reputation for undue emphasis on formality in the court of Louis XVI. She carried on an extended correspondence with the Virgin Mary, the Virgin Mary being—shall we say—ghosted by her confessor. One day the Virgin Mary made an appalling betise, socially speaking. The Duchess explained the episode to her household forgivingly: "You see, she only married into the House of David."*

And only the English could have produced the actor David Niven. He was at a fancy ball, standing at the bottom of a grand staircase, talking to a man he'd only just met. Two women appeared at the top of the stairs and began to descend.

Niven said to the man, "I say, that must be the ugliest woman I've ever seen."

The man stiffened. "That's my wife."

Niven quickly said, "I meant the *other* one."

"That's my daughter."

Niven looked the man calmly in the eye. "I didn't say it!"

Maybe I'll try that next time.

—*Forbes FYI*, May 1998

THANK YOU FOR NOT WARNING ME

The Department of Health and Human Services has announced that cigarette packages and advertisements will soon be required to feature "frank, honest and powerful depictions of the health risks of smoking." These depictions include smoke streaming from a hole in a man's neck, a set of cancer-ravaged gums, nicotine-baked autopsied lungs, and a illustration showing a baby born to a smoking mother, gasping for breath. Got a light?

Several U.S. tobacco companies, proudly holding high the torch of individual responsibility, tried to block the government action, calling the images "nonfactual and controversial" and what's more "intended to elicit loathing, disgust and repulsion."

Where is the Marlboro Man when you need him? Unavailable, alas. Wayne McLaren died of lung cancer, age fifty-one, and may he rest in peace. The poor guy spent his declining months haunting stockholder meetings of the Philip Morris company—now Altria, which sounds less smoky—trying to get its officers to acknowledge corporate complicity in the disease that was killing him. Philip Morris executives were about as forthcoming and apologetic with poor McLaren as the heads of Fannie Mae, Goldman Sachs, AIG, and other exemplars of American capitalism have been with their victims.

The new warning labels are, on the one hand, impactful (apologies for that awful word). As a precocious juvenile delinquent, I started smoking at age thirteen, filching my mother's Philip Morris–made Marlboros. Would I have lit up so gleefully had the flip-top box been festooned with a photograph of a pair of gray, tumor-eaten lungs?

Possibly not, though never underestimate the blitheness of an adolescent bent on looking cool, never mind the costs. My mother died years later of smoking-related illness. And as it happens, my father died of emphysema, not from cigarettes, but from cigars. Unlike a certain U.S. president, he inhaled.

But to pose the question bluntly: Is it necessary—really—at this late stage to slap gruesome decals on a product that any human being with an IQ above cretinous knows to be lethal? Or is it more prudent to continue on the assumption that we are a nation of idiots?

U.S. Surgeon General Luther Terry's epic report on the link between smoking and mortality became public in 1964. (I just looked him up and learned that this splendid American's middle name was Leonidas, presumably derived from the heroic Spartan leader at Thermopylae who was as lethal to invading Persians as Marlboros are to smokers today.) Surely by now, anyone reaching for that match knows that he's lighting not just a cigarette but a fuse.

There are two competing American behavioral archetypes: Uncle Sam and Lady Liberty. Uncle Sam is stern but loving. He exhorts us to defend our country and to be good citizens. Lady Liberty stands for—well, freedom. Her statue, rising above the waters of New York

Harbor, announces that this is the country where you can be anyone you want, do anything you want—so long as you don't do it in the street and frighten the horses.

Occupying the middle ground between Uncle Sam and Lady Liberty is what we libertarians call the Nanny State. Nanny State is the national bossypants, telling us what not to do. Don't smoke. Don't eat so much. Don't drink. Put down that 36-ounce Coca-Cola! What are you doing on that bicycle without a helmet? Put it on—now! And brush your teeth.

Some decades ago, not content with snatching Marlboros and Twinkies and soda pops from our hands, Nanny decided that she should also be in charge of the national sense of humor. This new rule became Political Correctness. PC is the voice we hear from the back of the room after the laughter has subsided, saying, "*That's* not funny." The importance of being earnest, but not quite Oscar Wilde's version.

I'm not against the new cigarette labels. But I'm not sure I'm for them. Is this a thoughtful position, or just wishy-wash?

Cigarettes kill—no argument there. So does alcohol. So logically, if that pack of Boros is to be decorated to look like a page from a medical textbook, shouldn't bottles of booze depict car crashes, cirrhotic livers, and beaten wives? And why stop there? Shouldn't Big Macs and Burger King Whoppers come with Before photos of those sad souls who appear on TV's *The Biggest Loser*?

For that matter, shouldn't French directors of the International Monetary Fund be required to wear signs saying: CAUTION: MAY BE HARMFUL TO HOTEL MAIDS? And since the new cigarette labels will take effect at the height of the presidential campaign, surely the candidates should be required to wears buttons that say: "WARNING: WILL PROMISE ANYTHING TO GET ELECTED."

—*The Washington Post*, June 2011

HOW TO WRITE WITTY E-MAIL

(Hint: Pretend They're Telegrams)

I got an e-mail the other day that clocked in at 1,286 words. Mark Twain once famously apologized to a correspondent for a long letter, saying he hadn't had time to write a short one.

In the not-so-old days, when electronically transmitted messages were generally urgent, every letter counted. Quite literally. I remember going over the wording of a telegram with the Western Union operator, trying to figure out how to cut it down to the fifteen-word economy-rate limit. They were great editors, those operators; and sticklers who wouldn't let you get away with, say, turning multiple words into one merely by adding a hyphen. Say, *Love-and-kisses*. "Sorry, sir. That's *three* words."

It occurred to me that it had been a long time since I had gotten or sent a telegram. Cheap long-distance telephone, faxes, and now e-mail have made it possible to be as wordy as we want, but in our rush to communicate instantly (and incessantly), we did not pause either to mourn the passing of the telegram as a literary form or to reflect upon its legacy. As those distinctive yellow forms pasted with teletype strips of tape passed from our lives, so did a certain poetry, drama, and wit.

When I was growing up in the fifties and sixties, a knock on the door from the Western Union messenger, always smart in cap and uniform, often signaled a significant moment—more often than not, bad news. The generation before mine had trembled at the approach of the same messengers, who might be bringing a message that began, THE SECRETARY OF WAR DESIRES ME TO EXPRESS HIS DEEP REGRET. . . .

Telegrams had their own code words, such as STOP, SOONEST, PROCEEDING, -WISE, ADVISE. The form itself was designed for concision. The American architect and engineer Buckminster Fuller once famously sent a cable to the Japanese artist Isamu Noguchi, explaining the key equation in Einstein's Theory of Relativity in 249 words. It's considered a masterpiece of compression. What makes Robert Benchley's classic telegram from Venice to his travel agent—STREETS FULL OF WATER. PLEASE ADVISE—so perfect is the superfluous PLEASE.

In his introduction to Joyce Denebrink's *Barbed Wires*, a delightful collection of telegrams, Marvin Kitman wrote that as an art form, the telegram is even more demanding than Japanese haiku, since haiku allows seventeen syllables, and the former only fifteen words. With wit worthy of the form he was illuminating, Kitman tells us that the inventor of the telegraph, Samuel Finley Breese Morse, had been seeking to instill a new, simple literary form that would displace the "flowery New England transcendentalists who dominated the literary Establishment. Unlike those chatterboxes Thoreau, Emerson, and especially Whitman, Morse loved the brief, the clear, the bold, a style epitomized in his code. The Morse code was popular with the avant garde not only because it pruned the deadwood out of the language, but because it couldn't be understood by the masses." Who knew that the Morse code was about elitism?

The very first telegraph message ever sent, on May 24, 1844, was only four words long. Morse tapped them out in the old Supreme Court Chamber (now the Law Library) in the U.S. Capitol, in the presence of Dolly Madison and Henry Clay. As you already know, they were: WHAT HATH GOD WROUGHT! Thus was the Age of Communication ushered in. His partner, Alfred Vail, sitting in a railroad station forty miles away in Baltimore, tapped back, YES, ushering in the Age of Miscommunication. (Morse's somewhat portentous four-letter message was not of his own choosing; that honor had for political reasons gone to the daughter of the commissioner of patents. Vail had been Morse's fellow student at Yale, and had persuaded his father to put up the money for their prototype telegraph device. When they were ready to test it, Vail asked Dad to suggest something to transmit through the three miles of wire stretched around their lab in New Jersey. He proposed: A PATIENT WAITER IS NO LOSER.

It's an ironic choice, considering that they were inaugurating an era of instant communication. Try quoting that the next time sometime phones you in a rage from Hong Kong because the 5,800-page document you e-mailed to him two minutes ago *still hasn't arrived.*

Between the first taps on Morse's telegraph keypad and the playing of taps for the telegram 130-odd years later, the wires (and wirelesses) vibrated with precisely chosen *bon mots*. If you wanted to tell someone off, there was no medium more suited to the task than a well-chosen telegram. The best example of that genre may be the one someone sent Lord Home, the foreign secretary: TO HELL WITH YOU. OFFENSIVE LETTER FOLLOWS. IRATE CITIZEN.

It was especially satisfying when two dynamos of repartee got going, as in the exchange between George Bernard Shaw and Winston Churchill. Shaw invited Churchill to the opening of his new play: HAVE RESERVED TWO TICKETS FOR MY FIRST NIGHT. COME AND BRING A FRIEND IF YOU HAVE ONE. Churchill's reply: IMPOSSIBLE TO COME FIRST NIGHT. WILL COME TO SECOND NIGHT IF YOU HAVE ONE.

There was the Tango Telegram, with one partner functioning as the straight man. Jesse Lasky, head of Paramount Pictures, wired the playwright George S. Kaufman: OFFER $40,000 FOR SCREEN RIGHTS TO ONCE IN A LIFETIME. Kaufman wired back: OFFER $40,000 FOR PARAMOUNT COMPANY. When Cary Grant, notoriously touchy about his age, received a telegram from a magazine editor asking HOW OLD CARY GRANT?, he replied, OLD CARY GRANT FINE. HOW YOU?

Telegrams recorded imperiousness high and low. When Frederick Remington cabled William Randolph Hearst from Havana in 1897 to report, THERE WILL BE NO WAR. I WISH TO RETURN, Hearst famously cabled back, PLEASE REMAIN. YOU FURNISH THE PICTURES AND ILL FURNISH THE WAR. (Actually, this exchange turns out to be apochryphal, but why let that ruin the story?) Less well known is the telegram Mrs. Peter Sellers got one afternoon while she was working in the kitchen and her actor husband was upstairs in his study: BRING ME A CUP OF COFFEE. PETER.

The telegram traffic between war correspondents and their editors back home provided some good moments. The correspondent for the London *Express* got this from his boss: DAILY MAIL MAN SHOT. WHY YOU UNSHOT? The same prefix allowed Evelyn Waugh to trump his editor in 1935, when Waugh was covering the Italian invasion of Ethiopia. The comic novel that resulted from that experience, *Scoop*, teems with cables from Boot to his paper, *The Daily Beast*: NOTHING MUCH HAS HAPPENED EXCEPT TO THE PRESIDENT WHO HAS BEEN IMPRISONED IN HIS OWN PALACE BY REVOLUTIONARY JUNTA HEADED BY SUPERIOR BLACK NAMED BENITO . . . LOVELY WEATHER BUBONIC PLAGUE RAGING. When a rumor began circulating that an English nurse had been killed in an air raid, Waugh's editor cabled, SEND TWO HUNDRED WORDS UPBLOWN NURSE. After checking it out and ascertaining there was no story, Waugh cabled back, NURSE UNUPBLOWN.

Concision sometimes leads to confusion. In 1933, the U.S. ambassador in Sofia, Bulgaria, cabled the Balkan desk of the State Department as follows: QUEEN HAS GIVEN BIRTH TO A DAUGHTER. HAVE CONGRATULATED PRIME MINISTER. The Maud Committee, which in 1940 advised the British government that a fission bomb was feasible, owed its name to a somewhat garbled understanding of a telegram. When the German army occupied Denmark, the Danish physicist Niels Bohr sent a telegram to friends in England informing them that he was safe. It ended with the sentence, PLEASE INFORM COCKCROFT AND MAUD RAY, KENT. British intelligence thought it was code and, after great labor, decrypted the sentence to mean, "Make uranium day and night." They subsequently learned that Maud Ray had been Bohr's English nanny.

What you read in a telegram depended on where you stood. When a lawyer unexpectedly won a difficult case for a client, he wired, JUSTICE HAS TRIUMPHED! The client immediately cabled back, APPEAL THE CASE AT ONCE! The weak link might be the clerk taking down the message, as in the case of the farmer in England who was anxiously awaiting delivery of a shipment of ewes, only to receive this alarming news: TWENTY BLACK-FACED YOUTHS DESPATCHED BY RAIL 9 PM.

Sometimes of course the idea *was* to deceive, and telegrams could be artful instruments of dodging. The French violinist Jacques Thibaud (1880–1953) once embarked on an extended *liaison amoureuse*, arranging for his wife to receive a series of telegrams: CONCERT IN BERLIN FANTASTIC SUCCESS. SEVEN ENCORES, LOVE JACQUES. ROME RECITAL SOLD OUT. IMMEDIATELY RE-ENGAGED. JE T'EMBRASSE. JACQUES. WARSAW CONCERT UNBELIEVABLE SUCCESS. MILLE BAISERS. And so on. When he got home, he and his wife were in the middle of dinner when the maid brought a telegram: BRUSSELS APPEARANCE SENSATIONAL. RAVE REVIEWS. I MISS YOU. JACQUES. However sensational Brussels might have been, the scene at the Thibaud dinner table was surely more so.

In a medium that depended on brevity, the smallest error could be tantamount to a Freudian blip. The wife of a Hollywood director who was on location with a foxy leading lady received this puzzler: HAVING A FANTASTIC TIME. WISH YOU WERE HER. Usually, Hollywood was more direct than that. The producer Walter Wanger cabled the agent Leland Hayward in 1936 after Hayward eloped with his client Margaret Sullavan: CONGRATULATIONS ON ACQUIRING THE OTHER 90%.

Brief as telegrams were, military cables had to be briefer yet, and sometimes they were witty into the bargain. After firing a string of torpedoes at a Japanese convoy in the Makassar Strait in 1942, Lieutenant Commander John Burnside, commanding officer of the U.S. Submarine *Sturgeon*, memorably cabled, STURGEON NO LONGER VIRGIN. When the commander of the U.S. military garrison on Wake Island was about to be overwhelmed by the Japanese on December 23, 1941, he flashed the poignant message ENEMY ON ISLAND—ISSUE IN DOUBT. One of the most famous telegrams of the war (SIGHTED SUB, SANK SAME), attributed to the crew member of a Navy patrol boat, turns out to be the invention of a Navy public relations officer.

The military does not as a rule try to be funny in its cables, of course; but sometimes it turns out that way. Back in the days of the British Grand Fleet, the commander aboard the admiral's squadron flagship, wanting to make sure the admiral had fresh clothing and linens after a tour at sea, cabled to shore: HAVE ADMIRAL'S WOMAN REPORT TO FLAGSHIP. This was quickly followed with one saying, INSERT WASHER BETWEEN ADMIRAL AND WOMAN.

At a critical moment of the Battle of Leyte Gulf in October 1944, the greatest naval battle ever fought, a few extra words tacked on to a cable had enormous consequence. Admiral Nimitz and his strategists knew that Admiral "Bull" Halsey had a battle plan to send his Task Force 34 ships to attack Japanese warships under the command of Admiral Ozawa, but as the critical hours wore on and they didn't hear from Halsey, their anxiety increased. Nimitz resisted sending any cable that his tactical commanders might misconstrue as questioning their authority, but he finally relented to the considerable pressure and gave permission to flash Halsey, asking where his ships were.

The story, as told in John Prados's book, *Combined Fleet Decoded*:

> *. . . a radioman caught the emphasis on the question by repeating its operative phrase. Finally the ensign who encoded it added "padding"—words at the beginning and end that were designed to frustrate cryptanalysts. In this case the wording, possibly drawn from Alfred, Lord Tennyson's poem "The Charge of the Light Brigade," set during the 1853–56 Crimean War (the charge had also occurred on October 25), sounded too much like an integral part of the message. When the dispatch arrived aboard Third Fleet flagship New Jersey it was handled just that way, and read* WHERE IS REPEAT WHERE IS TASK FORCE 34. THE WORLD WONDERS.
>
> *Admiral Halsey was incensed that his tactical judgment should be questioned in this fashion. The Bull tore the baseball cap from his head and threw it on the deck with a few choice words. He had begun activating the battleship unit to pursue Ozawa, but responded to the implied criticism by ordering [U.S. Admiral] Ching Lee back to Philippine waters with carrier groups to follow. That move permitted the escape of Ozawa's remaining warships.*

A good argument for keeping it brief, no matter what the circumstances. General Eisenhower displayed his talent—and genius—for simplicity. The occasion was the end of World War II. He had gathered his SHAEF officers around him for photographs and newsreels. Then it was time to sit down and write the cable informing the Allied commanders that they had at last prevailed in the greatest military effort in history. One by one, Ike's officers sat down to compose the message, each more flowery and self-consciously historical than the last. Finally, Eisenhower thanked them all and wrote it himself: THE MISSION OF THIS ALLIED FORCE WAS FULFILLED AT 0241, LOCAL TIME, MAY 7TH, 1945.

But the most concise military dispatch of all time was sent in 1844—the same year the telegraph was invented—by General Sir Charles Napier, after he had successfully captured the Indian province of Sind, now in Pakistan. It was all of one word long: PECCAVI. In Latin, that translates: "I have sinned."

Latin's not in use much anymore among battlefield commanders, and now we live in a time when machines can transmit the entire text of *Moby-Dick* in less than a second. Who's got time to be brief? But for a while there, the sending was awfully good.

—*Forbes FYI*, November 1998

WHAT'S A BODY TO DO?

Since the Soviet Union folded in 1991, Russia has been tippy-toeing around the dead mouse on the national living room floor, namely Lenin's embalmed corpse.

Every few years, someone suggests doing something about it. Some weeks ago, Vladimir Medinsky, Russia's minister of culture, said in a radio interview that he thought it was time Lenin was put to use pushing up the daisies. Not his exact words, but that was the basic drift.

When the subject came up in 2009, the Community Party leader, Gennadi A. Zyuganov, went predictably ballistic. These periodic suggestions send Russia's old hard-line Communists into a sputtering rage. Yes, Russia still has a Communist Party; some myths really do die hard.

"Discussions about removal and reburial are simply provocative," he declared. "Any attempt to vulgarize or rewrite the Soviet period and diminish the memory of Lenin . . . is an attempt to undermine the integrity of the Russian federation."

Mr. Zyuganov runs for president on a regular basis, making him the Harold Stassen of Russian politics, only snarly and frightening.

According to an April opinion poll cited by the British newspaper *The Guardian*, more than half of Russians now favor burying the god that failed. In his radio interview, Mr. Medinsky pledged to make it an occasion to remember and to observe all the obsequies.

If nothing else, the prospect of a state funeral poses questions of protocol, like—who gets to represent the United States?

Answer: This is why we have vice presidents. Really, it would be worth it just for the look on Joe Biden's face as the cortege moves past. And what an opportunity for some unscripted Bidenesque remarks.

I've just read a 1998 book called *Lenin's Embalmers*, by Ilya Zbarsky and Samuel Hutchinson. It's fascinating, in a horrible sort of way. Over the last eighty-eight years, Lenin's corpse has had more adventures than most live people. In the words of the Grateful Dead, "what a long, strange trip it's been." The author, who died in 2007, was the son of Boris Zbarsky, one of Lenin's original embalmers. Boris was keeper of the body for nearly thirty years, earning a pretty good living (by Soviet standards) and, better still, immunity from Stalin's terror.

Dictator Remains Management was not at the time a huge field;

more of a boutique industry. There just weren't all that many scientists back then who knew how to keep a body fresh and pinkish. Stalin couldn't afford to toss Boris into the Gulag along with tens of millions of other Russians. Boris wasn't arrested and thrown into prison—for no particular reason—until 1952, one year before Stalin died. He almost made it to the finish line.

Many sons follow Dad into the family business, but when Ilya Zbarsky entered the mausoleum in 1934, age twenty-one, it was surely a Guinness World Record moment. By the time he ran afoul of the government—like Dad, for no particular reason—he'd been in charge of the remains for almost twenty years. A good run, all in all.

After 1991, Ilya looked up his file in the KGB archives and learned that he and his father had been denounced in 1949 for "counterrevolutionary conversations." There in the margin of the report he saw Stalin's handwriting: "Must not be touched until a substitute is found." That was job security in Soviet Russia, circa 1949.

Soviet history is often indistinguishable from Orwell's fiction. When Lenin died, Stalin appointed a Committee for the Immortalization of Lenin's Memory. Immediately there were fierce disagreements as to how, exactly, to immortalize the actual remains.

I'll spare you the details, but suffice to say the committee gave the job to Ilya's father and another scientist named Vorobiev. Both recognized that a lot more than their scientific reputations was on the line. Next time you think you're under pressure at work, consider Comrades Zbarsky and Vorobiev, with Stalin and Dzerzhinsky breathing over their shoulders. How is it coming? Wonderfully! Couldn't be better! Look—no tan lines! It took them four months, but they got it right.

When World War II arrived in the form of General Heinz Guderian's tanks, Zbarsky and son were charged with spiriting the body out of Moscow—to Siberia, which seems apt, karmawise.

Lenin had a good war, unlike 25 million other Russians. In far-off Tyumen, the Zbarskys had all the time in the world to attend to Himself's maintenance. Indeed, by 1945, Ilya wrote, "the condition of the corpse had improved considerably." You look great! You been exercising?

The saga of Lenin's remains is a uniquely *Russian* story. His caretakers got drunk on the alcohol used in embalming Lenin's corpse, and in one instance, one of them was caught groping the other's daughter. What fun it must have been. There are group photos of them striking jaunty poses, as if they've gathered for a picnic.

And here was Khrushchev in 1956, growling, "The mausoleum stinks of Stalin's corpse." Stalin was embalmed and laid out beside Lenin between 1953 to 1961, when Khrushchev said enough and ordered him buried beneath the Kremlin wall.

Lenin remains, the Sleeping Beauty from Hell. Perhaps when his heir, President Vladimir V. Putin, is finished shipping combat helicopters to shore up his friend Bashar al-Assad of Syria he'll have time to consider his minister of culture's modest proposal.

Footnote: In 1991, when I was editing a publication for Forbes, I engaged in a hoax and briefly persuaded the world that the Russian government was preparing to auction off the body.

The story garnered quite a lot of play. A none-too-happy Russian interior minister denounced me for my "impudent lie" and called it "an unpardonable provocation." It kind of made my day.

But a number of readers of the magazine apparently didn't get the memo that it was all a hoax. The Kremlin was deluged with offers.

My favorite came from the head of a Virginia printing company, who accompanied his bid with this note:

"We are in the final planning stages of our new corporate headquarters. We were recently discussing the new lobby and saw the need for an appropriate centerpiece. Our interior designer has agreed with us, and feels that suitable arrangements can be made to house Mr. Lenin's body here."

—*The New York Times*, July 2012

AS I WAS SAYING TO HENRY KISSINGER

The Fine but Tricky Art of Name-Dropping (with apologies and a curtsey to Master Upman Stephen Potter)

THE SURNAME DROP

Many novices ask: When is it appropriate to drop the surname while dropping the name? The surest sign of the amateur is the Superfluous Surname Gambit. Classically: *I ran into Warren Beatty and Jack Nicholson.*

Many a gambit has come to grief this way. Contrast with the much cleaner: *I ran into Warren and Jack.* (See the Counter Warren Gambit, below.) Note that the Surname Drop should be employed only when the given name is *distinctive*.

THE COUNTER-SURNAME DROP

Our friend B. Conrad, of San Francisco, is an aficionado of this technique.

So you call him David, do you? I've known him for twenty years now. We're close as can be, but I still call him "Mr. Rockefeller." Maybe I'm old-fashioned, but this first-name stuff these days drives me batty.

THE COUNTER-WARREN GAMBIT

Grandmaster J. Tierney, of New York, New York, introduced this one memorably at a dinner party. The guest, himself adept at the Surname Drop, had been going on at length about his great pal Warren. Tierney let him exhaust himself, then suavely countered: *Oh, you mean the* actor.

"Actor" was pronounced disparagingly, as in "pig farmer." This was swiftly followed with *I assumed you meant Warren* Buffett.

While the guest was fumbling, Tierney finished him off with: *I wish I had more time for things like movies.*

Grandmaster Tierney will be familiar to readers as the inventor of the famous Out-Box Ploy. The dinner guest is steered into Tierney's study on some pretext. Lying in the Out tray on his desk is an eight-by-eleven-inch glossy photo of himself, signed in large lettering: *To Bill Gates, Glad I could help. Best, JT.*

Alternately, *To Meryl Streep, With deepest affection, J.*

ROYALS

Extreme caution must be exercised while royal-name-dropping within the United States. The correct stance is that while one is of course delighted to be on intimate terms with the royal families of Europe, one is *always* conscious of the Revolution, Valley Forge, Bill of Rights, etc. This republican imperative can be used to advantage. A variation of it is the Confused Commoner Gambit, which has been used with effect by R. Atkinson, a British subject. He lets it slip that he has just spent some quality time with the Prince of Wales. Then adds:

One minute you're calling him "Sir," and the next, you're stuffing a crumpet down his trousers.

This can be adapted to American usage. P. Cooke of Lakeville, Connecticut, gets the ball rolling by serving his guests Pimm's Cups, then shrugs:

It's one thing not to bow. It is our American birthright. But even though he's asked me to—repeatedly—I just can't bring myself to call him "Charles."

A more modest approach is to steer the conversation toward an apparently unrelated topic, such as tanning lotions, and then casually announce:

The Queen Mother has the most remarkable skin.

This should be quickly followed with: *Strictly between us, I find her the sweetest of the whole bunch. Giggly. Fun. Loves her gin and tonic. And puts you right at ease.*

Immediately rebuke yourself for having revealed this "out of school," and suggest forcefully that you do *not* want to see yourself quoted on Facebook, especially with Ascot approaching. Finish with:

It would only make things in the Royal Enclosure bloody awkward for me.

THE POSTHUMOUS DROP

Safest of all, as chances of contradiction or being challenged are minimized. R. Clements, of Blue Hill, Maine, uses this approach.

RC: (looking up from magazine, sighing heavily): *Well, thank God, is all I can say.*
Listener: *About what?*
RC: *That it never got out about us. Miracle, really.*
Listener: *About who?*
RC: Oh, nothing.

At this point, Clements excuses himself, leaving the magazine opened to an article about Princess Diana.

RC (returning, wiping his eyes with tissue): *Can I fix you another?*
Listener: *What did you mean by that?*
RC (with a hint of defiance, fighting back tears): *Nothing. I shouldn't have brought it up in the first place.*

Variation openings

—I told her not to marry Charles in the first place.

—It's at times like this that I miss her the most.

—I really wish that brother hadn't turned Althorp into a damned petting zoo.

Followed by

—Of course, I'm no one to ask. I did practically live *there for a while.*

Clements then adamantly refuses to discuss it further. A few minutes later, he morosely interjects: *Couldn't see a thing at the funeral.*

Wouldn't you know, I was seated directly behind Luciano Pavarotti. Just my luck.

OTHER ROYALS

Some novice droppers prefer to start off by invoking intimacy with Lesser Royalty. This is considered okay technique, but notoriety should be imputed to the Lesser Royal in order to compensate for his/her obscurity. T. Wilder, of Bethesda, Maryland, an advanced gamesman, typically begins as follows:

So, have you spent much time in Umvig-Glumstein?

The answer usually reliably no, he proceeds:

Well, if you ever get there, let me know and I'll arrange for you to see Schloss Schlitz. For my money, it's far more dramatic than Mad Ludwig's desperate attempt at attention getting, and yet it manages to be so—I don't know—gemütlich at the same time.

If he suspects the listener knows a few words of rudimentary German, Wilder deploys the Teutonic Escalator. In place of *gemütlich*, substituting: *Oh what* is *the German for it? Farbleflemmerchinzengespritz?* (chuckling to himself) *Yes, that's it*—Parsifal, *Act Two, scene three. Why can't I* ever *remember?*

Note that Wilder has audaciously put several balls in play simultaneously: his privileged access to the nonexistent castle, and Listener's assumed lack of knowledge of European geography and conversational German.

Listener now on the defensive on several fronts, Wilder continues:

The current Graf is an old, old friend. Last of a line, direct descendant of Philip of Swabia; for my money, one of the less gaga Holy Roman Emperors. Isaiah Berlin and I used to get into fisticuffs over it. I miss Isaiah.

Wilder has now deftly insinuated that his views on the Holy Roman Emperors are controversial and have been a cause of tension between him and a leading intellectual. Continuing:

Anyway, the Graf is a dear old thing. Gives us the run of the place every August. Of course there are *236 bedrooms, so it's not as though we're constantly bumping into each other in the hallway.*

Wilder now moves in for the kill:

Anyway, if you're in the vicinity, I could try to fix it for you to stick your head in and have a poke around. I'd arrange for you to meet him, but he can be a bit, you know, formal.

THE DNA INSINUATOR

If no royal opening presents itself, steer the conversation around to how you faint at the doctor's office every time they take blood. Then in a tone of mild annoyance:

I just got another letter from the Kremlin. They're after me to give them a DNA sample so they can settle this damned authenticity question about the czar's bones. (Sighing.) *I've been ignoring them for months. Well, they say they only need a drop or two. I suppose I owe it to the family.*

THE CONVERSATIONAL OBJECTIVE CORRELATIVE

Place a misshapen lump—any nondescript material will do—inside a glass display case along with a temperature gauge and mount it in a prominent place. Deflect initial inquiries, then in a world-weary tone, say it is the preserved heart of George III, king of Britain:

My great-great-great-great-grandfather was Nathan Hale. His brother, my great-great-great-whatever uncle, never quite forgave the Brits for hanging him. When he was visiting England he stole into the royal tomb and removed it. A bit gruesome, I know, but I can't bring myself just to put it in a safe deposit box. I must get around to giving it back one of these days, except I'm not really sure how to go about it. Don't let on. It would only create a huge to-do.

THE STAR AND BAR

Extreme care must be exercised here, as many Southerners are meticulously versed in genealogy. Disaster befell P. Harding of Athens, Georgia, in the course of gambiting that he was a direct descendant of General Jubal Early, only to be icily informed by someone present that the general had died without issue. Harding countercountered by saying that the general had had a liaison with a (beautiful) farm girl on the eve of the Battle of Cedar Creek, and that the resulting love child was Harding's great-great-grandfather.

Unfortunately, this only inflamed present company as it implied moral turpitude on the part of the Confederate god, and the evening ended in acrimony and remonstration.

One way to flush out any genealogically savvy Southerners is the Auto-Derogator Gambit. Declare, in a voice loud enough to carry the room, that it is now "universally conceded" that T. J. "Stonewall" Jackson was "vastly overrated" as a strategist. If no one approaches you with a fire poker, then the way is cleared for you to say how much this new scholarship pains you, inasmuch as you are the general's great-great-nephew. The rest of the evening can now be devoted to refuting the new scholarship. (Note: This is a variation on the Macedonian Sacrifice, perfected by D. Reigeluth of Harrison, New York, who uses it to affect aloofness while claiming direct descent from Alexander the Great. *Or as we in the family call him, Alexander the* Occasionally *Great*.

THE GEOGRAPHICAL PREEMPT

Extremely adaptable. Can be easily inserted into any lull in the dinner conversation.

(With a trace of annoyance) *Really, a week in Monaco is just too much. Frankly three days would be more than enough. Rainiers, Hapbsurgs, Hohenzollerns, Romanovs. After a while, one yearns to be among* ordinary *people.*

Or:

(With exasperation) *Five* days *at Balmoral! Shoot me! I have only so much conversation about grouse. On the other hand, I'm devoted to Princess Anne.* (Adding casually) *You going over this year?*

When a listener replies that he is not, nod sympathetically.

Just as well. Anne says the shooting's off this year.

THE GNOSTIC PARRY

G. Semler of Barcelona has written several well-regarded monographs on Counter Strategies. His most popular is the Kissinger Refuse:

Guest: *I just spent the weekend with Henry Kissinger.*
GS: *Isn't it exciting, his news?*
Guest: *News? What news?*
GS: *He didn't mention? Oh. Henry does like to play his cards close to his chest. Still, if he had you out to the house, I'm surprised he didn't . . . well, probably for the best.*

ALL-PURPOSE LINES IN CASE OF EMERGENCY

—*That's certainly not what Spielberg told* me.

—(Cupping hand over the phone) *It's the White House. Do you have another phone I could use?*

—*I'm being stalked myself. And let me tell you, it's a damned nuisance.*

—*Forbes FYI*, November 1998

MY ENTOURAGE IS BIGGER THAN YOUR ENTOURAGE

President Clinton recently went to China with a staff of eight hundred. President Lincoln began in office with a White House staff of one assistant. By the time he had won the Civil War, it had ballooned to—three people. Imagine what he could have accomplished with eight hundred. The Union would probably still be dug in around Petersburg. For that matter, imagine what Clinton could have accomplished over there with a staff of three.

It was an ironic photo opportunity at Xian, as the president gazed out on those six thousand terra-cotta warriors buried more than two thousand years ago with their emperor. His entourage was even larger than Clinton's, but the gap is closing. Richard Nixon, Quaker piker that he was, took a measly 200 staffers with him to China in 1972. In 1984, Ronald Reagan, champion of small government, took 350.

It's fun to fly around the world with an entourage as big as the Ritz. As Mel Brooks, playing Louis XIV, put it, "It's good to be the king."

In world entourages, the United States appears to rule. When Queen Elizabeth visited Ghana early this year, she brought with her a relatively tight retinue of a few dozen. Of course, Her Majesty doesn't require a military aide to carry a briefcase with nuclear launch codes. (I was once the custodian of one of our own nuclear footballs for a few heady moments, but more on that later.)

According to a recent *Debrett's Peerage and Baronetage*, the social register of the British classes, the queen's official household (excluding butlers, footmen, maids, cooks, postillions, and all the rest) numbers thirty-four, from the Lord Chamberlain to Temporary Equerry, including along the way two Baronesses in Waiting and an Extra Lady of the Bedchamber. The queen's household in Scotland, meanwhile, lists twenty-two, including Hereditary Carver of Scotland, Dean of the Order of the Thistle, Apothecary to the Household at the Palace at Holyroodhouse, and Captain-General and Gold Stick for Scotland. Wouldn't that look great on a business card? (The former husband of Prince Charles's consort, Camilla Parker Bowles, was Silver Stick in Waiting.) But there are even cooler titles in the Lord Chamberlain's office, the entourage within an entourage: Poet Laureate, Master of the Queen's Music, and Clerk of the Closet.

The Groom of the Stole, the person charged with laying the grand cloth over the monarch's shoulder during coronations, is apparently a sanitized spelling of a medieval word for a quite different function: the groom who was in charge of the king's privy. Monarchies have never been reticent about such matters. According to my scholarly friend Timothy Dickinson, who knows everything, "It is well attested that on one occasion Louis XIV was having an enema, and his *marchal de loge* (the marshall of the bedchamber) emerged and announced that since the king was having an enema, only the sixty senior ladies could be admitted." *That's* protocol.

When President Jiang Zemin of China visited the United States in 1997, he came with only eighty people, and he had more than a billion to choose from. The late King Faisal of Saudi Arabia traveled with a hundred. The late, unlamented President Mobuto Sese Seko of Zaire arrived in America in 1982 with an escort of a hundred—for a vacation. They spent $2 million in two weeks. Fidel Castro took a hundred comrades with him when he visited the Vatican in 1996, but then he may have been anticipating a firefight with the Swiss Guard.

The sultan of Brunei (until Bill Gates came along, the richest man on earth) visited London in 1992 with only twenty. However, he did celebrate the twenty-fifth anniversary of his coronation at home by riding though the streets of the capital in a chariot drawn by forty men. The sultan sounds like a decent fellow. He once left a $170,000 cash tip at the Four Seasons Hotel in Nicosia, Cyprus. Another time, while shopping in New York, he wanted to charge some purchases, and the clerk asked him for ID. He didn't carry any—a common trait among those who have entourages—so one of his ten bodyguards produced a wad of Brunei cash with His Majesty's face on it. Wouldn't you love to be able to do that at the airport when they ask for photo ID?

What private-sector entourages lack in volume, they make up for in vanity. A movie director marveled once to a reporter about the entourage of the actor Don Johnson. "The only person I've ever seen with an entourage like that was Elvis Presley, but they were his cousins." He totted up Mr. Johnson's traveling staff: a makeup person, hairstylist, wardrobe person, helicopter pilot, two drivers, two bodyguards, a trainer, a cook, and a secretary. Don—you ask—*who*? But where do you cut? The nineteenth-century duke of Buckingham went bankrupt, but adamantly refused to alter his lifestyle. His creditors finally persuaded his nephew Charles Greville to take the matter up with his uncle.

"But good heavens," the duke protested, "you have no idea. I've cut back to the bone."

"Well, Uncle, no doubt, but you do still have six personal confectioners."

"Upon my word, things have come to a pretty pass when a man can't send out for a biscuit!"

Once, at a party for a Condé Nast magazine executive, I noticed bulky men with earpieces. Was the president attending, I asked? My attention was directed to a nondescript, rather unkempt woman at a table having an intense conversation with a young man wearing a rather conspicuous fur hat. Madonna and her retinue. There might have been fifteen security men.

Another time, I watched Frank Sinatra move through a Las Vegas casino inside a phalanx of plainclothes centurions led by his faithful friend, a walleyed immensity named Jilly Rizzo. It was a spectacle worthy of the place's name: Caesars Palace. Sinatra never went anywhere—other than to the bathroom in the middle of the night—without an entourage. His Rat Packs varied in quality, from Dean Martin and Sammy Davis, Jr., to the bodyguards he sometimes used as a private police force. He was at his least sublime at such moments, as when he unleashed them on a man who'd had the temerity to protest when Ol' Blue Eyes made a pass at his wife in the restaurant. The bodyguards followed him to the *pissoir* and gave the insolent wretch a good lesson in respect.

There have been some peculiar entourages throughout history.

Friedrich Wilhelm I of Prussia (d. 1740) had a thing for giants. He dispatched his agents all over Europe to kidnap them. On one occasion, a tall priest in Savoy was sandbagged at the altar and packed off to Potsdam.

Certainly one of the more consequential bizarre entourages would be the one maintained by Ferdinando I and Francesco II, brothers and dukes of Mantua in the early seventeenth century. Their penchant was the opposite of Wilhelm's—for dwarves. They were insatiable. In the process of collecting them, they managed to bankrupt the Mantuan state, hard as it may be to imagine packing a palace to the rafters with dwarves.

Their family, the Gonzagas, had amassed what was at the time probably the greatest private art collection ever assembled. But as the saying goes, there is no such thing as a free dwarf, and eventually they had to sell the art to support their fetish for leprechauns. The buyer was Charles I of England. He wasn't on very good terms with Parliament, and the purchase of the Gonzaga art collection helped put him over the line into the red, triggering the English Civil War. So in a way, constitutional government in Great Britain owes its origin to a pair of Italian princes' insatiable need for dwarves.

The mid-eighteenth-century duke of Somerset once mischievously gave a dinner for a large circle of his acquaintances, none of whom knew one another, and all of whom stammered. That was the point of the dinner. Since no one knew the others, they didn't know whether the others were imitating them. Did anyone stick around for brandy and cigars that night?

Normally, entourages consisting of the differently abled had a more functional value. The Ming emperor maintained a court staffed by seventy thousand eunuchs. These were no lisping sissies. Au contraire—you wouldn't want to mess with these guys. There were grand eunuchs, one of whom, Grand Eunuch Zheng He, was put in charge of important naval expeditions. "He led," according to the historian John King Fairbank, "a can-do group of eunuchs." (This may be the only recorded instance of the phrase "can-do group of eunuchs.") Being a eunuch back then was a bit like having a law degree these days—the essential union card for getting ahead in government.

According to the historian Jonathan Spence, the noncastrated males were restricted to the outer edges of the court, beyond the inner gates. All things considered, I'd have been content to work on the fringes of power. Spence notes that Hong Xiuquan, a mid-nineteenth-century Chinese taiping, employed *no* eunuchs, so his inner palaces were run entirely by two thousand women under his general supervision. To paraphrase Mel Brooks, it's good to be the taiping.

> *One group of attendants is assigned to the care of his upper body, one for his lower. His beard is trimmed, his hair is combed and neatly coiled, his nose is wiped, his feet and lower parts kept clean, and the area near his navel cleansed with special care. Carefully they see to the rugs and quilts and braziers that will keep him warm, prepare his heated ginseng and shaved deer horn to give him strength, massage his head and feet, ankles, arms and knees to ease the tiredness of his body . . .*
>
> *His anger can be provoked by anything from a misplaced swing of a fan to the late arrival of his hot towels. Anyone making a mistake twice is considered a habitual offender . . . beating is the commonest punishment—those enduring the blows are expected to look cheerful and even to praise their Heavenly King as the blows fall.*

One of the advantages of being a future monarch was that you got to have a whipping boy, whose job was to be beaten senseless whenever *you* misbehaved. But the whole point of having an entourage is to be able to assign idiosyncratic individual duties. JFK kept a man in his inner circle whose function was pretty much to sing "Sweet Adeline" to him whenever he was feeling blue.

Roman senators employed *nomenclators*, whose job was to hiss into their ears the names of approaching people of importance. Roman emperors kept a sort of shadow entourage of professional zealots whose job was to shout flattery at them in public places—*We hail you as God, not Caesar!*—a forerunner of the modern-day floor demonstration at political conventions, when the assembly "spontaneously" erupts with frenzy as the candidate enters the hall.

Napoleon Bonaparte is said to have kept a man on his staff with the exact same size feet as his, whose only job was to break in the emperor's new shoes. One of the duties of Prince Charles's valet is to iron the five-pound notes that he puts in the collection plate at Sunday church service, folded so that Queen Elizabeth's head is facing outward. Kenneth Clarke, the art historian, had his butler iron the daily newspapers. FDR liked to surround himself with homeless royals, particularly Dutch and Yugoslav, so that he could call them by their Christian names, while they had to address him as "Mr. President." The Jain merchants of India sent their servants on ahead to the next town to sleep in their beds and become infested with all the bugs that would otherwise ruin their own night's sleep. Nice work, if you can get it.

Not all entourages are equal. One of LBJ's former Secret Service agents told me that one cold, shivering night at the Johnson ranch in Texas, he was standing post outside the presidential bedchamber. The president emerged, buck naked—*what* a sight that must have been—and began urinating on the agent's leg. (Johnson was surely our crudest chief executive. He once received the Israeli foreign minister Abba Eban in the Oval Office while sitting on the presidential crapper.) Relieving himself on his employees seems to have been one of his favored pastimes. He did it on another occasion. This time, when the hapless agent protested, "Sir, that's my leg you are urinating on," Johnson replied, "It's my prerogative." It could have been worse. The Moroccan emperor Moulai Ismail's favorite pastime was leaping onto horseback while simultaneously beheading a slave.

There are a thousand reasons not to have been a member of Hitler's entourage, but for me a very big one would have been the sausages. Hitler's disastrous obsession with blood and blood purity is well documented, but according to the historian Robert G. L. Waite's excellent book, *The Psychopathic God: Adolf Hitler*, the Führer was an even stranger camper than you might imagine. He was fascinated by his own blood. He would periodically have vials of it drawn, which he kept in a cabinet in his office. One of the regular rituals in a German household was the killing of the pig and the making of *blutwurst*, blood sausage. In a twisted parody of the Last Supper, come sausage-making season, Hitler would offer vials of his precious hemoglobin to his inner circle so their fraus could mix it in with the sausage and give it a little sacral tang. Their response isn't recorded. What do you say in such a situation? *I couldn't—really.*

I played a very modest part in a fairly large White House entourage for a while. It was interesting, even exciting work, and no one peed on my leg. One time I got to have possession of the football, the briefcase with the nuclear launch codes. We were at a baseball game and the Air Force colonel who carried it didn't want to walk with it alone through the crowds to the men's room. Sitting there with this thing wedged between my knees was an I-don't-think-we're-in-Kansas-anymore-Toto kind of moment.

I had my own code name—"Typewriter"—and once in South Korea, I even had my own car and motorcycle escort. (It's a memorable sensation, driving through crowded streets in Seoul at 90 miles an hour, watching people hurl themselves out of the way.) Normally, I rode in the rear of the motorcade, in a van with staff secretaries and the medical technician and the beach cooler that contained emergency blood for the vice president. The doctor, an Air Force major, once reached into his pocket and took out a white packet stamped in military lettering: BATTLE DRESSING.

It was an edgy time. President Reagan had just been shot. The pope had been shot, and there was evidence suggesting that this might have been done on orders from the Kremlin. Martial law was being declared in Poland, Libyan hit squads were rumored to be on their way to the United States, and the White House was declaring its war on Colombian drug cartels. At one point, Reagan's three senior staff, James Baker, Michael Deaver, and Edwin Meese, had their own Secret Service protection; even the entourage needed an entourage. You'd see them at events shadowed by agents carrying what looked like garment bags slung over their shoulders. They were easy-access Velcro carrying cases for their Uzi submachine guns. (Uncovered Uzis tend to change the tone of a cocktail party.) When we were in Puerto Rico, I peeked into the back of the CAT (Counter-Assault Team) vehicle that tailed the vice president's limousine and saw a Stinger anti-aircraft missile. The ultimate option in a Chevy Blazer.

The Secret Service gave a memorable orientation briefing to members of the traveling staff. It consisted of home assassination movies: Zapruder, Bremer shooting Wallace, Hinckley, an attempt on President Park of Korea in which one of his security people bravely took cover behind Mrs. Park.

In Bogota, they found 75 pounds of C-4 explosive under our runway; in London—London, of all places—we drove through angry crowds of protestors who screamed obscenities and spat on us. I gave them the finger, and it was satisfying. Vice President Nelson Rockefeller once did that to a crowd of hecklers in New York, but then he didn't care about getting reelected.

Being in a White House entourage, where the office is a downtown fortress surrounded by armed guards, where you fly around on Air Force planes, where you chopper into a tropical city at night in Army helicopters, where you drive in motorcades that don't have to stop for lights and snarl rush-hour city traffic for hours, where you pick up the phone and tell the White House operator to get you so-and-so, and so-and-so, no matter how important he is, takes your call every time—all this does not do wonders for your humility and sense of insignificance in the cosmic scheme of things. You need to be on the lookout for creeping signs of self-importance. It was amusing to watch staff members jockeying like Indy race car drivers for position in the motorcade. *For God's sake, you can't seriously expect me to ride in the same car as the speechwriter!*

The most fun to watch were the advance men, possibly the most empowered human beings on earth. No one says no to a White House advance person. The Chinese emperors had their eunuchs; White House advance men turn other people into eunuchs. I watched them reduce important people, masters of their own universes, to impotent, spluttering, vein-bulging rage and indignation—and there was *nothing they could do*. The Bermudan government officials had a hard time with our twenty-nine-vehicle motorcade, which was more or less the length of Bermuda. I was present once when the custodian of one of Europe's most exquisite palaces, where an event was to be held, was informed by a cocky twenty-something, "The facilities will be adequate."

If being a member of the entourage swells the head, imagine what having an entourage of eight hundred must do to it. Do presidents ever stop and say to themselves, *Do I really* need *all these people?* If President Nixon was able to open China with a staff of two hundred, why does it now take eight hundred just to keep it open? To think Jimmy Carter carried his own garment bag.

About a hundred years ago, an eighteen-year-old George Marshall, seeking a commission in the Army, walked into the White House holding a letter of introduction. He asked, "Where's the president?" The butler told him, "He's in there, but you can't go in." He walked in anyway and there was President McKinley, talking with some folks. In due course the people left and McKinley turned to Marshall and said, "And what can I do for you, young man?" Try *that* today.

When my ship comes in and I get an entourage of my own, there'll be someone to iron my church collection money, another to call up the American Express overdue accounts department and tell them that's *my* face on the national currency. I'll have zealots scattered throughout the frozen-food section at the supermarket to hail me as God, not Caesar, as I push my cart along, and someone with size-ten feet to break in my new shoes. Maybe with all this *E. coli* beef mooing, it would be a good idea to have a taster on retainer. And I'm tempted by the person with a cooler full of type-O blood. And I'll be needing an Apothecary to the Household, for that late-night heartburn after the double-jalapeño pizza.

—*Forbes FYI*, November 1998

TRUST NO ONE

In every movie involving spies invariably comes the moment when the good guy turns to the co–good guy—best friend, lover, dog Fido, whoever—and says, "Trust no one." Invariably a few scenes later, he finds himself staring into the muzzle of a pistol held by one of the above saying, "You *said* not to trust anyone. Didn't you?"

If it's a commercial sort of movie with the obligatory happy ending, this is followed by the loud click of the gun dry-firing. Our hero then pulls *his* gun and says with a smirk, "I took the precaution of removing the firing pin." And shoots the blighter and finishes his martini.

If it's a film noir of the kind, say, made from any John le Carré novel or directed by a German who grew up on a diet of too much Brecht, the hero doesn't remove the firing pin. Trusting fool! And gets blown away. A beautiful death, but a death nonetheless, leaving the audience to wonder whether we can trust anyone, especially those we trust.

A few weeks ago the FBI arrested a dozen deep-cover Russian agents who have been living among their American neighbors in various suburban locales, mowing the lawns, chatting amiably over the fences, exchanging casserole recipes. John le Carré, meet John Cheever.

Most of us probably don't live next door to Russian sleeper spies, but an episode like this raises the question, in a typically melodramatic American way: Whom—the hell—can we trust? To judge from the number of lawsuits by groups determined to get "In God We Trust" removed from courthouses and other government buildings, some of us aren't even sure about trusting the Big Guy anymore.

The arrest of the Russians also reminds us that one of the worst aspects of the old Soviet—or any totalitarian—regime is the vacuum of trust, especially familial. In Soviet Russia, children spied on their parents. How many fathers were sent off to die in the Gulag because little Boris was mad at him for making him do his homework and decided to tell the KGB that he'd made a joke about Comrade Stalin's mustache? The only witty thing Stalin ever said was "I trust no one, even myself."

Aeschylus grasped the idea two thousand years before Uncle Joe: "For somehow this is tyranny's disease, to trust no friends." In *1984*, Winston Smith aurally hallucinates a song whose lyrics are "Under the spreading chestnut tree, I sold you and you sold me." As Brecht put it, with Germanic—and Communist—mordancy, "I don't trust him. We're friends."

How grim and sere to contemplate a world in which one lived in constant fear of one's friends? I've lived happily in Washington, D.C., for almost thirty years, but it can at times be a bottle full of scorpions. There's an old joke we tell here: "What's the definition of a 'friend' in Washington? Someone who stabs you in the chest." Funny, huh?

A few paragraphs above I deployed the phrase "trusting fool." I pause to ask: Why should someone who trusts be open to the charge of "fool," under any circumstances? Does the cliché derive from a quietly understood universal truth that humans are by nature duplicitous? Was Stalin a fool for trusting Hitler? Was Elie Wiesel a fool for trusting his Holocaust foundation funds to Bernard Madoff?

Thirty or forty times a year I board an airplane and buckle myself in, trusting that the pilot has not spent the night doing shots of Jägermeister and snorting lines of cocaine off the breasts of a hooker. Some years ago I read in the news a comical (*sort* of) item about a pilot who, as the plane lumbered down the taxiway, was heard by the tower singing, "Some-*wherrrre* o-ver the rain-*bowwwwww*." He was blotto. So in the end we're all trusting fools, one way or another. At the practical level, we don't really have much choice.

I came of age during (but did not participate in) the war in Vietnam, the great trust-busting event of its day. (Followed by another beaut called Watergate.) Shocking to my then-naïve sensibility were the stories—perhaps overmythologized—of fragging, when disgruntled grunts rolled hand grenades under the bunks of their lieutenants. When soldiers, the ultimate band of brothers, start turning on one another, it's probably time to fold and go home.

That dismal war produced two memorable utterances on the theme. The first by LBJ, whose war it was: "I never trust a man unless I've got his pecker in my pocket." The second is anonymous but sounds like it sprang from some miserable hooch somewhere in LBJ's quagmire: "Just because you're paranoid doesn't mean the little bastards aren't out to get you."

What a tricky world we live in. Trust me.

—*Forbes*, August 2010

THE ART OF SACKING

There's been a lot of *Sturm und Drang* in the American corporate boardroom recently. Carol Bartz, the now former CEO of Yahoo!, was fired by the board's chairman—by phone. Ms. Bartz thought this was shabby exit etiquette and wasted no time ventilating her displeasure, telling *Fortune* magazine: "These people f— me over." She described them as "the worst board in the country," and—for good measure—"doofuses." As the famous telegram put it: F— YOU. STRONG LETTER FOLLOWS.

Refreshing as it is to hear straight talk from our captains of industry, these comments may prove costly to Ms. Bartz, inasmuch as she had a "non-disparagement clause" in her contracts. Ten million dollars is a steep price for steam venting.

Then came the "sudden removal" of Hewlett-Packard's CEO Léo Apotheker, just a year after the untidy firing of his predecessor, Mark Hurd. Mr. Apotheker refrained from dropping the f-bomb or calling the board doofuses, but then he's German and disciplined. He was content to walk away with an estimated $28 million to $33 million in separation fees.

The UBS chief Oswald Grübel might have been fired if he hadn't resigned, following the revelations that one of his thirty-one-year-old traders had managed to hide $2.3 billion in losses. Will Kweku Adoboli be getting severance pay? No? Then how come he's smiling in those photographs of him in handcuffs?

Firings—or to use the neater British term, sackings—are often occasions of drama. Suddenly protocol, punctilio, and politesse are out the window, leaving Tennyson's "Nature, red in tooth and claw." But let's review Ms. Bartz's messy departure in the larger historical scheme of things: Where does a Silicon Valley bigwig's sacking by phone rank in the pantheon?

It's a long, long list, so let's limit ourselves to: Satan, Adam and Eve, Judas Iscariot, Nicolas Fouquet, Sir John Falstaff, Generals McClellan, Patton, and MacArthur, the Nixon White House, Don Regan, and one or two Hollywood episodes.

Starting at the top (as it were): Satan, Adam and Eve, Judas. We're *still* dealing with the fallout from their sackings. The former angel Satan, "the brightest in the sky," attempted a corporate takeover of the heavens. But God, an experienced and canny chairman of the board, managed to hold on to his seat and down went Satan—and no golden parachute for him. Satan, however, was not the kind to go off and write a book about fly-fishing or do some consulting. He's the Barry Diller of the book of Revelation. He came back with a poison pill, forcing God to fire Adam and Eve. (Maybe He should have offered Satan that parachute after all.)

The Last Supper could be viewed as Jesus's last meeting with the twelve directors on his board. It was a productive session: Jesus instituted the Eucharist and correctly predicted that his successor would screw up three times before getting his act together. But he had to fire one of the board members, and that led to—well, you know the rest. If Jesus had offered Judas a severance package, how differently things might have turned out.

Skipping ahead to the seventeenth century, we come to Nicolas Fouquet, superintendent of finances under Louis XIV. As the minister in charge of *le Roi Soleil's* tax collectors, Fouquet managed to become a very, very wealthy public servant. Perhaps you've visited his modest country home, Vaux-le-Vicomte. It's *good* to be the superintendent of finances. His mistake was inviting the king to Vaux-le-Vicomte for a fête that made Stephen Schwarzman's birthday parties look like beggars' banquets. Louis, whose motto was *L'etat c'est moi, pas vous*—tossed Fouquet into jail, where he died nineteen years later.

Shakespeare is full of sackings. The ones that come most vividly to mind are Hamlet's (unauthorized and messy) firing of Polonius, Elsinore's chief of staff; and Henry V's dismissal of his old mentor and drinking buddy, Sir John Falstaff. Polonius's severance consisted of a sword through the arras. Henry terminated Falstaff with less prejudice: "I banish thee, on pain of death . . . not to come near our person by ten mile"—a fifteenth-century restraining order. Kings didn't bother much with nondisparagement clauses. Would Carol Bartz have called Henry a doofus? Methinks not.

Reviewing an abbreviated roster of American military sackees, two common denominators stick out: disrespect and an excess of initiative. The Civil War general George McClellan was always going on about what a dolt President Lincoln was. (He was the General Stanley McChrystal of his day, not to equate President Lincoln and Vice President Joe Biden). Patton and MacArthur were angrily dismissed by their commanders in chief, but getting the heave-ho added a certain luster to their legends.

Nixon's White House was white, but what a lot of red blood was left on those walls. Watergate was a Death by a Hundred Cuts *and* a Night of the Long Knives, the latter being the Saturday Night Massacre. Archibald Cox, Elliot Richardson, and William Ruckelshaus—trifecta. A year later, Richard Nixon, facing the presidential version of being fired, wisely took early retirement.

When CNN ushered in the 24/7 news cycle, the joke around the White House—not thigh-slapping but funny in a grim kind of way—was that you might very well learn that you'd been fired by hearing it on TV. The sacking of Don Regan, grumpy chief of staff in the Reagan Götterdämmerung, is the stuff of high comedy (see Richard Reeves's excellent *President Reagan: The Triumph of Imagination*):

"As Regan calmed down, [Vice President] Bush asked him about the President's schedule . . .

"'That's in the hands of an astrologer in San Francisco, George.'

"The Vice President looked mystified. Regan poured out his frustrations about the woman Mrs. Reagan called 'My friend,' Joan Quigley. 'Good God,' said Bush."

Moving now to Hollywood: David O. Selznick famously fired the director George Cukor from *Gone With the Wind* after only three weeks of shooting. More recently, Walt Disney's chairman, Michael Eisner, fired his president, Michael Ovitz, after only a year on the job. It was nasty, but Ovitz landed softly, and who wouldn't, with a parachute worth an estimated $170 million. (By my math, it worked out to $465,000 of severance for every day.) Later on, Eisner sacked Jeffrey Katzenberg with a package valued at an estimated quarter billion. Eisner may have been the Boss from Hell, but he didn't stint on the severances. This generosity was not popular among Disney's shareholders.

The 2009 movie *Up in the Air* starred George Clooney as a corporate downsizer who flies around the country sacking entire companies at a time. In the midst of filming, the director, Jason Reitman, decided to cast instead of actors actual people who had been fired by this brutal, impersonal process.

There's a term used in kayaking when you capsize and can't upright yourself—a "wet exit." Ms. Bartz's departure from Yahoo was an example of the wet exit. A dry exit is generally preferable, especially if it comes with $10 million.

—*Bloomberg BusinessWeek*, 2011

I LIKE TO DRINK A MARTINI

In one of the many, many scenes in *Mad Men* having to do with drinking, Roger Sterling, played to perfection by John Slattery, goes mano a mano with Don Draper over oysters and martinis. Roger instructs the waiter, "And don't let me see the bottom of this glass."

At the end of this ethyl alcoholic orgy, they walk up the stairs and Roger casually vomits. Oh, for the early 1960s, when America ruled the world and its captains of industry drank three martinis for lunch. Now, in our decline, they drink fizzy water.

I was about ten then, still virginal in matters alcoholic, but already aware that the word *martini* had iconic—or *hic*-onic—resonance. Does not the very shape of the martini glass connote cocktail?

My parents did not drink them. It was bourbon for my mother, scotch for my father; but it seemed that all the other grown-ups did. Once I tagged along to the Oak Room at the old Plaza Hotel. In my memory, everyone ordered them, which made the Oak Room seem not so much a bar as a church in which the martini was the sacrament served to the congregation.

At about this time the first James Bond movie appeared, in which Sean Connery memorably orders the barman: "Vodka martini. Shaken, not stirred."

"Shaken, not stirred" entered the language as the sine qua non of sophistication. (Or affectation.) Years later, reading one of the Ian Fleming novels, I came across Bond's actual formula: "Medium vodka dry martini, shaken not stirred." It was not only the method of preparation, but also the vodka by which Fleming was signaling us that Bond was exotic, a rebel, an iconoclast, a man apart from the herd. Most self-respecting Brits or Americans of the day considered a proper martini to be made from gin.

According to my friend Barnaby Conrad III, who wrote the book on the martini (literally), its origins are obscure and much debated. He posits, however, that the likeliest first recipe for this holy grail was in an 1896 manual by Thomas Stuart titled *Stuart's Fancy Drinks and How to Mix Them*. It was called a "Marguerite Cocktail," and into it went one dash of orange bitters, two-thirds Plymouth gin, and one-third French vermouth. "By 1900," Barnaby writes, "the word Martini was in common usage among bartenders on both sides of the Atlantic."

The martini is to modern American literature and lore what mead wine was to Norse sagas or claret to eighteenth-century English literature. Dorothy Parker remains its leading laureate, having given us the imperishable quatrain:

I like to drink a Martini
But only two at the most.
Three I'm under the table,
Four I'm under the host.

A memorable scene in Evan Thomas's biography of the legendary Washington lawyer Edward Bennett Williams: Williams is meeting with his prospective client Bobby Baker, the disgraced D.C. lobbyist-operator of his day.

These two alpha males couldn't resist the ritual pecker flexing as they sized each other up. One martini led to another. And another. And still more. Finally each had downed—ten. Pause for a moment to consider that heroic tally: *ten*. They shook hands, Williams went to his car, parked in the basement, and drove it through the garage door.

A quintessential martini moment. Never let them see the bottom of the glass.

—*Newsweek*, March 2012

YOU CAN DO IT!

A Short History of the Pep Talk

> *When Aeschines spoke, the people said, "How well he speaks." But when Demosthenes spoke, they said, "Let us march!"*
>
> —UNKNOWN

> *Over? Did you say over? NOTHING is over until WE decide it is! Was it over when the Germans bombed Pearl Harbor? HELL, NO!*
>
> —BLUTO BLUTARSKY, IN *ANIMAL HOUSE*

History does not record who gave the first pep talk or what the occasion was, but at some point, a long, long time ago when the chips were down and things were looking bleak, someone, probably wearing fur, stood atop a boulder in some Neolithic locker room and said, "Okay, guys, we had a rough first half out there. We weren't counting on the volcano erupting and the velociraptors. But are we going to let a bunch of woolly mammoths walk all over us and eat our lunch? Or are we going to show them what Neanderthal Man is made of?" To which the reply was, surely, "Huah! Huah!"

Give me a lever, said Archimedes, and I'll move the world. A few well-chosen words can do the same. George W. Bush stood on the rubble at Ground Zero and told the rescue workers through a bullhorn, "I can hear you. The rest of the world hears you, and the people who knocked these buildings down will hear all of us soon." Nothing stirs the blood like the prospect of spilling the enemy's.

Ronald Reagan went on TV hours after the space shuttle *Challenger* tragically Roman-candled over Florida and said, "The future doesn't belong to the fainthearted; it belongs to the brave. The *Challenger* crew was pulling us into the future, and we'll continue to follow them." His most memorable movie role was playing George

Gipp—"the Gipper"—who inspired the 1928 Notre Dame team to go back out there and beat Army.

In life as in the movies, Reagan was always upbeat, always urging others on, even when he was being wheeled into the Emergency Room with a bullet in his chest. "I hope you're all Republicans," he said as they took him into surgery, no doubt aware that doctors who suddenly find themselves tasked with saving the life of the president of the United States are themselves experiencing a bit of stress.

Pep talks are formally delivered in locker rooms at halftime, on the threshold of battlefields, from marble podiums after Japanese bombers have ruined an otherwise lovely Sunday morning in Hawaii. They can have a sinister aspect, as anyone will attest who has stood before the front gate at Auschwitz and seen the slogan *Arbeit Macht Frei* ("Work Makes Freedom").

They can take the form of asserting a negative. "Failure is not an option!" Apollo 13's Mission Control flight director Gene Kranz famously barked to his brigade of crew-cut, white-shirt engineers. In the movie *Glengarry Glen Ross*, the tyrannical sales manager incentivizes his Willy Lomans by telling them, "As you all know, first prize is a Cadillac Eldorado. Anybody want to see second prize? Second prize is a set of steak knives. Third prize is you're fired."

A pep talk can have a self-consciously melodramatic air. The valet of the Duc de Saint-Simon's nephew would wake him with the words "*Levez-vous, Monsieur le Comte, vous avez de grandes choses à faire aujourd'hui.*" ("Wake up, Count, you have big things to accomplish today.") The other day, the hotel operator gave me my wake-up call, saying, "You have a fantastic day!" Apparently the hotel management had decided that wishing the guest a "good" day was no longer adequate.

It can have a somber, fatalistic air: "Let us eat and drink; for tomorrow we shall die" (Isaiah 22:13). A promissory note: "Blessed are they which are persecuted for righteousness' sake: for theirs is the kingdom of heaven" (Matthew 5:10). Reassurance: "Let not your heart be troubled, neither let it be afraid" (John 14:27). Hope, in the midst of excruciation: "Today shalt thou be with me in paradise" (Luke 23:43).

It doesn't have to be a proper "talk" at all: "The corner has definitely been turned toward victory in Vietnam" (Defense Department announcement, May 1963).

But the great ones tend to be delivered formally, script in hand. They also tend to become the signature utterances of whoever said them. History favors the uplifter over the doomsayer.

On December 8, 1941, with the USS *Arizona* still smoking and hissing in Pearl Harbor, President Roosevelt spoke plainly to the nation. "We are now in this war. We are in it—all the way." He didn't sugarcoat: "It will not only be a long war, it will be a hard war. . . . We don't like it—we didn't want to get in it—but we are in it and we're going to fight it with everything we've got."

Churchill also inspired by straight talk. His prose was more polished that FDR's. It sounded as though it had been written by firelight, quill pen on parchment.

> *You ask, what is our policy? I say it is to wage war by land, sea and air. War with all our might and with all the strength God has given us, and to wage war against a monstrous tyranny never surpassed in the dark and lamentable catalogue of human crime. That is our policy.*
>
> *You ask, what is our aim? I can answer in one word. It is victory. Victory at all costs—victory in spite of all terrors—victory, however long and hard the road may be, for without victory there is no survival.*

Churchill made defiance a virtue, even after 226,000 British troops and 110,000 French had to be rescued off the beaches at Dunkirk. "We shall defend our island whatever the cost may be; we shall fight on beaches, landing grounds, in fields, in streets and on the hills. We shall never surrender . . ."

Two weeks later, on June 18, 1940, Churchill delivered his most famous speech of all.

> *The Battle of Britain is about to begin. On this battle depends the survival of Christian civilization . . . Hitler knows he will have to break us in this island or lose the war.*

If we can stand up to him all Europe may be freed and the life of the world may move forward into broad sunlit uplands; but if we fail, the whole world, including the United States and all that we have known and cared for, will sink into the abyss of a new dark age made more sinister and perhaps more prolonged by the lights of a perverted science.

Let us therefore brace ourselves to our duty and so bear ourselves that if the British Commonwealth and Empire last for a thousand years, men will still say, "This was their finest hour."

Churchill was a painter. "Broad sunlit uplands" is a painter's metaphor: He was showing the British people what the landscape would look like after victory. He was also a historian. "New dark age" is a vivid, resonant, terrifying image, even if to our generation, it might sound like Gandalf trying to rally a bunch of wobbly hobbits. Churchill's speech is marmoreal; this is prose, sixty-three years later, to raise the hairs on your arm.

Arguably the most famous speech in all Shakespeare is a pep talk. There are two, actually, both in *Henry V*. There's not a shred of evidence the real Henry ever said a word of them, but no matter.

Henry, no longer the callow frat boy Prince Hal, is on the Continent reasserting his claim to the throne of France. (English kings were always having to do this; it went with the job.) Rallying his exhausted men before the walls of Harfleur, Henry cries, "Once more unto the breach, dear friends, once more . . .

I see you stand like greyhounds in the slips,
Straining upon the start. The game's afoot:
Follow your spirit, and upon this charge
Cry, 'God for Harry, England, and Saint George!'"

Three centuries later "The game's afoot" became the cry of another famous Englishman. Elementary, my dear Watson.

On his march back to Calais, Henry finds his way blocked at Agincourt by 25,000 hopping-mad French. He is down to 6,000 archers and a few thousand foot soldiers. On the eve of battle, his aide-de-camp, Westmoreland—a resonant military name—moans,

O that we now had here
But one ten thousand of those men in England
That do no work to-day!

This is Henry's cue to riff magnificently on the general superiority of the English. "Wogs begin at Calais," as the saying goes.

If we are mark'd to die,
we are enow
To do our country loss;
and if to live,
The fewer men, the greater
share of honor . . .

We few, we happy few,
we band of brothers;
For he to-day that sheds
his blood with me
Shall be my brother;
be he ne'er so vile,
This day shall gentle
his condition;
And gentlemen in
England now a-bed
Shall think themselves
accursed they were not here,
And hold their manhoods
cheap whiles any speaks
That fought with us
upon Saint Crispin's day.

The next day, Henry's army of grunts disemboweled the shiny French noblesse with sharpened stakes and porcupined them with arrows shot from longbows. French body count: 5,000. English body count: 100. (This body count is disputed by some historians.)

Kenneth Branagh's rendition of the speech in his 1989 movie is so stirring you want to gallop up to the nearest French embassy and ride a horse through the front door. The Laurence Olivier version, filmed in 1944 while World War II was being waged on the same ground where Henry had fought, was a pep talk delivered in real time.*

Mel Gibson gives a goose-bump-inducing talk to his troops in the movie *Braveheart*, before the Battle of Stirling. The lads need some bucking up, since they've just had a good long look at the English army and those lethal archers. Braveheart gallops up to put the lead back in their sporrans.

"Will you fight?"

He's met with dubious looks.

"Aye, fight and you may die. Run and you'll live—at least a while. And dying in your beds many years from now, would you be willing to trade all the days from this day to that for one chance, just one chance to come back here and tell our enemies that they may take our lives, but they'll never take our freedom?"

Giving a speech on horseback seems to have twice the impact as just standing there whacking your shins with a riding crop. Soon Braveheart's men are lifting their kilts, mooning the English, and on their way to becoming a nation that distills three hundred types of single malt. That's a pep talk.

In the movie *Gladiator*, Russell Crowe plays the Roman general Maximus. (Why can't our generals have names like that, instead of Norman and Tommy?) Maximus is up against the skankiest-looking barbarians in movie history—Germans, natch. Even Kofi Annan

* Convalescing from his wounds in an Italian hospital during World War I, Ernest Hemingway met a British soldier who wrote out a line from *Henry IV, Part II*. The words became Hemingway's mantra. He quoted them in his short story "The Short Happy Life of Francis Macomber." The line is spoken in the play by a character named Feeble: "By my troth, I care not: a man can die but once; we owe God a death . . . and let it go which way it will, he that dies this year is quit for the next."

and Dominique de Villepin wouldn't bother with inspections on this bunch, who've just returned the Roman negotiator tied to his horse, minus his head.

Maximus addresses his men in the charged dawn mists: "Archers! Three weeks from now I will be harvesting my crops. Imagine where you will be, and it will be so." Then he's thundering up behind the barbarian front line, blade drawn, shouting to his captains, "Stay with me! If you find yourself alone, riding in green fields with the sun on your face, do not be troubled—for you are in Elysium, and you are *already* dead!"

The centurions chortle. They love it. *That Maximus—what a cutup!* That's leadership, getting a chuckle out of men about to go toe-to-toe with second-century Huns armed with hammers and axes.

Germany, ancient and modern, has been the setting for memorable pep talks. The most stirring of my youth was given in Berlin by John F. Kennedy on June 26, 1963. It was remarkable at even the technical level: One key line is Latin, the punch line in German. Don't try this at home.

"Two thousand years ago the proudest boast was *civis Romanus sum*. Today, in the world of freedom, the proudest boast is *Ich bin ein Berliner*." The words were spelled out phonetically in Kennedy's speech text as "ISH BEEN OIN BEAR-LEE-NER."*

Berliners needed some cheering up. They'd been through rather a lot, what with World War I, Weimar, World War II, and now the Cold War. Two years prior to Kennedy's visit, the East Germans had built a wall through the city. Every night, they went to sleep to the sound of guards shooting escapees and Russian tanks on the other side revving their engines.

Onto that stage climbed the handsome young American president to tell them:

* Legend has it that this translates literally as "I am a jelly doughnut," *ein Berliner* being a local pastry, and *Berliner* being an inhabitant of the city. Maybe, but the Berliners who heard Kennedy speak knew perfectly what he meant. As I type, today's *New York Times* carries the obituary of Robert H. Lochner, eighty-four, Kennedy's translator on that day.

> *I want to say, on behalf of my countrymen, who live many miles away on the other side of the Atlantic, who are far distant from you, that they take the greatest pride that they have been able to share with you, even from a distance, the story of the last eighteen years. I know of no town, no city, that has been besieged for eighteen years that still lives with the vitality and the force, and the hope and the determination of the city of West Berlin.*

When they got back aboard Air Force One, the adrenaline was still pumping. Kennedy said to his speechwriter Ted Sorensen, "We'll never have another day like this one, as long as we live." Prophetically correct, as it turned out.

The speech marked the high point of transatlantic relations. These days, German politicians tend to run *against* the United States—and win. But in 1987, Ronald Reagan gave West Berliners a pep talk that turned out to sound the first death knell for Soviet communism.

"Mr. Gorbachev," he said, looking uncharacteristically grave, "tear . . . down . . . this . . . wall!"

Leni Riefenstahl died this September at age 101. Her 1934 film *Triumph of the Will* documented the twentieth century's most ominous pep talk—Hitler's, at Nuremberg. Hitler was by all accounts one of the most powerful speakers of the twentieth century. Even before he got to "in conclusion," the audience was reaching for the keys to the Panzers and the Baedeker guide to Poland. And yet—can you quote a single thing he said, other than "Is Paris burning?" Hitler is a paradox: the great orator who left no memorable quotes.

It's similarly difficult, poring over the pep talks of other twentieth-century monsters, Stalin, Mao, Mussolini, Castro, Saddam Hussein—and not much fun, really—to find notable lines. Perhaps it's that pep talks given by dictators are organically flawed: They lack sincerity. Dictators don't have to bring their crowds to their feet. The audience will do that automatically.

Say it's you sitting there in Row 3 at the Eighteenth Party Congress, into the fourth hour of Stalin's speech about how you, comrade, can increase tractor and hydroelectric output under the new

Five Year Plan. Are you inspired? See the guy sitting at the end of the row, in the KGB-issue black leather raincoat, checking to see how loudly you're applauding? You bet you're inspired. *Boy, the Boss is really cooking tonight!*

Dictators not only give Potemkin pep talks, but also Trojan Horses. In 1957, Chairman Mao Tse-tung gave an uplifting speech in which he urged—demanded—that the Chinese express themselves freely, no matter if it was contrary to the party line. "Let a hundred flowers bloom," he said, "and a hundred schools of thought contend." Harvard professors cheered! What followed was the Cultural Revolution, in which all the free-thinkers found themselves being dragged through the streets wearing dunce caps, on their way to being reeducated, or worse.

Saddam Hussein's inspirational style is somewhat harder to characterize. Last March 20, on the eve of Shock and Awe, he appeared on television to stiffen the doubtless quavering spines—and sphincters—of his followers. He called the Iraqi people "Dear friends." Under his rule, an estimated quarter of a million people were detained or murdered. As a rule, the more of his own people a dictator has murdered, the more affectionately he addresses them in public.

"We love peace," he said. He urged Iraqis to "Go use the sword. Draw your sword, and I'm not afraid. Draw your sword. The enemy is making a fuss." (This may have sounded more inspiring in the original Arabic.) Like FDR and Churchill, he told it straight, telling the "brave" Iraqi people what they were up against: "the criminal junior Bush" and "the criminal Zionists . . . who have agendas." Well, who doesn't have an agenda these days? He signed off, "Long live jihad!" This gets my vote for the year's Worst Cheerleading Routine.

But it was Saddam's information minister, Mohammed Saeed al-Sahaf, who showed himself a true master of the pep talk. "Baghdad Bob," as he was nicknamed, had Americans cheering for him. He was the ur-cheerleader, the Super Pangloss, Anthony Robbins on LSD.

"Today we slaughtered them at the airport!" he announced on TV, even as U.S. troops were taking smoke breaks in the control tower.

"The infidels are committing suicide by the hundreds on the gates of Baghdad!" he said, with so many U.S. tanks rolling through that MPs had to direct traffic.

"As our leader Saddam Hussein said, 'God is grilling their stomachs in hell!'" If I'd been a "brave" Iraqi soldier, cowering in the basement of a hospital or orphanage and I'd heard that on the TV, I like to think I'd have rushed right out and shot some woman in the back.

On a cheerier note, if the killing of whales can be called that, are the pep talks given by the three mates in *Moby-Dick* to their respective crews as they pull—pull!—at their oars. Here's Stubb, the second mate, urging on his crew:

> *Pull, pull, my fine hearts-alive; pull, my children; pull, my little ones . . . Why don't you break your backbones, my boys? What is it you stare at? Those chaps in yonder boat? Tut! They are only five more hands come to help us—never mind from where—the more the merrier. Pull, then, do pull; never mind the brimstone—devils are good fellows enough. So, so; there you are now; that's the stroke for a thousand pounds; that's the stroke to sweep the stakes! Hurrah for the gold cup of sperm oil, my heroes! . . . Pull, babes—pull, suckings—pull, all . . .*

Wouldn't you break your back for a coxswain like that? Chief mate Starbuck, whose name has now become synonymous with "grande nonfat mocha latte with an extra shot," urged on his crew more economically. All he said was, "Pull, pull, my good boys." Whereas Flask, the *Pequod*'s third mate and its most eager whale hunter, could barely contain himself:

> *Sing out and say something, my hearties. Roar and pull, my thunderbolts! Beach me, beach me on their black backs, boys; only do that for me, and I'll sign over to you my Martha's Vineyard plantation, boys; including wife and children, boys. Lay me on—lay me on! O Lord, Lord! but I shall go stark, staring mad: See! See that white water!*

As for the whaleboat management secrets of Captain Ahab, Melville was coy: "But what it was that inscrutable Ahab said to that tiger-yellow crew of his—these were words best omitted here; for you live under the blessed light of the evangelical land." But Ahab knew how to incentivize. Want to improve your third quarter? Try nailing a gold doubloon above the water cooler. Business schools could use these four disparate styles of pep-talking as case studies on how to motivate employees, though it's possible that human resources might have a problem with "Pull, sucklings!"

Then there's what might be called the Anti-Pep Talk, which seeks to inspire by scaring the bejeezus out of the audience. One of the most memorable of this genre was surely delivered by the late Herb Brooks, the U.S. Olympic hockey coach whose team performed the "Miracle on Ice" by beating the Soviets in 1980. On that occasion, the famously abrasive Brooks went into the locker room and told his men, "You're meant to be here. This moment is yours. You're meant to be here at this time."

Very calm, almost Zen-like. And boy did it work. Before the next game, with Finland, he told them, "If you lose this game, you'll take it to your f—g grave." He turned to leave, pausing at the door to add, "Your f—g *grave*."

Vince Lombardi, legendary coach of the Green Bay Packers, inspired by evincing contempt for anything less than total victory. "There is a second-place bowl game," he said, "but it is a game for losers played by losers. It is and always has been an American zeal to be first in anything we do, and to win, and to win, and to win."

This American will to win is most grandiloquently showcased in the opening scene of the movie *Patton*—a pep talk to the troops on the eve of the invasion of Europe. George C. Scott strides out on stage, exquisitely accoutered in chrome helmet, ivory-handled .45s, riding crop, and breeches.

"The Americans love a winner," he says, "and cannot tolerate a loser. Americans despise cowards. Americans play to win—all the time. I wouldn't give a hoot for a man who lost and laughed. That's why Americans have never lost and will never lose a war, for the very thought of losing is hateful to an American."

The above is from the actual speech Patton gave in the spring of 1944. Historians call it "The Speech." It was carefully rehearsed and staged, and he gave it four or more times on the eve of invasion. In contrast to the quiet invigorations of Ike and Omar Bradley, Patton's is pure trumpet, the Mother of All Pep Talks. The movie version—written in part by a young Francis Ford Coppola—is actually less profane than the real article: "An army is a team. It lives, sleeps, eats, fights as a team. This individual heroic stuff is a lot of crap. The bilious bastards who wrote that kind of stuff for the *Saturday Evening Post* don't know any more about real battle than they do about f—g."

It ends on a high-comic note: "There is one thing you all will be able to say when you go home. You may all thank God for it. Thank God that at least thirty years from now, when you are sitting around the fireside with your brat on your knee, and he asks you what you did in the great World War Two, you won't have to say that you shoveled s— in Louisiana."

Contrast that with the pep-talk scene in the war movie *A Bridge Too Far*. Allied troops are about to embark on the ill-fated Operation Market Garden mission in Holland. Lieutenant General Brian Horrocks of the British Army, played by the excellent Edward Fox, tells them, "Gentleman, this is a tale you will tell your grandchildren—and mightily bored they'll *be*!"

On the eve of Operation Iraqi Freedom, the forty-two-year-old commander of the First Battalion of the Royal Irish Regiment gave a remarkable talk to his men. It's worth quoting nearly in entirety:

> *The enemy should be in no doubt that we are his nemesis and that we are bringing about his rightful destruction. There are many regional commanders who have stains on their souls and they are stoking the fires of hell for Saddam. He and his forces will be destroyed by this coalition for what they have done. As they die they will know that their deeds have brought them to this place. Show them no pity.*
>
> *There are some who are alive at this moment who will not be alive shortly. It is my foremost intention to bring every sin-*

gle one of you out alive, but there may be some among us who will not see the end of this campaign. We will put them in their sleeping bags and send them back. There will be no time for sorrow.

Those who do not wish to go on that journey, we will not send. As for the others, I expect you to rock their world. Wipe them out if that is what they choose. But if you are ferocious in battle, remember to be magnanimous in victory. It is a big step to take another human life. It is not to be done lightly.

I know of men who have taken life needlessly in other conflicts. I can assure you they live with the mark of Cain upon them. If someone surrenders to you, then remember they have that right in international law and ensure that one day they can go home to their family. The ones who wish to fight, well, we aim to please.

If you harm the regiment or its history by overenthusiasm in killing or in cowardice, know it is your family who will suffer. . . .

We go to liberate, not to conquer. We will not fly our flags in their country. . . . Iraq is steeped in history. It is the site of the Garden of Eden, of the Great Flood and the birthplace of Abraham. Tread lightly there. . . .

You will see things that no man could pay to see . . .

Lieutenant Colonel Tim Collins is from Belfast. The Irish, North and South, are known for their gift with the spoken word. His speech to his troops became a sensation—which ended up being ironic, as he was subsequently accused of pistol-whipping an Iraqi civil leader and shooting at the feet of civilians. He was cleared by the Ministry of Defence, but his battalion is being investigated for other incidents. The colonel, whose nickname is "Nails," is on his way to Pattonization.

Perhaps the most inspiring speech in history was given by a soldier. They are the few short words spoken two and a half millennia ago in a tent by the mountain pass of Thermopylae, in Greece.

The entire Persian army was about to come through the pass, defended, as you well know, by a small unit of Spartans. Herodotus tells the story:

> *. . . one man is said to have distinguished himself above all the rest, Dieneces the Spartan. A speech which he made before the Greeks engaged the Medes [Persians] remains on record. One of the Trachinians told him, "Such was the number of barbarians, that when they shot forth their arrows the sun would be darkened by their multitude." Dieneces, not at all frightened at these words, but making light of the Median numbers, answered, "Our Trachinian friend brings us excellent tidings. If the Medes darken the sun, we shall have our fight in the shade!"*

Now go out there and kick ass.

—*Forbes FYI*, November 2003

ACKNOWLEDGMENTS

Many of the essays here were originally published in *The New York Times*, *The New Yorker*, *The Atlantic Monthly*, *The Wall Street Journal*, *The Washington Post*, *The Daily Beast*, *Time*, *Newsweek*, *National Review*, *New Republic*, *Bloomberg/BusinessWeek*, *Smithsonian*, and in the magazine that was my happy professional base for almost twenty years, *Forbes FYI*, now *ForbesLife*.

Special thanks—and then some—to two people who have been my professional north stars for over twenty years (one north star is good; two is even better): Jonathan Karp and Binky (née Amanda) Urban. Bless you both. Every author should be so lucky.

I have been the beneficiary of hugely talented editors over the years. To name a few to whom I owe so much: Tina Brown, Cullen Murphy, Patrick Cooke, Susan Morrison. As for family and friends who generously—and often valiantly—served as first responders: John Tierney, Gregory Zorthian, Lloyd Grove, Lucy Buckley, and my precociously talented daughter, Cat.

Special thanks and devoted love to my wife, Katy Close, without whom nothing would be worthwhile.

Finally, another large Milk-Bone to the Faithful Hound Jake, who as the author banged away, vigilantly stood guard, albeit recumbently.

Index

About the Author

Christopher Buckley is the pen name of Christopher Buckley.